LORD CHIEF JUSTICE
MANSFIELD

Chief Author of the American Revolution

ERNEST B. LOWRIE

ISBN: 979-8-88640-019-9 (sc)
ISBN: 979-8-88640-020-5 (hc)
ISBN: 979-8-88640-021-2 (e)

Because of the dynamic nature of the Internet, any web addresses or
links contained in this book may have changed since publication and
may no longer be valid. The views expressed in this work are solely those
of the author and do not necessarily reflect the views of the publisher,
and the publisher hereby disclaims any responsibility for them.

THE EWINGS
PUBLISHING

One Galleria Blvd., Suite 1900, Metairie, LA 70001
1-888-421-2397

CONTENTS

Acknowledgments..v

I. Introduction 1
II. Background...7
III. Early Years 14
IV. Solicitor General in the Whig Establishment 24
V. Attorney General in the Newcastle Administration 45
VI. The Rise of Pitt to Power 66
VII. The Transformation of the English Common Law Heritage .. 79
VIII. Some Early Decisions...93
IX. Young King George III in the Hands of the Scots 109
X. Thomas Hutchinson: Revisionist Historian.............................120
XI. The Opening of the Constitutional Crisis 132
XII. The Repeal of the Stamp Act..160
XIII. The Chatham Administration... 185
XIV. The Grafton Administration..208
XV. The Opening Years of the North Administration 242
XVI. Thomas Hutchinson: Lord Mansfield's Foremost
        American Disciple 272
XVII. The Intolerable Acts of 1774 309
XVIII. Thomas Jefferson: A Summary View 341
XIX. Thomas Hutchinson's Entry Into England 350
XX. The First Continental Congress..360
XXI. The Final Descent...368
XXII. Novanglus V. Massachusettensis 387

XXIII. The Empire Goes to War 397

XXIV. The War of Independence 419

XXV. Three Judgments Against Lord Mansfield...........................432

XXVI. Lord Mansfield's Final Years 439

Notes 445

Bibliography...483

ACKNOWLEDGMENTS

Several scholars have contributed in providing this book with the clarity it now has achieved. Chris Elston read major portions of an initial version. Michael Armstrong reviewed the entire manuscript and made several suggestions that improved the whole. Jon Gunnemann contributed more than he could imagine to the project from the beginning to the end. Throughout the writing, my wife Joyce and daughter Michèle have been constant companions and helpful critics. Of course, I alone am responsible for the full story, one that has needed to be told for a very long time.

INTRODUCTION

L ORD CHIEF JUSTICE MANSFIELD WAS BORN AT THE SCONE PALACE ON THE NORTHERN outskirts of Perth, Scotland, on 2 March 1704 (O.S.) with the given name of William Murray. Because he fully shared his family's commitment to the restoration of the line of descent from the dethroned King James II, nothing would be gained from attempting to soften the claim that he had been a conspicuous Jacobite in his youth and early manhood. Although it is not clear exactly when or how he embraced the Protestant Succession, that he did so is simply the case. It does not follow, however, that he altered his fundamental orientation to the law that he had learned while studying the Scottish Civil Law.

The more important honors King George II and King George III showered upon this eleventh child and the fourth son of the Fifth Viscount Stormont are carved in stone on his massive monument that dominates the West Aisle of the North Transept in Westminster Abbey:

HE WAS APPOINTED SOLICITOR GENERAL 1742
ATTORNEY GENERAL 1754
LORD CHIEF JUSTICE AND BARON MANSFIELD 1756
EARL OF MANSFIELD 1776

Those four dates specify some of the most critical turning points in eighteenth-century British public life.

1742 marks the *Fall of the Walpole Administration.* Soon after the long political career of Sir Robert Walpole came to an abrupt end during the War of Austrian Succession, William Murray emerged as the *Solicitor General.* Over the next decade the most powerful players among the *Old Corps Whigs* were Prime Minister Henry Pelham, his older brother, the Duke of Newcastle, Lord Chancellor Hardwicke, and the new Solicitor General, William Murray.

1754 marks the *Splintering of the Old Corps Whigs.* As the General Election of 1754 was reaching a climax, the Whig Oligarchy was traumatized by the unexpected death of Prime Minister Henry Pelham. Continuity was the end-in-view when George II chose the Duke of Newcastle to head the new ministry, but that decision carried with it an intractable structural problem, for Newcastle sat in the House of Lords while political power had shifted to the House of Commons. Worse still, the designated Leader of the House of Commons was not even a participant in the deliberations of the short-lived Newcastle Administration. Given this awkward situation, William Murray quickly became the principal though unofficial spokesman for the ministry from the moment he was appointed *Attorney General* in 1754.

1756 marks the formal opening of the *Seven Years War.* Austria had been a close English ally, while Prussia had been allied with France, but the breathtaking *Diplomatic Revolution of 1756* reversed that balance of power. The new alliances now pitted France and Austria against the British Empire and its new ally, Prussia. Soon Sweden and Russia—and before the fighting was over, Spain—intervened on the side of this novel Franco-Austrian Alliance. Following a steady stream of military disasters, the Newcastle Administration simply dissolved in October 1756, but in its dying moments Newcastle somehow persuaded George II into appointing William Murray *Lord Chief Justice and Baron Mansfield.*

Throughout the opening months of the Seven Years War the imperial government was in desperate straits because the King wanted the spokesman for the Duke of Cumberland—Henry Fox—to become the new Prime Minister, but this gambit triggered a horrendous opposition led by the Dowager Princess of Wales and her advisor, the Earl of Bute. The quarrel within the political nation raged on, rendering military strategy completely incoherent and hopelessly ineffective. Then in June 1757 the newly installed Lord Chief Justice somehow managed to convince the King that the only plausible way to resolve the chronic crisis of confidence was to place executive power directly in the hands of his life-long rival, William Pitt. Given Pitt's outstanding leadership, by the time the young George III inherited the throne from his grandfather in October 1760 the First British Empire was rapidly approaching an astonishing victory. The 1763 Peace of Paris humiliated France, signaled the emergence of Prussia as a Great Power, and added Quebec to the British Empire.

Soon after this stunning moment of triumph, however, it quickly became apparent that the British Empire was caught in the coils of a constitutional crisis. For a long decade the disputants on both sides of the Atlantic engaged in a sustained argument over the proper interpretation of the Constitution of the British Empire. The constitutional argument finally gave way to armed conflict on the Lexington Green in the Province of the Massachusetts Bay during the early hours of 19 April 1775.

1776 marks the *Declaration of Independence by the United States of America*. After receiving news of this declaration, George III responded by honoring the Lord Chief Justice of King's Bench with the handsome title of the *Earl of Mansfield*.

So simple a rehearsal of the pivotal years 1742, 1754, 1756, and 1776 marks this Scottish Law Lord as one of the most influential political judges in the entire history of England. From the moment he was appointed to the Court of King's Bench in late 1756 till he retired in 1788—thirty-two tumultuous years that match rather nicely the

Age of the American Revolution—Lord Chief Justice Mansfield was the acknowledged Head of British Jurisprudence.

WHILE addressing the constitutional issues that dominated public policy after the end of the Seven Years War, three different levels or arenas need to be kept firmly in mind. First, *the Unwritten Constitution of Great Britain.* Since the Union of 1707 Scotland had become *within the realm* and, therefore, subject to the jurisdiction of the British Parliament. Second, *the Constitutions of the Numerous Colonies in the Extensive British Empire.* Each of the twenty-six British colonies had its own distinctive polity, subject to the King, but each was *without the realm* and, therefore, not subject to the authority of Parliament in regard to its internal affairs. Third, *the Evolving Constitution of the British Empire Itself.* Prior to 1763 imperial governance had remained under the purview of the King-in-Council, while the jurisdiction of Parliament had been limited to the governance of the imperial trade for the good order of the whole. That defined Parliament's role during the Old Colonial System. The New Colonial System that was introduced immediately after the Seven Years War was grounded in the belief that Parliament also held authority to legislate for—and raise taxes on—the colonies.

This novel system has ordinarily been discussed in terms of the Doctrine of Parliamentary Supremacy. That doctrine, however, could be understood in three different ways. First, for traditionalists it carried the meaning it had carried for generations, namely, that Parliament held jurisdiction over the imperial trade alone. William Pitt's imperial vision would fall under this reading. Second, it could be understood to mean that Parliament—in addition to its jurisdiction over the imperial trade—also held reserved powers to tax, but these powers should seldom be acted upon, and then only as a last resort. This version acknowledged Parliament's right to tax the colonies as a theoretical possibility but not as a practical option. The persons associated with Edmund Burke as the spokesman for the Rockingham party championed this interpretation of the doctrine. Third, it could be understood to mean that Parliament held unlimited sovereignty over all the various entities throughout the polycentric Empire. By right Parliament could tax and legislate for those *without the realm* exactly as it taxed and legislated for those *within the realm*. Prime Minister Grenville introduced this novel theory in 1764, and Prime Minister North carried it into the Revolution itself, but Lord Chief Justice Mansfield remains the person most directly responsible for this maximal reading of the Doctrine of Parliamentary Supremacy.

After becoming the Lord Chief Justice of King's Bench in the midst of the Seven Years War, Mansfield laid the foundation for the coming crisis. Regardless of whatever else might need to be said about the causes of the American Revolution, few today would care to quarrel with the claim that the violent adjudication arose after a full decade of intense probing of what Mansfield himself called "the true bone of contention" at the core of the constitutional conflict.

LORD Chief Justice Mansfield never visited the American colonies, and very few Americans actually met him face to face. One of those few was Benjamin Franklin (1705-1790). As almost an exact contemporary, he was positioned to understand in depth the subtle implications of Mansfield's doctrines. When the Continental Congress became bogged down over the vexed issue of representation, with the small colonies insisting upon equal weight with the larger colonies (each colony to have one vote), and the larger colonies wanting representation to be based on population (each colony to carry proportional weight), Benjamin Franklin cut through the predicted fears (according to Thomas Jefferson's recollection) by reminding the delegates that prior to the Union of 1707 the Scottish lawyers had "prognosticated that it would again happen as in times of old, that the whale would swallow Jonas," only to discover to their surprise after Scotland and England were united that "Jonas had swallowed the whale, for the Scotch had in fact got possession of the government and gave laws to the English."[1]

Exactly when Franklin picked up this clever saying remains unknown, but it is reasonable to suppose that he first heard it during his six-week tour through Scotland occasioned by his receiving the honorary degree of Doctor of Laws from the University of Saint

Andrews. In fact, Franklin had prepared *An Historical Review of the Constitution and Government of Pennsylvania* to deliver to Archibald Campbell in preparation for a forthcoming trial in Lord Chief Justice Mansfield's Court.

One of the more memorable events on this excursion occurred on 30 September 1759 when the Reverend William Robertson escorted him on the standard pilgrimage to the abandoned Scone Palace just north of Perth. Since Robertson had recently published his *History of Scotland, during the Reigns of Queen Mary and of King James VI*, this erudite historian undoubtedly treated his distinguished American guest to a profound commentary on the institutional significance of this ancient capital of the Picts.

While much that was said remains unknown, years later Robertson would bitterly recall the cryptic comment that Doctor Franklin did make on this solemn occasion: "Who knows but St. James's may some time or other lie in ruins as Scone does now."[2] Our latter-day Jonas was "Born at Scone 2d March 1704" according to the Old Style dating on Lord Chief Justice Mansfield's massive monument that dominates the West Aisle of the North Transept in Westminster Abbey.

BACKGROUND

THE LEGAL TRADITION OF SCOTLAND WAS ROOTED IN THE *CORPUS JURIS CIVILIS* OF THE Roman Emperor Justinian (circa 482-565). Because Justinian's *Corpus* was eclipsed throughout the so-called Dark Ages, the story only began its historical career after the code was rediscovered in medieval Europe. According to Ephraim Chambers in his monumental 1728 *Cyclopaedia*, "Irnerius first made profession of [the Roman Civil Law] at Bologna" in the year 1128, and soon it became known as *Lex scripta*. This was the historic groundwork for the education and orientation of Lord Chief Justice Mansfield. He knew intimately the developing tradition through his detailed studies of the Continental and Scottish legal systems.

Over against this sterling performance Chambers juxtaposed the English Common Law as an example of *Lex non-scripta*. Although it had been "written in the old *Norman* Dialect," the English Common Law Heritage was still deemed to be *Lex non-scripta* "because it cannot be made by Charter or Parliament; for those are always Matters of Record, whereas Customs are only Matters of Fact, and are no where but in the Memory of the People." The English preferred customs because "the Written *Laws* made by King and Parliament, are imposed upon the Subjects before any Probation or Trial whether they are beneficial to the Nation, or agreeable to the Nature of the

People." Customs, on the other hand, "bind not till they have been tried and approved Time out of Mind." Since that enduring deposit of customary law was locked in "the Memory of the People" and had been worked up through countless precedents, this *Lex non-scripta* protected those Common Law Rights that were the proud boast of Englishmen.[1]

Before Edward I of England forcibly removed the Coronation Stone of Destiny in the late Thirteenth Century and had it placed next to the tomb of Edward the Confessor behind the high altar in Westminster Abbey, the Scottish Kings had been crowned on the Stone of Scone. The Abbey of Scone (in William Shakespeare's telling) had witnessed the death of Macbeth followed by the coronation of Malcolm. And here it was that the Bishop of Saint Andrews crowned Robert the Bruce with a golden circlet. Although this ancient Abbey of Augustinian Canons had been razed during the Protestant Reformation, the Earl of Gowrie soon began restoring the Abbey.

When Mary Queen of Scots was forced to abdicate in 1567, her one-year-old son became King James VI. During his minority a series of regents ruled Scotland, and that was when Gowrie captured the King at the Scone Palace. Because Gowrie's foul plot was foiled by the adroit responses of David Murray, this distinguished "Master of the Horse, Comptroller of the Household, and Captain of the Body-guard" was rewarded with "a considerable portion of the forfeited estates" of the fallen Earl of Gowrie. David Murray became the First Lord Scone and Viscount Stormont. Although he died without issue, he had prudently obtained a special remainder of his titles so they could pass down through his extended family.[2]

James VI of Scotland inherited the English throne as James I (1603-1625). Soon after the Scottish King became King of England as well, James I "expressed himself with great disparagement of the common law of England, and [gave] the preference, in the strongest terms, to the civil law" with which he had governed in Scotland. That is David Hume's opening statement in his revisionist interpretation of the English constitution in the 1754 volume of his *History of England*.[3]

One of the most prominent leaders in Parliament who opposed the proclivities of the House of Stuart was Sir Edward Coke (1552-1634). In 1606 Coke became Chief Justice of Common Pleas; then in 1613 Chief Justice of King's Bench. Coke's *Institutes of the Laws of England* formed the bedrock of legal studies in the various Inns of Court—except in Doctors Common, where candidates for the Spiritual Courts and the Admiralty Courts were schooled in Canon and Civil Law respectively. And that is why Ephraim Chambers expressly emphasized in his *Cyclopaedia* that in England's legal systems the shaping power of the Roman Civil Law had been limited to "the ecclesiastical courts" and "the courts of admiralty," but even in those judicial systems it had been "restrained and directed by the common law."

Shortly after the execution of Charles I during the English Civil War, Charles II was crowned at the Scone Palace before fleeing to the Continent. And before the Duke of York was crowned the King of England in 1685, James II laid out the troubled doctrine of "the divine right of kings" for the benefit of the learned at Cambridge: "We will still believe and maintain that our Kings derive not their title from the people but from God; that to him only are they accountable; that it belongs not to subjects, either to create or censure, but to honour and obey their Sovereign."[4] Although the policies flowing from this theorem of Renaissance Absolutism had cost Charles I his head in 1649 and James II his crown in 1688, the Glorious Revolution did not reject the doctrine *in toto*, for Revolution Principles were elastic enough to embrace a version of the divine right of kings so long as that vexed doctrine included a constitutional place for the people represented in Parliament. Technically put, while virtually all shades of opinion were committed to a monarchical form of government through a hereditary descent, Jacobitism championed "the hereditary indefeasible right" of a divinely anointed monarch.[5]

Even after the Glorious Revolution had transformed the situation rather thoroughly, the conflict over the constitutional heritage was still being fought out in pamphlet wars of the most serious type. For example, in the early 1690s James Tyrrell published a series of dialogues (amounting to "968 closely printed pages" in the final edition) between—mark the qualifiers—"Mr Freeman, a Gentleman" and "Mr Meanwell, a Civilian."[6]

"Civilian" carried only a technical meaning at the time, one that seems rather odd today. In Samuel Johnson's 1755 *Dictionary of the English Language* one finds *civilian* defined this way: "One that professes the knowledge of the old Roman law, and of general equity." With citations reaching all the way back to Wyclif's translation of the Bible in the fourteenth century, the *Oxford English Dictionary* amplifies Johnson's definition:

> One who makes or has made the Civil Law (chiefly as distinguished originally from the Canon Law, and later from the Common Law) the object of his study; the practitioner, doctor, professor, or student of the Civil Law, a writer or authority on the Civil Law.

This standard eighteenth-century meaning can be seen, for example, in *The Tatler* when "Isaac Bickerstaff" repeatedly presents himself as a *civilian*, namely, as "a doctor, professor or student of the civil law" (see especially #69 on 17 September 1709). And while explicating the roots of the Scottish Civil Law, the first edition of the *Encyclopaedia Britannica* (serially published in Edinburgh between 1768 and 1771) is quite explicit:

> CIVILIAN, in general, denotes something belonging to the civil law; but more especially the doctors and professors thereof are called civilians ... The civil or Roman and canon laws, though they are not perhaps to be deemed proper parts of our written law, have undoubtedly had the greatest influence in Scotland. It continues to have great authority in all cases where it is not derogated from by statute or

custom. And where the genius of our law suffers us
to apply it.

Few things could be more transparent than the extraordinary
difference between Scotland's Civil Law and England's Common Law.

AFTER the Glorious Revolution the exiled James II lived rather
handsomely in the magnificent Chateau of Saint Germain-en -Laye
twenty miles west of Paris made available by the generosity of Louis
XIV living at Versailles. When James II died, his thirteen-year-old
son, James Francis Edward Stuart, became the Old Pretender to the
throne of His Britannic Majesty. The Catholic House of Stuart in
exile posed an enduring threat to the Protestant monarchs reigning
in London throughout the first half of the eighteenth century.

The first indication of what lay in store for Lord Chief Justice
Mansfield's family came in the Rising of 1708. Because significant
portions of Scotland did not relish the new order established by the
1707 Act of Union, Louis XIV surmised that the time might be ripe
for a diversion through the British north in order to relieve some of
the pressure pouring down upon Flanders from the armies of the
Grand Alliance under the command of the Duke of Marlborough.
James Francis Edward Stuart—now nineteen years old—sailed from
Dunkirk for Edinburgh on 9 March 1708, but the French navy under
the command of the Chevalier de Forbin overshot the mark and was
almost captured by the superior British navy under the command
of Sir George Byng. The government, however, did not take lightly
the possibility of an invasion in the Firth of Forth. Not only was
the Fifth Viscount Stormont among those Scottish nobles forced to
post substantial bonds because of their questionable loyalty to the
government of Queen Anne, one of his ambitious sons was even
kept under lock and key in Edinburgh Castle for the duration of the
crisis.[7]

Given the abortive Rising of 1708, the Stuart Court in exile
decided to postpone any further military action and wait patiently for
the ripened fruit to fall into its lap upon the death of Queen Anne. As

a daughter of James II from a previous marriage, the pretender's half-sister had been reared as a Protestant. Alas, not one of her seventeen children survived, the last dying two years before she became queen in 1702. Since no Protestants remained in the direct Stuart line, the 1701 Act of Settlement stipulated that no Roman Catholic could be the monarch of England. The Protestant Succession dictated that the crown would pass through the granddaughter of James I, namely, the Electress of Hanover in Germany.[8]

Soon after the Elector of Hanover became George I the Jacobites launched the Rebellion of 1715. Few families could have been more thoroughly implicated in the Rebellion than the family of the future Lord Chief Justice. A widely held legend even has it that sometime between the landing at Peterhead and the flight six weeks later from Montrose, the Old Pretender was actually crowned James VIII of Scotland at the Scone Palace.[9] His closest confidante was John Hay, the husband of Marjorie Murray, who was the older sister of young William. Not only were her father and oldest brother arrested on suspicion of high treason, another brother, James Murray, was Lord Bolinbroke's private secretary, and from the highest levels in the government Bolingbroke had controlled the principal center for the Rebellion before he fled from London in 1714. James Murray was also the secret agent who arrived incognito from France on 28 September 1715 with the Old Pretender's commission of Commander-in-Chief for Lord Mar, plus the critical information that Louis XIV would support the Rebellion with 12,000 muskets, 18,000 swords, 4,000 barrels of powder, 12 brass field pieces, and nearly 2,000 men on board twelve ships. These Jacobites on the march, however, did not know until it was too late that this critical shipment would never arrive because the absolute monarchy of the Sun King had come to its end.

After spending a month in Newgate Prison, James Murray somehow managed to return safely to France and join "the Chevalier de St. George" (as the Old Pretender began referring to himself) first at Avignon, then at the papal palace in Urbino, Italy. For his services he was soon honored with the Jacobite title, the Earl of

Dunbar. Nothing could document more convincingly just how close the Murray family was to the Jacobite Court in exile than the fact that James Murray served as the proxy in the marriage of the "King over the water" to the beautiful seventeen-year-old Princess Clementina Sobieski of Poland in May 1719. Before long Charles Edward Louis Philip John Casimir Silvester Severino Maria Stuart (better known historically as "Bonnie Prince Charlie") was born on 31 December 1720. As the Governor of the Young Pretender, James Murray and his sister, Marjorie Hay, moved within the innermost circle of the exiled Stuart Court in Catholic Italy.[10]

William Murray's life-long ambition was to assimilate the English Common Law Heritage to the Roman Civil Law Tradition as issues came up in the Court of King's Bench. The future Lord Chief Justice Mansfield never intended for this strategy to be comprehensive, but it was to be consistent and gradual. This gradual assimilation provides the key that promises to unlock the hidden sources of the American Revolution.

EARLY YEARS

R EGARDLESS OF HIS JACOBITE FAMILY BACKGROUND, WILLIAM MURRAY'S FUTURE possibilities in the larger world of English public life were opened up considerably when this studious thirteen-year-old teenager set his face toward London in order to pursue his education at Westminster Public School. While studying at Westminster, young William was ideally located to observe at close range the wild speculative fever that drove the shares of the South Sea Company "from 150 per cent in January to 1,000 per cent in August," only to have the bottom fall out of the market and bring down the Stanhope Administration when the South Sea Bubble burst.[1]

In response to this catastrophic collapse of public credit, the *London Journal* began publishing on Saturday 5 November 1720 an extraordinarily influential series of *Essays on Liberty, Civil and Religious, and Other Important Subjects* under the pseudonym "Cato." Over the next three years John Trenchard and Thomas Gordon wrote *Cato's Letters* "with such vigor and eloquence" across so vast a range of topics that these 138 *Essays on Liberty* "soon made the *London Journal* the nation's most influential paper and a particularly vexatious irritant to the administration."[2]

The first principle of Trenchard's and Gordon's political thought is frankly metaphysical, indeed, theological: "All men are born free;

liberty is a gift which they receive from God himself; nor can they alienate the same by consent, though possibly they may forfeit it by crimes." This God-given gift of liberty is "the unalienable Right of all Mankind" precisely because it is written into human nature as such—regardless of whether a given people were in some political society or left in a state of nature.[3]

What was meant by "a state of nature" should be understood with care, for it definitely does not refer to some primal, pre-historical "golden age" of innocence. As with the medieval and early modern meaning, it simply denotes a social situation in which there was no recognizable government in place. For example, while discussing a Roman revolution our latter-day Cato writes, "The government becoming incapable of acting, suffered a political demise: The constitution was dissolved; and there being no government in being, the people were in *the state of nature* again" (my emphasis).[4] Upon leaving this state of nature and "entering into political society," those who consented to a particular social contract must have deliberately stipulated "certain terms of union and society" in order to promote the collective interests of the commonwealth and protect their rights within an *ordered liberty*.[5] These "terms" are "laws" and these laws are binding upon the governors as well as the governed, because power that is "lawless" or "boundless" or "absolute" is "something so wanton and monstrous" that no "free people" would ever consent to such a "wicked and ridiculous bargain." Alas, just about everywhere in the world, "Despotick power has defaced the Creation, and laid the world waste." And even England herself had come ever so close to losing her freedom on more than a few occasions.[6]

Apostles of the Enlightenment though they were, Trenchard and Gordon thoroughly embraced a version of the Fall of Man. Notice how casually they use "before the fall" and "the sins of our first parents" and "the depravity transmitted to us by our first parents."[7] In their reading of the deep past "Slavery" has been the fate of most of mankind. Why? Because the ordered liberty secured by the social contract had been lost over time through the machinations of the abusers of "Power." Since power had "degenerated" it had to be viewed with an "exceedingly jealous" eye because of its incessant struggle with liberty:

> Power is naturally active, vigilant, and distrustful ... Power has many advantages over her [i.e., liberty]; it has generally numerous guards, many creatures, and much treasure; besides, it has more craft and experience, less honesty and innocence: And whereas power can, and for the most part does, subsist where liberty is not, liberty cannot subsist without power; so that she has, as it were, the enemy always at her gates.

Liberty is the passive defender of innocence, while power is the active aggressor in this ongoing struggle.[8]

While Cato the Younger was the celebrated hero of these provocative Whigs, Julius Caesar was the paradigmatic villain. Whereas the cornerstone of Cato's constitutional vision is inscribed with the motto, "the rule of law and not of men" (*imperium legum non hominum*), the active encroachment of power upon liberty finds its enduring expression in Justinian's pronouncement, "Though we are above the law, yet we live according to the law" (*Etsi legibus soluti summus, tamen legibus vivimus*), a principle that contains "more turn than truth," because magistrates who "think themselves above law, act almost constantly against all law." According to Trenchard and Gordon, "Power is like fire; it warms, scorches, or destroys, according as it is watched, provoked, or increased." In brief, Cato "watched" fire, while Caesar "increased" it.[9]

One of the cardinal themes running throughout *Cato's Letters* is captured succinctly in the opening sentence of an extended quotation lifted from Algernon Sidney's *Discourses Concerning Government*, first published in 1698, fifteen years after he was executed by "the Hanging Judge" Jeffreys: "Liberty cannot be preserved, if the manners of the people are corrupted." And Trenchard and Gordon were more than convinced that "the principles of our nobility and gentry" were now being thoroughly "debauched in our universities" because Oxford and Cambridge were under the control of the Tories.[10]

Corruption stood at the core of these schemes by the modern "projectors" just as it had stood with those ancient actors who exploited "lawless power" in the name of their uncontrolled masters. For example, Sejanus isolated the Roman Emperor Tiberius on the island of Capri in order to "devour his dominions, and plunder his subjects." The Sejanuses of this world were forever "contriving and forming wicked and dangerous projects, to make the people poor, and themselves rich." They love "ridiculous, expensive, fantastical wars" so as to distract the populace; they "create parties in the commonwealth" so as to divide loyalties; they "promote luxury, idleness, and expense, and a general depravation of manners" so as to destroy "private virtue" as well as "publick liberty." "The Roman virtue and the Roman liberty expired together," according to *Cato's Letters*; "tyranny and corruption came upon them almost hand in hand."[11]

All of this attention given to the ancient Romans served as a canvas upon which Trenchard and Gordon could paint in historical depth the current "struggle for old English liberty" as the polar opposite of French slavery under its absolute monarchy. As champions of "the glorious cause" of liberty they transparently credited the belief that the English Civil War that resulted in the execution of Charles I turned directly upon the fact that the House of Stuart located "absolute power in the crown" with the support of "complaisant bishops and judges." And the current churchman they most vigorously attacked as the inheritor of the seditious tradition of the Stuarts was none other than the Dean of Westminster Public School, the Bishop of Rochester, Dr. Francis Atterbury.[12]

Directly against Atterbury's convictions, *Cato's Letters* advanced the position that "the Pretender's game" was "altogether desperate" simply because there was "no possibility of restoring" to the throne of His Britannic Majesty any person "educated in the religion and maxims of France and Rome." In their treatment of "the Spirit of the Conspirators" Trenchard and Gordon minced no words—"no means were too black, no pitch of iniquity and cruelty too horrid,

17

for the accomplishment of their treason" against George I.[13] So, in direct polar opposition to "the hereditary indefeasible right" of divinely anointed kings so dear to the heart of the Jacobites, the Whig supporters of the Protestant Succession championed "the providential right" of a hereditary monarch divinely appointed by Parliament.

WILLIAM Murray was a student in Westminster Public School when Bishop Atterbury was condemned for organizing yet another Jacobite plot and sent into exile, never to return to England.[14] And it should not go unnoticed that over the coming years Westminster Public School graduated a considerable number of participants in the American Revolution. For example, Sir Francis Bernard, the Governor of Massachusetts (1760-1770); William Legge, the Earl of Dartmouth, Secretary of State for the Colonies (1772-1775); Lord George Germain, Viscount Sackville, Secretary of State for the Colonies (1775-1782); General Thomas Gage, Commander-in-Chief of the British Army in North America (1763-1775); Viscount Richard Howe, Commander-in-Chief of the British Navy in North America (1776-1778); and General John Burgoyne, who surrendered a British Army at Saratoga in October 1777.[15] And our brilliant young scholar from Scotland was clearly under Atterbury's influence when he graduated at the head of the class of 1723.

Regardless of his Jacobite political proclivities, William Murray was appointed one of the King's Scholars and pursued his education in that training ground for Tories, Christ Church, Oxford. As an undergraduate at Oxford he visited his older brother, James, in Paris during the Long Vacation. While in Paris he sent this 6 August 1725 letter to the Old Pretender now in Rome:

> I flatter myself you will excuse the ambition of a young man, if I make use of the freedom I at present have, to desire you to make a tender of my duty and loyalty to the King; a very small present, but all I have to offer. 'Twill in some measure excuse my presumption for offering my service, though in

so private a station as not to be able to render any
considerable, that I do it at a time when so many are
wanting in their duty, that 'tis some merit to protest
against it … The chief end I would propose from my
studies and education, and the greatest glory I can
aim at is to be able to serve his Majesty in any way
that he pleases to command me.[16]

While this letter thoroughly documents his Jacobite loyalties, he sent
it at a most unfortunate moment, for the movement itself was in the
grips of a profound crisis.

Around the time Prince Henry Benedict Stuart was born on 6
March 1725 in the Palazzo Muti that Pope Clement XI had settled
upon the Stuart Court in Rome, the Chevalier de St. George and the
young Queen had fallen out, and so serious was their marital conflict
that the emotionally unstable Clementina incarcerated herself in an
Ursuline convent. The cause? She had been led to believe that the
Chevalier de St. George had adopted as his mistress Marjorie Hay,
the wife of the Secretary of State, and William Murray's older sister.

Both the Pope and the King of Spain were so convinced by
Clementina's complaint that they cancelled the Old Pretender's
pensions. Before he could coax Clementina out of the convent,
Marjorie Hay and her husband had to abandon the Stuart Court in
Rome and move to the Papal State of Avignon. (John Hay died there
in 1740; Marjorie Hay lived on until 1760.)

Soon after rejoining her husband Clementina intensified the
volatile situation by nursing "a spiritual passion for the new Pope
Clement XII." By openly riding in the Pope's carriage through
the streets of Rome, she set "the tongues of the salacious Romans
wagging furiously." Given to "religious mania," the youthful Stuart
Queen in Exile soon wasted away into the emptiness of a melancholy
death.[17] James Murray—now the Secretary of State as well as the
Governor of both Prince Henry and Bonnie Prince Charlie—realized
full well that the prospects for the exiled House of Stuart were rather
bleak indeed.

ALTHOUGH William Murray's political world had begun to disintegrate, and his financial world had grown truly desperate, Lord Foley generously advanced him "the requisite supplies" to follow his "*calling* for the profession of law," first at Christ Church, Oxford, then in Lincoln's Inn.[18] After being admitted to the bar in November 1730, Murray soon moved into chambers on King's Bench Walk. At first the business was slow but before long his cultivated eloquence was conspicuously displayed when he argued a case deriving from the South Sea Bubble. In a fantastic action caused by the "prodigious splendor" of the funeral for the Marquis of Annandale, he evoked "the principles of the Roman Civil Law." Soon the dazzling orator argued before the bar in Parliament in one of the most sensational murder trials of the century, namely, the 1736 lynching of Captain Porteus by the people of Edinburgh. The Scots had been caught up in an anti-English riot fueled by "Mother Gin" and fired by some new excise duties. In retaliation a bill had been introduced that would disenfranchise the entire town, but after William Murray argued down the crown lawyers, all Scotland adopted him as their hero. Because of his winning way with words, he was voted "the freedom of the City of Edinburgh."

More sensational still was a scandal that erupted when Mrs. Cibber engaged in a public quarrel with Mrs. Clive over which of these lovelies "should perform the part of Polly Peachum in the Beggar's Opera." What had all of Hogarth's London gossiping was the fact that Mrs. Cibber had been found *in flagrante delecto* with one Colonel Sloper. That the Colonel was guilty was not under dispute in this entertaining adultery trial. So, the sophisticated defense attorney set out to defend the "unwary young gentleman" by arguing that the "good-natured boy" had been entrapped by a well-laid snare deliberately set by an artful husband and his willing wife. "Gentlemen of the jury," William Murray pleaded, "if it be thought requisite to find a verdict for the plaintiff, we have not a denomination of coin small enough to measure the damages." All the intriguing couple won for their refined endeavor was "a piece of bank paper of the smallest value at that period in circulation."[19]

The rising scholar did not spend all of his youthful years pouring over old black-letter law books. As Samuel Johnson has it, even in the midst of his more severe studies, he found ample time to drink "champagne with the wits."[20] His "most intimate and familiar friend" during his early years was none other than the most famous versifier of the age, Alexander Pope. On a regular basis Pope spent endless hours teaching him "varying attitudes and intonations," not only to clean out his Scottish accent, but to improve his already impressive oratorical abilities. Pope even tried to reconcile Lord Bolingbroke and Warburton by arranging an informal dinner party for these literary titans at William Murray's house. Not only did Pope dedicate "the Sixth Epistle of the First Book of Horace Imitated" to him, he even willed to him his spectacular bust of Homer carved by the young Bernini.[21]

Trials of imbeciles and lynch mobs, wild speculators and wilder women, catapulted William Murray into such prominence that in 1738 the successful young lawyer won the hand of Lady Elizabeth Finch. Jacobite though his extended family remained, and intimate with the politically disgraced Lord Bolingbroke though he was, his marriage brought him into the family of one of the most substantial pillars upholding Hanoverian England, the Earl of Winchelsea.

According to Lord Campbell's calculations, the odds were "many milliards to one" that the fourth son and eleventh child in one of the most thoroughly disaffected families—whose roots reached back to at least the twelfth century in Scotland's misty past and whose branches reached out into an extensive Jacobite conspiracy in Scotland's mysterious present—would ever have cut so splendid a figure in Hanoverian England. But it is reasonable to suppose that he had already come to the steady realization that his mission in life could never be accomplished through the exiled House of Stuart in Catholic Rome, but that it might be carried to completion through the Protestant House of Hanover in London. What did not change during his conversion from Jacobitism to the Protestant Succession—and this claim should carry the heaviest emphasis—was his "high feeling that his destiny called him to reform the jurisprudence" of England.[22]

WILLIAM Murray's entrance upon the larger stage of the political nation was due to a considerable extent to the influence of one of his closest friends from Westminster Public School and Christ Church, Oxford, Andrew Stone (1703-1773). In 1732 Stone was introduced to the Duke of Newcastle, a Secretary of State in the Walpole Administration. Soon after becoming the Duke's private secretary, Stone was promoted to the office of Under-Secretary of State. Through Stone's good offices, Murray was introduced to Newcastle, exactly when is unknown but probably shortly after the time of his marriage in 1738. In any event, these two "Cabinet Counsellors" would do more than a little of the Duke's thinking for him over the coming years.[23]

Murray burst upon the scene as Great Britain began preparations for what has been called the War of Jenkins's Ear. For years Spain had been vexing the British by claiming a right to search English vessels involved in the American trade. To work up the populace against the Spanish pretension that America remained within the domain of His Most Catholic Majesty, the London merchants needed a dramatic incident and they found one in a bizarre story that Robert Jenkins was prepared to repeat for public consumption. Jenkins claimed that a Spanish "guarda-costa" had cut off one of his ears while he was returning the *Rebecca* from the West Indies.

Although this atrocity had passed unnoticed for seven long years, Murray now presented a petition from the London merchants and paraded Jenkins before a committee of the House of Commons. By leading Jenkins into expressing how he had felt when his ear had been cut off—what purported to be his ear was dramatically exhibited—he elicited from his star witness this confession: "I recommended my soul to God, and my cause to my country."[24]

Murray's "private friendships and acquaintances" at this moment, according to the Duke of Newcastle's recollection many years later, were "with those at the head of the opposition, Sir Wm. Wyndham, Lord Bath, Lord Granville, etc." When the future Earl of Granville, John Carteret, mobilized the opposition to prevail upon Parliament to declare war on Spain, Sir Robert Walpole threatened to resign as

Prime Minister, but to no avail, for George II refused to accept his resignation. Badly split though the Walpole Administration was, on 23 October 1739 the hawks prevailed. After war was officially declared, events soon proved that Walpole knew what he was talking about when he hurled this charge into the teeth of those clamoring for Carteret in the Cabinet and for war in the Caribbean: "They may ring their bells now; before long they will be wringing their hands."[25]

The day before this official declaration of war, British forces entered the port of La Guaira—flying Spanish flags—only to be defeated after three hours of heavy shelling by the Spanish forces. Soon, however, the British prevailed in the Battle of Porto Bello on the coast of Panama. This was followed by a series of assaults on Cartagena de Indias in present day Columbia. In early 1741 the British pulled together an enormous fleet of 186 ships carrying over 27,000 men. To be precise, that number included 12,600 sailors, 10,000 soldiers, 4,000 Virginians, and 1,000 slaves. The Spanish defenders included 3,000 soldiers, 600 militia and some native Indians. With such superiority word went out that victory was at hand. Metals depicting the British victory were cast in London. When the British reached the decisive Spanish fort, however, they discovered that an enormous trench had been dug around the walls, thereby rendering the British ladders too short to reach the top of the walls. Because this heavy equipment bogged them down, when the Spanish counterattacked, the British were decisively defeated in one of the greatest contests in the annals of the British navy.[26]

As the conflict expanded into the larger War of the Austrian Succession the situation grew desperate. By "divinely" defending the opposition candidates in the contested elections of 1741, William Murray set the stage for the *Fall of the Walpole Administration*. Even though Horace Walpole readily acknowledged that the eloquence of this up and coming legal luminary from Scotland clearly surpassed "what was ever heard at the bar," Sir Robert Walpole's youngest son never forgave him for aiding and abetting the eclipse of his father's long political career.[27]

SOLICITOR GENERAL IN THE WHIG ESTABLISHMENT

WHEN THE SHORT-LIVED BROAD-BOTTOM ADMINISTRATION TOOK OVER AFTER THE FALL of Sir Robert Walpole, the Duke of Newcastle handed William Murray the safe seat of Boroughbridge in the House of Commons. Then on 27 November 1742 he was appointed *Solicitor General*. For some time— exactly how long remains unclear—our rising star from Scotland had secured his position by cordially embracing the Whig Oligarchy. The government soon settled into a predictable pattern under the guiding hand of the new Prime Minister, Henry Pelham, Newcastle's younger brother.[1]

Bringing William Murray into the ministry was considered something of a masterstroke. "The only objection that can be made to him," the Duke of Richmond wrote to Newcastle, "is what he can't help, which is that he is a Scotch man; which (as I have a great regard for him) I am extremely sorry for." Newcastle even assured Lord Chancellor Hardwicke that the new administration could "absolutely depend upon Mr Murray." Not only would he provide a solid contact with the Tory Opposition headed by his old friend, Lord Bolingbroke, he could also shoulder the primary responsibility for answering the Opposition Whigs in general and William Pitt in particular on the floor of the House of Commons.[2]

Upon hearing Murray's maiden speech in the House of Commons, Horace Walpole reported to Horace Mann in Florence that it was received "with the greatest applause; Pitt answered him with all his force and art of language, but on an ill-founded argument. In all appearances they will be great rivals."[3] Appearances did not deceive, for they had been avid competitors since Murray placed first and Pitt second in an undergraduate poetry contest at Oxford occasioned by the death of George I in 1727. Now the rhetorical war of the two Williams would be waged on the floor of Parliament as the two greatest orators of the age engaged in the grand parliamentary debates. According to the refined taste of Lord Chesterfield, they were "beyond comparison the best speakers" on a political stage still moved by the magical power of words to shape propositions for public argument. "They alone can inflame or quiet the House," Chesterfield observed; "they alone are so attended to in that numerous and noisy assembly that you might hear a pin fall while either of them is speaking."[4]

William Pitt had already made a name for himself by pouring down high-minded scorn upon the policies and procedures of Sir Robert Walpole's corrupt system, and the political patterns of the new Pelham Administration pleased him no better. By the end of 1743 when the War of Austrian Succession was not going so well as expected, this latter-day "Demosthenes"—as Pitt was called—was arguing furiously that British forces should promptly replace the standing army of 16,000 Hanoverian troops in the pay of the British Crown. Our latter-day "Cicero"—as Murray was called—responded "that to the King alone it belongs not only to declare war, but to determine how the war, when declared, shall be carried on." One witness of their initial interchange in Parliament filed this report: "Murray *gains* your attention by the perspicuity of his arguments and the elegance of his diction. Pitt *commands* your attention and respect by the nobleness, the greatness of his sentiments, the strength and energy of his expression, and the certainty you are in of his always rising to a greater elevation both of thought and style." But time and again Pitt's commanding "thought and style" were overwhelmed by Murray's "perspicuity" and "elegance" when votes were taken in the House of Commons. And after defeating Pitt 231 to 181 at this critical juncture, the Solicitor General became "a special favorite of George II" and "the Government leader in the House of Commons."[5]

FROM the moment he was appointed Solicitor General, William Murray was closely associated with another legal luminary, Philip Yorke. In *Lives of the Lord Chancellors and Keepers of the Great Seal of England*, Lord Campbell carefully explained that "like most English lawyers, in preparing for the bar," Yorke "had hardly paid the slightest attention" to the Civil Law Code deriving from Roman antiquity. After Yorke was appointed Solicitor General, however, that jurisprudence captured his interest. Indeed, the brilliance of his long career was due to his "familiar knowledge ... of the Roman civil law," a competency that he acquired over time. He began to relish "the taste for this study ... from the necessity of preparing himself first to argue as an advocate, and then to decide, as a judge, appeals to the House of Lords from the Court of Session in Scotland." When he became the Attorney General he was "obliged to dip into the *Pandects* and into the commentaries upon them" because "the Roman civil laws" regulated "the enjoyment and succession of personal property" in Scotland. And when he served as the Lord Chief Justice of King's Bench he even "assisted a little in adapting ... the principles of the old common law ... to the new commercial transactions and changed manners which were gradually springing up." But only after he became Lord Chancellor Hardwicke in 1737 did his appreciation of Justinian's *Pandects* intensify radically. He plunged in a careful study of "Mackenzie, Bankton, and Stair" and then proceeded from these experts on the Scottish Civil Law to "the *Corpus Juris Civilis* with Vinnius, Voet, and other commentators." Because he now "sat in the House of Lords as sole judge to decide all appeals from Scotland," Lord Chancellor Hardwicke quickly discovered "the necessity of making himself a profound Scotch lawyer, and he found that this was impossible without being a good *civilian*" (my emphasis).

Because Hardwicke's "mind was thoroughly imbued with the truly *equitable* maxims of this noble jurisprudence," the Court of Chancery once again achieved high esteem as a Court of Equity. In Campbell's considered opinion, "Lord Hardwicke, in a few years, raised a reputation which no one presiding in the Court of Chancery has ever enjoyed, and which was not exceeded by that of the great Lord Mansfield as a common-law Judge." Hardwicke held the Great Seal from 1737 to 1756. During the better part of that transitional period "the first counsel in the Court of Chancery" was William Murray.[6]

REGARDLESS of how the War of Austrian Succession had been going, George II was determined that the Prince of Wales should not participate in the war effort. Because the relations between Prince Frederick and the King had been strained by their long-standing disagreement over the importance of Hanover, to carry out his continental strategy, the King turned to his third and favorite son, the Duke of Cumberland, William Augustus (1721-1765).

At the tender age of twenty-one Cumberland was appointed Major-General, only to be promptly promoted to Lieutenant-General after he was wounded in the battle of Dettingen in 1743. (Dettingen would be the last battle actually witnessed by a British king.) By 1745 the twenty-four-year-old Duke became the Commander-in-Chief of the British, Hanoverian, Austrian and Dutch land forces fighting the French in Flanders, an allied army that was defeated at Fontenoy by Marshall Saxe.

Given the military situation on the continent, another young Duke, the twenty-five-year-old Bonnie Prince Charlie, persuaded himself that the time was now ripe for the restoration of the House of Stuart. Lord Chancellor Hardwicke had cautioned against such an alarming contingency from the moment Parliament began examining Jenkins' supposed ear, for he was convinced that "discontents with the government" were "now general and deep, and without prudence will soon lead to open rebellion." "I warn you," Hardwicke informed Parliament, "that before long an attempt will be made to subvert our present happy establishment," for Bonnie Prince Charlie was known to entertain "delusive hopes" of saddling Great Britain with "Popery and slavery." Indeed, "his family in their exile have *learned nothing and forgot nothing*" (my emphasis).[7]

As a true believer in the indefeasible divine right of the Old Pretender to the crown, the Young Pretender decided on his own to launch the Rebellion of 1745 in order to drive the Elector of Hanover (as he contemptuously referred to George II) from the throne his Germanic father had usurped from its divinely anointed legitimate heir now forced to live in exile in Italy. Without the blessing of the Old Pretender in Rome, without the support of Louis XV in Paris, and without the knowledge of George II now in Germany, two months after the French had defeated the allied armies at Fontenoy, Bonnie Prince Charlie embarked from Belle Isle off the western coast of France with a tiny group of Jacobites and after a harrowing sail set foot on British soil for the first time in his life. In short order "the gallant and handsome young Prince" (in the words of Sir Walter Scott) "threw himself upon the mercy of his countrymen, rather like a hero of romance than a calculating politician." More and more Highland chiefs soon joined in the proclamation of the Old Pretender as King James VIII of Scotland.[8]

The ancestral turf of the Murray and Hay clans around Perth formed the initial staging area for the Jacobite Rebellion of 1745. After taking Edinburgh without firing a shot, the rebels won a stunning victory at Prestonpans. By December they had marched all the way to Derby where they positioned themselves in full battle array scarcely more than a hundred miles north of London. If they had just pressed their luck a bit further instead of retreating, legend has it that Bonnie Prince Charlie would have taken the capital by storm and replaced the dull, Germanic Hanoverians with a brilliant Stuart Court fashioned on the refined French model. Alas, this romantic revolt commanded precious little substantial depth in England, and the Duke of Cumberland made sure that the Stuart cause was finally finished. By early April 1746 he mobilized his forces in Aberdeen and promptly crushed the Rebellion root and branch in the Battle of Culloden just north of Inverness.[9]

This battle proved to be a watershed in military strategy, according to Michael A. Bellesiles's account: "The Duke of Cumberland made it standard practice for British troops to hold their fire until the enemy came into effective firing range (about ten yards), fire once, and then use the bayonet against the enemy, stabbing at the man to the right, rather than against the one immediately in front, so as to catch the enemy under his lifted sword arm." Whereas Cumberland's forces suffered only around fifty casualties, almost one thousand Scots lost their lives, thereby demonstrating for all to see the vast superiority of a bayonet attached to the long barrel of the British Brown Bess over the traditional broadsword of the Scottish forces.[10]

Terrible was the retribution Cumberland forced the Jacobites to pay. "The victory of Culloden was followed by a reign of terror in the Highlands," according to R. L. Mackie; "Houses were burned, cattle driven off or killed, men dragged to prison or shot without warning, and women ravished."[11] The range of Cumberland's victory is exhibited in John Prebble's description of the Culloden Medal struck for the British army:

> Cast in gold for the officers, it bore a Roman bust of the Duke with the single word *Cumberland* in halo above it. On the reverse side the nude figure of Apollo transfixed the neck of a dragon with his arrow. The legend was in Latin, *Actum est ilicit periit*—The deed is done, it is all over.

The Duke of Cumberland smashed the spirit of the Stuarts so severely that until his premature death two decades later he was known as "the Butcher of Culloden."[12]

THE Rebellion of 1745 created a very delicate situation for the Solicitor General in the Pelham Administration. Lord George Murray was merely the most conspicuous military leader from within the clan to commit treason. Substantial evidence does more than suggest that William Murray's own mother provided "the rebels with provisions as they passed through Perth." His older sister, Majorie Hay, was still living in Stuart quarters in Avignon. And it was public knowledge that his older brother, James Murray, was the Secretary of State in the exiled Stuart Court in Italy.

Even though many of the rebels were "connected with his family by blood and alliance," the ambitious Solicitor General saw his calling clear and prosecuted the fallen Jacobites. The penalty for treason in eighteenth-century law is expressed in grisly detail by the judge who sentenced seventeen commoners to death:

> Let the several prisoners return to the gaol from whence they came; and from thence they must be drawn in the place of execution; and when they come there they must be severally hanged by the neck, but not till they be dead, for they must be cut down alive; then their bowels must be taken out and burned before their faces; then their heads must be severed from their bodies, and their bodies severally divided into four quarters; and these must be at the King's disposal.

The nobility, though, were dispatched more swiftly by the executioner's axe. And so gripping were the "eloquence and learning" of the Solicitor General at the trial of Lord Lovat that this cousin was moved to say on the night before his execution, "Mr. Solicitor is a great man, and he will meet with high promotion *if he is not too far north.*"[13]

From Scotland though he was, William Murray was not from the Highlands. And upon his shoulders fell the task of carrying through the House of Commons the punitive policies pursued by the Pelham Administration against the Scottish Highlands. Those wild parts of Scotland were "yet uncivilized" because they were still under the control of the clan chiefs. So absolute was the power of a clan chief that "if he sentenced an offender to death no complaint would come from his people." Their chief was "the only judge whose decrees the clan recognized," according to R. L. Mackie; not even a "royal proclamation could stop his clan if he had ordered it to follow him to battle."

To break down the identity of the various clans in so primitive a social system, a new dress code was imposed: "the wearing of the Highland dress, or even cloths made of tartan, was prohibited under the penalty of six months' imprisonment for the first offence and transportation for the second." A Disarming Act was relentlessly carried out in order to remove the material foundations of the ferocious fighting spirit of the Highland clans. Then Parliament abolished the "Heritable Jurisdictions" that still function as the legal system in the feudal north.[14]

Lord Chancellor Hardwicke argued in Parliament that the "private law" of the clan system nurtured "a dangerous and unconstitutional dependence" upon the clan chiefs: "The people will follow those, who have the power to protect or hurt them; and this dependence will operate most strongly in the uncivilized part of any country, remote from the seat of government." The only way to make sure that these "ill effects" would never again tear asunder the fabric of the kingdom was to "restore the powers of jurisdiction to the crown, as it now stands bounded by law since the [Glorious] Revolution."[15]

Arguing directly against this unfolding interpretation of the British Constitution, it should be noted, one speaker in the parliamentary debate boldly asserted that "our constitution will be undone" if Parliament took so much as a single step down the slippery slope of passing "an act for giving the king's proclamation the authority of an act of parliament":

> No one can tell how far our future princes and their fanciful ministers may push the authority of such a precedent: for from experience we know, that the imagination of ministers is mighty fertile, with respect to the dangers or inconveniences that may ensue from the rights or powers lodged in the people.

The lived experience of the English people had clearly indicated that an arbitrary government "will necessarily" follow along one of these three devious routes:

> It will necessarily and of course deviate [1] into an *absolute monarchy*, as it was for some time after the Conquest [of 1066], and again in the reign of Henry 8, after passing the law ... for rendering the King's proclamation of equal authority with an act of parliament; or it will deviate [2] into an *absolute aristocracy*, as it was for some time in the reign of Henry 3; or lastly, it will deviate [3] into a *democracy*, as it was for some time after the defeat of Charles I; and that of course, as such governments generally soon do, will deviate into a sole and arbitrary tyranny, as was our case under Oliver Cromwell [my emphases].

This constitutional lawyer then pressed on to claim that Hardwicke's novel interpretation of the British Constitution—one shared by Solicitor General Murray—exhibited "a vulgar error, which of late but too general prevails," namely, "that the executive power of our government is wholly and solely lodged in the crown; from whence it is inferred, that the jurisdictive power, being a part of the executive power, originally and properly belonged to the crown." After appealing directly to "the ancient and original form of our constitution" during the gorgeous past of Anglo-Saxon England, this parliamentary debater asserted—even in the face of all the historical evidence he had just marshaled—that "the dernier resort has always, and still does lie in the House."[16]

George Lyttelton would not let so quaint a celebration of those "Gothic constitutions" go unchallenged in this debate. He thought that enlightened, eighteenth-century legislators should readily see that during the Dark Ages "the people" never attained "any considerable share of wealth or freedom, till they had been emancipated from [heritable] jurisdictions." "The great feudal lords," in Lyttelton's judgment, were "petty tyrants, too potent for subjects, too weak for sovereigns, strong enough to oppress, but unable to protect." Nothing creative of social peace could possibly transpire until all those feudal privileges were "entirely absorbed in the more beneficial and salutary power of the crown." Only when "the wildest parts" of Scotland were blessed with "good government" could "all the virtues and sweets of civil life" blossom forth in grandeur. "Authority and justice must take the lead in this great work of reformation: discipline, peace, and civility, will follow after." But the path to "improvement" could only be cleared by "an active communication of the generous, free, and noble plan of the law of England."[17]

Although the heritable jurisdictions of the Highland Chiefs in Scotland's ancient traditions were removed, contrary to what Lyttelton suggested, "the generous, free, and noble plan of the law of England" was not extended throughout Scotland. What actually happened was the extension of the legal system of the Scottish Lowlands throughout the Scottish Highlands. The old clan chiefs now became landlords; the clansmen now became tenants; and the Highlands now became depopulated. So desperate a situation also focused some of the most powerful minds in Scotland upon the ways and means of coping with the "reformation of manners" that drove the "uncivilized" common people into a frantic search for a new way of life. Another year would pass before Montesquieu would publish his extraordinarily influential *Esprit des Lois*, which advanced the thesis that among the various peoples of Western Europe the English alone had somehow managed to preserve the "beautiful system" of "liberty" that they brought with them from "the woods" of barbaric Germany.[18]

THE War of Jenkins's Ear quickly led into the War of Austrian Succession (1740-1748). While devastating for the Scottish Highlands, it was inconclusive in the larger arena of European politics. In the considered opinion of the Oxford historian, Paul Langford, the conflict was "the true beginning of that total commitment to the pursuit of empire which was to dominate the middle years of the century." William Murray was one of the most influential persons who talked Great Britain into that contest, and he was the one who carried through the House of Commons the Treaty of Aix-la-Chapelle in 1748. Although the ensuing peace was widely viewed as one of "those great stalemates ... which made a new war inevitable," the Solicitor General thoroughly embraced the new imperial vision.[19] And his prominence in both foreign and domestic affairs caused people to begin calling attention to how he was "no less conspicuous for knowledge and virtue than for politeness of manners and a noble extraction." Indeed, he was widely acknowledged to be "the first counsel in the Court of Chancery" as well as the principal spokesman for the Pelham Administration in the House of Commons.[20]

WHEN Prince Frederick unexpectedly died in 1751, the succession to the throne went directly to his son, the future King George III. Because five years would pass before the young Prince of Wales would reach legal age—and George II was sixty-seven—the government rather urgently needed a Regency Act. The fear that moved on the surface was that if George II should die, the only Prince of the Blood of legal age—the King's favorite son, the Duke of Cumberland—might make a bid for supreme power. Indeed, a few months before Prince Frederick's death an anonymous pamphlet (attributed to Frederick's principal political consultant) had directly accused Cumberland of plotting a *coup d'état*.

Even more ominously, the King clearly wanted Cumberland to be designated Regent instead of the Dowager Princess of Wales, Prince George's mother, Augusta. With the shade of King Richard III still stalking the popular imagination—and with "the Butcher of Culloden" at the head of the military—the Pelham Administration handed to Solicitor General Murray the delicate task of negotiating a Regency Act. The upshot was that the Dowager Princess of Wales would become the Regent during her son's minority, but with the proviso that she could not act without the consent of a ministerial council headed by the Duke of Cumberland.[21]

Once that clever compromise had been shepherded through Parliament, the Pelham Administration turned its attention to the ways and means of providing a proper education for the Prince of Wales and his younger brother, Prince Edward, something that had escaped the notice of the government simply because it had been casually assumed that their father would soon become His Britannic Majesty. And truth to tell Prince Frederick had scarcely been any more attentive to their intellectual development than to his own. It is also important to remember that the offices of the Governor and Preceptor in the royal household were honorific positions—the real work, in typical eighteenth-century fashion, was carried on by the Sub-Governor and Sub-Preceptor. The new Sub-Governor the ministry chose was William Murray's close friend and intimate associate, Andrew Stone.

Not many months passed before the Governor, Lord Harcourt, and the Preceptor, Bishop Thomas Hayter, became alarmed over what they considered to be the arbitrary principles of government being instilled in the hearts and minds of the tender youths. By early summer 1752 the Duke of Newcastle learned while he was accompanying the King in Hanover that all was not well in Prince George's household. The conflict came to a head as soon as the royal entourage returned to England in the late fall, for on 21 November 1752 Lord Harcourt forced the issue into the open by submitting his resignation. Whereas Governor Harcourt and Preceptor Hayter thought that they had sniffed out the scent of Jacobitism in the princely curriculum, the elderly King saw fit to replace them because of their "fantastic allegations" against Sub-Governor, Andrew Stone, and Sub-Preceptor, George Lewis Scott.

This squabble over the proper education of Prince George and Prince Edward would scarcely deserve more than a passing comment had the affair ended there. That it did not was due primarily to the suspicious temperament of Horace Walpole. According to the conspiracy theory at the heart of his *Memoirs of King George II*, the "secret source" of this "prostitution of patriotism" was Lord Bolingbroke with his *Idea of a Patriot King*. Shortly after Bolingbroke bid his final adieu in December 1751, Walpole assured Horace Mann that "Lord Bolingbroke dead will govern, which he never could living," because the old Jacobite's dream had already begun to influence the inner circles of the ministry through the determined design of his two devoted disciples, Andrew Stone and William Murray.[22]

In Walpole's telling Murray had officiously told Bishop Hayter that Lord Harcourt was "a cipher, and must be a cipher, and was put in to be a cipher," and now both Bishop and Lord had no choice but to resign their positions. Soon Walpole would make this prognostication to Mann: "the foundations of a revolution in earnest are laying." And this threat was taken so seriously that he drew up a Memorial on the matter and clandestinely sent it under the cover of anonymity to five or six particular persons in high places. By mid-December several key figures in the government were pondering what Newcastle called "this scandalous and seditious libel," a veritable depth charge set to go off when it reached a sufficiently explosive level.

In this Memorial Walpole warned that it was "unwarrantable, dangerous and illegal" for "a faction to engross the education of a Prince of Wales." Especially dangerous because those in charge of shaping the heart and mind of the heir to the throne were "friends and pupils of the late Lord Bolingbroke." Not only had "books inculcating the worst maxims of government, and defending the most avowed tyrannies ... been put into the hands of the Prince of Wales," this "dangerous faction" was conspiring in a deep-laid plot "to overthrow the government and restore the exiled and arbitrary House of Stuart."

In Walpole's suspicious but informed opinion the "first disciple of Bolingbroke" was none other than William Murray. Furthermore, "to have a Scotchman of a most disaffected family, and allied in the nearest manner to the Pretender's first minister, consulted on the education of the Prince of Wales, and entrusted with the most important secrets of government, must tend to alarm and disgust the friends of the present Royal Family, and to encourage the hopes and attempts of the Jacobites." Walpole then pressed his conspiracy theory to the maximum:

there is a settled design in those low and suspected persons [i.e., Murray and Stone] to infuse such jealousies, caprices, and fickleness into the two Ministers whose confidence they engross [i.e., Pelham and Newcastle], as may render the Government ridiculous and contemptible, and facilitate the Revolution, which the Memorialists think they have but too much reason to fear is meditating.

With this anonymous Memorial one of the most knowledgeable commentator on the intrigues behind the scenes of the contemporary political world not only poisoned the well but launched a legend.[23]

One of the persons who received a copy of Walpole's Memorial was Lord Ravensworth and it jogged his memory about what he had heard at the Deanery of Durham during a party honoring George II's birthday on 10 November 1752. Over perhaps too much drink—Ravensworth never seemed to be able to recall exactly what he had actually heard—the Dean of Durham turned the conversation to Dr. James Johnson, who was another close friend of William Murray since school days in Westminster and had been elevated recently to the bishopric of Gloucester. The current gossip, according to the Dean's information, suggested that Johnson was now going to become the new Preceptor to the Prince of Wales. Unfounded though this rumor turned out to be, it did elicit from a local lawyer named Charles Fawcett a careless comment something along these lines: "I am glad Johnson gets on so well, for I remember him a Jacobite several years ago."[24]

Given Walpole's direct indictment as well as a host of vague rumors afloat—there was a genuine Jacobite Plot planned but scratched for the King's birthday—Prime Minister Pelham decided to investigate Fawcett's assertion soon after he got wind of it from Ravensworth in December. On 12 January 1753 Fawcett received an official letter demanding a written statement that either confirmed or denied his allegation against Bishop Johnson. Sensing that he had rushed in where angels fear to tread, Fawcett acknowledged in his response that when he was nineteen years old he had indeed met James Johnson at the home of one Vernon, a distant relative that Fawcett had visited for an extended period in the early 1730s, but he categorically denied that he had ever said that the good Bishop was a Jacobite. Soon Johnson demanded and got from Fawcett a written statement of denial as well.[25]

One would have thought that with his written denial in hand this rather trivial comment made over drinks during an after-dinner conversation would have passed into oblivion, but such was not the case. Before long Fawcett stumbled across Lord Ravensworth at a local club and in their heated exchange Fawcett confided that he could not substantiate his accusation against James Johnson without implicating William Murray and Andrew Stone as well. Fawcett's expanded version now claimed that twenty years or so ago, these Westminster friends had frequently come home with their schoolmate, Vernon, and all four of them had drunk toasts to the Stuart Pretender's health.

Lord Ravensworth was now so alarmed by this direct confirmation of Walpole's Memorial that he urged Fawcett to make a full and honest disclosure to the Prime Minister. In his retelling of the episode to Henry Pelham, however, Fawcett completely omitted any reference to Stone and Murray, and utterly denied that he had ever accused Johnson of Jacobitism. But to lend some semblance of plausibility to his tale of treason told in words of mirth, Fawcett rushed on to say that while he was visiting the Vernon household in the early 1730s the *disaffected father* of young Vernon had been much given to swearing loyalty to the exiled House of Stuart. And he had stood for William Murray's father at his wedding in 1738.

Conveniently, both the Vernons—father and son—had long since died. Alas, Lord Ravensworth was still very much alive and he was also very determined to distill the truth from the contradictory stories Fawcett seemed to be fabricating as the occasion demanded. Before long Ravensworth persuaded, or perhaps pressured, Fawcett into testifying under oath—not against James Johnson, who already had his written clearance—but now against Andrew Stone and William Murray.

For three days in mid-February 1753, according to Walpole's rendition of this crisis, "the Cabinet Council sat long and late, but with much secrecy, inquiring into this affair." On the first day Ravensworth testified under a voluntary oath and handed over to the Council some letters Fawcett had written to him, letters that failed to support what Fawcett had previously told the Prime Minister. On the second day Fawcett testified under oath that he could not remember very clearly whether Johnson had been present at the time but he was certain that "both Stone and Murray, on various occasions down so late as the year 1732, had, at Mr. Vernon's house, drunk the health of the Pretender, and once he was sure they had done so on their knees." Indeed, "the conversation was wont to be partly literature, partly treason; the customary healths THE CHEVALIER and THE EARL OF DUNBAR," that is, the Old Pretender and his Secretary of State, James Murray.

When Fawcett finished this fine speech the Council asked him to square his accusations with what he had written in his letters to Lord Ravensworth, letters that he only now discovered had been placed in the Council's possession. Once he realized that they knew that he was caught on the horns of his own contradictions, Fawcett threw it all up and openly declared that after so many years he just could not recall with precision what had actually transpired during his stay in the Vernon household so long ago. In his own words, "it is impossible that any credit should be given to what I say."[26]

When the Council interrogated Andrew Stone, the Sub-Governor of the Prince of Wales denied under oath that he had ever done or said anything like what Fawcett first claimed and then retracted. Bishop Johnson thoroughly supported Stone's testimony. Solicitor Murray went even further. On 23 February 1753 he gave (in Walpole's words) "an incomparable oration" that (in Newcastle's words) "made the greatest impression upon the Lords in Council."

In this moving vindication of his services to the Crown, William Murray made several interesting points:

> I saw very soon [in my youth] the blessings of a
> free government, and I did not, even then, argue so
> weakly as to think that a free government could be
> preserved but by allowing such a resistance as was
> necessary at the [Glorious] Revolution.

That covered over rather nicely his Jacobite background.

> When I went to the university, as I was upon a
> foundation, I took all the oaths to the Government.
> When I took them I well knew the force of those
> engagements. I was not ignorant of the nature of the
> question, if it can be called a question, for I never
> could see the doubt. That a Protestant should reason
> himself into a Jacobite is as incomprehensible in
> politics as it is in religion that a man should reason
> himself into an atheist.

That hid in deep darkness the 1725 letters he sent to the Old Pretender
from Paris during the Long Vacation of his second year at Oxford.

> Pleading in the courts at Westminster and at the bar
> of either House of Parliament, I never uttered a word
> to disparage the Protestant settlement, or to create
> any longing for the exiled family. I determined never
> to come into the House of Commons but upon *Whig
> principles* [my emphasis].

That final phrase would return to haunt William Murray for
years to come.

Nevertheless, his explanation of Fawcett's evolving contradictions
was more than convincing: "That wretched man, to figure in company
and outrun the cry, began with falsehood. He falsely accused the
Bishop of Gloucester, and alledged a false cause of knowledge.
Wanting afterwards to get rid of the personal accusation, and yet to
keep up some opinion of his veracity, he has plunged from falsehood

to falsehood, till he is, at last, irretrievably lost." The upshot? On 26 February 1753 it was agreed unanimously that Fawcett's prevarications were "scandalous, and malicious; and that there appears no ground for … the aspersions" he had so recklessly cast upon the good names of James Johnson, Andrew Stone, and William Murray.[27]

This princely affair, though, was not quite over. In March the Duke of Bedford gave notice that he wanted all the papers concerning this bizarre episode laid before the House of Lords. Because Bedford's demand was widely perceived to be the opening salvo in a steady effort by the Opposition to bring down the Pelham Administration, the members of the Council were released from their oaths of secrecy so that they could openly face the gathering storm.

At this critical juncture William Murray gained some unexpected support from his avowed rival, William Pitt. In unequivocal terms Pitt told Lord Temple (soon to become his brother-in-law) that it would be a profound mistake to follow Bedford in an assault upon the Pelham Administration: "If you should entertain any thought of supporting or going with the question, to lay it aside, as I am deeply persuaded that nothing could be so fatal to me and to all our views, so nothing imaginable could give me a concern equal to seeing your Lordship take such a step." Although the political nation braced itself for some fancy fireworks, the Duke of Bedford's roman candle failed to ignite. So this strange affair over the education of the Prince of Wales finally burned out without so much as a division.[28]

Jacobitism was still something more than a mere nuisance on the political landscape, a fact made abundantly clear that same March by the arrest of Dr. Archibald Cameron—one of the few who had escaped with Bonnie Prince Charlie after the defeat at Culloden. Cameron thought that after so many years in exile it might be safe to return clandestinely to Scotland. Alas, he was arrested, tried, and condemned for treason. In June 1753 this last known Jacobite within the realm to be executed was "taken to Tyburn," and in James Alan Renne's telling, "suspended by the neck for twenty minutes, cut down, his head haggled off and … his heart torn out and burned."[29]

Although it is reasonable to presume that William Murray had been (in the words of Paul Kléber Monod) "a raging Jacobite in his youth," the Solicitor General was thoroughly exonerated because of his steadfast loyalty to the Pelham Administration. His denial of his past, however, was met with more than a touch of skepticism within the political nation. Lord Chesterfield's prediction in a letter written on 6 April 1753 captures the essence of the unfolding situation:

> The evidence against them [i.e., William Murray and Andrew Stone] was really nothing; but, upon the whole, the affair has affected them both, and they will feel the weight of it as long as they live. No reasonable man, I believed, thinks them Jacobites now, whatever they may have been formerly. But parties do not reason, and every Whig party man, which is nine in ten of the Whig party, is fully convinced that they are at this time determined and dangerous Jacobites.

What Paul Langford calls this "ludicrous but damaging scandal," in Lord Campbell's narrative occasioned "infinite annoyance and vexation" for years to come, because "it somewhat damaged" William Murray's "reputation for sincerity, and it afforded a topic to his opponents of which they ever after unsparingly availed themselves." Years later, for example, *The Letters of Junius* hammered him with the accusation that he was "always a rank Jacobite." The proof? "Lord Ravensworth produced the most satisfactory Evidence of his having frequently drank the Pretender's health upon his knees."[30]

WEAKENED politically though William Murray was by this affair, the opinions he expressed while Solicitor General marked out the coming line of development within the imperial government in regard to the emerging understanding of the Constitution of the British Empire. In *Peripheries and Center: Constitutional Development in the Extended Polities of the British Empire and the United States, 1607-1788*, Jack P. Greene called attention to the fact that during the 1730s and 1740s Parliament had refused "on three separate occasions to use its legislative authority to strengthen royal authority in the colonies":

> In 1734, a House of Lords committee proposed a bill to prevent any colonial laws from taking effect until they had been approved by the crown, but the Lords never formulated this proposal into a bill. Similarly, two bills to regulate colonial paper currencies considered by the House of Commons in 1744 and 1749 contained clauses that would have given royal instructions the force of law in the colonies. When these clauses provoked a "general opposition" from the colonial agents in London, however, the Commons dropped both bills, and the currency law it finally did enact in 1751 included no such provision.[31]

That parliamentary restraint, however, would soon yield to a more aggressive pattern of governance. As early as 1744 Solicitor General Murray had reaffirmed the imperial doctrine that "a colony of English subjects cannot be taxed but by some representative body of their own *or by the Parliament of England*" (my emphasis). Given time he would advise Parliament to begin exercising that latent power. Soon he also insisted upon the importance of the controversial imperial doctrine that the various colonial assemblies existed "from the Grace and Favour of the Crowne alone."[32] Given the enhancement of these theoretical notions, one did not need to be a prophet to perceive that soon royal "instructions" to colonial governors would also undergo a significant expansion.

Solicitor General Murray received considerable support for his expansive doctrine of the authority of royal instructions from another key player in the decision-making process, Charles Townshend (1725-1767). After "reading Justinian" at Cambridge University, Townshend pursued "the course of civil law" under a Professor Schwartz in Leyden. Midway through the curriculum his father sent him a blistering letter that reads, "I think you have been there long enough, to gain as much knowledge in the civil law as may be necessary for a basis to your future study of the laws of your own country!" Charles, though, responded by saying that his knowledge of "the whole system" of that "science" would remain "imperfect" unless he stayed in the Netherlands until the end of the term in July 1746.

Soon after he returned to England Charles Townshend entered the House of Commons, and from 1749 to 1754 he served on the Board of Trade. According to Sir Lewis Namier's splendid biography of this emotionally unstable weathercock,

> In August 1753 instructions of a rather unusual character were issued to Sir Danvers Osborn, Governor of New York—Horace Walpole, writing about 1755, described them as "better calculated for the latitude of Mexico and for a Spanish tribunal, than for a free, rich British settlement." These instructions Charles Townshend subsequently avowed in the House to have "advised," that is, to have drafted.

Volatile though he was in his personal life—Namier does more than suggest that his personality was shaped by the fact that his father was a tyrant and his mother a tramp—the orientation that Charles Townshend received from his advanced studies in the Roman Civil Law Tradition meshed nicely with the grand vision for reforming the Old Colonial System championed by Solicitor General Murray.[33]

According to Leonard Woods Labaree in his 1930 study, *The Old Colonial System*, in 1753 "the Board of Trade, reconstituted under Lord Halifax, asked the attorney and solicitor general of Great Britain to prepare new regulations, because they felt that the instructions had become obsolete and improper in some respects."[34] Lord Halifax, Charles Townshend and William Murray put this critical expansion of the authority of royal instructions in motion as British North America was actively bracing itself for the French and Indian War. In retrospect the baseline of the constitutional conflict of the 1760s was already visible in the planning processes of the imperial bureaucracy.

ATTORNEY GENERAL
IN THE NEWCASTLE
ADMINISTRATION

A S THE GENERAL ELECTION WAS REACHING A CLIMAX, PRIME MINISTER HENRY PELHAM died suddenly on 6 March 1754. Upon hearing this shocking news, George II was moved to confess, "Now I shall have no more peace," and the elderly king was right. Horace Walpole immediately reported to Horace Mann, "all that calm, that supineness ... is at an end!" Pelham "could not have died at a more critical time." Stunned though the political nation was by this unexpected turn of events, the governing class was not silenced. "You can't imagine," Walpole continued, "how much a million of people can talk in a day" about who would "snatch at the rudder of the state, amidst this storm and danger."[1]

This election was something of a watershed because it registered the decisive end to the relative stability that had characterized the Walpole and the Pelham Administrations. That long period of stability now gave way to ministerial instability. And that is one of the controlling reasons why the editors of the comprehensive five volume *History of Parliament: The House of Commons from 1715 to 1790* selected the Election of 1754—not the transition from the reign of George II to George III in 1760—as the proper pivot for dividing the narrative of the institutional development of the House of Commons during the eighteenth century, with Romney Sedgwick editing the earlier half from 1715 to 1754 (two volumes, Oxford, 1970), and Sir Lewis Namier and John Brooke editing the latter half from 1754 and 1790 (three volumes, Oxford, 1964).[2]

Regardless of the adequacy of standard party labels, the Whigs had thoroughly vanquished the Tories ever since the Elector of Hanover had become George I in 1714. Over the years the country gentlemen who were the backbone of the Old Tory Tradition had, by and large, withdrawn to their more pastoral pleasures. As Lord Bolingbroke described the party situation in 1739, "The Whigs have always looked on the Protestant succession, and the Tories on the restoration of the Stuarts, as a sure means to throw the whole power of Government into the hands of one or the other of them, and to keep it there." Once the Jacobites had been crushed in the Rebellion of 1745 these Old Tories came to realize that they faced a lost future. That is precisely why Lord Chesterfield observed in regard to the Election of 1754: "The fury of this war is chiefly Whig against Whig, for the Tories are pretty much out of the question; so that, after the new Parliament shall be chosen, the greatest difficulty upon the administration will be, to find pasture enough for the beasts they must feed."

Broadly construed, the Whig Establishment splintered into three factions driven by personal loyalties and political favors, with each faction claiming to espouse "Revolution Principles" but obviously meaning quite different things by that common phrase. First, one faction was headed by Henry Fox under the guidance of the Duke of Cumberland. Second, the rather independent William Pitt had a small but tenacious following called the Patriot Whigs. And finally there was what remained of the Old Corps Whigs under the leadership of the newly appointed Prime Minister, the Duke of Newcastle.[3]

46

Whereas the Pelham Administration had controlled all the separate and distinct departmental responsibilities by centralizing everything in the office of the Prime Minister, the Newcastle Administration proceeded to divide the key offices, thereby losing a significant amount of control. Furthermore, since Newcastle was in the House of Lords, his enduring problem was to find someone who could manage the House of Commons with its commanding but volatile Whig majority.

From among a host of aspiring contenders for the leadership of the House of Commons, there were only three serious contenders: Henry Fox, William Pitt, and William Murray. All three of these publicly known enemies were in their late forties, but like three scorpions locked in a bottle, these ambitious politicians had been forced by organizational necessity to mute their differences in order to serve within the ranks of a secure political establishment under the guiding hand of Henry Pelham. That necessity dissolved dramatically, however, the moment the Duke of Newcastle tried to regroup and lead this unholy alliance after the Election of 1754.

Henry Fox had been the "ostensible second" in the House of Commons ever since Pelham had appointed him the Secretary at War. Because he was attached to the Duke of Cumberland it was generally assumed that George II would select Fox to become the new Leader of the House of Commons. That this did not happen was due in large part to the enduring hostility of Lord Chancellor Hardwicke. The Dowager Princess of Wales at Leicester House also shared Hardwicke's judgment that Fox was "a dark and insidious genius, the engine of personality and faction." Pitt, too, was determined to block Fox's pursuit of power.

William Pitt had a mighty voice but only a slim base in the House of Commons. As a free-floating Patriot Whig with an intensely loyal but small following, Pitt's power rested to a considerable extent upon the tacit but unreliable support of the Tories when it suited their purposes to team up with the Opposition Whigs. And the legend that the Great Commoner was already the darling of public opinion, it should be pointed out, results from reading back into this earlier period his later prominence and popularity. Pitt's tactical problem turned on the fact that His Britannic Majesty would not countenance even the suggestion that he should confide in a political leader who was assumed to be unalterably opposed to the continental interests of the Elector of Hanover.[4]

William Murray was clearly the first choice of Newcastle, but his chances for becoming the Leader of the House of Commons were "ruined by malice" churned up by the recent affair over the education of the Prince of Wales. The cry that made the rounds roasted the Solicitor General by calling attention to "the absurdity of having a Tory head ... on a Whig body." Perhaps even Lord Chancellor Hardwicke was a bit jealous of his commanding influence. William Pitt's stance, though, was much more refined. "Could Mr. Murray's situation have allow'd him to be placed at the head of the House of Commons," Pitt assured Newcastle, "I should have served under him with the greatest pleasure." What had so altered Murray's situation was the sudden death of Lord Chief Justice Lee, which opened the way for Attorney General Dudley Ryder to be appointed to the Court of King's Bench. And Ryder's advancement opened the way for William Murray to be appointed *Attorney General* on 2 May 1754.[5]

Since Henry Fox was blocked, and the King would not consider William Pitt, and William Murray could not serve, the new Prime Minister chose Sir Thomas Robinson to be the Leader of the House of Commons. This tactical maneuver, however, fooled precious few. As Newcastle candidly expressed the disguise, Robinson would "inform the House of facts," but Murray would "do the business of the King and the public" when Parliament reconvened in November.[6]

WHILE the Newcastle Administration was being patched together, the halcyon days of spring soon gave way to the storm clouds of summer now gathering hurricane force on the American frontier. As early as 28 August 1753 Secretary of State Holderness had sent a circular letter that called attention to the rising dangers posed by French Quebec. Soon the most exposed Province, New York, called for an inter-colonial Congress to meet at Albany during the summer of 1754 to address the common problem facing British North America on the verge of what promised to become one of the greatest world wars of the eighteenth century. But before the commissioners from Massachusetts, New Hampshire, Rhode Island, Connecticut, New York, Pennsylvania, and Maryland—as well as the Iroquois Nations—could begin their deliberations on how to defend the exposed frontier against the rapidly rising French menace, open hostilities had already broken out.

On 9 May 1754 the *Pennsylvania Gazette* posted this critical information: "Friday last an Express arrived here from Major Washington, with Advice, that Mr. Ward, Ensign of Capt. Trent's Company, was compelled to surrender his small Fort in the Forks of Monogahela to the French." The urgency of the situation was exhibited by a famous political cartoon that featured a snake divided into eight segments—marked S.C., N.C., V., M., P., N.J., N.Y., and N.E.—with its tail in South Carolina coiling up to its head in New England. The message was crystal clear—"JOIN, or DIE."[7]

Nothing could express more clearly the alarming situation of British North America that so troubled Benjamin Franklin (1705-1790). He epitomized what the eighteenth century called "a public man" from the moment he turned over his extraordinarily successful printing business to his foremen so that he could pursue on a full time basis both his scientific interests and political concerns. He was acutely aware of the dynamic controlling the settlement of British North America throughout the tumultuous seventeenth century, for it turned upon the transparent fact that England had exported her diversity, especially in the traditionally divisive area of religious beliefs and practices. Over time each colony stretched along the Atlantic seacoast had developed its own distinct identity. On any plausible set of topics, the planters of Charleston felt vastly closer to metropolitan London than to, say, provincial Boston. And the pluralistic province of Pennsylvania differed in the most fundamental ways from the aristocratic ethos of the Old Dominion. No single city in the New World even pretended to be the center of the multifarious colonies. What these English speaking colonies did share, though, was an enduring loyalty to a promising Empire. According to Franklin's demographic calculations "our People must at least be doubled every 20 years," a growth rate so astonishing that before long "the greatest Number of *Englishmen* will be on this Side the Water. What an Accession of Power to the *British* Empire by Sea as well as Land."[8] Briefly put, American attachment to the mother country had actually been increasing decade after decade since the Glorious Revolution.

Not only was Franklin one of the commissioners in the 1754 Albany Congress, he was a principal drafter of its ill-fated Plan of Union that was consciously designed to overcome the "present disunited State of the British Colonies, and the extreme Difficulty of bringing so many different Governments and Assemblies to agree in any speedy and effectual Measure for our Common Defence and Security." In lining out the different "Reasons and Motives for the Albany Plan of Union" the commissioners began with the sobering fact that "the assemblies of six (out of seven) colonies applied to, had granted no assistance to *Virginia*, when lately invaded by the *French*." Therefore, the First Resolution: "*That an union of the colonies is absolutely necessary for their preservation.*" But it was readily apparent that the colonial Americans would never unite on their own precisely because the various colonies with their divergent interests were "extremely jealous of each other." Therefore, the Second Resolution: "*That it was necessary the union should be established by act of parliament.*"[9]

Parliament carried extraordinary weight with Franklin as with most colonial Americans. He was fond of recalling, for example, how in 1744 the House of Commons had "thrown out" a pernicious "Clause in a Bill brought into Parliament by the Ministry" that "had propos'd to make the King's Instructions Laws in the Colonies." He also noticed how most colonies attempted to replicate a parliamentary form of government, with a Governor representing the King, over against an Assembly patterned upon the House of Commons representing the people. Between them stood a Council, which more or less resembled the House of Lords, minus, of course, any hereditary Peers or Lords Spiritual. While the match was less than perfect, the colonials had a "mixed constitution" derived from their English background. And they universally celebrated this "mixed constitution" with its limited government as a marvel of political ingenuity that stood in polar opposition to the absolute monarchy of the dreaded French.[10]

From the fact that the Albany Congress embraced the proposition that an inter-colonial "union should be established by act of parliament," it does not follow that the colonial Americans were asking for parliamentary interference in the internal affairs of the various colonies, as a close examination of the 1754 Plan clearly shows. To be precise, the proposed "general government" would be located in North America and it would be "administered by [1] a President General to be appointed and supported by the crown; and [2] a Grand Council to be chosen by the representatives of the people of the several colonies met in their respective assemblies." The formation of this Grand Council would preserve a critical constitutional principle, namely, "That it is essential to English liberty, that the subject should not be taxed but by his own consent or the consent of his elected representatives."

One of the principal reasons "the people" were given the sole voice to consent through their "elected representatives"—instead of permitting "the governors and council of the several provinces a share in the choice of the grand council"—is more than instructive:

> In some [of the colonies], both governor and council are appointed by the crown [e.g., Virginia]. In others, they are both appointed by the proprietors [e.g. Pennsylvania]. In some, the people have a share in the choice of the council [e.g., Massachusetts]; in others, both governor and council are wholly chosen by the people [e.g. Rhode Island and Connecticut].

Remarkably diverse though the polities and legal codes of the different colonies were, each had a lower house elected by "the people," and this branch of every colonial government jealously guarded its privileges, especially the power to tax.[11]

Most of the commissioners in Albany had served on the councils of their respective governments, and from long experience in colonial affairs they had become more than a little sensitive to the issue of taxation, for a steady stream of Royal Governors and British Officials had written a plethora of letters over the previous half-century that suggested that Parliament should levy a tax on the colonies. In fact, soon after the Albany Congress Governor Shirley communicated to Benjamin Franklin the "profound secret" that the Newcastle Administration was actively considering a novel parliamentary tax on the colonies.

Shirley's profound secret had substance behind it, for immediately prior to the Albany Congress the Board of Trade circulated a plan that proposed to finance a series of outposts on the American frontier by a parliamentary tax upon the colonies. Charles Townshend, recently promoted to the Admiralty Board, actively promoted this plan within the ministry. His lengthy response to Newcastle, which lines out the rationale for this new type of taxation, captures a pervasive sentiment among some key government officials:

> It is well known to those who have attended to the affairs of America that the provinces have been for many years engaged in a skillful design of drawing to themselves the ancient and established prerogatives wisely preserved in the crown as the only means of continuing the superintendency of the mother country and their manner of doing this has been by their annual bills of supply, in which they have appointed all the officers of the crown by name to be employed in the exchequer, substituted warrants for drawing out public money in the place of the governors' and in one word dispossessed the crown of almost every degree of executive power ever lodged in it … I am supported in the Opinion by the History of America for fifty years past.

After reviewing Townshend's letter, Attorney General Murray did more than agree "in all he says and proposes"; he even assured Newcastle that many more "Reasons … might be given" in support of the policy of a parliamentary tax upon the Americans. The plan was to consolidate the various colonial contributions "into one permanent and fixed Fund" which would be "applied by Directors from home to the Services for which it is appropriated in Such manner as His Majesty shall think best."[12]

Benjamin Franklin responded directly and vigorously to the suggested tax in the most explicit terms in December:

> That it is suppos'd an undoubted Right of Englishmen not to be taxed but by their own Consent given thro' their Representatives. That the Colonies have no Representatives in Parliament. That to propose taxing by Parliament, and refusing them the Liberty of chusing a Representative Council, to meet in the Colonies, and consider and judge of the Necessity of any General Tax and Quantum, shews a Suspicion of their Loyalty to the Crown, or Regard for their Country, or of their Common Sense and Understanding, which they have not deserv'd … . That if the Colonies in a Body may be well governed by Governors and Councils appointed by the Crown, without Representatives, particular Colonies may as well or better be so governed; a Tax may be laid on them all by Act of Parliament, for Support of Government, and their Assemblies be dismiss'd as a useless Part of their Constitution.[13]

Henry Fox also cautioned the House of Commons not to interfere in colonial matters, for "as our colonies are more immediately under the eye of the crown than any other part of the British dominions, it would, in my opinion, be too great an encroachment upon the prerogatives of the crown, or at least it would be an intermeddling in an affair with which we [i.e., the House of Commons] have no call to have any concern."[14] Technically put, as the spokesman for the traditional Whig mentality, Fox was maintaining that the colonies were under the jurisdiction of the King-in-Council, not the King-in-Parliament.

For reasons unknown the Newcastle Administration rejected the Board of Trade's plan—and the explicit advice of both Charles Townshend and William Murray. Events, in any case, were rapidly marginalizing constitutional considerations. From the moment the news of George Washington's defeat near present day Pittsburgh reached London on 3 September 1754, a reverberation was felt in "the stagnated politics of the Ministry."

On 10 October Newcastle informed the British ambassador in Paris, "A most ill-judged advertisement from the War Office has set all the ministers on fire and made them believe we are going to war, which is, I hope, the furtherest from our thoughts." Thoughts of war, however, were front and center in the collective mind of the ministers of Louis XV. As Horace Walpole commented, "The pacific genius of the house of Pelham was not unknown to France, and fell in very conveniently with their plan of extensive empire." France's "attempts in America grew daily more open, more avowed, more alarming." The aim was to block the expansion of British North America "by erecting a chain of garrisons from Canada to the mouths of the Mississippi." Although Washington's defeat was a "trifling" event, this border skirmish in the howling wilderness of North America marked the opening of what Lawrence Henry Gipson has called "the Great War for the Empire."[15]

THE rising tensions among the Great Powers of Europe fed the domestic frictions when Parliament opened on 14 November 1754. Although Sir Thomas Robinson was sitting in the vacated seat of Henry Pelham, he was not a member of the Cabinet. Neither was the Secretary at War (Henry Fox), nor the Paymaster General (William Pitt), nor the Chancellor of the Exchequer (Henry Legge). Not one of them was an active participant in the decision-making processes of the Newcastle Administration. Fox, Pitt, and Legge positioned themselves in that order to the immediate left of the designated Leader of the House. To Robinson's right was Attorney General Murray, and he alone knew the Cabinet's deliberations. Not even the most naïve could have failed to notice that he had "taken upon him[self] the air and appearance of the minister who was to lead the House." (Exactly when the "Secret Committee" of the Cabinet Council started to hold its meetings remains unknown, but surely Newcastle had continuously consulted Murray—the sketchy records document that he began attending no later than 21 January 1755.)[16]

Before the end of November William Pitt began warning the House that unless it asserted its independent power and constitutional position it would soon "degenerate into a little assembly, serving no other purpose than to register the arbitrary edicts of one, too powerful subject," for Newcastle's little arrangement with Robinson and Murray was a fatal step that Pitt thought would soon reduce the House of Commons to being "the contemptible appendix of he knew not what." According to the testimony of both Fox and Walpole, that indictment was leveled directly against the scarcely hidden leadership of the Attorney General.[17]

At a crucial moment in these parliamentary debates Pitt picked up an image Robert Nugent had used to make vivid his claim that the Jacobites had become an extinct breed. In his speech Nugent had resorted to the fable of the disappointed mother hen that had hatched duck's eggs only to be surprised when her chicks took to the water. Pitt seized upon this stock fable in his rejoinder to Nugent: "For, Sir, I know of such a hen, I was bred under such an one, and will tell the House what she has been doing for these twenty years—raising a succession of treason."

After lambasting Oxford University as a "seminary" of sedition, Pitt proceeded to inform the House how some of the students had shouted "rank treason" while he was enjoying "a party of pleasure" during the previous summer. Pitt mocked the youthful bravado of these misguided "boys" by suggesting that when they grew up and discovered that their seditious plots had led them into the wilderness, "the most zealous of them, when leader of the Government party in this House, may assure you that he always approved of *the Protestant succession*, and that he refused to enter parliament except upon *Whig principles*" (my emphases). Then with piercing eyes fixed on Attorney General Murray, he added: "Perhaps some of them might hereafter zealously fill the office of Attorney or Solicitor General to a Brunswick Sovereign."

According to Fox's report, for a full hour Murray suffered from Pitt's assault. Walpole's narrative was even more graphic. It disclosed that "colours, much less words, could not paint the confusion and agitation what worked in Murray's face during this almost apostrophe! His countenance spoke everything that Fawcett had been terrified to prevaricate away." On another occasion, according to a contemporary report on the parliamentary debates, "Pitt made use of an expression of savage triumph":

> Having for some time tortured his victim by general invective, he suddenly stopped, threw his eyes around, then, fixing their whole power on Murray, uttered these words in a low, solemn tone, which caused a breathless silence: "I must now address a few words to Mr. Attorney: they shall be few, but they shall be daggers." Murray was agitated; the look was continued; the agitation increased. "Judge Festus trembles!" exclaimed Pitt; "he shall hear me some other day."

Pitt's abuse of Murray was relentless in these parliamentary debates, for he had "more dread of arbitrary power dressing itself in the long robe, than even of military power," according to Walpole's account. So far as the Great Commoner was concerned, he "did not date his principles of the liberty of this country from the [Glorious] Revolution; they are eternal rights."

In one of his speeches Pitt claimed, "The constitution may be shaken to its centre and the lawyer will sit calm in his cabinet, but let a cobweb be disturbed in Westminster Hall, and out the bloated spider will crawl in its defence." After commending Murray's "abilities" on another occasion, Pitt proceeded to torture him on his "distinctions and refinements." "When master principles are concerned, he dreaded accuracy of distinction: he feared that sort of reasoning; if you class everything, you will soon reduce everything into a particular; you will then lose great general maxims." Convinced that "Gentlemen may analyze a question till it is lost," Pitt directly charged that Murray's foreshortening of the constitutional heritage of ordered liberty amounted to "constructive treason" against the Act of Settlement with King William and Queen Mary.[18]

Attorney General Murray's position as the "unofficial" Leader of the House of Commons was surely perilous. What brought it to an end was Newcastle's decision to bring Henry Fox into the Cabinet. Because Fox steadily advanced the military strategies and political interests of the Duke of Cumberland, William Pitt decided to go into formal opposition. So, he was turned out of office as Paymaster General on 20 November 1755. Five days later Secretary of State Henry Fox replaced Sir Thomas Robinson as Leader of the House of Commons, thereby removing Attorney General Murray from the line of fire.

ONCE the news of General Braddock's defeat and death on the frontier of America reached London, the Newcastle Administration could no longer hide the melancholy fact that the military situation had deteriorated because of a lack of coordination, incompetent planning, and administrative confusion. Now as a leader of the opposition Pitt launched a frontal assault upon the new Leader in the House in order to expose "the whole conduct of the administration during the whole summer, and the long neglect of our colonies preceding that time which had bred this war."

William Pitt's assault steadily increased until it reached a climax on 2 December 1755. The issue was whether to pass a bill to encourage the enlistment of seamen. Henry Fox was against taking precipitous actions "now" because he believed that "the allies of France" could mediate the conflict and persuade the French to agree to "reasonable terms of accommodation." William Murray backed Fox by saying that to act "now" would send the wrong diplomatic signal. William Pitt responded with ridicule:

> In this debate, it seems, the monosyllable, "now," is of equal consequence with the monosyllable, "aye" or "no." If it be, Sir, I must ask the hon. Gentleman, who lays so great a stress upon it, whether we ought to prepare for war before we declare war? If he answers by the important monosyllable, "aye," he must grant that the important monosyllable, "now," is in favour of the Bill proposed [for the encouragement of seamen], as nothing more is thereby designed, but a method of preparing for war which experience has taught us to be both proper and necessary.

William Murray was not intimidated:

> I must repeat the word "now," Sir, because notwithstanding the ridiculous light it has been placed in by the hon. Gentleman who spoke last, it is of the utmost consequence in this debate. He, indeed, has the happy faculty of being able to turn the most important word, the most serious argument, into ridicule, and to give a seeming weight and importance to the most useless words, the most trifling arguments, that can be made use of in any debate.

Brutal though the rhetorical war of the two Williams could sometimes be, what should not be overlooked is that William Murray almost always won these contests when the votes were counted in the House. At this critical moment the Attorney General so convincingly defeated Pitt that people began to notice that even Fox "cries up *Murray* to the stars." Walpole, however, more aptly captured the unfolding situation when he claimed that Murray had no choice but to be "equally the buckler of Newcastle against his ally, Fox, and his antagonist, Pitt."[19]

AS the pressure of events intensified, the Newcastle Administration found itself squeezed ever more tightly in the grip of a vice turned by the formidable conflict between Fox and Pitt. Toward the end of May 1756 the Duke of Newcastle finally came to the sober realization that the government was engulfed in a crisis of truly catastrophic proportions. "Our friend [Andrew] Stone said most wisely to me," Newcastle confided in a letter to Murray, "the attorney-general out of the House of Commons, Fox disobliged, the possibility (I wish I could not say the probability) of a breach in the royal family, an alliance between the House of Austria and France—four terrible events."[20] But he could no longer postpone the prospect of facing up to these four terrible events, considered here in reverse order.

An Alliance Between the House of Austria and France. Regardless of how successful the Attorney General might have been in defending the Newcastle Administration on the home front, on the international scene the government stumbled into a transformative process that carried staggering implications. Since the reign of William and Mary, London's anchor on the continent had been Austria. As early as 1752, however, Prince Kaunitz of Austria began dropping hints at Versailles that the Bourbons and the Hapsburgs should stand together against the rising power of Prussia. Those teasing flirtations began to bear fruit in 1755, primarily because of the diplomatic strategy the British government put into motion in order to protect Hanover's flank from Prussian maneuvers should the undeclared war in America spill over into Europe.

The initial tactic was to increase subsidies for Hesse and Russia to provide for mercenary armies in case of need. While this standard gambit was directed against France, it carried with it the added benefit—or so Newcastle thought—of keeping Frederick the Great of Prussia in awe. But one of the unintended consequences of the Administration's diplomacy was to set Frederick's fertile mind upon considering a novel possibility, namely, to assure the Elector of Hanover that Prussia had no interest whatsoever in threatening His Britannic Majesty's domains in Germany. So, on 16 January 1756 Prussia signed the Convention of Westminster with Great Britain, a treaty that was designed to preserve Prussian neutrality in the rapidly escalating conflict between the British and French Empires.

The French, though, never received from Frederick the Great a clarification of the defensive intent of this Convention, and that ambiguity in Newcastle's bold diplomacy soon drove Bourbon France into the waiting arms of the willing Hapsburgs. A few days after the First Austro-French Treaty of Versailles was sealed on 12 May 1756, Great Britain declared war on France. What radically expanded this conflict between these ancient foes into one of the greatest world war of the eighteenth century, however, was King Frederick's unilateral decision to invade Saxony.[21]

William Murray's favorite nephew, Viscount Stormont (1727-1796), was His Britannic Majesty's envoy extraordinary to Saxony when the Prussian armies invaded and Austria responded with armed force. After trying to mediate this bolt out of the blue, Stormont retreated to Warsaw with the Elector of Saxony, who was also the King of Poland. From his privileged post in Warsaw, Stormont was splendidly located to observe how Great Britain's new ally defended herself from the armies not only of Austria but of France, Russia, and Sweden as well. Because of the miscalculations arising from the *Diplomatic Revolution of 1756*, this war promised to be waged in India and the West Indies as well as on the continents of Europe and America.

A Breach in the Royal Family. Because the elderly King was well into his seventies when the Empire went to war with France, the last thing any experienced politician needed to learn was that prudence dictated that a steady effort should be made to cultivate the good will of the close circle around the heir to the throne. The key player in the politics of the Junior Court established at Leicester House when the Prince of Wales reached legal age on 4 June 1756 was the Third Earl of Bute, John Stuart (1713-1792).

During the 1740s this Scottish Lord had taken up residence at Kenwood House, a magnificent villa positioned between "the Villages of Hampstead & Highgate" with a splendid view of London. Indeed, Bute reports, "the whole city with 16 miles of the River appears from every window." In 1747 Bute chanced upon Prince Frederick and Princess Augusta at the Egham races. Because a torrential rain had upset their outing, Frederick decided to play a game of whist to pass the time, but the party needed another player. So, Bute was invited to join in the diversion. His elegant manners so charmed the Prince and Princess that he soon became the Lord of the Bedchamber, a position that apparently served him quite well when Princess Augusta discovered that she needed a little guidance in domestic affairs after the premature death of Prince Frederick in 1751. That Bute became the favorite of the Princess Dowager of Wales and the surrogate father of her teenager son is beyond dispute. What is not so clear is exactly when he gained so commanding a position, though it would seem fair to surmise that the decisive development occurred some time before 1754 when he suddenly sold Kenwood House to William Murray and moved to South Audley Street in the heart of London.[22]

Whether the Lord of the Bedchamber was actually having an affair with the future King George III's mother is something historians can weigh in the balance of a rumor mill lacking any hard evidence. Horace Walpole certainly credited the notion that Prince George "lived shut up with his mother and Lord Bute," an uncomfortable situation that "must have thrown them under some difficulties." And the gossiping public was more than a little scandalized by the fact that Bute was "by no means desirous of concealing his conquest." Walpole explicitly dated the beginning of "Bute's influence over the Princess of Wales … from the summer of 1755," though he carefully noted that only after Prince George came of age on 4 June 1756 did it become "generally known" that this charming Scottish Lord was "directing the policies of Leicester House."[23] The policies flowing from the Junior Court caused a breach in the royal family precisely because Lord Bute was guided by a simple principle—oppose all measures and men advanced by the dreaded Duke of Cumberland, especially his political henchman in the House of Commons, Henry Fox.

Fox Disobliged. When Henry Fox became the Secretary of State, he tried to stretch a continental strategy over the war effort, but the harder he pressed Cumberland's policies, the more Newcastle reached for support from Leicester House. The ocean was the element most favorable to the British forces; therefore, William Pitt and the Princess favored a blue water strategy that would promote the interests of the oceanic empire of liberty. The Duke of Cumberland, though, was the commander of the land forces and he could not take lightly the exposed situation of Hanover so dear to the heart of the King. An army on the European continent, however, spelled horrendous expenses—and the House of Commons held the purse strings. "All the world revolted against subsidiary treaties," according to Walpole's report; "nobody was left to defend them but Murray, and he did not care to venture."[24] The conflict was brought to a head when Henry Fox resigned on 13 October 1756.

The Attorney General Out of the House of Commons. For well over a year Attorney General Murray had been striving mightily to defend the badly split Newcastle Administration caught between Pitt's hammer and Fox's anvil. Weary to the point of abject despair, he had repeatedly and publicly proclaimed "that he meant to rise by his profession, not by the House of Commons." And a splendid way up and out unexpectedly opened when Lord Chief Justice Ryder died on 25 May 1756. With transparent relief and steady resolve William Murray demanded the vacated seat, plus a peerage.

Opposition forces were more than delighted with the promotion to the Court of King's Bench of Newcastle's "political henchman" (as Sir Lewis Namier designated Murray). Charles Townshend, for example, politely informed him, "I wish you joy, Mr. Attorney," but then added, "or, to speak truly, I may wish joy to myself, for you will ruin the Duke of Newcastle by quitting the House of Commons, and [ruin] the Chancellor [Hardwicke] by going into the House of Lords."[25]

AS the political situation grew ever more desperate the Duke of Newcastle came to the steady realization that his administration was boxed in an untenable position. On 29 May he sent an urgent note to Murray that did more than suggest that the end was at hand: "The experience of this last session [of Parliament] shows me that nobody but yourself will or can support me; and I will go further, will or can, in this House of Commons, support the King and his measures against such a formal opposition and at such a critical conjunction." The next day Newcastle wrote again: "Every man who pretends to be Minister in this country, *is a fool*, if he acts a day without the House of Commons; and a greater fool, if he depends upon any, of whom he cannot be sure." But nothing Newcastle could say would soften Murray's resolve. Arguments failing, Newcastle tried bribes. Initially he offered him the Duchy of Lancaster for life. Before giving up Newcastle went so far as to try to lure him with a six thousand pound "pension … a year if he would only stay in the House of Commons till the [King's] address was carried and the new sessions fairly begun."

But regardless of how high the administration was prepared to go, William Murray would not bend, for he realized full well that no better opportunity was ever likely to come open for him to put into motion his longstanding ambition to reform the jurisprudence of England. The Attorney General's final response to Newcastle's desperate overtures was adroit: "I have, with your judgment and approbation, carefully avoided the appearance of being the minister in, or being the head of, the House of Commons. If I should be now marked as such your enemies will run at you through me, and those who are politically connected with you will grow jealous." From the moment Sir Dudley Ryder died, William Murray never wavered in his resolve to become the Lord Chief Justice of King's Bench. And even his most determined enemies readily acknowledged that he was certainly the most qualified person within the realm to fill this important post, though Walpole did not have the grace to scratch this stinger: "He knew it was safer to expound laws than to be exposed to them."[26]

After much soul searching the King reluctantly appointed William Murray *Lord Chief Justice and Baron Mansfield*. According to a lengthy letter Newcastle sent to Andrew Stone long after the event, he made an extraordinary effort to persuade the King. This letter rehearses Murray's Jacobite family background, his early position in the Opposition, and his surprising ascent in the King's service made possible by the Duke's sustained commitment to this legal luminary from Scotland. It deserves to be quoted extensively:

> Men of my Lord Mansfield's parts and abilities generally can make their own way in this country; but in his Lordship's case it was impossible. He had the misfortune to be so nearly allied to the most declared enemies of the Protestant succession; his own character not known in that respect; his first appearance in the world marked with the most intimate connection with the late Lord Bolingbroke and Mr. Pope; and his public performances as council and his private friendships and acquaintances with those at the head of the opposition, Sir Wm. Wyndham, Lord Bath, Lord Granville, etc.; that nothing but the most determined resolution and support from me, not tainted with those principles or those acquaintances, could have forced his way to the great stations he has been in. That task was left to me; and I may say, many an uneasy moment did it give me; but perseverance, supported by friendship and opinion, carried me thro' it, contrary, I may aver, to the *real wish and inclination* of the King himself, to the very last instance of the peerage, and of every single friend that I had, except yourself.

Another letter written by Lord Bute seven years after the event claims that it was his influence that brought Lord Mansfield "into office," but Bute's claim is less than convincing.[27]

Both King George II and the Duke of Newcastle wanted Murray to remain in the House of Commons because the Attorney General's forensic gifts and political skills were the only known line of defense sufficiently strong to shield the government from the assaults of Pitt in the Commons, the intrigues of the Princess in Leicester House, and the clamor of the people in the streets. But neither the King nor the Duke could find a way around this ultimate either/or that he forced them to face—either he would serve the Crown as the Lord Chief Justice of King's Bench with the title, Baron Mansfield, or he would no longer serve the Crown as the Attorney General. Given that choice, the King reluctantly agreed, thereby permitting William Murray to become the first Scottish Law Lord to be acknowledged as "the Head of British Jurisprudence."[28]

FOR six agonizing months—from May through October—the Duke of Newcastle struggled valiantly against staggering odds to pursue a foreign policy dominated by the Duke of Cumberland, in a Cabinet split by Henry Fox, with a House of Commons increasingly willing to listen to the voice of William Pitt in formal opposition. An administration in such profound disarray was soon overwhelmed by events vastly beyond its power to control.

On 12 May the Austro-French Treaty of Versailles was signed. On 15 May George II declared war on Louis XV. On 25 May Lord Chief Justice Ryder died. On 4 June the Prince of Wales came of legal age and established his Junior Court at Leicester House. On 28 June British forces surrendered Minorca in the Mediterranean. On 28 August Prussia unilaterally invaded Saxony. On 30 September news reached London that the French had driven the Americans from the Great Lakes. On 13 October Henry Fox resigned from the Cabinet. On 25 October George II consented to appoint William Murray *Lord Chief Justice and Baron Mansfield*. The very next day the Duke of Newcastle submitted his resignation. Great was the *Fall of the Newcastle Administration*—but the worst was yet to come.

VI

THE RISE OF PITT TO POWER

NO SOONER HAD LORD MANSFIELD BEEN APPOINTED
TO THE COURT OF KING'S BENCH than Lord Chancellor
Hardwicke followed the Duke of Newcastle's example and also
resigned. Since nobody could be found within the realm to shoulder
the responsibilities of the vacated office, this key political post was
"given in commission to Lord Chief Justice Willes, Mr. Justice
Wilmot, and Mr. Baron Smyth." What that legal fiction masked
throughout the ensuing limbo was that in everything but name the
new Lord Chief Justice of King's Bench also exercised the powers
of the Great Seal itself, an institutional pattern that found a way of
repeating itself at critical moments over the coming decades.

As the most conspicuous political judge of the era Lord Mansfield
was remarkably well connected, too. His man in the diplomatic corps
was his favorite nephew now in Warsaw, David Murray. His man in
the Duke of Cumberland's camp was his brother-in-law, Admiral
Winchelsea. His man in the Junior Court at Leicester House was
his closest friend since school days, Andrew Stone. And his man in
the King's Closet was—himself. As Newcastle told the Duchess, "it
is very material to have my lord Mansfield on our side; for he is now
so well with the King and will have access to him." Because the new
Lord Chief Justice and acting Lord Chancellor was now in the House

of Lords, he could stand, so to speak, above the conflicted powers centered in the Closet and the Commons.[1]

Horace Walpole described the chaotic situation in the wake of the Duke of Newcastle's resignation as being left "with no ministry, no plans for supplies, no communication for the foreign ministers, all government at a stand." And what he saw during the profound paralysis that gripped the British Empire while our sleeping Gulliver writhed in confusion and impotence over the next eight months amply satisfied his satirical wit as he looked down "on the mischief of civil disturbances as a lively amusement" from the serenity of Strawberry Hill. At the head of this section of his *Memoirs* Walpole affixed this saying by La Bruyère: "Plus on étudie le monde, plus on y découvre le ridicule."[2]

STRANGE though it may seem to a later generation schooled in the notion of parliamentary responsibility, the Duke of Newcastle was forced to resign even though he had not come even close to losing a single vote in Parliament, and there were more than four years to run before the next regularly scheduled General Election. Assuming that all those in Opposition would stand together—a most dubious assumption at best—Newcastle's "friends" would still have command of a sweeping majority of 120 or so votes in the House of Commons! But the King chose his ministers. So, Newcastle was out of favor, out of office, and out of sorts—but not out of power.

From the moment Newcastle resigned the House of Commons was thrown into turmoil. George II turned to Henry Fox to form a new ministry, and for four furious days Fox tried to stitch together a new administration. Pressing for power so close that he could smell it, he actively reached out to his antagonist, William Pitt, for he realized that he could never succeed without the Great Commoner's support. Pitt stunned Fox, however, when he unequivocally declared in a face-to-face encounter that he would have nothing whatsoever to do with any Cabinet formed by him, period. Pitt's categorical refusal, plus Newcastle's fury over Fox's betrayal, quickly brought matters to a stand. "Since the Duke of Newcastle's retreat," Henry Digby wrote on 10 November, "it has been a most extraordinary scene and varied so often that it is hardly possible to relate all the turns it has had."

After Henry Fox failed in his attempt to form a new ministry, for all intents and purposes the imperial government went into receivership under the reluctant leadership of Lord Devonshire, considered by Walpole to be one of "those baby politicians" who could only flirt with power. Although Devonshire was the Prime Minister, operational power devolved upon the new Secretary of State for the Southern Department, William Pitt. Within moments a "paper war of the most inveterate kind" between Fox's *Test* and Pitt's *Con-Test* enflamed the volatile situation all the way to the breaking point. By the Christmas Recess Sir Thomas Robinson even cautioned Newcastle that unless some enduring ministry could be empowered to act with authority "the whole would fall at once into a total anarchy, and that the gates of the King's palace and the two Houses of Parliament would be besieged by mobs, clamouring for some government." "At such a crisis," according to Walpole's sober account, "heated as the passions of men were, even a civil war might ensue." Nobody dared believe the Devonshire-Pitt Administration carried any substantial weight with the King or much sustaining depth in Parliament. Walpole's prognostication that "Pitt would not last six months" missed the mark by only a few days.[3]

What brought down this short-lived, caretaker ministry was a vicious controversy occasioned by the condemnation of Admiral Byng, the lackluster loser of Minorca in the summer of 1756. At his 27 January 1757 court martial Byng was found guilty under the Twelfth Article of War. While that carried the sentence of death, the court recommended a pardon. And Walpole spoke for a considerable portion of the political nation when he noted that it was "a notorious violation of the customs of England (and the common law itself is scarce more than custom) to put him to death after such earnest recommendations of the judges." The Great Commoner expressed the sense of the House of Commons when he argued that "more benefit would accrue, more honour redound to King and country from the pardon of the unhappy admiral than from his execution." The Great

Lord Mansfield, however, responded in the House of Lords with "a panegyric on the twelfth article," claiming that Byng's execution would restore discipline in the demoralized navy. After he "censured the House of Commons for precipitate proceedings," the new Lord Chief Justice "went indecently into the question of the Admiral's behaviour." Walpole could not resist the temptation to suggest acidly that "the real criminal, ... with no ignorance to plead, found such an outrageous violation of law no impediment to his succeeding as Chief Justice." Because of the disasters so richly descending upon the Empire, George II shared with the people a potent desire to offer up a scapegoat to propitiate the wrathful political gods. And given Mansfield's control over the judiciary, the judges ruled unanimously that the verdict was binding. Justified or not, Admiral Byng was shot on the quarter-deck of the *Monarque* on 14 March 1757.[4]

The execution of Admiral Byng provided both King and country with their scapegoat, but (as Lord Halifax expressed it) "nobody but a witch could have thought" up the turmoil that immediately engulfed the political nation. "I think we are at the verge of another ministerial revolution," in the opinion of Lord Holdernesse, Secretary of State for the Northern Department; "the conduct of my colleagues [Pitt and Lord Admiral Temple] in the affair of *Byng*, has greatly lowered their popularity, and so exasperated the King that I think they cannot long keep in the saddle. This must be followed by a reconciliation between Newcastle and Fox, which the friends of the latter seem earnestly to wish." Although George II was determined to remove William Pitt (whom he found intolerable) and Lord Temple (whom he found insufferable), their dismissal presupposed "a reconciliation between Newcastle and Fox," a precondition that any politically sensitive analyst would have realized could never hold.

Mansfield cautioned Fox against entertaining his earnest wish at this critical juncture. He also directly warned Newcastle that Fox's scheme amounted to little more than luring him to lay his *"head down upon a table to be struck at."* And he informed George II that nothing could be put together with Newcastle until after his fallen administration had been cleared by the forthcoming inquiry into who was responsible for the loss of Minorca. But the King was not at all pleased with Newcastle's refusal to deal with Fox. "I shall see," he bluntly told Secretary Holdernesse, "which is King of this country, the Duke of Newcastle or myself."[5]

The signal that George II was going to sack William Pitt and appoint Henry Fox came when Lord Winchelsea (Mansfield's brother-in-law) replaced Lord Temple (Pitt's brother-in-law). Although it was expected that Pitt would resign in protest, he simply decided to do nothing, thereby forcing the King to initiate the next round in this ongoing crisis. So, on the evening of 6 April 1757 Holdernesse was handed the hard assignment of collecting the Seals of his office from the Great Commoner.

Now that it was assumed that Henry Fox would be guiding the ship of state, the Duke of Cumberland convinced himself that he would be sailing on a sound bottom when he set out to command the army of observation in Germany on 10 April. "I have been told," Hardwicke reported to Newcastle, "that Horace Walpole said publicly the other day, that the D[uke] of C[umberland] was going to command in Germany; held England *in commendam*; and left Mr Fox his viceroy to command in his absence."

Cumberland's calculations, however, were quickly shattered because neither Newcastle's friends nor the Junior Court's forces would tolerate a ministry headed by Henry Fox as the political henchman of the King's favorite son. As Newcastle wrote to Hardwicke, "an administration, with a Prince of the Blood, Captain General, at the head of it, with Mr Fox the principal or sole agent, or instrument under him, is what your lordship and I cannot concur in, or take a share of, without evident prejudice to the King's service, and the greatest danger, and strongest imputation upon ourselves." Hardwicke needed no convincing, for he thought that the King had "absolutely resigned" effective power into the hands of the Duke of Cumberland. And there was no disguising the transparent fact that the Junior Court at Leicester House was in a towering rage because such "a *Ducal Government*" would be founded upon an "unconstitutional bottom."[6]

FOR some time William Pitt and Lord Bute had been reaching out toward each other. Indeed, on the very day Admiral Byng was executed on the quarter-deck of the *Monarque,* the Great Commoner escorted Lady Bute to the opening at Covent Garden of John Home's masterpiece, *The Tragedy of Douglas.* Those with eyes to see could not help but notice this budding alliance.

Although every man of sense realized that Newcastle held the balance of power in the House of Commons, in a lengthy letter Newcastle sent to Hardwicke he schematized what he perceived to be the structure of the dilemma facing his wing of the shattered Whig Party. On the one hand, if Henry Fox were allowed to form a new ministry, "we then involve ourselves, not only in the unpopularity, but even in the inconveniences, and mischiefs that may arise … ; and to the public, it is the same, as if we were parties to the administration." On the other hand, if Fox were blocked, then George II would hold the parliamentary majority responsible for bringing the governmental machine to a grinding halt squarely in the midst of a shooting war. But Newcastle was clearly searching for a middle way that would escape the sharp horns of this acute dilemma.

Hardwicke responded immediately to Newcastle's analysis by rejecting forthrightly the very idea of joining forces with the opposition in Parliament to block Fox: "For my own part, I am determined not to go into *a formed general opposition.* I have seen so much of them I am convinced they are the most wicked combinations, that men can enter into—worse, and more corrupt than any administration, that I ever yet saw." And Mansfield backed Hardwicke's stance. In a 15 April letter to Newcastle the Lord Chief Justice wrote:

> To mix in factious opposition, after so many years of honourable service, wou'd blast your fame and reputation forever. Specious pretences are never wanting; but in the present distress, it is impossible for any Court, how desperate soever, to make unconstitutional attempts. But I speak of opposition

to [the King's] right or indifferent measures to force
a change of hands. I desire for one to subscribe to
Lord Hardwicke's declaration as the sentiments of a
virtuous and loyal mind, to which I will inviolably
adhere. I had much rather not exist than join at
this time factiously in opposition to the King,
whomsoever he employs. For his sake, for the sake
of his successor, for the sake of Government itself I
wou'd not do it.

From the rejection of one horn of the perceived dilemma, however, it
did not follow that Newcastle's friends had to embrace the other and
consent to a Fox Administration. Why? Because Henry Fox's scheme
had split the Royal Family. Given that advice from two of his most
trusted advisors, Newcastle found it more than convenient to remain
"entirely free" from "any immediate engagement with either party"
polarized around Henry Fox and the Junior Court.

What the volatile situation called for was patience in a waiting
game. According to the lucid analysis Mansfield shared with
Newcastle, for any "scheme of general conciliation" to emerge, "the
public exigency of affairs is such, that the different parties in the
state must sooner or later be reconciled … In the present factions (as
in a state of war) he that holds out longest will have the advantage
in terms of peace." Any resolution of the impasse, according to
Hardwicke, would have to "bring the *succession* to support and give
quiet to the *possession*" of the government. Furthermore, he was
more than persuaded "that it would become necessary either to make
up with Mr Pitt or Mr Fox." Henry Fox was unacceptable; therefore,
like it or not, William Pitt was necessary. But nothing much could
happen until events—and the Junior Court at Leicester House—put
so much pressure on George II that he would be forced to see that
there was no viable alternative to handing over executive power to
the Great Commoner.

On the same day that Newcastle penned his despairing
analysis, George II invited Lord Chief Justice Mansfield into the

Closet for a lengthy consultation. After condemning Pitt's policies and commending Mansfield's measures, the King brought up his frustration with the Duke of Newcastle and his refusal to bring his commanding majority in the House of Commons into line by supporting a ministry headed by Henry Fox. Mansfield carefully explained that "the Duke of Newcastle has given his opinion to your Majesty, that those gentlemen [i.e., Pitt and Temple] should not be removed *at present*; and if he had promised to support their successors, it might have encouraged a measure, which he had thought not for your Majesty's service."

George II then posed a critical question: "But, will he go into opposition?" Mansfield responded adroitly: "He will never do anything contrary to his duty and zeal for your Majesty's service." The King then pressed on to ask the decisive question: "But, tell me your opinion, if the Duke of Newcastle should go into *Opposition, would the Whigs in the House of Commons follow him?*" Mansfield answered directly: "Since your Majesty commands me to tell you my opinion, *I think they would.*" Given Mansfield's "strong answer" the King could no longer entertain any illusions about the fact that "the Duke of Newcastle *could do it*," that is, he could make him a "prisoner" by storming the Closet.[7]

THE impasse reached truly desperate proportions in early June. On Monday 6 June George II pressed Newcastle "very strongly to come in." After explaining that he could not serve "in conjunction with Fox," he added, "I can't come in, without bringing in my enemy, Mr Pitt." When the King cautioned that Pitt would surely be unreasonable, Newcastle countered that Pitt was indispensable. The next day the King demanded that Newcastle promise his support for yet another attempt by Henry Fox to form a new ministry. When the Duke "waived any such promise, … the King dismissed him in wrath."[8]

For four furious days Fox tried yet once again to patch together a new administration directly against the collective will of Newcastle, Pitt, the Princess, and the people. So many people were lining up to protest against Fox's project that Walpole predicted that "by tomorrow it will rain resignations as it did in the year '46." On Thursday 9 June Secretary of State Holdernesse actually turned in the Seals of his office. On Friday 10 June Walpole declared,

> after the House of Commons had sat near an hour in silence and suspense, Sir Francis Dashwood mentioned that they had met several days without having any business to do to the great fatigue of the Speaker and the House and moved to adjourn to Monday. Col. [George] Townshend seconded the motion and said he was glad it was moved for no longer time for that in the present dreadful situation of this country without the appearance of a government he hoped the House would that day resume its ancient right (too long disused) of advising the Crown in this dangerous crisis, and that he wished the House would then be full as he should offer some proposal of that kind.

Although the Empire was tottering on the brink of a precipice the depth of which no man knew, "the people hating Fox, neglected by Pitt, and despising Newcastle, waited with patience to see which of them was to be their master."[9]

The daunting task at hand was to forge a new ministry, one that would command the steady support of Newcastle's friends in the House of Commons, one that could nurture the good will of the Junior Court, and one that should hold the genuine confidence of George II in the Closet. No easy task that! When Lord Chief Justice Mansfield took it up, he was not only the acting Lord Chancellor— from the moment Henry Legge resigned when Pitt was turned out, he even temporarily assumed the Office of Chancellor of the Exchequer as well![10]

EARLY on the morning of Saturday 11 June 1757 Mansfield met with Devonshire and asked the caretaker Prime Minister "whether the King expected him to bring the Seals that day to Court" so that

George II could hand them over to Henry Fox. When Devonshire answered in the affirmative, Mansfield carefully explained to him "that it was plain to demonstration that Mr Fox could not carry on the King's affairs, that it would be the ruin of the King and the country." Devonshire was "clearly of the same opinion," too. Everything was now hung upon our latter-day Cicero's capacity to convince the King. Unless appearances deceive, Mansfield was just about the only person left standing with a range of power sufficiently broad to persuade George II in the Closet.

Henry Fox was already in the antechamber waiting to receive the Seals—and both Lord Rockingham and the Duke of Rutland were also there to submit their resignations—when Lord Mansfield arrived and was immediately ushered into the Closet. To the astonishment of the gathered host, when he came out he had even more than the Seals in his hand, for George II had given him a commission that carried "full powers" to negotiate a new ministry, although he did attach two conditions to Mansfield's mandate: (1) Henry Fox must be made the Paymaster; and (2) Lord Temple must not be provided with any office that would require his presence in the Closet very often.

Mansfield whispered the secret of this palace revolution to Henry Fox. He also told Lord Rockingham to keep his resignation in his pocket, and Rockingham passed the good word along to the Duke of Rutland. Although Lords Bedford, Gower, Devonshire, Marlborough, Winchelsea, and Bridgewater had gathered to witness Henry Fox's moment of triumph, the "good company attending in the antechamber were amazed" by this breathtaking turn of events.[11]

The report Mansfield sent to Hardwicke at 4 PM that Saturday afternoon captures the urgency of the moment:

> I am just come from Kensington, where I was by order to deliver the seal, & Mr. Fox was there to receive it. Upon my going into the closet, the King did me the honour to talk to me of the present melancholy situation, & bid me tell him what I thought. I did so very sincerely, & made a great impression. The result

> was, that I have brought the seal back, and am to
> speak to the D[uke] of N[ewcastle] & your L[ordshi]
> p … I beg your Lordship wou'd not take the trouble
> to write, but to send me word how late I may venture
> to come if your L'p is to be at home to-night.

The Duke of Newcastle, though, was the most astonished of all. He learned about this startling reversal in a chance encounter with Mansfield at Hyde Park Corner. According to his report to Holdernesse that evening, Mansfield had somehow managed to persuade George II that Fox's project "could not succeed":

> [Mansfield] was sure of it and was so positive in his
> opinion, that he was ready to give it in the presence
> of any of those who were in the other room (the
> Duke of Bedford etc.) if His Majesty would please
> to call them in. This had such an effect upon the
> King that his Majesty immediately suspended his
> new ministry, Lord Mansfield took back his seal,
> and had orders to speak to my lord Hardwicke and
> me, to renew our conference with my lord Bute and
> Mr Pitt, which we shall accordingly do on Monday.

Realizing full well that William Pitt was jealous of him, the Lord Chief Justice removed himself from the center of the action by having Devonshire arrange for Hardwicke to conduct the final negotiations leading into the new ministry. Nevertheless, years later he would remind the House of Lords that he "had a hand in that negotiation," a negotiation that resulted in "a full and comprehensive union of all parties" when the Empire was threatened not only by determined enemies from without but more especially by deadly divisions from within. According to his memory, "Two persons only [i.e., William Pitt and Henry Fox], after some fluctuation were taken in; yet by so immaterial a change the nation was satisfied, a coalition ensued, and the effect of that seasonable union was the immense accession of territory made in the course of the late glorious war." And his claim that he knew "more of all the springs which have moved upon this occasion, than perhaps anybody" was not an empty boast, for the Great Lord Mansfield had opened the path to power for his life-long rival, William Pitt.[12]

THE entire political nation thoroughly understood that the Great Commoner would rule the roost when the Pitt-Newcastle Administration came into power on 29 June 1757, even though on technical grounds Newcastle was officially the Prime Minister once again. The arrangement meant that Pitt would control foreign affairs and the war effort, while Newcastle would attend to domestic policy. Interestingly, the Lord Chief Justice was included in the ministry. According to a contemporary report on the inner workings of the executive branch of the government, "The Duke of Newcastle, the Lord President [Granville], Lord Hardwicke, Lord Mansfield, the two Secretaries of State [i.e., William Pitt and Lord Holdernesse] and Lord Anson form what Lord Granville calls *the Conciliabulum*. They meet continually, and their opinion is the advice given to the King."[13] Newcastle insisted upon Mansfield's inclusion in this *conciliabulum*, and that was the price that Pitt had to pay in order to gain control of the imperial government in the midst of this global contest with France.

THE military situation had grown truly alarming. For three straight years the British Empire had lost one battle after another. Major George Washington surrendered Fort Necessity in 1754. Then came General Braddock's crushing defeat and death near Fort Duquesne in 1755, the same year in which the French secured their hold on Lake Champlain and erected Fort Carillon (Fort Ticonderoga). During 1756 Oswego—the Anglo-American trading emporium on Lake Ontario—fell to the French and Indians. In 1757 British forces were repulsed in their assault on Louisbourg—France's "Gibraltar" guarding the St. Lawrence seaway into the heart of Quebec. Then in August disaster struck—the French captured and destroyed Fort William Henry on Lake George in New York. At all the critical points

British North America was on the defensive and facing defeat. In Europe the situation was no better. The strategic island of Minorca in the Mediterranean was abandoned. Then on the continent the Duke of Cumberland was reduced to signing the ignominious capitulation of Kloster-Seven on 8 September 1757.

By the end of autumn "it would have seemed to all detached observers," according to Lawrence Henry Gipson's account in his monumental narrative of *The Great War for the Empire*, "that hostilities must soon come to a close in favor of the great coalition of powers … that Great Britain and the British Empire, Prusssia, and the little states of Hanover and Hesse-Cassel were obliged to face." Indeed, "France with its overseas possessions, Austria with its dependencies, the Imperial Circles of Germany, Russia, and Sweden, not only were arrayed against them in overwhelming force but everywhere were victorious." While almost unrestrained joy and confidence pervaded the atmosphere in Paris and Vienna and Quebec, "gloom and foreboding" enveloped London and Berlin and British North America.[14]

Although the Empire had been on the defensive for three years, a radical transformation occurred the moment George II handed over executive power to William Pitt. Robert Clive decisively defeated the French at Plassey, north of Calcutta in India. A few months later Frederick the Great scored a stunning victory at Rossbach on 5 November 1757, followed shortly by another at Leuthen. In America the French surrendered Louisbourg on 26 July 1758, lost Fort Frontenace in August, and were forced to destroy Fort Duquesne in November. The path into French Canada now lay open, and the fate of Quebec was sealed on the Plains of Abraham when James Wolfe defeated Montcalm on 17 September 1759. After the Battle of Minden the French army never recovered on the European continent and the French navy was soon driven from the seven seas. One can hardly begin to imagine what fate would have awaited the British Empire had the Lord Chief Justice of King's Bench failed to persuade George II to hand over operational power to William Pitt in June 1757.[15]

THE TRANSFORMATION
OF THE ENGLISH
COMMON LAW HERITAGE

T HE LEGAL ESTABLISHMENT WAS SET FOR A RADICAL DEPARTURE WHEN LORD CHIEF JUSTICE Mansfield was appointed to the Court of King's Bench. By 1757 he was shocking the "Friends of Liberty" in London by openly championing the proposition that the received English Common Law Heritage was badly out of tune with the progressive ethos of the times and now needed a systematic update to make it relevant to the rapidly expanding social and commercial needs of the contemporary world.

The magnitude of his influence over the development of the English Common Law can be conveniently measured by the space dedicated to him in *The Lives of the Chief Justices of England* by Lord John Campbell (1779-1861). In this massive multi-volume survey of the historical embodiment of institutional law from the Norman Conquest of 1066 to, say, the Reform Bill of 1832, about one-sixth of the entire narrative—just under 450 pages in the revised edition—is dedicated to Lord Chief Justice Mansfield, three times the amount of space allotted to Sir Edward Coke, and vastly more than is given to anyone else.[1]

It is hard to imagine how any serious commentator could disagree with Lord Campbell's conviction that "the history of a country cannot be well understood without the study of its jurisprudence." The enduring roots of Mansfield's jurisprudential orientation were thoroughly planted in the richly variegated historical soil long before he completed his advanced legal studies in Lincoln's Inn. Campbell emphatically reports that he consistently maintained that "the foundation of jurisprudence" was laid in the Roman Civil Law Tradition: "Thence he proceeded to the international law, doing full justice to the learning and genius of Grotius, its codifier and almost its founder. Next he entered on the feudal law, without which our law of real property must be very imperfectly understood. Here he showed his discernment by taking for his guide and his favorite his countryman CRAIG, whose treatise DE FEUDIS he justly thought was much to be preferred to any juridical work which England had then produced." Indeed, "the methodical arrangement and precise definitions of Mackenzie and Stair"—the gifted expounders of the Scottish Civil Law—resonated deeply with his judicial temperament.

By the same token he "formed a very low ... estimate of the Common Law of England" because it was still slumbering "in the same style as in the days of Sir Robert Tresilian and Sir William Gascoigne." As he searched through the "very crabbed and uncouth compositions" that established English precedents, he was "often filled ... with disgust and sometimes with despair." Campbell continues: "He was pleased with Bracton, and could not deny the terseness and perspicuity of Littleton; but he never could be made to fall down and worship Lord Coke, whom we are taught to regard as the god of our idolatry. Nay, he was ... constantly to be laughing at [Coke's] etymologies." Not only did our savant from Scotland find *Coke-upon -Littleton* "uncouth," even "the merits of the old common law" were wasted upon him. And given the disgust that the expressions of the English Common Law Heritage released within his brilliant but tidy mind, it is not at all surprising to discover that from his formative years he had nursed a "high feeling that his destiny called him to reform the jurisprudence" of England by gradually assimilating the English Common Law Heritage to the Roman Civil Law Tradition.[2]

From the moment Lord Chief Justice Mansfield was appointed to the Court of King's Bench, he made it unmistakably clear that the judiciary was facing a procedural transformation. Because "the heavy arrears" that burdened the business of the legal system had long troubled him, he introduced "a rule ... that the counsel could only make one motion apiece in rotation; and that if by chance the court rose before the whole bar had been gone through, the motion should begin next morning with him whose turn it was to move at the adjournment." So simple a procedural change broke "the monopoly of the leaders" of the bar and opened the way for "young men of promise" to present their briefs. To everybody's astonishment the new Lord Chief Justice also moved straightforwardly toward a decision as soon as the argument was closed in order to short-circuit the standard lawyer's device of prolonging the litigation so as to increase legal fees. The business of the Court moved forward much more expeditiously the moment these procedural innovations were instituted.

More significant still was the rule that Mansfield imposed that the judges on the bench should caucus with him in order to "communicate our sentiments with great freedom" and "form our conclusions without any prepossession to first thoughts." Whereas previously each judge had handed down his own opinion, now virtually "every order, rule, judgment, and opinion" exhibited a steady uniformity. A recent study has shown that "in the period 1756-1765 not a single decision was given which was not unanimous." Indeed, because these caucuses were so adroitly handled, the Court reached unanimity in almost all the different cases while he presided over the Court of King's Bench. What impressed Campbell even more was the extraordinary fact that "of the many thousand judgments which Lord Mansfield pronounced" during his thirty-two years on the bench "two only were reversed" on appeal to the High Court of Parliament. So convincing were his arguments that "the business of the King's Bench increased amazingly, while that of the other courts of common law dwindled away almost to nothing."[3]

Procedural changes were only the opening wedge in the mentality of the Lord Chief Justice. The spirit of the laws exhibited in his numerous innovations is succinctly captured in the best remembered piece of advice that he ever gave to his fellow judges: "Consider what you think justice requires and decide accordingly. But never give your reasons; for your judgment will probably be right but your reasons will certainly be wrong."[4] While he was Solicitor General and Attorney General that discretionary spirit had been conspicuously displayed in the Court of Chancery under the guiding hands of his mentor, Lord Chancellor Hardwicke. In that legal system "equity" and "reason" and "conscience" were nurtured by a learned tradition rooted in the ancient body of Roman Civil Law, a tradition of interpretation that shaped the legal codes of Scotland as well as Continental Europe.

How central this continental orientation was to Mansfield's approach is exhibited in "On the Study of Ancient and Modern History," an extensive guide that he drew up to direct the education of the "heir of the ducal house of Portland." After mapping "the causes of the decline of the Roman Empire," he focused the young man's studies upon the institutional development of medieval and early modern France. According to Campbell's exposition, he "seems to have carried in his memory every remark of every French historical writer from Philip de Comines to Voltaire, and by a few masterly strokes he gives a better notion of Clovis, Charlemagne, Louis XI, and Henry IV, than is to be gathered from perusing many tomes of ordinary bookmakers." But his "true delight," in Campbell's opinion, "was to dip into the juridical writers of France, that he might see how the Roman and feudal laws had been blended in the different provinces of that kingdom." Of particular importance was "to pore over the admirable commercial code recently promulgated there under the title of ORDINANCE DE LA MARINE, which he hoped one day to introduce here by well-considered judicial decisions,—a bright vision which was afterwards realized." The realization of that "bright vision" over time is precisely why Sir Francis Buller in his eulogy for Mansfield openly declared that our Scottish Law Lord was "the founder of the commercial law of this country."

His strategy was to implement his jurisprudential reforms gradually through judicial decisions as concrete issues came before the Court of King's Bench. Campbell is quite emphatic upon his incremental approach to the questions troubling so turbulent a time:

> Instead of proceeding by legislation, and attempting to *codify* as the French had done very successfully in the COUSTUMIER DE PARIS, and the ORDINANCE DE LA MARINE, he wisely thought it more according to the genius of our institutions to introduce his improvements by way of judicial decision ... His plan seems to have been to avail himself, as often as opportunity admitted, of his ample stores of knowledge, acquired from his study of the Roman civil law, and of the judicial writers produced in modern times by France, Germany, Holland, and Italy.

According to Campbell, "The learned on the continent of Europe had hitherto looked upon English lawyers as very contracted in their view of jurisprudence, and had never regarded the decisions of our courts as settling any international question." But precisely because the historical groundwork for our Scottish Law Lord's transformative "innovations" was laid in the legal systems arising within the Roman Civil Law Tradition, when his substantive reforms started to take real effect, the continental authorities discovered "that a great jurist had at last been raised up among us." They even placed his "bust by the side of Grotius and D'Aguesseau." Campbell's hero—"THE GREAT LORD MANSFIELD"—would always tower over his many illustrious contemporaries with "the unclouded majesty of Mont Blanc."[5]

NEVER did Lord Chief Justice Mansfield entertain the idea that the Roman Civil Law should replace the English Common Law completely. He pursued a gradual strategy of slowly revising the law as concrete cases came up for review in his court. And the process was random but consistent. For example, commercial law was addressed in 1758, followed by marine insurance in 1761 and religious toleration in 1762. In 1766 he addressed insurance fraud; in 1768 marriage contracts; in 1770 freedom of the press; in 1774 international law; in 1776 the impressment of sailors; in 1778 the right of privacy; in 1782 expert witnesses; in 1783 labor unions. And on it went, slowly, deliberately bringing the English Common Law Heritage more into alignment with the Roman Civil Law Tradition. What did not change, however, was his enduring commitment to a particular reading of the unwritten British Constitution. He believed that by right Parliament held unlimited authority over the colonies within the polycentric Empire. And he had championed that belief long before he was appointed Solicitor General, although it had not been acted upon. Perhaps one should say the idea was *latent, not manifest* before the Stamp Act Crisis brought the issue explosively to the surface.

FEW aided Mansfield more in his project than Sir William Blackstone (1723-1780). After graduating from Pembroke College, Oxford, Blackstone entered the Inner Temple; then he became a fellow of All Souls, Oxford, where he received his Doctor of Civil Law degree in 1744. When the Regius Professorship of Civil Law fell vacant, the future Lord Mansfield recommended Blackstone for the distinguished position, a patronage plum under the control of the Duke of Newcastle. Moved more by political considerations than by any academic acumen, Newcastle turned down this sage advice from his trusted counselor, but students of the law have never regretted that Blackstone failed to obtain that chair precisely because it would have required him to lecture in the Roman Civil Law Tradition. Blackstone was pointed down the path toward professional fame, however, when Mansfield had the insight to suggest that he take up residence at Oxford anyway and "read law-lectures to such students as were disposed to attend him," a suggestion Blackstone embraced with enthusiasm in 1753. Oxford students would soon begin mapping the maze of English laws with an *Analysis* that he circulated privately in a format that closely followed the "analysis of the Civil Part of the Laws" by Sir Matthew Hale (1609-1676). Pirated copies of Blackstone's *Analysis* soon began to circulate rather widely throughout the English-speaking world. Then in 1758 he was appointed to the newly endowed Vinerian Professorship of Common Law.[6]

Emphasis on the heaviest possible sort should be placed upon the fact that Blackstone *introduced* the historical study of the English Common Law Heritage in the university world. As would be expected, the new Vinerian Professor of the Common Law brought his orientation in the Roman Civil Law Tradition to bear directly upon his *Analysis* in the 1750s, which prepared the way for his masterpiece, *Commentaries on the Laws of England* (1765-1769). In the Preface he explained how he embarked upon his lifework with more than a little trepidation, because "the novelty of such an attempt in this age and country" had to run the gauntlet straight across "the prejudices usually conceived against any innovations in the established mode of education." But he had persuaded himself that "our laws and constitution" should be studied historically "as a liberal science."

Within moments he reminds his students that they surely were sensible of the need for "a masterly acquaintance with *the general spirit of laws and principles of universal jurisprudence*" (my emphasis). Only after orienting students within the "universal jurisprudence" of the Roman Civil Law Tradition did he proceed to add the need for "an accurate knowledge of our own municipal constitutions, their original, reason, and history." Given that mode of approach to the material, the predictable result lies right on the surface, namely, the student would discover that such a procedure "hath given a beauty and energy to many modern judicial decisions, with which our ancestors were wholly unacquainted."

These "many modern judicial decisions" that reflected so much "beauty and energy" were primarily the work of Lord Chancellor Hardwicke and Lord Chief Justice Mansfield. Their admiration was mutual, too. When Mansfield was asked for his opinion on which books the son of a fellow Lord should study in order to pursue a successful career in the law, he did not have to reflect for long:

> My good Lord, till of late I could never with any satisfaction to myself answer such a question; but since the publication of Mr. Blackstone's *Commentaries*, I can never be at a loss. There your son will find analytical reasoning, diffused in a pleasing and perspicuous style. There he may inhale imperceptibly the first principles on which our excellent laws are founded; and there he may become acquainted with the uncouth crabbed author, Coke upon Littleton, who has disgusted and disheartened many a tyro, but who cannot fail to please in the modern attire in which he is now decked out.[7]

Sir William Blackstone's *Commentaries on the Laws of England* decked out in a most pleasing and perspicuous style the numerous innovations at the heart of Lord Chief Justice Mansfield's enduring project.

William Blackstone advanced the thesis in his *Commentaries* that Parliament's god-like sovereignty was "so transcendent and absolute, that it cannot be confined, either for causes or persons, within any bounds."

> It hath sovereign and uncontrollable authority in making, confirming, enlarging, restraining, abrogating, repealing, reviving, and expounding of laws, concerning matters of all possible denominations ... : this being the place where that absolute despotic power, which must in all governments reside somewhere, is entrusted by the

> constitution of these kingdoms ... It can, in short,
> do every thing that is not naturally impossible; and
> therefore some have not scrupled to call its power,
> by a figure rather too bold, the omnipotence of
> parliament.

To labor the obvious, "What Parliament doth no power on earth can undo."

Care should be taken to understand how Blackstone understood the definition of "Parliament." With analytical precision he studiously opened his exposition with the observation that "the constituent parts of a parliament" are "the king's majesty ... and the three estates of the realm." These three estates are (1) "the lords spiritual"; (2) "the lords temporal"; and (3) "the commons." The first two estates "sit, together with the king, in one house," while the third estate sits separately in the House of Commons. In order to "make any new law that shall bind the subject," the King, the Lords Spiritual and Temporal (the first and second estate voting together), and the Commons (the third estate voting separately) must all consent before a bill can become an Act of Parliament. According to Blackstone, "the king and these three estates, together, form the great corporation or body politic of the kingdom."[8]

With these distinctions held consciously in mind, it should be transparent that when Blackstone speaks of Parliament he includes the King. Technically put, his understanding of the constitutional settlement after the Glorious Revolution located that "absolute despotic power, which must in all governments reside somewhere" in what is sometimes referred to as "the King-in-Parliament." Gone now was the standard juxtaposition of "King" and "Parliament" that had so plagued the seventeenth century from the beginning of the reign of James I in 1603 to the abdication of James II in 1688.

Because the Glorious Revolution was such an important fact in that "noble pile" called the British Constitution, Blackstone could never come out and say that revolutions *per se* were unconstitutional. But given the resolution of that monumental crisis, he did maintain that "Revolution Principles" now supported the opinion "that the people's right to remove the legislature existed in theory only and was no longer of practical value."[9] According to Pauline Maier's careful exposition of this development,

> Sir William Blackstone tried to explain away Locke's fundamental assertion that "there remains ... inherent in the people supreme power to remove or alter the legislative, when they find the legislative act contrary to the trust reposed in them." However just this may be "in theory," the jurist wrote in early editions of his *Commentaries on the Laws of England*, "we cannot adopt it, nor argue from it, under any dispensation or government at present actually existing."

Indeed, Blackstone relocated "revolutionary beliefs to the purer realm of philosophy," while "denying that the people in real life had the right to resist a legislative power that abuses its trust—denying, in effect, the notion that public officials *ipso facto* surrendered legal authority by violating their trust." His emergent doctrine of Parliamentary Supremacy was designed to strengthen radically the power of the government over against the liberties of the people. Limited though the people's rights were in Great Britain, they far surpassed any thing relevant to the colonies, for English rights did not extend fully to the colonial Americans.[10]

William Blackstone was prepared to pay Parliament so many metaphysical, indeed, theological compliments—and scale down the liberties of the people, especially the Americans—precisely because he thoroughly shared the fundamental principles operative in the interpretation of the British Constitution championed by Lord Chief Justice Mansfield, an interpretation of Revolution Principles that rendered unconstitutional any further revolutionary changes after the Glorious Revolution of 1688.

TO exhibit how thoroughly Sir William Blackstone transformed legal education one need look no further than the career of John Dickinson (1732-1808). Born in Maryland but reared in Kent in the new colony of Delaware, where his father, Samuel Dickinson, served as the judge of the Court of Common Pleas, John showed promise as a young man. In 1750 he began working in the Philadelphia office of John Moland, the king's attorney in the proprietary province of Pennsylvania. After three years of service as a clerk in Moland's office, this studious fourth generation American followed his mentor's example and pursued legal studies in the Middle Temple near Westminster Hall in the imperial capital in 1753.

For three dense years of study, Dickinson soaked up English history and legal lore in London. "Law, based on precedent, has an affinity with history," according to Milton E. Flower's treatment of Colonial America's most influential constitutional lawyer during the constitutional crisis of the 1760s. Dickinson soon "found himself inspired by the thoughts that Coke and Plowden had lived in the same Inns of Courts as he did, that the halls where he daily heard cases debated once had witnessed the defenses of Hampden and Holt against the tyranny of injustice." And that tradition was still alive in current practice as well as in conscious memory.

In a letter to his father in Philadelphia about the time that the French and Indian War was getting under way on the western frontier, Dickinson made this fundamental disclosure:

> There is great variety & entertainment in the study
> of our profession, especially in England. We see how
> the courts of justice are crowded by people who
> know nothing of the law; how much more agreeable
> then must it be to us who understand everything
> that is said. Here we are not always plodding over
> books: Westminster Hall is a school of law where
> we not only hear what we have read repeated, but
> disputed & sifted in the most curious & learned
> manner, nay frequently hear things quite new, have

our doubts cleared up, & our errors corrected. The
bar is a perfect comment upon the written law, &
every great man at it is in some measure a master
& instructor to these young students who have the
wisdom to attend there.

Because all that subject matter stood in need of so much critical
commentary and close reading, Dickinson "purchased many books,
legal and historical, and made appropriate marginal notes in their
pages." Indeed,

He transcribed Servienti's *Doctrine Placitandi* with
notes into three large volumes and studied the *Art
of Reading*, which Coke had pronounced the "very
life of the law." He continued with Coke's *Institutues*
and the reports of Plowden, Ventris, and Salkend.
But it was Bacon from whom Dickinson seemed to
profit most and whom he admired for his brilliant
use of language, phrase, and allusion.

Before Lord Chief Justice Mansfield handed down any of his famous
decisions in the Court of King's Bench, John Dickinson—"the
Penman of the American Revolution"—was called to the English
bar on 8 February 1757.[11]

JUXAPOSE now the educational experience in the same institution
just the following year by Benjamin Franklin's son, William Franklin
(circa 1729-1813). This future Loyalist succeeded his father as the
clerk of the Pennsylvania Assembly and served as his aide while the
newly appointed Colonel Franklin was organizing the defenses along
the Pennsylvania frontier after the defeat of General Braddock and
a British army in 1755. When his father was appointed the Agent of
the Pennsylvania Assembly in early 1757, William accompanied him
to London and there he began his legal studies in the Middle Temple
shortly after Lord Chief Justice Mansfield was appointed to the Court
of King's Bench. According to Willard Sterne Randall's study of the

two Franklins, "During his first year in London, William crammed massive doses of law. Besides memorizing the ancient Pandects of the Roman Emperor Justinian (which he read in Latin), he had to keep abreast of Blackstone's latest interpretations and add to his store of knowledge by taking notes at major trials in the Court of King's Bench in Westminster Hall." Sir William Blackstone's *Analysis* had now begun to circulate more widely within the Inns of Court and our Scottish Law Lord's decisions had now begun to take effect in the Court of King's Bench.

Benjamin Franklin's son was more than impressed by the "beauty and energy" found in the "many modern judicial decisions, with which our ancestors were wholly unacquainted." Before he was called to the English bar on 10 November 1758 William Franklin had received from Justinian in the library, Sir William Blackstone in the corridors, and Lord Chief Justice Mansfield in the Court of King's Bench, an enduring jurisprudential orientation that shaped his actions as the Loyalist Royal Governor of New Jersey throughout the coming constitutional crisis of the 1760s and 1770s.[12]

WHEN the new Pitt-Newcastle Administration came into power on 29 June 1757, William Pitt made sure that the new Attorney General would be none other than Charles Pratt (1714-1794). Pratt was fond of recalling Lord Bacon's comment that the Court of Star Chamber (abolished in 1641) was one of the *"courts of criminal equity."* Convictions about "equity" in the English Common Law Heritage can be gathered from statements such as this from Selden's *Table Talk*:

> Equity is a rogish thing; for law we have a measure. Equity is according to the conscience of him who is Chancellor, and as that is larger or narrower, so is equity. It is all one as if they should make the standard for the measure we call a *foot* 'a chancellor's foot.' What an uncertain measure would this be! One chancellor has a long foot; another a short foot;

> a third, an indifferent foot: it is the same thing in the
> chancellor's *conscience*.

Directly against the uncertainty caused by Mansfield's jurisprudential orientation, Pratt championed the certainty of publicly known law: "The discretion of a judge is the law of tyrants; it is always unknown; it is different in different men; it is casual, and depends upon constitution, temper, and passion. In the best [judges], it is often times caprice; in the worst it is every vice, folly, and passion to which human nature is liable." He was under the persuasion that Mansfield's eloquent tongue served an indifferent conscience that directed a very long foot. And truth to tell, the Attorney General's mild "constitution, temper, and passion" boiled over when the new Lord Chief Justice began acting upon his "high feeling that his destiny called him to reform the jurisprudence of his country" through "judicial decisions" rather than "proceeding by legislation."

The differences between Pratt and Mansfield turned not upon this particular reading or that precious ruling but upon fundamental principles that were philosophical in nature and constitutional in scope, with Pratt defending English Liberties in direct opposition to the spirit of the laws moving through our Scottish Law Lord's jurisprudential reform project. Horace Walpole even reported that Pratt "personally hated" the Lord Chief Justice of King's Bench.[13]

VIII

SOME EARLY DECISIONS

LORD CHIEF JUSTICE MANSFIELD HAD LONG CHAMPIONED THE POSITION THAT IN LIBEL cases the truth or falsity of the issue was something the judges alone were sufficiently capable of determining. As early as 1723 Lord Chancellor Hardwicke (then Solicitor General Philip Yorke) had claimed that "the jury were only to decide upon the sufficiency of evidence, and upon innuendoes"—"the lawfulness or criminality of the writings" was something well beyond the competence of juries. In this arcane context "innuendoes" pointed toward those blanks spaces that a reader should be able to fill in with ease. If a document mentioned "L—d C–f J—e M—sf–d," the reader should have no difficulty in figuring out the person intended. Juries dealt with "facts"; judges alone dealt with "laws."[1] Not many months would pass before a publication on the periphery of polite society joined the issue. In Horace Walpole's words, "the Chief Justice Mansfield caused to be seized at an auction, a well-known tale, called *The Woman of Pleasure*, a work that simplified novels to their original intention."[2]

The steamy career of the *Memoirs of a Woman of Pleasure*, better known by its subtitle, *Fanny Hill*, is more than a little obscure even for salacious books. What can be maintained with confidence is that the book would never have given rise to so much notoriety without the tender loving care of John Cleland (1710-1789). Cleland was not only of Scottish descent; he spent two years in Westminster Public School at precisely the same time that Mansfield was a student there. And later they both moved in the same literary circle around Alexander Pope.

The book had been around for years. Hints that this pornographic tale had circulated in manuscript from as early as the 1730s can be found in Peter Wagner's informative Introduction to the 1985 Penguin edition of the first published version of 1749: "The records of 'The Most Ancient and Puissant Order of the Beggar's Benison and Merryland', a club of would-be libertines flourishing from 1732 to 1836, contain an interesting entry on St Andrew's Day, 1737, when 'two nymphs, eighteen and nineteen, [were] exhibited' and 'Fanny Hill was read'." Wagner then added, "In Boswell's journals there are also two passages where Cleland asserts that a first version of *Memoirs* was written in the 1730s."

Cleland directly stated in a 13 November 1749 letter to the Law Clerk in the office of the Secretary of State that "the plan of the first Part was originally given to me by a young gentleman of the greatest hopes that ever I knew, (Brother to a nobleman now Ambassadour at a Foreign Court,) above eighteen years ago." Although this young gentleman remains unknown and the earlier manuscript of this first Part has never been uncovered, it does seem reasonable to suppose that for decades some pieces of *Fanny Hill* had been working their clandestine way through some rather advanced social circles of ill repute.

Well connected though he was, Cleland still did not fare so well in life. After serving in the East India Company from 1728 to 1740, he left Bombay and "joined the poorly paid crowd of Grubb Street hacks." The plot only began to thicken, however, after Cleland was thrown into Fleet Prison for debt on 23 February 1748, for now he found the leisure time under rather forced financial circumstances to polish the manuscript. Soon 750 cheap copies of *Fanny Hill* in an expanded version began working the streets of London. Ralph

Griffiths published this first printed edition, and it was so successful that Griffiths paid off Cleland's debts.

Although Cleland was released from prison on 6 March 1749, both publisher and author were arrested again on 10 November 1749, but Griffiths and Cleland were immediately "released on a recognizance of £100." By 8 March 1750 sales were coming along so well that "an abridged and bowdlerized version" came out to titillate or scandalize, depending upon one's point of view. Arrested yet again on 16 March 1750, things now took a surprisingly different turn, for Lord Granville, the Lord President of the Privy Council, was so impressed by Cleland's literary talents that he thought the government could direct his potent pen toward a more socially useful end. So it was arranged that the author of *Fanny Hill* would become a secret scribbler for the Pelham Administration with a pension of £100 per annum!

This dirty little secret arrangement with England's most notorious pornographer could not have remained unknown to Lord Chief Justice Mansfield, who was the Solicitor General at the time. And this observation might go some way toward clearing up a minor mystery in literary history. "After 1750," according to Peter Wagner's exposition, the abridged and bowdlerized version of *Fanny Hill* "kept selling slowly but steadily, in several versions and numerous pirate editions, though the text of the first edition [of 1749] was apparently not reprinted after Drybutter's unsuccessful attempt in 1757."

The major difference between the toned-down second edition of 1750 and this 1757 reprint of the sexier first edition of 1749 lies in the inclusion of a homosexual act of anal intercourse that Fanny witnesses through "a peep-hole" in a closet of a roadhouse. Fascinated by the proper workings of the male "machine" though the young charmer with lesbian experiences certainly was, at least one sexual act offended her delicate sensibilities. And what she had laid her innocent eyes upon was punishable by death, according to eighteenth-century English law. Burning with such "rage and indignation" over "so criminal a scene," our closet voyeur just happened to stumble while jumping off her chair and made so much noise that those nasty homosexuals somehow managed to escape from the roadhouse before our enterprising whore had time to screw up her virtue and sound the alarm.[3]

Unless appearances deceive the manuscript that Mansfield had seized at an auction in 1757 was "Drybutter's unsuccessful attempt" to reprint the original, juicier 1749 version. If yes, then it would seem that Cleland had already agreed with the government not to permit the 1749 version to be reprinted. In any event, that version was effectively suppressed for two centuries while the cleaned-up 1750 version moved from triumph to triumph through the dark underworld of dirty books. The publisher of the new version is said to have netted £10,000 for a sterling performance still relished by those whose taste extends beyond the conventional canon of British literature. When the 1749 version finally became publicly available again in 1963, it occasioned yet another obscenity trial, even though, truth to tell, not a single four letter word can be found in this most explicitly pornographic extravaganza written by an eighteenth-century British libertine.

That Lord Mansfield was primarily interested in keeping the political machine in good working order received considerable support from the trial of a Dr. Shebbeare that soon followed the Fanny Hill Affair. "The most remarkable part of this trial," according to Walpole's *Memoirs*, "was the Chief Justice Mansfield laying down the law, that satires even on dead kings were punishable." Walpole could scarcely contain his outrage: "Whatever obsolete statutes may pronounce, can anything be more foreign to the genius of the English constitution, nay, to the practice even of arbitrary countries! Where are tyrants sacred, when once dead? Adieu, veracity and history, if the King's Bench is to appreciate your expressions!"[4]

The spirit moving through Mansfield's rulings against the satires of Shebbeare and the immorality of Cleland promised to land our Scottish Law Lord in repeated controversies over the meaning of the freedom of the press throughout the decades to come. And soon after laying the tender hands of the government upon *Fanny Hill* he focused his attention upon the proper interpretation of a very different type of body, namely, Habeas Corpus.

IN 1679 Parliament passed the Act of Habeas Corpus, an Act that brought forward and codified a long tradition that reached all the way back to at least Magna Charta in 1215. Time out of mind a writ of Habeas Corpus commanded "the person to whom it is directed to bring the body of a person in his custody" before a proper tribunal to be charged. Because Habeas Corpus protected somebody in custody from arbitrary arrest by securing the right to be brought to trial, it was widely considered to be "the corner stone of our liberty."

Lord Mansfield, however, saw the matter in a rather different light. When the military impressed a man in 1757, he peremptorily pronounced "against that universal immunity from uncertain detention of their persons, which the English with so much reason think their birthright." In Mansfield's opinion, two technicalities in the case were transparent. First, no "criminal charge" had been filed against the man; therefore, there could not be any justification for evoking Habeas Corpus. In his reasoning, "A pressed sailor is not a slave. No compulsion can be put upon him except to serve his country; and, while doing so, he is entitled to claim all the rights of an Englishman." Second, because the courts were on "legal vacation" at the time of the action, "Lord Mansfield decided that it lay within the discretion of the judge to issue a writ of habeas corpus or not."

William Pitt, as would be expected, was "aghast at the discovery that a writ of habeas corpus might be a matter not of obligation but of discretion of the judges." According to Basil William's rendition of this affair, Pitt declared in the House of Commons that "he would never be entangled in the cobwebs of Westminster Hall, but would force any judge who nibbled at the liberties of the people to hide his head. To have every Englishman's birthright at the discretion of a judge was dangerous, since there was no trusting to the multiform, clashing, inconsistent opinions of Westminster Hall." So, to keep Mansfield from "compounding a great law of liberty," the Great Commoner had Attorney General Pratt draw up a bill that would strengthen the 1679 Act by requiring the judges to issue a writ of Habeas Corpus regardless of the technicalities within any given circumstance. And Pratt was so eager to comply, according to

Walpole's report to Horace Mann, that "the interpreting world" ascribed his "motive to a want of affection for my Lord Mansfield."

Since this bill sailed "almost unanimously" through the House of Commons, Pitt thought that he was in a strong position to make a clean sweep of the cobwebs Mansfield had been weaving around Westminster Hall. According to Basil Williams's narrative of this episode,

> [Pitt] dined with Newcastle on April 14 and had a long legal argument with him. "I have read," he told him, "as I suppose you have, Littleton, Coke, Selden, and Sir Simon D'Ewes and can talk upon this question as any lawyer." He then expounded his view at great length—that Mansfield had willfully misinterpreted the law: "judges had frequently given up law and liberty," he said, and made dark allusions to the fate of the ship-money judges.

Ominous words those surely were, for "the ship-money judges" had triggered the constitutional crisis that resulted in the English Civil War in the seventeenth century.[5]

Nevertheless, Mansfield's cobwebs withstood the slashes of Pitt's daggers, for King George II was determined to block what he conceived to be an encroachment upon his prerogative. And the Lords Spiritual and Temporal were fondly nursing their "privileges" because they looked "on themselves as distinct from the rest of the nation." During the 1750s, in Walpole's analysis, these privileged Lords were "a tame, subservient, incapable set of men, governed entirely by the Duke of Newcastle, and the two lawyers, Hardwicke and Mansfield." So far as Walpole could see, "Those lawyers were instances of the discrimination that ought to be made between the spirit of the laws and the profession of them. Nobody better read in them, nobody more warm to enforce them, nobody less actuated by the essence of them." Neither Hardwicke nor Mansfield "ever took the side of liberty." After the court lawyers had thoroughly exhausted "the subtleties, distinctions, chicaneries and absurdities of their profession" during three long days of tedious debate, Mansfield felt called upon to elucidate the bone of contention by laying out his full position in a moving oration on the true meaning and proper scope of Habeas Corpus.

According to a first-person report, Mansfield publicly asserted in the House of Lords that the people who supported Pratt's Bill did so "from the groundless imagination that liberty was concerned in it, whereas it had as little to do with liberty as the Navigation Laws." While he conceded that "ignorance on subjects of this nature was extremely pardonable, since the knowledge of particular laws required a particular study of them," he hastened to add that "the greatest genius, without such study, could no more become master of them than of Japanese literature without understanding the language of the country." Because both Pitt and Pratt lacked any such ingenious expertise, they failed to understand that "the writ of Habeas Corpus at common law was a sufficient remedy against all those abuses" which their bill was supposed to rectify.

Walpole's report on how Mansfield's appeal to expert authority prevailed over the appeal of ancient experience is quite moving:

> [Lord Mansfield] spoke for two hours and half; his voice and manner composed of harmonious solemnity were the least grace of his speech. I am not averse to own, that I never heard so much argument, so much sense, so much oratory, united. His deviations into the abstruse minutiae of the law, served but as a foil to the luminous parts of the oration. Perhaps it was the only speech, that, in my times at least, had real effect, that is, convinced many people.

After filing that glowing report Walpole troubled to add this pointed comment: "Nor did I ever know how true a votary I was to liberty, till I found that I was not one of the number staggered by that speech."[6]

Because William Pitt realized that his coalition ministry could not withstand the impact of a contest that pressed these constitutional contentions all the way to the breaking point, he yielded to political necessity and withdrew the bill. But he did get in one last word. When Lady Yarmouth observed that all the crown lawyers had lined up solidly against his understanding of that birthright liberty protected by Habeas Corpus, the Great Commoner responded with this rhetorical question: "Madam, if all the Bishops on the Bench were to say the people should not have use of the Bible, would the people part with their Bibles?"[7] While the Bishops on the Bench in eighteenth-century Great Britain were not known for their close reading of the Bible, many were zealous promoters of a longstanding project to introduce bishops in the American colonies, a project many Americans believed would undermine the freedom of religion.

THE Lords Spiritual were associated historically with the prerogative Court of High Commission that gave the House of Stuart such a bad name among what Anglicans called "Dissenters," that is, all those Congregationalists, Baptists, and Quakers spun out by the conflicts of the turbulent seventeenth century and now so conspicuously dominated the religious life of colonial America, especially north of the Mason-Dixon Line. Because the attempt to introduce Anglican bishops had been repeatedly portrayed in the colonial press as an assault upon the "unalienable ... right of conscience and private judgment" as well as "the precious jewel of religious liberty," even in those Southern colonies where the Church of England was legally established, the laity was not eager to embrace the blessings of bishops. For decades, though, ardent Anglican missionaries supported by the Society for the Propagation of the Gospel in Foreign Parts had agitated for American bishops. And now that the politically astute Thomas Secker had been installed as the Archbishop of Canterbury, plans were put into high gear for the establishment of an ecclesiastical hierarchy upon American soil.[8]

A REPORT was filed in the imperial bureaucracy in 1759 that "memorialized the Privy Council advocating, among other things, a uniform plan for establishing the judicature of the courts of vice-admiralty in the colonies on a more certain foundation that justice in all cases might be diligently and impartially administered and such regulations as parliament thought proper to make might be duly carried into execution." According to Charles M. Andrews's careful exposition, the High Court of Admiralty was introduced into England in the fourteenth century, then in the sixteenth century it was "raised by King Henry VIII to a position of equal importance with the common law courts at Westminster Hall." But "during the seventeenth century the common law courts, judges, and lawyers entered upon a persistent effort to restrict the jurisdiction of the admiralty courts and to extend that of the courts of common law. Sir Edward Coke and his common law successors demanded that admiralty jurisdiction be confined to the open seas only." Needless to say, "These common law prohibitions carried great weight in the seventeenth century, because the admiralty courts, as prerogative courts sitting without juries, were associated in the popular mind with the prerogative claims of the Stuarts."

Regardless of the differences between these legal traditions, on 15 May 1696 Parliament passed a famous Navigation Act that created the Board of Trade and established Admiralty Courts with jurisdiction over the colonial trade. These courts, however, were guided by an earlier "Act for preventing Frauds and regulating Abuses in the Plantation Trade," and this act contained a notorious ambiguity. Sections 2 and 7 of the Navigation Act clearly "required that trials for breaches of the acts of trade should be held in courts of vice-admiralty, which were courts of civil law without juries." Nevertheless, section 11 directly stated that in plantation suits involving "a ship or goods to be forfeited by reason of any unlawful importations or exportation, there shall not be any jury, *but of such only as are natives of England* " (my emphasis). Since the colonials were considered *natives of England*, section 11 specified that "such trials were to take place in the common law courts with juries." While that ambiguity had been allowed to fester for six decades, the standard practice in colonial America kept the proceedings under the control of local juries. This 1759 recommendation, however, was consciously designed to resolve the ambiguity in favor of the civil law procedures operative in the Admiralty Courts, where expert judges handed down verdicts instead of juries.[9]

FREEDOM of the Press, Habeas Corpus, Religious Liberty, and Trial by Jury—these were not the only rights up for review during the last few years of the reign of George II. Lord Chief Justice Mansfield's understanding of the Constitution of the British Empire would also undermine the authority of the representative assemblies within all of the colonies, regardless of whether they were charter, proprietary, or royal colonies. When he was the Solicitor General in the Pelham Administration, he had argued that the various colonies existed merely "from the Grace and Favour of the Crowne alone."[10]

During the opening years of the Seven Years War the Pennsylvania Assembly passed a Quartering Act to pay for housing the British army, a decision consciously designed to preserve provincial autonomy. Shortly before Attorney General Murray became the Lord Chief Justice of King's Bench, however, he advised the Council to reject Pennsylvania's Quartering Act precisely because the Assembly had assumed that Pennsylvania held the same "immunities from forced quartering of soldiers in private houses" that pertained in England, *but not in Scotland*. In his opinion "propositions true in the mother country" were not applicable "to a colony in time of war in the case of troops raised for their protection."[11]

This act, it should not go unnoticed, was up for action before the Privy Council, not a committee of Parliament. The reason lies right on the surface, for imperial jurisdiction over the various colonies was held by the King-in-Council, not the King-in-Parliament. And that is why Benjamin Franklin—the new agent for the Pennsylvania Assembly—focused his attention upon the Council from the moment he and his son William took up lodgings with Mrs. Margaret Stevenson at 7 Craven Street, London, on 30 July 1757.

Franklin's most detailed analysis of the inner workings of the imperial government can be found in his 19 March 1759 letter to

Isaac Norris in Philadelphia. This "unusually full and explicit letter" deserves careful scrutiny, according to the editors of the *Papers of Benjamin Franklin*, because it "describes more clearly than virtually any other contemporary document the attitude of leading members of the ministry on some of the constitutional questions which were to become increasingly important in the relations between the colonies and the mother country during the next fifteen or sixteen years."

Franklin opened his analysis with this observation: "The Prevailing Opinion ... among the Ministers and great Men here [in London], is, that the Colonies have too many and too great Privileges; and that it is not only the Interest of the Crown but of the Nation to reduce them." Then followed his recollection of a 1757 "Discourse" by the Lord President of the Council, Lord Granville:

> Your People in the Colonies refuse Obedience to the King's *Instructions*, and treat them with great Slight, as *not binding*, and *no Law*, in the Colonies; whereas, says his L__p, those Instructions are not like little Pocket Instructions given to the Ambassador or Envoy, in which much may be left to Discretion; they are first drawn up by grave and wise Men learned in the Laws and Constitution of the Nation; they are then brought to the Council Board, where they are solemnly weigh'd and maturely consider'd, and after receiving such Amendments as are found proper and necessary, they are agreed upon and establish'd. The Council is *over all* the Colonies; your last Resort is to the Council to decide your Differences, and you must be sensible it is for your Good, for otherwise you often could not obtain Justice. The King in Council is the LEGISLATOR of the Colonies; and when his Majesty's Instructions come there, they are the LAW OF THE LAND; *they are*, said his L__p, repeating it, the Law of the Land, and as such *ought to be* OBEYED.

Franklin responded diplomatically—and any fair-minded historian would also add that it is a much more accurate description of the received Constitution of the Empire:

> I told his Lordship this was new Doctrine to me. I had always understood from our Charters, that our Laws were to be made by our Assemblies, to be presented indeed to the King for his Royal Assent, but that being once given the King could not repeal or alter them. And as the Assemblies could not make permanent Laws without his Assent, so neither could he make a Law for them without theirs. He assur'd me I was totally mistaken. I did not think so however.

Regardless of their radically different understandings of the received constitution, it should not be overlooked that neither Granville's discourse nor Franklin's response so much as hinted that Parliament was involved in the governance of the internal affairs of the various colonies in any way whatsoever.

Lord Granville was not alone in his opinion, either. Next on the Council Board was the former Chancellor, Lord Hardwicke, and his exaltation of the royal prerogative easily matched Granville's. Since Granville and Hardwicke were both on the Board, Franklin thought that "one may easily conjecture what Reception a Petition concerning Privileges from the Colonies may meet with from those who are known to think that even the People of England have too many." Even more discouraging was the opinion of Lord Halifax at the head of the Board of Trade. His attitude was exhibited in the fact that he favored a military government for the new colony of Nova Scotia.

Discouraged though he happened to be, Franklin hastened on to add a description of a countervailing weight in the balance of power within the system: "The Speaker of the House [of Commons, Arthur Onslow], indeed, is look'd on as a staunch Friend to Liberty; and so is the Secretary Mr. Pitt; the Attorney General [Charles Pratt] is likewise *inclin'd* to that Side in all Questions." He even troubled to point out that Pratt was "greatly perplex'd, angry with the Council for referring the Affair" over the refusal of the proprietors to pay their fair share of taxes to his office. Finally, Franklin included a quoted statement, probably from Richard Jackson, that summarized the substance of Pratt's opinion on the issue:

> [T]he Council he knows are for Clipping the Wings of [the colonial] Assemblies in their Claims of all the Privileges of a House of Commons; the House of Commons are thought to claim too many [Privileges], some very unfit and unreasonable, and not for the common Good; but the Council have let the Colonies go on so long in this Way that it will now be difficult to restrain them; and the Council would now make the Attorney and Sollicitor the first Instruments of so odious a Measure; that they (the Council) should have carried it into Parliament, but they are afraid the Parliament would establish more Liberty in the Colonies than is proper or necessary, and therefore do not care the Parliament should meddle at all with the Government of the Colonies; they rather chuse to carry every Thing there by the *Weight of Prerogative*, which by Degrees may bring Things to a proper Situation. Most Attorney Generals (he said) would immediately do what they knew would be pleasing to the Council; but he could not: He must however make some kind of Report.

To conclude Franklin added this stinger: "It is some Comfort that the Council are doubtful of the Parliament."[12]

MISSING from Franklin's analysis was any consideration of Lord Mansfield. Why? The answer is this simple. The Lord Chief Justice had quarreled with the Great Commoner so often and so bitterly that he simply chose to not attend. Nevertheless, he was the only member of the *Conciliabulum* positively known to champion the idea of involving Parliament in the internal affairs of the colonies. However, he did hold some trump cards, for the unwritten British Constitution was governed by precedents, and in the same year that Franklin penned this detailed letter, our Scottish Law Lord handed down what promised to become a decisive precedent in the 1759 case of *Rex v. Cowle*.

While Benjamin Franklin did not comment on this 1759 case, Lord Chief Justice Mansfield was very much on his mind. The organizing purpose of his mission was to lobby in London to force the proprietor of Pennsylvania to pay his fair share of taxes for the war effort. With his eyes fixed upon a coming hearing before the Privy Council, he set out on an extensive tour of Scotland to receive the honorary degree of Doctor of Laws from the University of Saint Andrews, a tour that brought him into contact with many of the leading lights of the Scottish Enlightenment.

To gain maximal political effect Franklin had rushed into print *An Historical Review of the Constitution and Government of Pennsylvania*. One of the key persons who received this detailed rehearsal was the political leader of the Scottish bloc in Parliament and a member of the Privy Council, Lord Bute's uncle, Archibald Campbell. After enjoying the charmed company of the most advanced savants in Scotland, Franklin was driven back over the border into England by that "master of British law," Lord Kames.[13]

Franklin's long awaited hearing before the Privy Council— notice, not before a Committee of Parliament—finally came on 27 August 1760. According to his *Autobiography*, in the midst of all the wrangling among the lawyers arguing both sides in the Cockpit,

> Lord Mansfield, one of the Council rose, & beckoning to me, took me into the Clerk's Chambers, while the Lawyers were pleading, and ask'd me if I was really of Opinion that no Injury would be done the Proprietary Estate in the Execution of the Act. I said, Certainly. Then says he, you can have little

objection to enter into an Engagement to assure that
Point. I answer'd None, at all.

So, the Supply Act was allowed to pass.[14] (Curiously, this episode with
Lord Chief Justice Mansfield forms the climax of Benjamin Franklin's
Autobiography, even though he lived another three eventful decades.)

Given this type of evidence, Paul Langford convincingly argued
that "the mentality of mid-eighteenth century Whigs" pivoted upon
"the conviction that the colonies were peculiarly the concern of
the executive, and except in matters of commercial regulation,
outside the natural purview, if not the competence, of Parliament."[15]
Technically put, *the colonies were dependent upon the King in all
matters other than the regulation of the imperial trade.*

IN the late 1750s Horace Walpole ranked Lord Chief Justice
Mansfield alongside Sir Robert Walpole, the Duke of Cumberland,
Lord Granville, and William Pitt as one of the five Great Men who
graced this most "unBritish an age as ever was!" Sir Robert Walpole
had died in 1745. The Duke of Cumberland's fame rested upon his
military prowess—during the Rebellion of 1745 he had crushed
Bonnie Prince Charlie, and during the opening years of the Seven
Years War he was in command of the campaign on the Continent.
And Lord Granville exercised considerable influence as the President
of the Council until his death in 1763. But the principal players on the
political landscape that Walpole wanted to lay bare for the benefit of
posterity were the Great Commoner and the Great Lord Mansfield.

William Pitt remained "an unfinished greatness" in comparison
to Lord Mansfield's more brilliant qualities. Whereas Pitt was
impetuous, Mansfield was deliberate. Whereas Pitt spoke in
flourishes, Mansfield spoke with precision. Whereas Pitt was an
outsider born to lead boldly in full public view, Mansfield was an
insider bred to work through others from a concealed position
behind the public screen. If Walpole were forced to chose between
these two titans who should be ranked as the "brightest genius," he
would not hesitate in awarding that distinction to Mansfield, for this

savant from Scotland coupled "a most accurate understanding" with such "great powers of eloquence" that his debating techniques were "formed to convince, even where Pitt had dazzled."

Eloquent, yes—too eloquent for Walpole's taste. Persuasive, yes—way too persuasive in Walpole's judgment. From the moment Lord Chief Justice Mansfield presided over the Court of King's Bench, Walpole nursed a conviction that a steady stream of evil consequences would flow from our Scottish Law Lord's rulings. It would not be an exaggeration to claim that he despised the Lord Chief Justice of King's Bench with a malice that bordered upon the pathological. Profound hostility against the jurisprudential orientation of this sophisticated connoisseur of French refinements veritably drips from his poison pen as he pours down scorn upon those "grave personages" who "affect to authenticate our liberties by history and precedent," thereby making "the plainest thing in the world, *the right to freedom*, the most obscure." This common error sprang from the spurious hope that liberty would somehow become more intelligible once men finally uncovered "through what genealogy of terms this blessing had been derived to them." Especially dangerous was this moral mistake when the legal lessons were to be learned before the bar of a political judge who so thoroughly adored "the reality ... of despotism" and was just beginning to expand those "principles that favoured an arbitrary king" to embrace "an arbitrary government."[16]

AFTER becoming the Lord Chief Justice of King's Bench, our Scottish Law Lord deliberately brought up for review both the Freedom of the Press and Habeas Corpus. Planning for the transformation of the Old Colonial System was also under active consideration during the late 1750s, plans that the Americans would consider to be direct threats to Religious Liberty, Trial by Jury, and Representative Assemblies. Unless appearances deceive, the groundwork for the constitutional crisis that gripped the British Empire in the 1760s was laid during the final years of the reign of King George II.

IX

YOUNG KING GEORGE III IN THE HANDS OF THE SCOTS

L ORD MANSFIELD WAS SO PLEASED BY HOW THE BRITISH EMPIRE WAS WAGING WAR WITH France that he composed a stately Thanksgiving Sermon that his old friend, Dr. James Johnson, preached in Westminster Abbey on 29 November 1759. This solemn celebration of the reign of George II was brought to a fitting climax with a standard refrain: "And may the happiness we enjoy by his government be perpetuated to us under his family to the latest generation."[1]

Less than a year would pass before the tender twenty-two-year-old Prince of Wales inherited the throne of the most promising Empire in the world. Horace Walpole opened the next volume of his *Memoirs* with the claim that "No British monarch had ascended the throne with so many advantages as George the Third."[2] The guarded welcome that greeted the new regime, however, is captured with a little more circumspection in a pungent letter Dr. Samuel Johnson sent to a friend in Italy:

> We were so weary of our old King, that we are much
> pleased with his successor; of whom we are so much
> inclined to hope great things, that most of us begin

> already to believe them. The young man is hitherto
> blameless; but it would be unreasonable to expect
> much from the immaturity of juvenile years, and the
> ignorance of princely education. He has been long
> in the hands of the Scots, and has already favoured
> them more than the English will contentedly
> endure. But, perhaps, he scarcely knows whom he
> has distinguished, or whom he has disgusted.[3]

Much to the disgust of the political nation, in "the immaturity of juvenile years" George III actively promoted the persons, patterns, and principles that prevailed in the Junior Court at Leicester House where his princely education had long been "in the hands of the Scots."

Johnson was emphatically calling attention to the commanding influence of the King's "Dear Friend," John Stuart, the Third Earl of Bute, but the learned Doctor's use of the plural points to an intimate circle within the royal entourage, beginning with John Home. In 1754 this dashing young dramatist ventured down to London to promote his historical drama, *The Tragedy of Douglas*. Although David Garrick turned *Douglas* down for Drury Lane, Lord Bute picked up John Home for Leicester House, where he became (in the words of Sir Walter Scott) "the favourite of the favourite" of the Prince of Wales.

As Bute's private secretary Home was splendidly located to open more than a few doors for his numerous friends, many of whom were in the Cast of Characters for a private reading of *The Tragedy of Douglas* in Edinburgh during 1756:

Lord Randolph	William Robertson
Lady Randolph	Adam Ferguson
Norval	Alexander Carlyle
Glenalvon	David Hume
The Maid	Hugh Blair
Douglas	John Home

Simply by adding the name of Lord Kames—who was in the audience—one has an impressive list of so many of the shining lights of the Scottish Enlightenment.[4]

Seldom has an intellectual movement ever enjoyed so direct a connection with so promising a center of political power. When Bute was in need of a tutor for his sons, the Scottish Moral Philosopher, Adam Ferguson, came readily to mind. When William Robertson came to London with a manuscript, he easily found a publisher for his *History of Scotland, during the Reigns of Queen Mary and of King James VI* (1759). When Lord Hertford needed a private secretary for the British Embassy in France, David Hume landed the position. And it is reasonable to suppose that Dr. Samuel Johnson also realized that as North Britons the Scottish Lords Bute and Mansfield had shared (in Campbell's words) "a secret sympathy" from at least 1754, when Bute sold his magnificent estate of Kenwood to Mansfield.[5]

Regardless of how much refined taste and prodigious talent Bute could import from the literati of Edinburgh, when the elderly George II died in October 1760 Bute remained (in Walpole's telling) "unknown, ungracious, and a Scot." This *unknown* mentor of the Prince of Wales had never so much as spoken even once during more than two decades in Parliament. Nevertheless, within a matter of days George III appointed him to the Privy Council. This *ungracious* favorite had so flaunted his connection with the young King's mother that the "passionate, domineering" Dowager had become "an object of scandal." Nevertheless, within a matter weeks Bute became the honored Groom of the Stole and First Gentleman of the Bed Chamber. And this *Scot* bore the Jacobite name that evoked the worst of all possible memories of the House of Stuart. Nevertheless, within a matter of months "*Prerogative* became a fashionable word," for, as Walpole troubled to point out, "the language of the times was altered, before the favourite dared to make any variation in the Ministry."[6]

The King's speech to his council at the opening of the reign was drafted by Bute without consulting any of the King's servants. Bute's draft and Pitt's response, according to Walpole's record, reads:

> It talked *of a bloody and expensive war, and of
> obtaining an honourable and lasting peace.* Thus
> was it delivered: but Mr Pitt went to Lord Bute that
> evening, and after an altercation of three hours,
> prevailed that in the printed copy the words should
> be changed to *an expensive but just and necessary
> war*; and that after the words *honourable peace*
> should be inserted, *in concert with our allies.* Lord
> Mansfield and others counselled these palliatives
> too; but it was two o'clock of the following afternoon,
> before the King would yield to the alteration.

In the next paragraph Walpole added that Pitt "had for some time been on the coldest terms with Lord Bute."[7]

At the beginning of a new regime all of the crown officers are required to submit their resignations. While some would receive their old commissions back, others would receive commissions with a different wording. Bute made sure that all the colonial commissions contained the proviso that the designated officers served at *the pleasure of the crown.* For example, the Chief Justice of New Jersey had held a commission that spelled out his tenure to continue "during good behavior"; his new commission was deliberately changed to read "during pleasure." When the New Jersey Assembly refused to appropriate a penny to pay the salary of the Chief Justice unless the earlier wording was restored, the Royal Governor reluctantly caved in to that demand. The moment this "premeditated and unprecedented act of disobedience" became known, Bute had the Governor sacked without so much as a hearing. And it is a curious fact that in a matter of months Benjamin Franklin's illegitimate son, William Franklin, became the new Royal Governor of New Jersey.[8]

The signal that significant structural change was in the making at home as well as in the colonies came on 25 March 1761 when the culturally disliked, socially despised, and politically distrusted Earl of Bute replaced Holdernesse as Secretary of State. The predictable conflict within the Pitt-Newcastle Administration, however, did not come to a head until a confidential report on 31 August 1761 informed the government that Spain was definitely going to intervene in the war effort because of its Family Compact with France.

Whereas the Great Commoner pressed for an immediate declaration of war against Spain, the Cabinet refused to support Pitt's bold policy on 18 September. On the very next day, Newcastle, Devonshire, Mansfield, and Bute held an urgent meeting at Devonshire's house to "discuss the situation … their own audacity in opposing Pitt's judgment" had precipitated. Two days later Pitt conferred with George III. When the Cabinet met again on 2 October, Mansfield tried to mediate the conflict, only to have his life-long rival silence him with the cutting remark, "the Chief Justice of England has no opinion to give in this matter."[9]

The Great Lord Mansfield was silenced, but he endured. The Great Commoner did not. Claiming "he would not remain in a situation which made him responsible for measures he was no longer allowed to guide," William Pitt submitted his resignation on 5 October 1761. According to Walpole's *Memoirs*, "The nation was thunderstruck, alarmed, and indignant" over this sudden turn of events—*thunderstruck* over the King's acceptance of the resignation of such a popular War Leader, *alarmed* over the gathering power of the unknown Earl of Bute, and *indignant* over the seduction of the Great Commoner, who was promised the title of Lord Chatham with a £3,000 pension for Lady "Cheat'em."[10]

Within a matter of months the ministry—nominally headed by the Duke of Newcastle but controlled by the Earl of Bute—came to the sober conclusion that an armed confrontation with Spain could no longer be postponed. When war was finally declared against His Most Catholic Majesty in January, "The City and Country had so mean an opinion of those who were to direct [the war with Spain], that the Stocks immediately fell to 66½, though in the Rebellion [of 1745] they had never been lower than 72." Reduced to impotence, Newcastle finally resigned, but only after "Lord Mansfield … had *pleaded* with Lord Bute for above an hour, and could not extract from him a wish that the Duke should continue in the Treasury." When Henry Fox pressed Mansfield on whether this claim was true, he replied: "Not an hour, for I soon saw it was to no purpose." With Newcastle's resignation on 26 May 1762 the young King's "Dear Friend" became the Prime Minister in name as well as fact.[11]

JOHN Wilkes immediately launched a severe attack upon the new Bute Administration. Since 1757 he had represented Aylesbury as a loyal follower of Pitt, and now this extraordinary agitator positioned himself as a propagandist for the Opposition.[12] When the Scottish author, Tobias Smollett, introduced a weekly called the *Briton* as the chosen mouthpiece for the Bute Administration, Wilkes and his partner, Charles Churchill, responded with the *North Briton*, a title deliberately chosen to point up the satirical purpose of this scurrilous weekly. On the first issue of 5 June 1762, the *North Briton* proclaimed this guiding principle: "The *liberty of the press* is the birthright of a BRITON, and is justly esteemed the firmest bulwark of the liberties of this country. It has been the terror of all bad ministers."

What catapulted this radical rascal into prominence was how he repeatedly pressed close to the edge of libel—or several degrees beyond, in the opinion of the Court. His vision of the freedom of the press was on a collision course with the received legal opinion championed by the Lord Chief Justice of King's Bench.

Over the coming years Walpole devoted considerable space in his *Memoirs* to Wilkes's ever evolving power to shape public opinion. According to his report on the wildly popular *North Briton,* "The highest names, whether of statesmen or magistrates, were printed at length and the insinuations went still higher. In general favouritism was the topic, and the partiality of the court to the Scots. Every obsolete anecdote, every illiberal invective, was raked up and set forth in strong and witty colours against Scotland. One of the first numbers was one of the most outrageous, the theme taken from the loves of Queen Isabella and Mortimer." The reading public did not need to be coached on how Bute had long been playing the role of Mortimer with the King's mother.[13]

A significant portion of Wilkes's talent derived from his biting wit. When Lord Sandwich assured the Hell Fire Club that Wilkes would

YOUNG KING GEORGE III IN THE HANDS OF THE SCOTS

"die either by hanging or the pox," the jester cleverly replied with spirit, "That depends, My Lord, whether I embrace your lordship's principles or your mistress."[14] And his flair for repartee spiced his writing style. The *North Briton* (in Walpole's telling) exhibited "an acrimony, a spirit, and a licentiousness unheard of before even in this country." "To laugh and riot and scatter firebrands, with him was liberty." In point of fact, "despotism will for ever reproach freedom with the profligacy of such a saint!" And profligate this libertine surely was in the universal opinion of his contemporaries, a scandalous reputation that Wilkes cultivated to the amusement of his numerous followers—and to the horror of polite society. Walpole's organizing point, however, cut to a deeper level: "The virtuous are too scrupulous to go the lengths that are necessary to rouse the people against their tyrants." It did not take long before Wilkes had mastered the art of provoking the government into making mistakes that would spontaneously generate popular support for "Wilkes and Liberty"—the enduring banner of English Radicalism.[15]

ALTHOUGH the political nation was in profound disarray throughout 1762, France had already been defeated, and now Spain learned to its sorrow that it was no match for the British fleet. Havana fell in Cuba on 13 August. Manila fell in the Philippines on 5 October. Soon Spain joined the ongoing negotiations for a peace treaty at Fontainebleau, where the preliminaries were signed on 3 November 1762. Soon after the terms of the coming peace were made public, the *North Briton* escalated its assault upon the Bute Administration. Before long "the Favourite was assaulted in his chair by a formidable mob," in Walpole's report, "and had not the Guards arrived opportunely, would hardly have escaped with his life." "*No Petticoat Government; No Scotch Favourite*" was the chant in the streets as the mob convulsed London. In the House of Lords, "The Duke of Grafton, with great weight and greater warmth, attacked [the terms of the Peace] severely, and looking full on Lord Bute, imputed to him corruption and worse acts." Soon William Pitt took up his position in the House of Commons and spoke for three hours and twenty-five minutes, primarily to remind the House that it was *"the indubitable and fundamental right of Parliament to offer advice"* to the Crown in such matters, but also to castigate any "cobber" who might try his hand at remodeling "this old constitution."[16] After all these fireworks on the floor, however, the vote against the preliminaries in the House of Commons added up to only 96— the Great Commoner even abandoned his seat before the vote was taken.[17]

The day after the preliminaries had been signed George III confided in a letter to his Dear Friend that he had been "provok'd to the greatest degree at having seen Ld Mansfield." Why? Because he had "so much self sufficiency concerning his own judgement." The King thought he was "but half a man" whose "timidity and refinement made him unfit for the present turbulent scene." The young King particularly disliked the way the Lord Chief Justice "cries out against everything but *moderation*."[18] While it is not clear what the King was protesting, it is reasonable to suppose that Lord Mansfield had been cautioning him about the Earl of Bute's plans to transform the government. In any event, *moderation* was not an operative word in Bute's working vocabulary.

In Walpole's analysis of the political situation that unfolded during the dénouement of the Seven Years War, "Lord Bute's object was, peace at any rate, that he might pursue his plans of power at home." Bute struck back ferociously against any opposition through the Leader of the House, Henry Fox. "A more severe political persecution never raged" throughout the government. "Newcastle, Grafton, and Rockingham were dismissed from their lord-lieutenancies, and even the humblest of officials who owed their appointment to Whig patronage were deprived of their post." Punishment was the order of the day as every office holder who had voted against the preliminaries was instantly dismissed from office, and "the measures of the House of Stuart were so thoroughly copied, that even the rankest friends of that family were adopted at St James's." Walpole was even persuaded that "a clear indication of the principles of the new court" became apparent on 30 January

1763 when "that Jacobite holiday," the anniversary of the execution of Charles I was conspicuously celebrated in the most blatant manner.[19]

Nasty though the political situation was, this vicious episode was fueled much more by partisan considerations than by any particulars in these preliminaries, for on the face of it the Peace of Paris humiliated France and Spain by granting to the British Empire an extraordinary preeminence in both India and North America. Spain surrendered the vast region known as "East and West Florida," but she did gain the strategic French city of New Orleans. France not only yielded Quebec—she was forced to remove her flag from the North American continent altogether. (France, however, did retain two small islands off the coast of Canada to support her fishing fleets.) British North America now stretched from the Atlantic Ocean to the Mississippi River, and from the Gulf of Mexico to the North Pole.

Moderate though he was deemed to be by the young King, Lord Mansfield made a "fine defence of the treaty," so fine that it was approved by the House of Lords without even a division. And it sailed through the House of Commons, because, as Henry Fox observed, there never was a House "so well disposed to be governed."[20]

THE Peace of Paris brought to an end the most devastating but decisive war fought between the French and British Empires since the Glorious Revolution. What it failed to bring was peace at home. For weeks the political climate was more than drenched with foreboding as tension steadily mounted—until Bute abruptly resigned on 8 April 1763.

Although Bute's friends had been told that he planned on retiring after the peace had been secured, this was taken as a calculated political gambit to strengthen his hand. But Henry Fox discovered on 2 March that he had resolutely set his mind upon retreating from the scene, for he asked this Leader of the House of Commons to begin preparing for a new ministry. That Bute wanted Fox to be appointed Prime Minister was a proposition that profoundly shocked the inexperienced young King, for he had always viewed Fox as a front for his dreaded uncle, the Duke of Cumberland. Reluctantly

George III consented—only to have Henry Fox decline the offer! The choice then fell upon George Grenville to form a new ministry.

Even though the King told Bute that he "must not be surprised that the seeing him resolved to quit the scene of business is the most cruel political blow that could have happen'd," he realized full well that his Dear Friend was "heartily sick of his situation." Bute's pathetic letter of resignation openly labored the isolation of his solitary command:

> Single in a cabinet of my own forming, no aid in the House of Lords to support me except two peers (Lords Denbigh and Pomfret), both the Secretaries of State silent, and the Lord Chief Justice, whom I myself brought into office, voting for me, yet speaking against me, the ground I tread upon is so hollow, that I am afraid not only of falling myself, but of involving my royal master in my ruin. It is time for me to retire.

The short-lived Bute Administration fell by its own weight—or lack thereof.[21]

What "shook the Favourite's power," in Walpole's rendering of the messy affair, "was his ignorance of the world." Not only was his "head unadapted to government," his heart was infected with a "morose and recluse pride … that made him embark imprudently, and retreat as unadvisedly."[22]

Never again would the Lord Bute hold any political office during the reign of George III. Marginal though he quickly became, he was represented in the iconography of the age by a large boot—with a devil crawling up and out. A pervasive myth even claimed that for years to come he would be pulling the strings from behind the curtain, a popular notion dismissed by serious commentators as a wild delusion shared by too many of his contemporaries. John Stuart, the Third Earl of Bute, earned through his brief foray into the political arena, the dubious distinction of being the most thoroughly despised political leader in the entire history of the British Isles.

ALTHOUGH the Scottish Lords Bute and Mansfield were closely identified in the public mind, they operated on profoundly different political principles. Few things could be more transparent than the fact that the Earl of Bute sought to rule by the royal prerogative, while Lord Mansfield was (in Macaulay's words) "the father of modern toryism, of toryism modified to suit an order of things in which the House of Commons is the most powerful body in the state."[23] The distinction is critical, for Mansfield consistently argued for the supremacy of Parliament as the instrument through which the King ruled. In Lord Campbell considered opinion, "Hitherto Lord Mansfield had always called himself a Whig, although entertaining and not disguising what are considered Tory principles; but now that on the accession of George III there was to be a new distribution of parties, and that the Tory flag was openly hoisted by royalty, he rallied under it."[24]

The transition, however, did not go smoothly for Mansfield. It cost him the support of the Duke of Newcastle. And it did not gain him the support of the Earl of Bute. But he guarded his options with care. The King even came to realize that his advice was splendid. And one thing was utterly transparent—what Great Britain needed more than anything else was more revenue, for the victory over France had left the Empire with an enormous debt. By no means was Lord Chief Justice Mansfield the only one looking for new sources of revenue to be located in America.

THOMAS HUTCHINSON: REVISIONIST HISTORIAN

T HE AMERICAN MOST SYMPATHETIC TO LORD CHIEF
JUSTICE MANSFIELD'S UNDERSTANDING of the Constitution
of the British Empire was none other than the Lieutenant Governor
and Chief Justice of Massachusetts, Thomas Hutchinson (1711-1780).[1]
His family tree stretched all the way back to the Great Migration of
the 1630s when William and Anne Hutchinson arrived on the shores
of the howling wilderness known as the Massachusetts Bay. Over five
generations his extended family had grown quite wealthy through
hard work as merchants—and quite prominent by avoiding religious
controversies that had led to the destruction of Anne Hutchinson in
the Antinomian Crisis.

At the tender age of twelve Hutchinson enrolled in Harvard
College. Before long he made a conscious decision to pursue a
vocation in public service. By 1737 he was elected to represent Boston
in the Massachusetts General Court, a position he held almost
continuously for over a decade. At the Albany Congress he shared
with Benjamin Franklin the distinction of being one of the prime
movers in drafting the ill-fated Albany Plan of Union. During the
ensuing French and Indian War he was Massachusetts's agent to

the commanding general in North America. Then in 1758 he was appointed the Lieutenant Governor of Massachusetts. Few things pleased him more than the arrival of Sir Francis Bernard as the new Royal Governor of Massachusetts in 1760.

It did not take long before Bernard began writing letters to officials in the imperial government suggesting "when a Revisal and settlement of the political state of North American should have a place in the British Councils, I might possibly be of some service."[2] Given time he worked up his imperial vision into 97 propositions published as *Principles of Law and Polity, Applied to the Government of the British Colonies in America*. Several of these propositions exhibit how his understanding of the Constitution of the Empire matched Sir William Blackstone's and Lord Chief Justice Mansfield's—and shaped the mentality of Thomas Hutchinson:

> #2. In all *imperial* states there resides somewhere or other an absolute power, which we will call the *Sovereignty*.

> #4. The *King in Parliament* has the sole right of legislation, and the supreme superintendency of the government; and, in this plenitude of power, is absolute, uncontrollable, and accountable to none; and therefore, in a political sense, can do no wrong ...

> #10. The *King in Parliament*, is the sole and absolute Sovereign of the whole *British Empire*.

> #30. The *Parliament* of *Great Britain*, as well from its rights of *Sovereignty*, as from occasional exigencies, has a right to make laws for, and impose taxes upon its subjects in its external dominions, although they are not represented in such *Parliament*.

Needless to say, in Bernard's vision the King-in-Parliament exercised unlimited power. And he thoroughly shared Mansfield's opinion that colonial charters were "no more than temporary provisions" to get things under way and now should be elevated to a more mature model. Bernard was also convinced the King should appoint "a Nobility for life," because "there is no Government in *America* at present, whose powers are properly balanced" (propositions 86 to 88). The Royal Governor, however, had been in America long enough to realize, according to proposition 44, that "it would be most advisable to leave the Provincial Legislatures the raising of internal taxes."[3]

Sir Francis Bernard's detailed plans to revise the governing principles of the Province of Massachusetts were not widely known at the time, but rumors somehow had begun to spread. Suspicions had been aroused. And his appointment of Lieutenant Governor Hutchison to the office of Chief Justice had poisoned the well.

SOON after Bernard arrived in Boston, Chief Justice Sewall died on 10 September 1760. Immediately the Speaker of the House of Representatives, James Otis, Sr., let it be known that "the first surviving judge" should be elevated to the open post of Chief Justice, thereby opening a position on the bench for Otis himself, who believed that he was entitled to the promotion because a former governor had promised him a seat as soon as it became available. Governor Bernard, though, took that prior promise lightly. And to find his way through the thicket of Massachusetts politics he was more than willing to listen to the advice of members of the Court where "the first surviving judge, and two other judges, together with several of the principal gentlemen of the bar, signified their desire ... that he would appoint the lieutenant-governor to be the successor" of Chief Justice Sewall.[4]

Although Thomas Hutchinson lacked formal legal education—the standard complaint focused on the fact that he was "not ... bred to the law"—diligent student and devoted public servant that he was, the newly appointed Chief Justice "applied his intervals to reading the law," beginning with the legal developments of the Bay Colony under the Old Charter.

To prepare for this task he gathered up four different bodies of materials besides those in the public record. First, "many ... came to me from my ancestors, who, for four successive generations, had been principal actors in public affairs." Second, he generously acknowledged that the "manuscript history of Mr. William Hubbard ... has been of great use to me," especially in regard to the history of the early decades. Third, he collected as many "private papers of others of our first settlers" as he could, though he admitted that in this endeavor "I have not had the success I desired." And finally his brother-in-law, the Reverend Samuel Mather, had opened his library to him, a library that included much of the source material for Cotton Mather's monumental *Magnalia Christi Americana* (1702).[5]

With documents drawn from all these sources Hutchinson realized that he had in front of him the most comprehensive and authoritative collection of original materials on the history of early New England ever assembled in one place, in one mind. Scholarly by inclination and habit—and "being very loath, that what had cost me some pains to bring together, should be again scattered and utterly lost"—he put pen to paper.[6] With prodigious energy and incredible speed he bent the entire force of his fertile mind—when he could escape from pressing public business—in a steady effort to understand and explain what actually happened between the Founding of Massachusetts and the New Charter of 1691.

IN a letter to Ezra Stiles in Newport, Rhode Island, Hutchinson confessed that his manuscript was written in "about twelve months."[7] One suspects that it took much longer to bring it all together, and surely he had begun collecting the materials much earlier. Suffice it to say, planning for this first volume in the three volume series must have entered his mind soon after becoming Chief Justice in 1760; writing commenced around the time the Peace of Paris was signed on 10 February 1763; and the manuscript was finished around the time the first hint of the forthcoming Sugar Act surfaced on 7 March 1764.

In reviewing the work Stiles informed him rather bluntly that he had been misinformed when he maintained, "The Pequod tribe was wholly extinguished." In fact, the tribe still lived not far away. (Curiously, Herman Melville adopted that spelling instead of the more accurate "Pequot" in his narrative of the voyage of the Pequod in pursuit of the White Whale.[8]) On 4 July 1764 Hutchinson again informed Stiles, "I have let the manuscript rest for 4 to 5 months," because he had wanted his tome to be published in England. Since that had proved to be impractical, and the political situation he wanted to address was growing urgent, he had begun "to think of printing it here" in Boston. *The History of the Colony of Massachusetts-Bay, from the First Settlement thereof in 1628, until its Incorporation with the Colony of Plimouth, Province of Main, &c. by the Charter of King William and Queen Mary, in 1691*, covering 566 densely packed pages simply overflowing with extensive notes and direct testimony from original sources, plus 21 crucial documents from the seventeenth-century archives in an Appendix, appeared in the Boston bookshops during the latter part of 1764—right when the constitutional issue was joined by the Sugar Act of 1764.

AFTER a cursory review of earlier attempts to settle New England from "the voyage made by Bartholomew Gosnold" in 1602, through the landing of the Pilgrims at New Plymouth in 1620, to the initial ventures along the Bay, Hutchinson moved directly to the crucial meeting that occurred in England on 28 July 1629: "Several gentlemen of figure and estate, Isaac Johnson, John Winthrop, Thomas Dudley, and divers others, who were dissatisfied with the arbitrary proceedings both in church and state, pleased themselves with the prospect of liberty in both, to be enjoyed in America; but upon this condition only, that the patent and charter should remove with them." The original design of the charter, according to Hutchinson's close reading of the text, was "to constitute a *corporation in England, like to that of the East-India and other great companies*" (my emphasis). While the governing body of this joint stock company was supposed to remain in England, these Founding Fathers of New England in fact brought the company and the charter with them across the Atlantic, even though there was "a doubt whether such a transfer was legal."[9]

During the opening decades the first generation acted as though they were "at full liberty, without any charter from the crown, to establish such sort of government as they thought proper, and to form a new state as fully to all intent and purposes as if they had been in a state of nature, and were making their first entrance into civil society."[10] And experiment they emphatically did, with every deviation from the letter of their charter pointed out by our learned historian with a critical eye focused upon the legality of these unwarranted developments.

While Oliver Cromwell was the Lord Protector after the execution of King Charles I, Massachusetts was something of a "favorite"— the communications between the Bay Colony and "home" were conducted in "a style more proper for one ally to another, than for the head of a sovereign state to one of its branches or dependencies." In Hutchinson's considered opinion, "the reasonable and necessary connexion, between a colony and the state from which it springs, perhaps, was not fully understood" at the time.[11] But by their very daring, the builders of the Bay Colony had positioned themselves to be disciplined by events vastly beyond their control at the restoration of the House of Stuart in 1660.

Beginning with the reign of Charles II a sea change occurred in the relationship between Massachusetts and England. Whereas "the people had been without any apprehensions of danger to their religious and civil privileges," all of a sudden "they were alarmed from all quarters" because the new royal government threatened them with a basic "change in the form of their government, both in church and state."[12] (This was no empty treat either, for in 1662 the New Haven Colony was absorbed into Connecticut for harboring the three regicides, Whaley, Dixwell, and Goffe. Three of the major thoroughfares radiating out from the campus of Yale University are named after these three judges who signed the death warrant of Charles I.)

Given this critical situation the General Court of Massachusetts appealed directly to their "Dread Soveraign": "Let our government live, our patent live, our magistrates live, so shall we all yet have further cause to say, from our hearts, let the King live for ever." For some time Charles II did let them continue to live under their original charter, but, as Hutchinson labored the point, "the colony never stood well in England" from "the restoration until the vacating of the charter" in 1684.[13]

While that third generation never forgot that they were "colonists, and therefore subject to the controul of the parent state," one letter sent to their agents in London advanced this understanding of the constitution of the evolving empire: "they not being represent in parliament, and according to the usual saying of the learned in the law, the laws of England were bounded within the four seas, and did not reach America." Because they were *without the realm* their obedience extended merely to ceremonial niceties—"The King's arms were ordered to be carved and put up in the court-house." But on substantive matters the Bay Colony ignored the imperial regulations: "No custom-house was established. The acts of parliament of the 12 and 15th of King Charles the Second, for regulating the plantation trade were in force, but the governor, whose business it was to carry them into execution, was annually to be elected by the people, whose interest it was that they should not be observed." Because of such flagrant abuses "the whole colony of the Massachusetts suffered the loss of their charter."[14]

Hutchinson went to considerable lengths in trying to track down "the wrong sense they had of the relation they stood in to England," a mistake they shared with "the people of Ireland," especially with William Molineux's 1698 treatise, *The Case of Ireland's being bound by Act of Parliament stated*. The conceptual error that Hutchinson found in this traditional political thought turned upon a wrong sense of "civil subjection" that was drawn between a *necessary* and a *voluntary* subjection. What the former meant, according to his exposition, was that some kind of civil government was *necessary* in the nature of things because of an "actual residence" in a place.

A *voluntary* civil subjection was quite different, for its foundation was rooted in a "compact" with the King. By this compact "they acknowledged they were so bound, that they were not at liberty to subject themselves to, or to seek protection from, any other prince, they were to pay a fifth part of all silver and gold mines, they were to make no laws repugnant to the laws of England, &c; but on the other hand, they were to be governed by laws made by themselves, and by officers elected by themselves &c." These subtle distinctions, however, were foreign to Hutchinson's own mentality. In his own understanding, "the allegiance of English subjects ... is not considered as local, but perpetual and unalienable." And he firmly believed the early Puritans were quite wrong in their approach: "But however pleasing these principles were in speculation, or whatever foundation they may have in nature, yet they could not continue to practice upon them, nor would they bear the test when adopted by English subjects."[15]

Because of the earlier generation's conceptual confusion, the Old Charter was vacated and Massachusetts was absorbed into the Dominion of New England—which included New York as well— under the governance of Sir Edmund Andros, a Royal Governor appointed over the entire region with its capital in Boston. Hutchinson opened his detailed chronicle of the train of evil consequences flowing from this disastrous turn of events with the observation that "Nero concealed his tyrannical disposition more years than Sir Edmund and his creatures did months."

First, the New Englanders "must not think the privileges of Englishmen would follow them to the ends of the world." Second, "the press" was put under the thumb of the new government. ("There was not so much room to complain of this proceeding," however, simply because the press "only changed its keeper, having been long under restraint during the former administration.") Third, "a restraint upon marriage" was put in effect. (Because marriage had been strictly a civil matter in Puritan New England, magistrates, not the clergy, officiated at weddings. Under English law the ceremony had to be conducted by properly ordained ministers, but there was only one Anglican minister in residence in Boston. So, the new regime had no choice but to permit the civil magistrates to "continue to join people in matrimony," but these vows lacked legal standing until the parties "entered into bonds with sureties to the governor.") Fourth, the people had reason to believe "that public worship in the congregational way" would no longer be "tolerated." (At the Old South Meeting House the congregation was forced to wait outside until the Governor and his entourage finished their Anglican services on Sunday mornings.) Fifth, "these harpies" raised "fees to all officers" to an "exorbitant" level. Sixth, "the people were told that their titles to their estates were of no value." (To fleece the people thoroughly and systematically, "prudence was used" so that their "titles were not questioned all at once" but stretched out for maximal advantage.) Seventh, "an entire new model of government was intended" to replace the Old Charter.[16]

This endless tale of woe stretched from December 1686 to April 1689. As Hutchinson touched all the bases his rising fury veritably breathes through the pages of his straightforward narrative. The tension even rises to incredible heights when he retells how his grandfather, Elisha Hutchinson, and the President of Harvard, Increase Mather, slipped away "in the night and in disguise" to board a ship for England in a desperate attempt to petition the King for relief from the arbitrary edicts of the oriental despot he had visited upon them. Alas, "solicitations in England had not the least influence" upon King James II now so closely associated with the absolute monarchy of the Sun King in France.[17]

The narrative tone shifts radically, however, when Hutchinson records how a rumor began to spread that William of Orange had landed on the English coast to liberate the land from its Catholic King. In Boston Sir Edmund Andros charged "all officers and people to be in readiness to hinder the landing of any forces which the Prince of Orange might send into those parts of the world." What actually happened in New England during this revolutionary situation was told with passion as well as skill:

> The old magistrates and heads of the people silently wished, and secretly prayed, for success of the glorious undertaking, and determined quietly to wait the event. The body of the people were more impatient. The flame, which had been long smothered in their breasts, burst forth with violence, Thursday the 18th of April, when the governor and such of the council as had been most active, and other obnoxious persons, about fifty in the whole, were seized and confined, and the old magistrates were reinstated.

Even though this was "a rash precipitate proceeding," Hutchinson cheerfully celebrated the liberation of New England:

> The 26th (being Sunday) a ship arrived from England, with advice of the proclaiming King William and Queen Mary. This was the most joyful news ever received in New England. The fears of the people of any very bad consequences from their late actions, were over. On the 29th, the proclamation was published in Boston, with greater ceremony than had been known, the [reinstated old] governor and council, civil and military officers, merchants of the town, the principal gentlemen of the town and country being on horseback, the regiment of the town, and many companies of horse and foot from the country, appearing in arms; a grand entertainment was prepared in the town-house, and wine was served out to the soldiers.

Nobody understood better than Thomas Hutchinson that the Glorious Revolution had happened in New England as well as in the British Isles.[18]

The 1691 Charter granted by King William and Queen Mary transformed Massachusetts from a Colony into a Province that included the small Plymouth Colony and the enormous area now known as the State of Maine. (Maine became a separate state in the Missouri Compromise of 1820.) Hutchinson concluded the narrative portion of *The History of the Colony of Massachusetts-Bay* by straightforwardly observing, "Seventy years practice under a new charter, in many respects to be preferred to the old, has taken away, not only all expectation, but all desire of ever returning to the old charter." He then slipped in this sly comment about Rhode Island and Connecticut: "We [in Massachusetts] do not envy the neighbouring governments which retained, and have ever since practiced upon, their ancient charters. Many of the most sensible men in those governments, would be glad to be under the same constitution that the Massachusetts province happily enjoys."[19] Not many months would pass before he would learn to his sorrow that there were not very many "sensible men" in New England.

Thomas Hutchison's *History of the Colony of Massachusetts-Bay* was consciously designed to instruct. Lord Chief Justice Mansfield's foremost American disciple did not entertain the slightest doubt that the Glorious Revolution had resolved once and for all the constitutional conflicts that had so vexed the seventeenth century. The absolutist pretensions of the House of Stuart had been utterly defeated. Public liberty rested upon the solid foundation of King, Lords, and Commons, while sovereignty rested on the solid foundation of the King-in-Parliament. The lived experience of Massachusetts had conclusively proven that a corporation would lose its "charter" by abusing its "privileges." The province had not entered into a *voluntary compact* with the Crown. The lesson of history plainly taught that *perpetual and unalienable allegiance* was due to the parent state. The constitutional settlement with William and Mary was the most perfect establishment ever to grace the face of the earth.

WHEN Boston received the joyful news that the Peace of Paris had been signed, James Otis, Jr. opened his address to the Boston Town Meeting by stretching this expansive vision over an imagined future for the British Empire: "We in America have certainly abundant reasons to rejoice. The heathen [Indians] are not only driven out, but the [French] Canadians, much more formidable enemies, are conquered and become 'fellow subjects.' The British dominion and power may now be said, literally, to extend from sea to sea, and from the great river to the ends of the earth." The biblical allusion was not wasted upon the sons of Puritan New England. The standard Palm Sunday text reads: "Rejoice greatly, O daughter of Zion; shout, O daughter of Jerusalem: behold, thy King cometh unto thee: ... and he shall speak peace unto the heathen: and his dominion shall be from sea even to sea, and from the river even to the ends of the earth" (Zechariah 9:9-10, KJV).

Now that the French and Indians had been forced to hear the King "speak peace," Otis entertained the belief that "we may safely conclude from his majesty's wise administration hitherto, that liberty and knowledge, civil and religious, will be co-extended, improved, and preserved to the latest posterity. No other constitution of civil government has yet appeared in the world, so admirably adapted to these great purposes, as that of Great Britain." Toward the end, nonetheless, he added the shocking disclosure that "some weak and wicked minds had endeavoured to infuse ... jealousies" between the mother country and her obedient colonies, jealousies that had their birth "in the blackness of darkness." That powerful image comes from the tiny book of Jude in the New Testament where heretics are likened unto "clouds without water, carried about of winds; trees whose fruit withereth, without fruit, twice dead, plucked up by the roots; raging waves of the sea, foaming out their own shame; wandering stars, to whom is reserved *the blackness of darkness for ever*" (my emphasis, verses 12-13, KJV). In one of the shortest sentences in his enormous three-volume study of Massachusetts, Thomas Hutchinson pointedly observed, "From so small a spark a great fire seems to have been kindled."[20]

THE OPENING OF THE CONSTITUTIONAL CRISIS

AS THE BRITISH EMPIRE REACHED THE PINNACLE OF POWER AND PRESTIGE IN THE EARLY 1760s, the Scottish Lords Bute and Mansfield were clearly in charge of public affairs. Although Lord Bute would quickly fall into oblivion, the Lord Chief Justice of King's Bench would exercise considerable influence within the executive branch of the government. Indeed, he "acquired great political consequence, and for fifteen years to come there was probably no individual who more influenced the counsels of the nation both at home and abroad," according to Lord Campbell's narrative.

The distinction between Mansfield and Bute needs to be understood with care. Bute attempted to rule by the royal prerogative and came to a bad end at home. Mansfield articulated a new tack, namely, that sovereignty flowed from the King through Parliament to the people *both at home and abroad*. Of course, Mansfield did not hold a political office; therefore, he worked through others who did. And his understanding of the Constitution of the British Empire became fully operational in the policies of George Grenville (1712-1770).

After entering Parliament in 1741, this younger brother of Lord Temple and the brother-in-law of William Pitt began a rapid rise to political prominence in the early 1760s. When Henry Fox declined to form a new ministry, Bute persuaded George III to choose Grenville as Prime Minister.[1] Horace Walpole candidly acknowledged that he welcomed George Grenville with a sigh of relief. Not only did he entertain "a most favourable opinion of his integrity," he even considered him to be "a grounded republican" because he had heard him "harangue by the hour against the despotic doctrines of Lord Mansfield." Alas, it did not take long before the scales fell from Walpole's eyes: "my late republican friend has become as strict a disciplinarian as the most arbitrary of his predecessors." And to his enduring chagrin, "Lord Mansfield retained great weight in a cabinet so framed [by Grenville] to embrace boldly any arbitrary measures that [Mansfield] was always ready to suggest, and always afraid to execute himself." Truth to tell, Grenville soon became "the staunchest champion of unwarrantable power."[2] According to John Brooke, a leading historian associated with the Lewis Namier school of interpretation, he remained "Lord Mansfield's favourite politician."[3]

THE first serious controversy to engulf the Grenville Administration was precipitated by John Wilkes, who was on his way home from a brief trip to Paris when Bute resigned on 8 April 1763. When he arrived at Calais, the governor of the port "asked him how far the liberty of the press extended in England." His response? "I cannot tell, but I am trying to know."[4]

Wilkes's man in change, Charles Churchill, had already prepared an edition of the *North Briton* to come out on 9 April 1763, but it was no longer relevant in the unfolding situation. Wilkes's revised version of *Number Forty-Five* directly attacked the celebration of the Peace of Paris in the King's Speech:

> Every friend of his county must lament that a prince
> of so many great and amiable qualities whom
> England truly revere, can be brought to give the

> sanction of his sacred name to the most odious
> measures, and to the most unjustifiable, public
> declarations, from a throne ever renowned for truth,
> honour, and unsullied virtue.

That was not all.

> The *prerogative* of the crown is to exert the
> constitutional powers entrusted to him in a way
> not of blind favour and partiality, but of wisdom
> and judgment. This is the spirit of our constitution.
> The people too have their *prerogative*, and I hope
> the fine words of Dryden will be engraved on our
> hearts: Freedom is the English Subject's Prerogative.

When *North Briton, Number Forty-Five* was finally published on Saturday 23 April 1763, it swept through the political world with hurricane force.

The Grenville Administration began consultations almost immediately on how to proceed against this outrageous performance. The Secretary of State for the Northern Department, Lord Halifax, signed a General Warrant for the arrest of "the authors, printers and publishers of a seditious and treasonable paper, entitled the North Briton, Number 45." The government agents soon arrested over a dozen printers, who had nothing to do with the publication. Caught in the net, however, was a bookseller who did point the investigation in the right direction by fingering the actual printer, Richard Balfe. By Saturday morning Wilkes was under arrest, and by that afternoon he was confined in the Tower of London. Before the opening phase of this ordeal was over, 49 persons had been arrested under Halifax's General Warrant.[5]

In his continuing struggle with Mansfield, Charles Pratt, the Chief Justice of Common Pleas, issued a writ of Habeas Corpus on Monday. Opposing arguments were heard when Wilkes appeared in his court on Tuesday. By Friday Pratt handed down his ruling that Wilkes be discharged from the Tower of London on the narrow ground that libel was not a breach of the peace and, therefore, he was protected from arrest because of his parliamentary privilege. The newspapers claimed that perhaps as many as 10,000 persons escorted Wilkes home in triumph.[6]

As the contest continued to intensify, Wilkes counter-attacked by filing charges against a host of government agents, including Lord Halifax, the Secretary of State who had issued the General Warrant. Two months later Wilkes took comfort in the defeat of the government before Judge Pratt in the trials of those printers who had been wrongly imprisoned for a few hours. With the encouragement of Pratt, the jury awarded William Huckwell £300 in damages, plus legal costs. The next day James Lindsay received £200, plus costs— and it was agreed that this verdict would hold for the twelve other printers innocently caught up by the government's actions. With the government losing a good £4,000 in damages and fines, Wilkes had clearly won the first round. And in good spirits he set off for a two-month excursion in France during the summer recess.[7]

GEORGE Grenville fully realized that his administration had not gotten off to a very promising start. Not only did he deeply resent how people were whispering that he was a phantom because Bute still exercised the real power from "behind the Curtain."[8] Not many months into the new administration at least three distinct attempts were made to replace the Prime Minister. First, Bute had Mansfield approach Lord Rockingham to see if "the opposition, as [Bute] called them, would come in, and serve the King." Second, the Duke of Bedford was sounded out, but he refused to deal unless William Pitt was included in the projected ministry, an option that was not in the realm of possibility, given Bedford's role in negotiating the Peace of Paris that had so offended Pitt's sensibilities. Finally, the King even conferred with the Great Commoner himself about leading a new administration, but Pitt's demands were so extravagant that the negotiation never got off the ground.[9]

One can only speculate upon what turn governmental affairs might have taken had Bute been able to control the political dynamics during the spring and summer of 1763. It is difficult to imagine how Lord Chief Justice Mansfield would have functioned in an administration headed by, say, Henry Fox, or the Duke of Rockingham, or the Duke of Bedford, or William Pitt. Quarrelling with Fox had occupied a significant portion of Mansfield's time and energy over the past decade. And Fox had also consistently maintained—directly contrary to Mansfield's known position—that Parliament had no business poking its nose into colonial affairs. The Duke of Rockingham and the Lord Chief Justice would find themselves on the opposite ends of almost every important issue over the coming years. Bedford and Mansfield had been declared enemies ever since the 1753 affair over the education of the Prince of Wales. Indeed, Mansfield delighted "in every opportunity of exposing and mortifying the Duke of Bedford." And of all the people the Great Commoner proscribed from a projected ministry, our Scottish Law Lord headed the list. Pitt even told George III that the Lord Chief Justice of King's Bench was "a Jacobite ... and means, Sir, to ruin your family."[10]

After the collapse of all of these attempts to find a more favorable Prime Minister, Bute persuaded the King on 29 August 1763 that there was no viable alternative to George Grenville. The Grenville Administration, moreover, was also in the process of a significant transformation because Lord Egremont had died of apoplexy as these maneuvers were coming to a head. Lord Halifax, who had been the Northern Secretary, now moved into Egremont's old post as the new Southern Secretary of State. And Lord Sandwich now became the new Northern Secretary. Sandwich was a disciple of the hard-liner, Lord Bedford, who now became the Lord President of the Council.

Satisfied that a suitable successor and a stable ministry had finally gained the confidence of the young King, John Stuart, the Third Earl of Bute, retreated to his country estate at Luton Hoo. While scholars may dispute exactly when his influence over George III dissolved completely, at least in terms of public policy it was now effectively over.[11]

DURING the summer recess the Grenville Administration consulted a variety of legal experts—including Lord Chief Justice Mansfield—on the question of whether seditious libel was protected by parliamentary privilege, as Judge Pratt had declared in the Court of Common Pleas. Even though the collective opinion was negative, it was decided on prudential grounds to postpone any action against John Wilkes until Parliament met on 15 November 1763.[12]

Whereas the ministry was learning to be cautious in its dealings with Wilkes, he threw all caution to the wind. Directly against the advice of Lord Temple, who was providing the money for all the legal actions against the ministry, he set up a printing press in his house and started reprinting all of the issues of *North Briton* in a collective booklet. He also had a number of copies of his *Essay on Woman* printed for his personal use. He had initially written this obscene parody of Alexander Pope's *Essay on Man* for the amusement of his friends in the Hell Fire Club, and, of course, improved it over time to bring it up to date. This new version included these lines: "Then in the scale of various Pricks, 'tis plain, Godlike erect, Bute stands the foremost Man." Alas, the ministry surreptitiously obtained a copy of his *Essay on Woman*.[13]

When Parliament convened Lord Sandwich led the assault. Because Sandwich was one of the most notorious womanizers in the Hell Fire Club—undoubtedly he had enjoyed hearing Wilkes recite the obscene piece—his fellow Lords were vastly amused by his hypocritical performance, and he never lived the incident down. Nevertheless, the satire shocked their refined sensibilities. Although the House was ready to take action against Wilkes as the author, they paused when "Lord Mansfield condemned so hasty and arbitrary a course." According to the Lord Chief Justice "it was necessary first to hear what Wilkes could say in his defence."[14]

While Lord Sandwich was leading the charge against Wilkes in the House of Lords, Lord North managed the attack on *Number Forty-Five* in the House of Commons. The substantive debate focused upon this proposition: "That Privilege of Parliament does not extend to the case of writing, and publishing seditious Libels."

That treason, felonies, and breaches of the peace were not covered by parliamentary privilege was clear from precedents. The question turned on whether civil offences such as libels were covered, as Judge Pratt had ruled in the Court of Common Pleas. The Opposition said civil offences were covered. The ministry argued they were not. And the ministry prevailed by a vote of 258 to 133.[15]

DURING the opening debate Samuel Martin denounced Wilkes as "a cowardly rascal." When Martin and Wilkes fought a duel with pistols in Hyde Park the next day, Wilkes was seriously wounded with a shot in his stomach. Then on 3 December *North Briton, Number Forty-Five* was scheduled "to be burned by the hangman at Cheapside." What actually happened (in Walpole's telling) was "a prodigious riot," with the crowd screaming, "Wilkes and Liberty." According to the sheriff's report, "the greatest mob ... that he has known in forty years" rose up to thwart the burning. In its stead "the mob's hieroglyphics for Lord Bute and the Princess"—"a jackboot and a petticoat"—"were burned with great triumph and acclamations." This "terrible uproar" continued for days as Wilkes's suit against the Undersecretary of State, Robert Wood, for trespass and seizure of papers was tried before Judge Pratt. Wilkes also won this case "after a trial of fourteen hours." And "the jury gave him damages of £1,000." Furthermore, the ministry's claim that Wilkes was the author of *North Briton, Number Forty-Five* "failed in the proof." Although Judge Pratt was catapulted into enduring fame, Wilkes was quick to read the handwriting on the wall. Because the House of Commons had declared that libels were not protected by parliamentary privilege, he realized that he would have to face trial before Lord Chief Justice Mansfield. Seriously wounded though he was, on 26 December 1763 he escaped to France.[16]

On 19 January 1764 Wilkes was formally expelled from the House of Commons. When he was tried in absentia in the Court of King's Bench, Mansfield instructed the jury not to even consider whether Wilkes had been the author but only whether he had republished *North Briton, Number Forty-Five*. The process was repeated with yet another jury on whether he had republished *Essay on Woman*. On this narrow ground the separate juries returned verdicts of guilty as charged. After refusing to respond to several court orders to appear to be sentenced, on 1 November 1764 Wilkes was declared an outlaw by Lord Chief Justice Mansfield.

YEARS had passed since Sir Robert Walpole had dismissed the possibility of taxing the Americans with this pungent statement: "I will leave that for some of my successors, who may have more courage than I have and less a friend to commerce than I am." After referring to this pronouncement by his father, Horace Walpole added, "That man was found in Grenville, who great in daring, and little in views, was charmed to have an untrodden field before him of calculation and experiment."[17]

Regardless of what one might think of his commercial acumen, even his most determined enemies never accused George Grenville of lacking courage. As early as October 1763 he had his assistant, Charles Jenkinson, draw up a memorial for consideration by the Privy Council. This paper, according to Carl Ubbelohde, became "a blueprint for the future, changing the course of the customs establishment, the vice-admiralty courts, and, in the end, the British Empire itself."[18]

On 7 March 1764 the Gentle Shepherd, as Grenville was called, "gave notice that on Friday next he would go at large into the ways and means … [of] taxing America." His plan, in the first instance, was to revise the Navigation Acts that had been in effect for generations. After calculating what was deemed a proper level for the duty on molasses, the administration actually *lowered the duty to three pence per gallon*, but with the proviso that now the law would be enforced, and that enforcement would be placed under the jurisdiction of the Vice-Admiralty Courts operating under the rules of the Civil Law Tradition, not under the local Common Law Courts where juries tried the cases.

Although this might look like a straightforward revision of the received regulations, Grenville did not even attempt to disguise the larger, second intention of the project, namely, the "raising a Revenue in the *British* Colonies and Plantations in *America*, toward defraying the necessary Charges of defending, protecting, and securing the same." Those charges were calculated at £359,000 per year. On that Friday he told the House of Commons, "We have expended much in America. Let us now avail ourselves of the fruits of that expense."

Grenville was fully conscious of the fact that "the officers of the revenue must strike in the dark" in executing his plan, precisely because there was precious little experience to draw upon. The closest thing to a direct tax on the colonies in the past was the postal service, but that was more than a stretch because it was not a tax but a service, and it had not yet begun to pay for itself. (In the following year the postal service did manage to bring in a little incidental revenue.) But he entertained not the slightest doubt about Parliament's right to tax the colonies. One report on his extensive oration reads rather cryptically:

> Britain has an inherent right to lay inland duties there. The very sovereignty of this kingdom depends on it. Were this doubted, he would go into it deeply, would assuredly take the sense of the House upon it. He concluded by saying that the path was thorny, but that still he would proceed, that upon these principles alone he thought this country could be saved.

When he finished Grenville received "the applause of the *whole* House." Not a single M.P. challenged his position. Even John Huske, who had resided in America for 24 years, agreed with the principle at stake. Parliament was convinced it held the right to tax America.

One hint on why the House of Commons could be so easily persuaded to embrace this novel but thorny path surfaced in this debate. A sketchy report on the comments by one of the debaters reads: "Thinks the power of the Crown extends no further over the colonies than it does in England. And yet this power has been exerted as by orders passed here by the *King in Council* which have gone to the plantations as kind of laws" (my emphasis). One suspects that in a direct recoil against Lord Bute's design to govern by the royal prerogative, Parliament was prepared to assert its own authority along lines something like this: if the King-in-Council could do it, then surely Parliament has the right to do it, too. Regardless of the reasons, soon the House of Commons thoroughly embraced Mansfield's long held opinion that Parliament had the undoubted right to tax the colonies. What had long been latent in *legal opinions* now would become manifest in *colonial policy*. The American Duties Act—popularly known as the Sugar Act—became law on 5 April 1764.[19]

USING the Royal Navy to stop the notorious smuggling would go a long way toward reaping the needed revenue, but enforcing the Sugar Act alone would still not go far enough. More revenue would be urgently needed down the road. So, while arguing over the Sugar Act Grenville threw out this hint: "Stamp duties [were] the least exceptionable because it requires few officers and even collects itself." On 17 May 1764 several colonial agents—Jasper Mauduit of Massachusetts and Charles Garth of South Carolina wrote extensive reports—met with Grenville to discuss the content of the forthcoming Stamp Bill. Because he refused to provide them with any concrete details—such as how much a particular colony was supposed to pay—they were frankly at a loss in knowing how to proceed. Although they dutifully reported to the colonies that Grenville had offered them the option of taxing themselves, no action on that option was conceivable, for reasons made abundantly clear by the Governor of Massachusetts.

Sir Francis Bernard on 18 August 1764 informed Richard Jackson in London that members of the Massachusetts Assembly had expressed "their desire that they might be allowed to tax themselves and not be taxed by the Parliament." But he told them that "it was impossible at present to proceed to an actual taxation, untill the demands of the ministry should be further explained." In his own words, "the particular sum expected from each province as their proportion must be first ascertained."[20]

After establishing a committee of correspondence to address the implications of the constitutional contention, Boston entered into a Non-Importation Agreement to protest the Sugar Act. Then on 18 October a Petition from New York to the House of Commons directly states, "this Innovation, will greatly affect the Interest of the Crown and the Nation, and reduce the Colony to absolute Ruin." Furthermore, "No History can furnish an Instance of a Constitution to permit one Part of a Dominion to be taxed by another." Directly against "the Prospect of an endless Train of the most distressing Mischiefs, naturally attendant upon such an Innovation," this petition celebrates "our antient Rights ... established in the first Dawn of our Constitution, founded upon the most substantial Reasons, confirmed by invariable Usage, conducive of the best Ends."

Virginia sent separate petitions to the King, the Lords, and the Commons. The Lords were informed bluntly, "Your Memorialists conceive it to be a fundamental Principle of the *British* Constitution, without which Freedom can no Where exist, that the people are not subject to any Taxes but such as are laid on them by their own Consent, or by those who are legally appointed to represent them." Virginia boldly concluded its petition to the House of Commons with the claim that "*British* Patriots will never consent to the Exercise of anticonstitutional Power, which even in this remote Corner may be dangerous in its Example to the interiour Parts of the *British* Empire, and will certainly be detrimental to its Commerce."[21]

Grenville knew full well that the Americans were opposed to the new imperial policy, but instead of looking for direction from past experience and invariable usage—instead of listening to the colonial agents or considering colonial petitions—in December 1764 he sought guidance from Lord Chief Justice Mansfield.

From before he became the Solicitor General in 1742 Mansfield had long experience with American affairs. He had represented several of the colonies before the Board of Trade. He was familiar with the border dispute between New Hampshire and Massachusetts, plus Rhode Island. He knew first hand about the dispute between Pennsylvania and Maryland over what became Delaware. He had extensive contact with Georgia in its dispute with South Carolina. Even Indian Affairs were not beyond his involvement. And from the outset of his political career, if not before, he had also claimed that Parliament by right *could* tax the Americans, and since at least the early 1750s it *should*. Now he told Grenville, "I wish you would employ somebody to look with this view into the origin of their [i.e., colonial assemblies'] power to tax themselves and raise money at all." Because he considered the colonial governments to be "on the same footing as our great corporations in London," what was problematical in his mind was whether the colonies had the right to levy taxes upon their own constituencies.[22]

Given Mansfield's reassuring advice, on 2 February 1765 Grenville held another shadow meeting with the colonial agents, who quickly discovered to their sorrow what Walpole already knew, namely, that Grenville "had no address, no manner, no insinuation, and had least of all the faculty of listening."[23] Four days later he opened the debate in the House of Commons on the Stamp Bill. After expressing the wish that "those who had gone before him had marked out a path to him which he might more easily follow," he acknowledged that over the last few months he had heard "strange language" in both "conversation and public writings" that denied the right of Parliament to tax the colonies. Besides the petitions just mentioned, in all probability he was alluding to James Otis's widely read and wildly popular pamphlet, *The Rights of the British Colonies Asserted and Proved*.

James Otis, Jr. wrote the piece and he was convinced that the Americans thoroughly shared this conviction: "I believe there is not one man in a hundred (except in Canada) who does not think himself under the best national civil constitution in the world." Nevertheless, the Sugar Act "has set people a-thinking in six months more than they had done in their whole lives before." What had focused so much thinking was Parliament's violation of "the fundamental laws." In Otis's constitutional theory, fundamental law requires "an American representation in Parliament" before any taxation can be imposed on the colonies. He even argued for colonial representation in the House of Commons in order to resolve this constitutional issue.[24]

Grenville, however, dismissed all that strange language with an excursion into the doctrine of "virtual representation." Thomas Whately, a key spokesman for the administration, explained the doctrine in a 1765 pamphlet, *The Regulations lately Made concerning the Colonies and the Taxes Imposed upon Them Considered*. In his opinion the Americans had claimed "the Privilege ... of being taxed only with their own Consent, given by their Representatives." And he continued: "may they ever enjoy the Privilege in all its Extent: May this sacred Pledge of Liberty be preserved inviolate, to the utmost Verge of our Dominions, and to the latest Page of our History." But after so fulsome an acknowledgement of colonial privileges, Whately proceeded: "the Fact is, that the Inhabitants of the Colonies are represented in Parliament," just as, say, "Women and Persons under Age" in Great Britain are represented, even though they cannot actually vote. Grenville agreed from top to bottom, saying, "The Parliament of Great Britain *virtually represents* the whole Kingdom, not *actually* great trading towns." In fact, "Not a twentieth part of the people are *actually represented*." According to the Administration, "The Colonies are in exactly the same Situation: All *British* Subjects are really in the same; none are *actually*, all are *virtually represented in Parliament*" (my emphases).[25]

In considering virtual representation, two important points should never be lost sight of. First, while the theory makes some sense *within the realm*, it is utterly unconvincing *without the realm*. Second, regardless of what one might think of the theory's adequacy, it definitely documents beyond equivocation that *taxation had always been dependent upon representation in some form or other*.

In this 6 February debate Charles Townshend avoided the issue of representation, but he "heard with great pleasure the right of taxing America asserted and not disputed." Fabulous orator that he was, he rushed on to say, "And now will these Americans, children planted by our care, nourished up by our indulgence until they are grown to a degree of strength & opulence, and protected by our arms, will they grudge to contribute their mite to relieve us from the heavy weight of that burden which we lie under?" Isaac Barré, who rightly claimed "to know more of America than most" of the members of the House, responded by disputing each point in Townshend's condescending speech. He also pointed out that "Civil law is the only law by which the Court of Admiralty is governed, and that is very oppressive." Furthermore, the Civil Law "was never made by the representatives of the people of England." According to an eye witness account, Barré's "sentiments were thrown out so entirely without premeditation, so forceably and so firmly, and the breaking off so beautifully abrupt, that the whole House sat awhile as amazed, intently looking and without answering a word."[26]

Amazed, yes; awakened, no. According to Charles Garth, agent of South Carolina, "The House declared they would not suffer a petition that should hint at questioning the supremacy and authority of Parliament to impose taxes in every part of the British Dominions."[27] Because the House of Commons had so thoroughly embraced Mansfield's revolutionary opinion, Grenville could sweep away—without any significant opposition whatsoever in Parliament—the received customs and usages that had for so long shaped the Old Colonial System. The triumph of the novel imperial doctrine was so complete that the House of Commons did not even formally vote after the second reading of the bill.

The novel Stamp Act authorized a direct tax upon America's very life and thought. It cut to where the marrow separates from the bone. For example,

> For every skin or piece of vellum or parchment, or sheet or piece of paper, on which shall be ingrossed, written or printed, any declaration, plea, replication, rejoinder, demurrer, or other pleading, or any copy thereof, in any court of law with the *British* colonies and plantations in *America*, a stamp duty of three pence.

> For every skin ... on which shall be ingrossed ...
> any donation, presentation, collation, or institution
> of or to any benefice, or any writ or instrument for
> the like purpose, or any register, entry, testimonial,
> or certificate of any degree taken in any university,
> academy, college, or seminary of learning ... a stamp
> duty of two pounds.

And the list goes on and on. Before finishing one discovered a tax on "every pack of playing cards, and all dice"; every "pamphlet"; every "almanack or calender"; even doubling the tax for anything written in "any other than the *English* language." Extensive duties were placed upon matriculating in college. In order to graduate required yet another. Entering a profession cost more than in England. All in all, the Stamp Act was very expensive, and this was only a beginning designed to soften the Americans for the coming regime.[28] The Stamp Act received the royal assent on 22 March 1765. It was scheduled to go into effect on 1 November 1765.

FOR reasons that had nothing to do with the Stamp Act, George III replaced the Grenville Administration in the summer of 1765. Simply put, he had grown weary of listening to the Prime Minister in the Closet. In the King's own words, "that gentleman's opinions are seldom formed from any other motives than such as may be expected to originate in the mind of a clerk in a counting house." According to the historian John Brooke, "George III is reputed to have said that he would rather see the Devil in his Closet than George Grenville."[29]

The Prime Minister, for example, completely misread the import as well as the intricacies of the Regency Act that Mansfield drew up in April in response to the King's serious illness. He wrongly assumed that the King secretly wanted to name his mother as Regent, who would obviously be a front for Lord Bute. A critical turning point occurred on 9 May, according to Walpole's *Memoirs*, when in a "cold, half-owning, half-denying speech" Grenville completed his ruin with the Princess Dowager and the Royal Family. Weakened but determined, on 22 May Grenville proceeded to lay down three conditions for remaining in charge: "1st. Would his Majesty promise on his royal word, not to consult Lord Bute any more, nor suffer him to interfere in business? 2ndly. Would he dismiss Mr Mackenzie from the direction of Scottish affairs? 3rdly. Would he immediately declare Lord Granby Captain-General?"[30]

George III was more than angry. He was furious because he was forced to give in to these three outrageous conditions. The first condition challenged his word of honor, which he knew he had kept in regard to excluding Lord Bute from public policy. The second condition was especially bitter, because he had personally promised Mackenzie—Bute's brother—that he would control Scottish patronage for the duration. As he told Grenville directly: "You will make me do, *as King* [that] which I should *be a scoundrel* to do, *as a private man.*" And the third condition was a direct assault upon the position of the Duke of Cumberland within the Royal Family. During the Silk Riots in May he had acted as the Captain-General of the Army, and now he had become one of the King's closest confidantes. Indeed, George III had already handed to his once dreaded but now trusted uncle the delicate task of securing a new ministry.[31]

AFTER much negotiating that tried the patience and skill of the Duke of Cumberland, on 10 July 1765 the Old Whigs returned to power with the Marquis of Rockingham as Prime Minister. Paul Langford concluded his introductory comments on *The First Rockingham Administration* with this observation: "The 'Old Whigs' had been invited to take office through no merits or efforts of their own, and had accepted it only with the utmost reluctance and doubt; in almost all respect they seemed ludicrously unsuited for the task of government, and there appeared to be every justification for the general skepticism and disapproval which greeted their return to place and power." Although Rockingham was the Prime Minister, for all intents and purposes the decision making power resided in the hands of the Duke of Cumberland.[32]

Because it was common knowledge that Rockingham was Mansfield's nephew, it was reasonable to assume that the two would work closely together in the new administration. After all, it was Mansfield who had approached Rockingham in the summer of 1763 to sound out whether he would head a new ministry. And in the new Rockingham Administration, Mansfield's brother-in-law, David Finch, the Earl of Winchelsea, was the Lord President of the Council. But it remains the case that there is not the slightest evidence to support the belief that Mansfield exercised any influence over Rockingham's appointment.

One of the controlling reasons why Mansfield kept his distance from the Rockingham Administration was the simple fact that it was designed to open the way for William Pitt to return as its head. In the words of the Duke of Newcastle, the ministry was formed "to appear as a summer suit, till Mr. Pitt could come [in] with his winter's dress." Serious efforts were made to accommodate Pitt's "Notions, and Ideas," and, one might add, his closest confidante, Charles Pratt. As the Chief Justice of Common Pleas, Pratt had pursued his enduring conflict with Mansfield over the freedom of the press and the libel laws in the John Wilkes Affair. Now that the new ministry granted him a peerage with the title of Lord Camden, Mansfield was less than pleased that so talented a rival would oppose him in the House of Lords. But regardless of what Rockingham and his friends would say or do, the Great Commoner remained aloof.[33]

NEWS of the *Virginia Resolves* of late May reached London a few days after the Rockingham Administration was launched on 10 July 1765. Soon the political nation would be reading a trenchant American commentary on the unfolding constitutional crisis by Daniel Dulany. This Maryland lawyer had been educated in England at Eton, then Clare College, Cambridge, and finally the Middle Temple in London. On 12 August Dulany published, *Considerations on the Propriety of Imposing Taxes in the British Colonies, for the Purpose of Raising a Revenue, by Act of Parliament*. One does not need to read very far into Dulany's *Considerations* before coming across this good confession: "I shall pin my faith upon the *dictum* of no lawyer in the universe; and when his *ipse dixit* is authoritatively urged I shall be at no pains to repress my suspicions that his reasons are concealed." He then proceeded to cite an opinion of "a general of the law" as a case in point, namely, the 1755 opinion on Pennsylvania's Quartering Act by Attorney General Murray, who would soon become the Lord Chief Justice of King's Bench.[34]

While Dulany surely realized he was attacking Mansfield's earlier opinion, it is not plausible to believe that he knew the full advice Mansfield had given to Grenville in December 1764. Nevertheless, Mansfield's pregnant suggestion came to fruition, by what route is unknown, in *The Claim of the Colonies to an Exemption from Internal Taxes imposed by Authority of Parliament, Examined* (London, 1765). Although historians know that the author was William Knox— Georgia's colonial agent in London who sold out the Americans—this information was not available until long afterwards. Dulany simply referred to the author as "the Examiner." And the Examiner's pivotal constitutional claim was this straightforward: "the inhabitants of the colonies shall be taxed by no other authority than that of the British *Parliament*."

The Examiner articulated the novel position with admirable clarity, pointing out that the constitutional tradition tied the right of taxation to Parliament. And truth to tell, the colonial assemblies had been conspicuously absent from the constitutional sources. This was the doctrine that led Dulany into asking how the Examiner could square his so-called principle with what had actually happened throughout the historical development of the colonies, for they had never been taxed before by Parliament. And he had no trouble pointing out that the Examiner's mentality was a fine example of accepting the "letter" while rejecting the "spirit" of the received understanding, for the colonial *Assemblies* held exactly the same position as *Parliament* in terms of *consent*, and that was precisely what the colonial charters were designed to protect, too. From "the necessary and essential principle of a free government that the people ought not to be taxed without their consent," he labored how the

Examiner inferred through "a new kind of logic" that "the colonies ought to be taxed by an authority in which their consent is not nor can be concerned." Wonderfully strange reasoning, no? "How awkwardly are the principles of the [Glorious] Revolution applied by some men!" And that is why Dulany contemptuously dismissed William Knox with this final blast: "If the Examiner is a lawyer, he has betrayed the most shameful ignorance; if an agent, the most infamous unfaithfulness."[35]

Although Dulany expended considerable energy pointing out the fallacious usage of the doctrine of "a *virtual* or *implied representation*" of the colonies, he apparently realized that this short-lived doctrine—while central to the initial argument of the Grenville Administration—was totally foreign to the emergent constitutional theory, one that did not rest upon representation whatsoever. It rested upon the sovereignty of Parliament alone. And Dulany held no monopoly on the conviction that this novel reading of parliamentary supremacy over the Empire violated a "necessary and essential principle of *British liberty*" as well as "the necessary and essential principle of a free government." This emergent interpretation of the Constitution in fact violated "every civil right" that the Americans considered their birthright, their "unalienable rights," their "fundamental rights," as well as "the natural rights of mankind."[36]

WHILE Daniel Dulany focused most of his attention upon the Stamp Act of 1765, he was acutely aware of the fact that the Sugar Act of 1764 had radically altered the jurisdiction of the Vice-Admiralty Court to be established in far off Halifax. This amounted to "the substitution of *an arbitrary civil-law court* in the place of the legal judicatories and that deserved favorite, *the common law trial by jury*" (my emphases).[37] Furthermore, the newly appointed Judge of the Vice-Admiralty Court, Dr. William Spry, had received his legal training in Doctors Commons, the only Inn of Court that moved within the orbit of the Roman Civil Law Tradition.

In a defense of the new colonial policy, Martin Howard maintained in *A Letter from a Gentleman in Halifax* that William Spry was "an able *civilian.*" Howard then concluded on this note: "It may become necessary for the supreme legislature of the nation [i.e., Parliament] to frame some code, and therein adjust the rights of the colonies with precision and certainty, otherwise Great Britain will always be teased with new claims about liberty and privileges."[38]

That final comment on the need for Parliament "to frame some code" touched off this climax to *A Vindication of the British Colonies, against the Aspersions of the Halifax Gentleman, in His Letter to a Rhode Island Friend* that James Otis published in 1765:

> We want no foreign codes nor canons here. The common law is our birthright, and the rights and privileges confirmed and secured to us by the British constitution and by acts of Parliament are our best inheritance. Codes, pandects, novels, decretals of popes, and the inventions of the d____l may suit the cold, bleak regions [of] Brandenburg and Prussia or the scorching heats of Jamaica or Gambia; but we live in a more temperate climate, and shall rest content with the laws, customs, and usages of our ancestors, bravely supported and defended with the monarch, and from age to age handed down.[39]

James Otis held in contempt the *Corpus Juris Civilis* with all its codes and pandects. And that is one reason why Carl Ubbelohde in his study, *The Vice-Admiralty Courts and the American Revolution,* maintained that "Doctor's Commons ... retained something of the ill repute of prerogative courts and the Star Chamber."[40]

IN early 1765 John Adams worked up his extensive historical research on the development of that "vast and various Collection of materials" that shaped "the structure of British Laws" for a presentation to a small group of leading lawyers in Boston that Adams called the Sodalitas—a local club that kept abreast of the unfolding constitutional contentions. He had been studying the complicated issue since 5 October 1758 when he disclosed in the privacy of his *Diary*: "I am this Day about beginning Justinian's Institutions with Arnold Vinnius's Notes." For two years he had been reading standard English law texts under the rather casual direction of James Putnam in Worcester, Massachusetts. Now the legal studies of this beginning law student took this surprising turn, for he realized that this rather radical decision would distance him from the customary pursuits of his fellow colonial lawyers. "Few of my Contemporary Beginners, in the Study of the Law, have the Resolution, to aim at much Knowledge in the Civil Law. Let me therefore distinguish my self from them, by the Study of the Civil Law, in its native languages, those of Greece and Rome. I shall gain Consideration and perhaps favour of Mr. Gridley and Mr. Pratt by this means."[41]

In less than a month Adams met with Jeremiah Gridley and in their initial conversation this leader of the Boston bar was more than impressed. Since Gridley thought that he had the only copy of Justinian's *Institutes* in New England, he pressed Adams on how he had obtained it. After Adams confessed that he had "borrowed it ... from Harvard Colledge Library, by the aid of a Friend," Gridley conjectured that "it was among the Books that Sir Harry Franklin lately presented to the Colledge." While Gridley readily agreed that "A Lawyer in this Country must study common Law and civil Law, and natural Law, and Admiralty Law," he advised Adams to make "the common Law ... your first and last Attention." Indeed, "He has conquered all the Difficulties of the Law, who is Master of the *Institutes*," not Justinian's but Sir Edward Coke's *Institutes of the Laws of England*.[42]

Captivated though he was by *Coke-upon-Littleton*, before the end of 1759 Adams was comparing "Dr. Cowells Institutes of the Law of England, with Justinians Institutes of the Laws of Rome, Title by Title, that each may reflect Light upon the other, and that I may advance my Knowledge of civil and common Law at the same Time." In an October 1759 letter to his friend, Jonathan Sewall, Adams acknowledged what young American lawyers were up against in these words: "And the structure of british Laws, is composed of such a vast and various Collection of materials ... that, 'tis impossible for any Builder to comprehend the whole vast Design, and see what is well and what [ill] contrived or jointed, without Acquainting himself with Saxon, Danish, Norman [as] well as Greek and Roman History, with *civil, feu]dal and Canon Law*" (my emphasis; brackets in critical edition; "cannon" altered to "canon").[43] Since he had been studying the Civil, Feudal and Canon Law, there can be no doubt that he had read with care whenever the Roman Civil Law Tradition was alluded to in print. For example, the word *civilian* would have jumped out from the page of the *Providence Gazette* when it troubled to publish this comment from a Plain Yeoman: "I could wish that some *civilian* would settle how far the *people of America* are dependant on the *people of Britain*. I know of no *dependance* or relation, only that we are all the common subjects of the same king."[44]

Adams polished his presentation to the Sodalitas into four anonymous essays that came out serially in the *Boston Gazette*, beginning on 12 August 1765. When Thomas Hollis republished them in London, this friend of New England gave them the title that they have retained ever since, "A Dissertation on the Canon and Feudal Law."[45]

Before the *Boston Gazette* had time to finish publishing the four installments of Adams's *Dissertation*, the Boston mob had finished off a considerable portion of British authority. On 14 August an effigy of Andrew Oliver, the announced Distributor of Stamps, was displayed, then his shop trashed, and finally his house severely damaged but not destroyed. And where was the Governor? Sir Francis Bernard found safety in Castle William, where he enjoyed the isolation of his solitary command. On 26 August the mob attacked the house of the Deputy Register of the Admiralty Court, William Story. On the same day Benjamin Hallowell, the Comptroller of Customs, shared the same fate. But the climax was postponed to the evening when the house of Lieutenant Governor Thomas Hutchinson was utterly ruined. According to Edmund S. and Helen M. Morgan, the mob "destroyed windows, doors, furniture, wainscoting, and paintings, and stole £900 in cash, as well as clothing and silverware. They cut down all the trees in the garden, beat down the partitions in the house and had even begun to remove the slate from the roof when daylight stopped them."[46]

John Adams was so preoccupied during these extraordinary events that he neglected "to keep a regular Journal," even though "the Year 1765 has been the most remarkable Year of my Life." When he took up his pen again, after castigating himself for his negligence, he entered this observation in his *Diary*:

> The People, even to the lowest Ranks, have become more attentive to their Liberties, more inquisitive about them, and more determined to defend them, than they were ever before known or had occasion to be. Innumerable have been the Monuments of Wit, Humour, Sense, Learning, Spirit, Patriotism, and Heroism, erected in the several Colonies and Provinces, the Course of this year. Our Presses have groaned, our Pulpits have thundered, our Legislatures have resolved, our Towns have voted, the Crown Officers have every where trembled, and all their little Tools and Creatures, been afraid to Speak and ashamed to be seen.

Before long Adams would report that some thought that Thomas Hutchinson's "House was pulled down, to prevent his writing any more [of his *History*] by destroying his Materials."[47]

JOHN Dickinson of Pennsylvania emerged as one of America's leading constitutional lawyers when the Stamp Act Congress met in New York City during October 1765. Of the fourteen Declarations drawn up after two weeks of deliberations, the opening eight addressed issues involving the Constitution of the British Empire. The first and second declarations claim for the Americans the same rights as those "born within the Realm." The third states "that no Taxes [can constitutionally] be imposed on them, but with their own Consent, given personally or by their Representatives." The fourth claims that the colonies are not or ever can be "Represented in the House of Commons." The sixth insists that the Stamp Act was "inconsistent with the Principles and Spirit of the *British* Constitution." The seventh and eighth claim that "by extending the Jurisdiction of the Courts of Admiralty beyond its ancient Limits," the new colonial policy has "a manifest Tendency to subvert the Rights and Liberties of the Colonists." Declarations nine through twelve concern the deleterious impact of the new regulations upon commerce. Thirteen declares "that it is the Right of the *British* Subjects in these Colonies, to Petition the King, or either House of Parliament." And the final declaration petitions for the repeal of both the Sugar Act of 1764 and the Stamp Act of 1765.[48]

Before the end of the year John Dickinson published *The Late Regulations Respecting the British Colonies on the Continent of America Considered*. He concluded this public letter "from a Gentleman in Philadelphia to his Friend in London" by laying out in capital letters his operative conviction: "THE FOUNDATIONS OF THE POWER AND GLORY OF GREAT BRITAIN ARE LAID IN AMERICA." Hard on the heels of this proposition followed the question of "whether it is better to take [America's money] in taxes or trade." If Parliament would choose trade, then the new trade regulations should be reversed. If Parliament continued to insist upon taxes, then Parliament would surely lose, just as "many states and kingdoms have lost their dominions by severity and an unjust jealousy."

As "an universal and unexampled grief and indignation" had spread across British North America because of the new colonial policy, Dickinson pressed this extended rhetorical question:

> What man who wishes the welfare of American can view without pity, without passion, her restricted and almost stagnated trade, with its numerous train of evils—taxes torn from her without her consent—her legislative Assemblies, the principal

> pillars of her liberty, crushed into insignificance—a formidable force established in the midst of peace, to bleed her into obedience—the sacred right of trial by jury violated by the erection of arbitrary and unconstitutional jurisdictions—and general poverty, discontent, and despondence stretching themselves over his country?

The climax reads: "In short, we never can be made an independent people except it be by Great Britain herself; and the only way for her to do it is to make us frugal, ingenious, united, and discontented."[49] That climax was pursued in a private letter Dickinson soon sent to William Pitt. *Discontented* he assumed the Great Commoner already realized the American people universally had become. *United* he was not so sure they would remain because the "different Interests" of the various colonies would "excite Jealousies" among them. But he made sure the Great Commoner understood that "their Contests are of an inferior Nature" which would quickly yield to "a common Cause" if Great Britain persisted in her folly. *An independent people* he feared they might become, even though he assured the Great Commoner, "I regard with inexpressible Detestation and Abhorrence the Notion of the Colonies becoming independent." But if it comes to war, then America would prevail, even though his imagination revolted against the horrid consequences that would follow: "A Multitude of Commonwealths, Crimes, and Calamities, of mutual Jealousies, Hatreds, Wars and Devastations; till at last the exhausted Provinces shall sink into Slavery under the yoke of some fortunate Conqueror." To avoid so dreadful a fate, Dickinson's letter appealed to the Great Commoner as "the Friend and Preserver not only of Great Britain but of these Colonies"—as "the Friend of Liberty and Justice"—to set the British Empire on a more fruitful course and "form a Plan of Policy that shall establish for Ages the Union of Great Britain and her Colonies."[50]

WHILE the Stamp Act Congress was meeting in New York City, the Rockingham Administration embraced a firm policy of enforcement of the Stamp Act at a 13 October meeting of the Cabinet at the Duke of Cumberland's house. Another meeting of the Cabinet was scheduled to address the evolving crisis at Cumberland's house on 31 October, but this meeting never took place because earlier that evening the Duke suddenly died. The opinion that Lord Chancellor Northington prepared for that meeting, however, did survive. It reads:

> I am of opinion that the Stamp Act ought to be carried into Execution in support of the Sovereignty of the British P[arliamen]t over the Colonies. That for this Purpose immediate Orders should be given to the Respective Governments to execute this Order and that they should be furnished with the Assistance of a military Force for this Purpose.

Over the coming weeks Attorney General Yorke and Paymaster General Townshend explicitly supported Northington's openly avowed policy of enforcing the Stamp Act within the deliberations of the Rockingham Administration.[51]

That Lord Chancellor Northington's opinion succinctly captured the constitutional position of Lord Chief Justice Mansfield in particular and the judiciary in general is beyond doubt. But early in November the imperial government began to see the burgeoning problem with the colonies in terms of British manufactures and trade. It did not take the eyes of a prophet to see that the colonial trade had been severely damaged and that this directly impacted British manufactures and employment, a point adroitly pressed by Sir George Savile and Barlow Trecothick in letters to Rockingham. And this line of reasoning dovetailed nicely with the mentality of Secretary of State, Henry Seymour Conway, and the Duke of Newcastle, as well as others in the Cabinet. By moving decisively away from a policy of enforcement toward a policy of conciliation, however, the ministry faced two remarkably different alternatives from a constitutional point of view, namely, either the *modification* or the *repeal* of the Stamp Act. The Rockingham Administration hesitated throughout December in making this choice.[52]

WHEN Parliament opened on 17 December 1765, the political nation realized (1) that the Americans from New England to Georgia had not only refused to allow the implementation of the Stamp Act but had entered into a Non-Importation Agreement that was to take effect on 1 January 1766; (2) that the London North America Merchants Committee had sent a circular letter "to the outports and to the manufacturing Towns" advocating a repeal of the Stamp Act; and (3) that the ministry would pursue a policy of conciliation toward the Americans, although a fixed and final plan of action had not yet been fought out within the Rockingham Administration.[53]

This opening session of Parliament before Christmas was designed to be brief, really "a formality to enable the issuing of writs (forty-one in all) for the re-election of those who had accepted office in July," according to Paul Langford's detailed study.[54] Although the opening Address indicated that the serious American business would be postponed until after the Christmas Recess, George Grenville introduced this amendment in the House of Commons:

> To express to His Majesty our deep Concern and Indignation at the dangerous Tumults and Insurrections, which have been raised and fomented in His Majesty's Dominions of *North America*, in Opposition to the Execution of the Laws, and in open Defiance of the parliamentary Right, of *Great Britain*: And that we embrace with Pleasure the earliest Opportunity in our Power to assure His Majesty, that, fully sensible of the indispensable Necessity of vindicating and establishing the just Power of the Legislature of *Great Britain*, we will cheerfully concur in every Measure, which may strengthen the Hands of Government, and

enforce the legal Obedience of the Colonies, and
their Constitutional Dependance on the Sovereign
Authority of this Kingdom.

Although this amendment was so weakly supported that Grenville
withdrew it from consideration in the House of Commons, it did
engender a serious debate with about twenty participants in the
House of Lords.

According to the report by William Strahan, "almost all seemed
to be for supporting and adhering to the Legislative Authority over
the Colonies, and their undoubted Right to impose taxes upon
them." An analysis sent to William Pitt claimed that some of the
Lords openly said that the Americans were in *rebellion,* while others
called them *traitors* and compared them "to the Scots at Derby" in
1745. "The prejudice against the Americans on the whole seemed
very great."

It should be pointed out that Lord Chief Justice Mansfield argued
against "a division, and did not himself divide." Nevertheless, the
Governor of Maryland received a report that stated that he explicitly
"denied the power of the Crown to emancipate the colonies from the
jurisdiction of the British legislature." As he braced himself for the
coming controversy over the Stamp Act, he fully understood that his
understanding of the Constitution of the British Empire was facing
a most serious challenge.[55]

THE REPEAL OF THE STAMP ACT

F ROM 14 JANUARY TO 18 MARCH 1766 PARLIAMENT
ENGAGED IN AN EXTENSIVE argument over the Constitution
of the British Empire that resulted in the Repeal of the Stamp Act. On
the side opposing the repeal, the major players were George Grenville
in the House of Commons and Lord Mansfield in the House of Lords.
On the side advocating the repeal, the major players were William
Pitt in the House of Commons and Lord Camden in the House of
Lords. And finally there was the Rockingham Administration itself,
which could not keep these two quarreling parties from pressing the
constitutional issues to the outer limits. The report on the opening
debate in the House of Commons in the Harris Diary captured the
overall situation of the inexperienced ministry: "For some hours the
debate lay between those two great masters [i.e., Pitt and Grenville]
and the ministry stood by, like the rabble at a boxing match."[1]

As William Pitt was taking up his seat in the House of Commons
during the opening debate, a speaker could be heard saying, "The tax
was not a twentieth part of what they could afford to pay; but that
was not the point: he had rather have a *peppercorn* to acknowledge
our sovereignty, than millions paid into the Treasury without it"

(my emphasis). In the reports of Walpole and West, Hans Stanley was the one who spoke those words, but according to the fuller record in the Almon Debates that distinction should go to Robert Nugent. Regardless of who introduced this "peppercorn" into the argument over imperial policies, it would periodically surface in future debates.[2]

In his opening speech the Great Commoner apparently labored under a felt necessity to explain why he had remained aloof from the Rockingham Administration. After "bowing to the Ministry," according to the Almon Debates, Pitt declared that "confidence is a plant of slow growth in an aged bosom: by comparing events with each other, reasoning from effects to causes, methinks, I plainly discovered the traces of *an over-ruling influence"* in the new ministry. West's letter to Newcastle states that Pitt "liked and approved of many in the present [administration], particularly those *he saw."* Then he added: *"Marks of undue influences somewhere which prevented him placing his confidence in them."* Horace Walpole has Pitt asking this rhetorical question: "Was there not an *invisible influence* from more quarters than one?" The report in the Harris Diary is quite different in detail as well as tone but it essentially supports these other statements: "Mr. Pitt [gave the Rockingham Administration] a severe lash, by saying that though he had a respect for many of them, yet that some of them were under *influences* (Lord Bute) which while they lasted, he could never place in them any confidence" (my emphases).

Although virtually the entire political nation assumed that Bute was still pulling levers from behind the curtain—and for months Pitt had been complaining about the Newcastle's prominence within the Rockingham Administration—when Rockingham directly asked Pitt whom he had in mind when he referred to these "influences," Pitt explicitly denied that he was alluding to either Bute or Newcastle.[3] It should also be pointed out that in this same parliamentary debate the Great Commoner recalled that "there were some, when I had the honour to serve his Majesty, to propose to me to burn my fingers with an *American* Stamp-Act." But neither Bute nor Newcastle could possibly have been among those advancing that proposal while Pitt had "the honour to serve his Majesty" from 1757 to 1761.

Attention has already been called to the fact that in 1754 Mansfield (then Attorney General Murray) and Charles Townshend supported the plan of the Board of Trade to tax the Americans. And according to Bernard Knollenberg, in 1755 "Lord Halifax, President of the Board of Trade, likewise suggested immediate Parliamentary taxation of the colonies, preferably by a *stamp tax*" (my emphasis).[4] But in 1755 Pitt was not yet in charge, and he was clearly positioning this initiative a year or two later, for he proceeded to add, "With the enemy at their back, with our bayonets at their breast, in the day of their distress, perhaps the *Americans* would have submitted to the imposition; but it would have been taking an ungenerous, and unjust advantage." At that juncture the most plausible person within the *conciliabulum* to propose to Pitt to burn his fingers "with an *American* Stamp-Act" was none other than Lord Chief Justice Mansfield. Furthermore, according to West's letter to Newcastle, "Mr. *Pitt* said he had at the feet of the Throne objected to act with a man born on the other side of the Tweed." It is more than plausible to believe that he was referring to his brief negotiation with George III during the summer of 1763 when he explicitly excluded Mansfield from his proposed ministry, for this was the moment when he avowed "at the feet of the Throne" that our Scottish Law Lord was "a Jacobite ... and means, Sir, to ruin your family." The Great Commoner apparently was acknowledging that in the summer of 1765 that he had entertained the erroneous belief that Mansfield would exercise an *over-ruling or undue or invisible influence* within the Rockingham Administration.

IN his speech on this 14 January 1766 William Pitt thought it was ridiculous for the Grenville Administration to be willing to forfeit, say, "the 2 or 3 millions" derived from the American trade for "a paltry £50 or £60 per annum" to be gained in taxes. Structured syllogistically in the report of the Harris Diary, Pitt's argument reads—Major Premise: "Taxes could be legally imposed *only on those,*

162

whom the imposers represented"; Minor Premise: "The Commons of Great Britain were *no* representatives of the people of America"; therefore, Conclusion: "Ergo, could impose *no* tax on them."

One can follow Pitt's constitutional argument in the fuller report in the Almon Debates, where that Major Premise is spelled out in detail:

> It is my opinion that this kingdom has no right to lay a tax upon the colonies ... They are the subjects of this kingdom, equally entitled with yourselves to all the natural rights of mankind and the peculiar privileges of *Englishmen*. Equally bound by its laws, and equally participating in the constitution of *England*. The *Americans* are the sons, not the bastards, of *England*. Taxation is no part of the governing or legislative power. The taxes are a voluntary gift of the Commons alone ... The Commons of *America*, represented in their several assemblies, have ever been in possession of the exercise of this, their constitutional right, of giving and granting their own money. They would have been slaves if they had not enjoyed it.

After evoking "the natural rights of mankind," and "the peculiar privileges of *Englishmen*," plus the transparent fact that from the beginning the Americans had been "represented in their several assemblies," he proceeded to the Minor Premise.

Pitt opened his argument by calling attention to the way the Grenville Administration had initially advanced the doctrine of virtual representation to cover the lack of actual representation of the colonies in Parliament. Pointedly he then pressed this question: "I would fain know by whom an *American* is represent here?" Then followed this frequently quoted statement: "The idea of a virtual representation of *America* in this House, is the most contemptible idea that ever entered into the head of a man—it does not deserve a serious refutation."

Pitt then turned directly to a rehearsal of *the received pattern of governance* within the Old Colonial System: "At the same time, this kingdom, as the supreme governing and legislative power, has always bound the colonies by her laws, by her regulations, and restrictions in trade, in navigation, in manufactures—in every thing, except that of taking their money out of their pockets without their consent. 'Here I would draw the line.'"[5] Pitt's *line* was so remarkably similar to the position advanced by the Americans that it is reasonable to assume that he had been reading some of their pamphlets and petitions with care.[6]

George Grenville now responded to Pitt's constitutional argument. According to the cryptic report in the Harris Diary, Grenville not only "Maintained the power of Parliament to tax America" he also "Denied the doctrine of legislation arising from representation." He then pressed this point in his rejoinder: "The seditious spirit of the colonies owes its birth to the factions in this House." After observing that the colonies "border on open rebellion," he added that "if the doctrine I have heard this day" from the lips of the Great Commoner were to be believed, then "The government over them being dissolved, a revolution will take place in *America*." The logic of Grenville's position was this stark—either Parliament had the inherent right to tax the colonies, or the Americans were already in a revolutionary situation. Parliament had or had not the right to impose both "external and internal taxes" upon the colonies. It was all or nothing.

Pitt addressed the House a second time, and in his response to Grenville's charge that he had given "birth to sedition in *America*" he rejoiced in the fact "that *America* has resisted": "Three millions of people, so dead to all the feelings of liberty, as voluntarily to submit to be slaves, would have been fit instruments to make slaves of the rest." Before he finished Pitt also troubled to answer Grenville's claim that he could not "understand the difference between external and internal taxes," a distinction that apparently Pitt had implicitly made at the outset, for in Walpole's record Pitt had said that the House of Commons "had no right to lay an *internal tax* upon America, that country not being represented" (emphasis modified). It is only fair to interpret Grenville's comment as meaning that he could not understand how Pitt could accept "external taxes" and then turn around and reject Parliament's right to impose "internal taxes" through the Stamp Act.

The task at hand is to determine the scope of both *external* and *internal* taxes in these 1766 proceedings, beginning with Pitt's response to Grenville: "If the gentleman does not understand the difference between internal and external taxes, I cannot help it; but there is a plain distinction between taxes levied for the purpose of raising a revenue, and duties imposed for the regulation of trade, ... although, in the consequences, some revenue might incidentally arise from the latter." In Pitt's universe of discourse *external taxes* denoted those traditional "duties imposed for the regulation of trade," while *internal taxes* encompassed all kinds of taxes "levied for the purpose of raising a revenue." The only plausible way to interpret Pitt's distinction is to say that Pitt thought that Parliament should stick to the traditional policy in the Old Colonial System and leave *all taxation levied for the purpose of raising revenue* to the various colonial assemblies. And Pitt was quite right in believing that the Americans were not protesting against those traditional "duties imposed for the regulation of trade."

Pitt was convinced that if Parliament attempted to enforce the Stamp Act the Americans would fight to preserve their freedom: "Will you, after the Peace [of Paris] you have made, ... sheathe your sword in the bowels of your brothers, the Americans? You may coerce and conquer, but when they fall, they will fall like the strong man embracing the pillars of this constitution, and bury it in ruin with them." In his sober judgment, Parliament's active pursuit of that *peppercorn* of acknowledgement of its right to tax the Americans had plunged the British Empire into a profound constitutional crisis precisely because the emergent imperial policy rejected the wisdom of the past and embraced a novel principle. Given so dire a prospect, Pitt concluded: "Upon the whole, I will beg leave to tell the House what is really my opinion. It is, that the Stamp Act be *repealed absolutely, totally*, and *immediately*. That the reason for the repeal be assigned, because it was founded on an erroneous principle."[7]

WILLIAM Pitt had grasped with conceptual clarity the American position on taxation, a claim documented when the House of Commons took up the Petition from the Stamp Act Congress on 27 January 1766. In this Petition for the full House to see, the Americans declared, "the several Acts of Parliament imposing divers Duties and Taxes on the Colonies" had "by these Means ... in Effect, unhappily deprived [them] of Two Privileges essential to Freedom, and which all *Englishmen* have ever considered as their best Birthrights."

One of those privileges was "Trial by their Peers." According to Walpole, Pitt "painted the Americans as people who, in all ill-fated hour, had left this country to fly from the Star Chamber and High Commission Courts," prerogative courts of the early Stuarts without juries. And now the new imperial policy had reopened that vexed issue by "extending the Jurisdiction of the Courts of Admiralty" in the colonies "beyond their ancient Limits."

The other privilege so "essential to Freedom" was "that of being free from *all Taxes* but such as they have consented to in Person, or by their Representatives" (my emphasis). The Americans in Congress assembled were claiming that the Stamp Act struck at the very vitals of the Constitution. Not only did Pitt agree with the Americans, according to Lord Holland's letter, Pitt openly declared that "in attempting to tax the colonies, we had broke the Original Covenant, and they were freed from all allegiance."

Sir Fletcher Norton, who was close to Mansfield, pronounced Pitt's doctrine "extremely dangerous" because—mark the words— "he *set the prerogative above all law*, when he supposed that the Crown could by its Charters emancipate and set free from the legislature of Great Britain" (my emphasis).[8]

ON 3 February 1766 the House of Lords in committee addressed "the late Tumults in America." Lyttelton set the stage by reaching deep into that "great principle of policy" known as *Imperium in imperio*, which he explicated as meaning that "in all states, democratical, aristocratical, or monarchical, or in mixed states, as Great Britain, the government must rest somewhere, and that must be fixed, or otherwise there is an end of all government." And of course it was "fixed" in Parliament.

Camden responded by arguing against the vaunted omnipotence of Parliament: "The sovereign authority, the omnipotence of the legislature, my lords, is a favourable doctrine, but there are some things they cannot do. They cannot enact any thing against the divine law, and may forfeit their right. They cannot take away any man's private property without making him a compensation." (Rockingham reported to the King that Camden spoke "with great ability—ingenuity and knowledge.")

Contrary to Camden's interpretation of the constitution, Lord Chancellor Northington shared Lyttelton's doctrine that "there must be a supreme dominion in every state"; he also thoroughly agreed with Mansfield's notion that colonial governments were "on the same footing as our great corporations in London," that is, their charters could be vacated as readily as they could be granted. Indeed, he believed the Americans had already "forfeited all their charters" because they had not only "called a meeting of their states" but had "entered into Resolutions" that implicitly denied the authority of Parliament. In any event, "the colonies are become too big to be governed by the laws they at first set out with. They have therefore run into confusion, and it will be the policy of this country to form a plan of laws for them." (Rockingham reported to the King that Northington treated Camden's "doctrines as *new* unconstitutional etc.")

After these introductory overtures Mansfield finished off the debate with an oration that cut Camden "to pieces upon every point of the argument." Gifted with a fine rhetorical strategy, Mansfield first castigated Lyttelton for totally dismissing James Otis's pamphlet, *The Rights of the British Colonies Asserted and Proved.* "It may be called silly and mad," Mansfield reminded the House, but "mad people, or persons who have entertained silly and mad ideas, have led the people to rebellion, and overturned empires." Against such madness entertained by the silly Americans, our learned Law Lord laid out his understanding of the British Constitution with technical precision in propositional form: "In every government the legislative power must be lodged somewhere, and the executive must likewise be lodged somewhere. *In Great Britain the legislative is in Parliament, the executive in the Crown*" (my capitalizations and emphasis). In explicating this doctrine, Mansfield maintained that England and Wales, and, since the Union of 1707, Scotland composed those parts *within the realm*. Those parts *without the realm* were all those governmental entities throughout the British Empire that *were not represented in the British Parliament.*

From this solid foundation Mansfield drew this inference for the Constitution of the British Empire: "That the British legislature, as to the power of making laws, represents the whole British empire and has authority to bind every part and every subject without the least distinction, whether such subjects have a right to vote or not, or whether the law binds places *within the realm or without*" (my emphasis). In his opinion, "never, by our constitution, was representation adopted as necessary." In the House of Commons Mansfield's disciple, Sir William Blackstone, explicitly denied "the right of imposing taxes arises from representation." Blackstone even added: "However this doctrine of representation held in this country, it certainly does not hold with respect to the colonies who are dependent upon us."

Mansfield's justification for the doctrine of Parliamentary Supremacy over "the whole British empire" turned on a technical point. After acknowledging that "it is an established rule of construction, that no parts *without the realm* are bound unless named in the act," he proceeded to say, "this rule establishes the right of Parliament; for unless they had a right to bind parts *out of the realm*, this distinction would never have been made" (my emphases and capitalization). Even though there was no connection between *representation and legislation*, Mansfield could find *no distinction between legislation and taxation*. Indeed, "as a distinction has been taken between the power of laying taxes and making laws, I must declare, that after the most diligent searches on this head, I cannot find any distinction or difference whatever." Furthermore, Mansfield's diligent searches turned up "no difference between laying *internal and external taxes*." Assuming that dubious distinction, however, he added, "the acts of *giving duties, customs, and erecting a post office*" should be considered "as laying an *internal tax*" (my emphases).

Mansfield drew out the full implication of his understanding of the Constitution of the British Empire in propositional form: "That the colonists, by the condition on which they migrated, settled, and now exist, are *more emphatically subjects of Great Britain than those within the realm*" (my emphasis). From Parliament's acknowledged right to regulate trade, it followed that there were no limits to Parliament's authority over the colonies, period. Indeed, one report says that the Lord Chief Justice of King's Bench "repeatedly called upon the advocates for America to draw the line, to move their exceptions and to say how far the sovereignty of the British Parliament should go and where stop."

After reducing the Constitution of the British Empire to being something less than the Constitution of Great Britain, Mansfield then proceeded to marginalize the constitutions of the various colonies, each of which had a distinct civil polity. All colonial governments were "on the same footing as our great corporations in London," that is, to quote his 18 March 1747 opinion when he was Solicitor General, they exist "from the Grace and Favour of the Crowne alone." He then cited a case in point: "And it is worth remarking, that Massachusetts Bay had a charter which in Charles 2's time was vacated in Chancery for their abuse of it. Now, is it possible to suppose that a legislature can exist with a sole power of laying taxes, which legislature may be destroyed here by a process in the courts of Chancery or King's-Bench?" Perhaps he had read the *History* that Thomas Hutchinson had so dutifully sent him.

More to the constitutional point of the right of Parliament to tax a colony, Mansfield cited this legal opinion:

In 1724, the assembly of Jamaica refused to raise taxes for their necessary support. Application was made to the council by their agent here, and a reference to Sir Clement Worge and Lord Hardwicke, to know whether the King could not lay a tax. They gave their opinion, that if Jamaica was to be considered as a conquered country, the King could lay taxes; if otherwise, the assembly must lay it, *or it must be raised by Act of Parliament*" [my emphasis and capitalizations].

Recall that in 1744 as Solicitor General he had reaffirmed the imperial doctrine that "a colony of English subjects cannot be taxed but by some representative body of their own *or by the Parliament of England*" (my emphasis).

Within our Scottish Law Lord's political thought it was axiomatic that sovereignty was unconditioned, uncontrollable, absolute. He even cautioned the House, "Take care, my lords, you do not abdicate your authority," for "When the supreme power abdicates, the government is dissolved. In such an event, your lordships would leave the worthy and innocent, as well as the unworthy and guilty, to the same confusion and ruin."

In the judgment of W. Rouet, Mansfield's oration was "the finest speech of two hours, that, in the opinion of all with whom I have conversed, was the strongest in reason and the most eloquent in words that ever was heard in that House." And Rouet was not an impartial commentator, for on the next day he added: "Never was a poor Chief-Justice so mauled as *Camden* was last night. He spoke like an Attorney's Clerk: but his noble adversary like a great orator, an intelligent legislator, and, what is more, a candid and virtuous man." (Rockingham informed the King, "Lord *Mansfield* made a very extraordinary able and conclusive speech—answering minutely all Lord Camden's arguments with great force.")[9]

The Lord Chief Justice of King's Bench carried the day with style. The House voted 125 to 5 in favor of the resolution.

WHILE the Rockingham Administration agreed with Mansfield, Northington, Blackstone and Grenville that Parliament had the *right* to levy taxes on the colonies, it also agreed with Pitt and Camden and the London merchants that the Stamp Act had proven to be *a catastrophic mistake in imperial policy*. Given this rather conflicted situation the ministry decided upon a path that would result in a total repeal of the Stamp Act on *prudential grounds* but would preserve the principle of Parliamentary Supremacy *in theory*.

With the 1719 Irish Declaratory Act held consciously in mind, the Administration introduced its 1766 Declaratory Bill that asserted that Parliament "had, hath, and of right ought to have, full power and authority to make laws and statutes of sufficient force and validity, to bind the colonies and people of *America*, subjects of the crown of *Great Britain*, in all cases whatsoever." But Parliament had never tried to tax the Irish! In the mentality of the Rockingham Administration, having a right and exercising it were two completely different things.

Secretary Conway confessed in the House of Commons, "He never was nor ever shall be a friend to internal taxation in America. He does not deny the legal right, but he thinks in point of policy and justice this ought not to have been attempted." Edmund Burke also argued, "Without subordination, it would not be one Empire. Without freedom, it would not be the British Empire." In his opinion, "The most anxious work for the understanding of men is to govern a large Empire upon a plan of freedom; but it is as noble as it is anxious, and it is necessary because it can be governed by no other."[10]

It should not go unnoticed that during the examination of expert witnesses in the second week of February, Paymaster General, Charles Townshend, opened the session by declaring that "he could not repeal the [Stamp] act on account of the right, whereby it was imposed, nor on account of the violence that had been used against it, but only if at all, on the *impracticability*, or *inexpediency* of it, or the *inability* of the colonies to pay the tax" (my emphases). Prudential considerations at this moment, in other words, would prevent him from following his enduring convictions that Parliament did have the right to tax the Americans.

FOR three days of close examination—a plethora of witnesses testified—the Rockingham Administration pursued a plan that would thoroughly expose the fatal flaws in the Stamp Act. Barlow Trecothick, for example, told the examiners that the trade in North America was "almost wholly" stopped: "the most considerable exporting colonies have sent orders under such restrictions as disable us to comply with them. All have restricted not to be shipped unless the Stamp Act is repealed." When he was asked whether it might be "so modified as the Americans will submit to it," he answered, "I believe no modification will satisfy them." When pressed, he added, "Because the people from one end of the continent/country to the other have set their faces against it."

Capel Hanbury supported Trecothick's belief that "Anything short of a total repeal will be inadequate. A modification would not answer." James Balfour observed from his years of experience in America that he had "never heard of a more loyal, affectionate people"—until the Grenville Administration introduced its novel policy. And on it went as one witness after another documented how devastating the Stamp Act had been to British commerce and American affection. But the witness who best captured the spirit of the moment was Benjamin Franklin.

As the star witness Franklin informed the House on 13 February that prior to the current crisis the "temper of America towards Great Britain" was "the best in the world." Indeed,

> They submitted willingly to the government of the crown, and paid, in all their courts, obedience to acts of parliament. Numerous as the people are in the several old provinces, they cost you nothing in forts, citadels, garrisons or armies, to keep them in subjection. They were governed by this country at the expense only of a little pen, ink and paper. They were led by a thread. They had not only a respect, but an affection for Great-Britain, for its laws, its customs and manners, and even a

THE REPEAL OF THE STAMP ACT

fondness for its fashions, that greatly increased the commerce. Natives of Britain were always treated with particular regard; to be an Old England-man was, of itself, a character of some respect, and gave a kind of rank among us.

All that, however, was now "very much altered."

In response to a question about "the authority of parliament to make laws," Franklin answered adroitly: "The authority of parliament was allowed to be valid in all laws, except such as should lay *internal taxes*." To be precise, "It was never disputed in laying *duties to regulate commerce*." Shortly thereafter he amplified his statement on the colonial attitude prior to 1764: "I never heard any objection to the right of laying *duties to regulate commerce*; but a right to lay *internal taxes* was never supposed to be in Parliament, as we are not represented there."

When pressed on whether the Americans would "object to the Parliament's right of *external taxation*," he declared that "By *taxes* they mean *internal taxes*; by *duties* they mean *customs*" to regulate trade. But he also observed with Mansfield's recent oration in mind, "Many arguments have been lately used here to shew them that there is no difference [between *external and internal taxes*], and that if you have no right to tax them *internally*, you have none to tax them *externally*, or make any other law to bind them. At present they do not reason so, but in time they may possibly be convinced by these arguments." The Notes taken by Nathaniel Ryder on his distinctions contain this important observation: "By the word *taxes* they have always considered *internal taxes only*, and when they mean *external taxes* they use the word *duties*" (my emphases).

On the face of it, Franklin was using the categories *external and internal taxes* the way Pitt had used them when he answered Grenville in January, namely, that *external taxes* were *custom duties* designed to regulate commerce, while *internal taxes* encompassed *all taxes* levied for the purpose of raising revenue. Although the burden of his testimony fell upon the deleterious impact upon trade, he also wanted the House of Commons to understand that the Americans would resolutely refuse "to acknowledge the right of parliament to tax them."[11]

BENJAMIN Franklin had been reflecting on how the Union of 1707 had impacted the constitutional heritage at least since his 1759 tour of Scotland to collect his honorary degree of Doctor of Laws. And for several months he had engaged in a rather playful, running argument with Vindex Patriae in *The Gazetteer and New Daily Advertiser*. It began with his poking fun at Vindex Patriae for his preposterous belief that through a legal fiction the Americans were "represented in parliament, because the manor of East Greenwich in Kent is represented there, and they all live in that manor." Then later, after Vindex Patriae claimed that "the laws, customs, and religion of New England were largely Scottish," Homespun directly responded: "The common law of England, is, I assure you, the common law of the colonies: and if the civil law is what you mean by the Scotch law, we have none of it but what is forced upon us by England, in the courts of Admiralty, depriving us of that inestimable part of the common law, trials by juries."

Franklin troubled to remind his readers "that the colonies were planted in times when the powers of parliament were not supposed so extensive, as they are become since the [Glorious] Revolution." Indeed, "the people went from hence by permission from the crown, purchased and conquered the territory, at the expence of their own private treasure and blood: That these territories thus became *new* dominions *of the crown*, settled under royal charters, and formed their several governments and constitutions, on which the parliament was *never consulted*; or had the *least participation*."[12]

The dominant tradition in American political thought is captured in Franklin's reply to "Tom Hint": "Your most celebrated writers on the constitution, your *Seldens*, your *Lockes*, and your *Sidney's*, have reasoned" the Americans into their constitutional beliefs, and he could have added *Cato's Letters* to round off the central library of traditional Whig political thought.[13] He evoked the royal prerogative in granting charters to the American colonies to register the actual historical facts of the matter as well as to secure American rights under *the jurisdiction and protection of the Crown.*

The Tory position championed by Mansfield, on the other hand, elevated the doctrine of Parliamentary Supremacy over the Royal Prerogative, thereby marginalizing all colonial assemblies to the point of uselessness. As Sir Fletcher Norton lined out the emergent doctrine on 27 January 1766, to so much as suggest "that the Crown could by its Charters emancipate and set [the Americans] free from the legislature of Great Britain" would "set the prerogative above all law."[14] The decisive difference lies not with either "King" or "Parliament" but with the notion that "the King-in-Parliament" was omnipotent not only *within the realm but also without.*

Franklin was a gifted journalist with a clever eye for images. Recently he had printed a political cartoon, "Magna Britannia: Her Colonies Reduc'd." A forlorn Britannia, with her severed limbs (marked "Virg" and "Pensyl" and "New York" and "New Eng") scattered before her on a desolate landscape dominated by a dead tree, lifts her eyes to heaven in abject despair. Three ships on a distant horizon have brooms tied to their masts to indicate that they were up for sale. Britannia has fallen off the globe. Her Union Jack Shield lies uselessly at her side. Her spear is aimed directly at her breast. And her truncated torso is draped with a banner that reads in Latin: *Date Obolum Belisario.*

When this cartoon was published in Philadelphia, this Latin motto was accompanied by a lengthy "Explanation" (probably not written by Franklin):

> Belisarius was one of the Greatest Heroes of the Antients. He lived under Justinian the Emperor: He gain'd a Victory over and concluded an Honourable Peace with Cabades King of Persia, Took Carthage and Subdued Gilimes the Usurper of the Crown of the Vandals, Overthrew Vitiges and refused the Throne of the Goths when offer'd to him; Rebuilt the

Walls of Rome after they were distroy'd by Totila, and performed many other Military Atchievements too tedious to enumerate. In this Part of his Character is represented the late Succesful and Flourishing State of Great Britain, which Aided the King of Prussia against the Powerful Armies of Hungary and Russia; Supported Portugal against the Spanish, and reduc'd France and Spain to the most Advantageous Terms of Accommodation.

After that generous rehearsal of the feats of "one of the Greatest Heroes of the Antients," one comes to this finale:

By the latter Part of Belisarius's Life is represented the Unhappy and Miserable State of Great Britain, should the late Measures against America take Place. This General at length being Accused of a Conspiracy against Justinian, That Emperor barbarously Ordered his Eyes to be pulled out, which reduced him to the Greatest Poverty, and Obliged him to Subsist on the Alms of others. The Motto is also Stricking, and elegantly Expressive of this Truth: DATE OBOLUM BELISARIO—Give Poor Belisarius a Penny.

According to "a contemporary longhand inscription" on a copy in the American Philosophical Society archives, Franklin "employd a Waiter to put one of [these political cartoons] in each Parliament Mans hand as he entered the house the day preceding the great debate of the Stamp Act."[15]

ON 21 February 1766 the Rockingham Administration introduced the Resolution for the Repeal of the Stamp Act. Secretary Conway opened the Debate with this observation: "The principal trade of this country [was] at an absolute stand." The Stamp Act "carried with it evil policy" because it "carries oppression and impracticability in its very nature." Furthermore, according to the Harris Diary, he called "our right of taxing a doubtful one, and never to be exercised with equity." Indeed, "*we* assert [the right] because *they* deny [it]." Edmund Burke's line of approach, according to Reverend R. Palmer, sidestepped the question of Parliament's "*right* of taxation" and focused on "constant *usage*." According to him, "*internal taxation* was never once thought of [by Parliament] since the first emigration of the Americans from this country, and that England never thought of any other power over them or interest in them, but that of regulating their commerce to the advantage of the mother country."[16]

Three days later Hussey argued that Parliament had acquiesced in "the privilege of the colonists" to tax themselves. Indeed, Parliament had passed thirty-three laws concerning North America and "None of them have laid an *internal tax*, at least no *internal tax* which can so fairly be called so as this Act." "If the legislators had known what would have happened," he was convinced "they would never have enacted the law. If they had, they would in his opinion have been in a state of actual delirium."[17] In Walpole's opinion, "it was the clamour of trade, of the merchants and the manufacturing towns, that had borne down all opposition."[18] Trade, not constitutional principles, induced the House of Commons to vote 275 to 167 for the Repeal of the Stamp Act.

IN the 21 February Commons Debate William Pitt warned the House, "There never was an instance where the whole country was united to a man in a revolt as in the case of America." Ominously he continued, "It was not so in our country in the civil war" of the seventeenth century. During the 4 March debate on the Declaratory Bill he carried his argument a notch even higher. According to the report in the Ryder Diary, he read from earlier pamphlets that proved that "imposing taxes upon colonies which were not represented was improper and against the Great Charter of English liberties." Pitt's motion "to leave out the words in the [Declaratory] Bill *in all cases whatever*" was rejected, however.[19]

After the Great Commoner's argument "had been treated in his absence as nonsense, as the child of ignorance, as the language of a foreigner who knew nothing of the constitution," he promptly returned to the floor to announce (in Walpole's words), "the *common law* was his guide"—"it was the *civil law* that was the foreigner" (my emphases). The Harris Diary records that in this interchange he pronounced "absurd" the idea that "representation was not connected with taxation." Then he added the stinger that such "nonsense" was based on *Roman Law.*[20]

LORD Camden and Lord Mansfield reengaged in an argument over Parliament's right to tax the colonies during the second reading of the Declaratory Bill in the House of Lords on 7 March 1766. In the opinion of Charlemont, their "excellent debate ... displayed their talents in the most masterly manner." According to W. G. Hamilton, "They each of them spoke twice, and spoke for a long time together. Lord *Camden* began by answering the speech which Lord Mansfield had made a month ago, in support of the *right*" of Parliament to tax the colonies. Camden also wanted the House to appreciate that in the 3 February debate he had been "very injuriously treated" because Mansfield had laid upon him the "heavy charge" of being "the broacher of new-fangled doctrines, contrary to the laws of this kingdom, and subversive of the rights of parliament." Speaking "as peer and judge, the defender of the law and the constitution," Camden now claimed that he had spent the last month in "the strictest review of my arguments; I re-examined all my authorities." What he found was that Mansfield had falsely quoted "an Act of Parliament from Rasdel's Statutes." (Three days later they had yet "another altercation ... upon the subject of that mis-quotation," too.)

After all this research and reflection over the past month, Camden was more convinced than ever "that the British parliament have no right to tax the Americans." In his opinion the Declaratory Bill was "illegal, absolutely illegal, contrary to the fundamental laws of nature, contrary to the fundamental laws of this constitution." Because "the affair is of the utmost importance, and in its consequences may involve the fate of kingdoms," he thought that Parliament should pursue "the sage advice of Machiavel" and return to "first principles," which he laid out in detail:

> A constitution grounded on the eternal and immutable laws of nature; a constitution whose foundation and centre is liberty, which sends liberty to every subject, that is or may happen to be within any part of its ample circumference. Nor, my lords, is the doctrine new, it is as old as the constitution: it grew up with it; indeed it is its support: *taxation and representation are inseparably united*; God hath joined them, no British parliament can separate them; to endeavour to do it, is to stab our very vitals [my emphasis].

Camden continued:

> My position is this—I repeat it—I will maintain it to my last hour;—*taxation and representation are inseparable*;—this position is founded on the laws of nature; it is more, it is itself an eternal law of nature: for whatever is a man's own, is absolutely his own; no man hath a right to take it from him without his consent, either expressed by himself or representative; whoever attempts to do it, attempts an injury; whoever does it, commits a robbery; throws down and destroys the distinction between liberty and slavery. *Taxation and representation are coeval with and essential to this constitution* [my emphases].

He proceeded to argue that "there is not a blade of grass growing in the most obscure corner of this kingdom which is not, which was not ever, represented since the constitution began; there is not a blade of grass, which when taxed, was not taxed by the consent of the proprietor." So long as the Americans could not be represented in the House of Commons, it was unconstitutional to tax them, the fancy doctrine of *virtual representation* to the contrary notwithstanding, for it was "so absurd as not to deserve an answer."

Mansfield now rose and ridiculed Camden's "set speech" by comparing it "to the words which are spoke in Nova Zembla, and which are said to be frozen for a month, before any body can get at their meaning." After dropping "a few hints about the want of quickness" in his opponent, "he entered not only into every member, but almost into every sentence, of Lord Camden's argument." Whereas Camden had appealed to "the Law of Reason and of Nature," Mansfield responded by saying this amounted to appealing to "no more than every Man's own Reason and was in itself a mere vague idea." Whereas Camden had argued "from Custom and Usage," with particular reference to "Wales, Calais, Durham, Chester, etc." (another report mentions "the Clergy, Wales, the Counties Palatine, Calais, and Ireland"), Mansfield dismissed all this as "quite superficial and futile." Whereas Camden had evoked the authority of John Locke, Mansfield acknowledged that Locke "had said that money could not be raised in a Free Government without your own consent," but then added, "it was no more than a general proposition never intended to extend to all particular circumstances whatever."

Mansfield, it should be pointed out, also emphatically opposed the Declaratory Bill. According to W. G. Hamilton's letter, he treated it "with the utmost contempt." He thought "that it was from beginning to end an absurdity; that it contained many falsehoods; that it would render the legislature, if it passed unaltered, ridiculous and contemptible." According to another letter, Parliament's "*Right of Taxing the Colonies*" was so axiomatic in his jurisprudential orientation that "a *Declaration* of that Right by a Bill in Parliament" would be "*nugatory.*" To even attempt to qualify Parliament's sovereignty would prove to be a slippery slope.[21]

Mansfield and Camden squared off again during the decisive Second Reading of the Bill to Repeal the Stamp Act. According to one report, Mansfield actually said, "The Americans have adopted on this fatal occasion a new principle that they are not subject to the legislative authority of Great Britain." Indeed, repealing the Stamp Act would be "the giving up the total Legislature of this Kingdom" over America. "If a Bill passes which destroys the landmarks of the Constitution, it is without remedy." Furthermore, "May not the passing this Bill put us in a situation of being dictated to by the Americans, who may think they have a right to an open trade and establishment of manufactures. What then will become of us?" (Rockingham cryptically informed the King, "Lord Mansfield spoke with his usual eloquence and ability but rather anticipating upon the gloomy prospect of the Colonies throwing off all allegiance and turned all his arguments—as if that question was immediately before the Lords.")

Camden directly refuted Mansfield's assertion "that the Colonies had disclaimed the Legislative Authority of Great Britain." In his reading of history,

> From the 15 Car. 2 down to this day there never was a murmur against the Legislative Authority of Great Britain. What is it has changed their minds. No other cause than the grievances heapt upon them by the late Revenue Acts. The projector must have seen that difficulties must attend the experiment, but this was rather an incentive than a discouragement, and a double plan of policy was to take place; 1st, to strip them of their purses, and then to tame their spirits.[22]

Camden did not need to point out that their spirits had not been tamed, but regardless of what constitutional principles either Camden or Mansfield advanced in the House of Lords, on 11 March 1766 the policy of *expediency* prevailed with a vote of 105 to 71 on the Second Reading of the Bill to Repeal the Stamp Act.

THIRTY-THREE Lords proceeded to file a Protest against the Repeal of the Stamp Act. After it became public, Benjamin Franklin carefully commented on it. Where the Protest claimed that it was "*not in the power of prerogative to bestow*" authority upon "the subordinate Provincial Legislatures," his marginalia reads, "Dispute this with the King my Lords, he has done it." Then he added the observation that the Lords do have a valid claim *within the realm,* but not *without the realm,* for the simple fact that the colonies "are different States, Subject to the King." When the fear is expressed that by repealing the Stamp Act the Americans would begin challenging all laws, he repeated his standard refrain: "It is so reason'd here, not there, but in time they may be convinc'd." Again, when the Lords argue that the repeal "must (if admitted) set them absolutely free from any obedience to the *power of the British Legislature,*" he responded, "but not to the Power of the Crown." He finally confessed: "The Sovereignty of the Crown I understand. The Sovereignty of the British Legislature out of Britain, I do not understand." Shortly thereafter: "America not in the Realm of England or G.B. No Man in America thinks himself exempt from the Jurisdiction of the Crown and their own Assemblies."

Franklin troubled to underline the names of the Scottish Lords who signed this Protest, then added: "I observe two or three Scotch Lords Prot[estor]s. Many more voted agst. the Repeal. Colonies settled before the Union." "How could Scotland acquire a Right to any Legislation over English Colonies, but by Consent of the Colonies themselves." He repeated this line of argument at the end of his comments on the next Protest by twenty-eight Lords after the Third Reading. His final comment on the right of colonial consent reads: "if I cannot defend that Right, I can retire cheerfully with my little Family into the Boundless Woods of America which are sure to afford Freedom and Subsistence to any Man who can bait a Hook or pull a Trigger."[23]

PUBLIC attention was not focused on the Declaratory Act but on the Repeal of the Stamp Act that passed into law the same day. Benjamin Wilson immediately published a famous cartoon, "The Repeal, or the Funeral Procession of Miss Americ-Stamp." The procession is moving toward a final resting place under a plaque that reads in part: "Within this Family Vault, Lie Interred, it is to be hoped never to rise again, The Star Chamber Court, Ship Money." "The Reverend Mr. Anti-Sejanus," with a dog pissing on his clerical gown, leads this solemn procession. Lord Chief Justice Mansfield and the former Attorney General, Fletcher Norton, follow in abject sorrow, carrying two black flags that interlock "the Stamps with the White Rose and Thistle." The former Prime Minister, George Grenville, is carrying the coffin, followed by five mourners—the Lords Bute, Bedford, Temple, Halifax and Sandwich. The two bishops, Warburton and Johnson, bring up the rear. A boxed statue of William Pitt is being loaded onto a boat to carry it out to three ships ready to sail for America—named for the key members of the ministry: *Conway, Rockingham* and *Grafton.*[24]

WITH the Repeal of the Stamp Act, the political nation assumed that Mansfield had clearly lost a critical round in the constitutional argument. And his situation was rendered even more desperate when rumors began to circulated that William Pitt might soon be asked to head a new ministry. As early as 4 March the Great Commoner announced in the House of Commons that he had "heard by a bird in the air" that a change of ministers was up for action. Then on 17 March, Bute—after openly declaring "he had taken a positive and fixed resolution never again to enter into the busy scene"— suggested "that the present Ministry ought to enlarge their bottom from different sides."[25] On 10 June Benjamin Franklin informed the Committee of Correspondence of the Pennsylvania Assembly, "all ministerial Dispositions are extreamly fluctuating," so unsettled that he had decided to take a two-month continental vacation in Germany with Sir John Pringle.[26]

What brought down the Rockingham Administration was its rejection of the advice of Lord Chancellor Northington to address the urgent situation of Quebec. He shared Mansfield's opinion that Quebec should be governed through an Act of Parliament, whereas Rockingham deemed it best to continue to operate under the status quo, at least for now. On 11 July 1766 this minor episode provided

George III with an excuse to replace Rockingham with William Pitt, who now received the title, the Earl of Chatham.[27]

ON his return from Germany, Benjamin Franklin filed this report on the recent changes: "we have the Satisfaction to find, that none of those whom we look'd upon as Adversaries of America in the late Struggles, are come into Power; and that tho' some of our Friends are gone out, other Friends are come in or promoted."[28] Prominent among those friends who had come in was Camden. He promptly replaced Lord Northington as the new Lord Chancellor. And Lord Chief Justice Mansfield thoroughly understood that he would have precious little influence over policy now that his bitter rival was the new Prime Minister.

So as to avoid all ambiguity, before the constitutional crisis erupted the Americans governed themselves according to their Charters, but the various colonies always stood under the jurisdiction of the Crown. While the Crown could veto colonial legislation, the Crown could not change it *once the legislation was allowed to stand.* Parliament was simply not involved with the internal affairs of the various colonies. When Bute over-emphasized the Royal Prerogative, however, Parliament responded by extending its own authority over the colonies in protest against the Earl of Bute. That is the path by which Mansfield elevated the doctrine of Parliamentary Supremacy over the Royal Prerogative. The upshot? The Americans were, at least at first, traditionalists. And imperial policy would now return to the traditional patterns of the Old Colonial System that held prior to 1764, or so it would seem.

XIII

THE CHATHAM
ADMINISTRATION

L ORD MANSFIELD SUFFERED A SERIOUS SETBACK WITH
THE REPEAL OF THE STAMP ACT, for he had vigorously
promoted its legitimacy and determinedly opposed its repeal.
Nevertheless, he noticed that the repeal itself was grounded on
prudential grounds, not *constitutional* principles. What prudence
giveth, prudence could take away. Because this action violated the
entire orientation of his judicial understanding, he set his mind on
reversing this prudential decision. And he was aided in this pursuit
by the way William Pitt established the Chatham Administration
(1766-1768). As Horace Walpole expressed it, the chaotic years of
the Chatham Administration exhibited "how little men are, though
riding at what is called *the top of the world*."[1]

William Pitt made two mistakes while forming his
Administration. First, he decided that now was the appropriate
moment to receive the promised Earldom of Chatham. By
attempting to govern from the House of Lords, however, he forfeited
the confidence of his countrymen. Walpole's *Memoirs* capture the
transformed mood of the political nation: "That fatal title blasted
all the affection which his country had borne to him, and which

185

he had deserved so well ... The people, though he had done no act to occasion reproach, thought he had sold them for a title, and, as words fascinate or enrage them, their idol Mr Pitt was forgotten in their detestation of the Lord Chatham." So long as he "held the love of the people, nothing was so formidable in Europe as his name"; by becoming the Earl of Chatham "the talons of the lion were drawn, when he was no longer awful in his own forests."[2]

The Earl of Chatham also stumbled badly while cobbling together an inherently unstable ministry. As Walpole candidly confessed, "Every public consideration concurred to excite my endeavours that Pitt and the late [Rockingham] administration should not separate." He even labored the point: "*They* were honest, and *he* inflamed with the love of national glory. All *they* wanted was activity and authority; *he* was proper to confer both. If he lost *them*, he must hang on Bute, or revert to his brothers [i.e., George Grenville and Lord Temple] and the Bedfords. He and the late ministers were popular; all other sets were odious from past experience of their actions." Although Chatham "meant to make the present administration the groundwork of his own," at a deeper level he fancied that he could rise above what he called "connections." In Walpole's opinion, "Lord Chatham ... had always determined to break all parties." What he actually brought into being was "A ministry composed of heterogeneous particles." And by alienating Lord Rockingham, he destroyed the only promising political alliance that could successfully govern in both domestic and colonial affairs.[3]

WHEN Parliament opened on 11 November 1766 Lord Chief Justice Mansfield registered his opposition by declaring that the Chatham Administration had acted illegally by resorting to the royal prerogative in placing an embargo on the exportation of grain. A two-year famine had produced a severe shortage of grain and "the farmers ... would not bring it to market in order to enhance the price." "In this emergency the Council advised the King, as Parliament was not sitting, to lay an embargo by his own authority on the exportation of corn." Although this was "an extension of prerogative not used for a number of years, but in a war, or on the imminent approach of one," the situation was so urgent that the ministry decided that the nation could not wait until Parliament convened that fall. Mansfield, however, was persuaded that this "act of Council ... was illegal" precisely because only Parliament could act *legislatively*, and the "King could do nothing but by law."

With sarcasm veritably dripping from his pen, Walpole commented, "Lord Mansfield, from aversion to Lord Chatham and his Chancellor Camden, was now the advocate of the constitution." The royal prerogative was even pronounced irrelevant. In a letter to Horace Mann, he reported that Mansfield had spoken *"against prerogative*, yes, yes."

On this occasion, "Lord Camden answered with firmness, and with sharp irony on the new Whiggism of the Chief Justice." He openly declared, "If it was not yet in our law, it ought to be so, that *salus populi suprema lex*. If this act was a stretch of prerogative, *it was but a tyranny of forty days*."[4] Regardless of what one might think of Camden's ironic comment about "the new Whiggism of the Chief Justice," there was nothing new in Mansfield's position, for he was articulating the same constitutional doctrine of Parliamentary Supremacy in legislative matters that defined what could be called New Toryism.

Shortly after this interchange on the legality of the embargo, a Bill of Indemnity provided Mansfield with an opportunity to expand upon his position in detail. In Walpole's telling, "Lord Mansfield went through a laborious history of the constitution; and vindicated himself from the reproach of being a prerogative lawyer: had always been a friend of the constitution; on that ground had supported former administrations, did support this, and would support succeeding administrations."[5]

While all schools of thought maintained that it was the prerogative of the King alone to declare war, to appoint his executive officers, to pardon offenders, and always remained free from arrest for debt, Mansfield insisted that since the Glorious Revolution *it was no longer a royal prerogative to legislate in domestic or colonial affairs* precisely because legislative authority rested in Parliament. The Administration had acted illegally, according to Mansfield's understanding, because it had acted through the King-in-Council and bypassed Parliament altogether in a legislative matter.

These critical constitutional distinctions surfaced again in the 10 April 1767 Lords Debate on the Massachusetts Indemnity Act, a debate that focused upon "the Validity of such Part of an Act granting Compensation to the Sufferers, passed by the Governor, Council, and Assembly, of *Massachusetts Bay* ... as purports to be a free and general Pardon, Indemnity, and Oblivion, to the Offenders in the late Times" of the Stamp Act Crisis. Now according to the Lord Chief Justice this was exactly where the royal prerogative alone was operative—the colonial legislature was acting completely illegally in assuming this exclusively royal right. And all sides in this debate agreed that this part of the colonial Act was "null and void" because it violated "the inherent and inseparable Right of His Majesty's Crown alone to pardon Offenders."

The Duke of Bedford had posed this question because he thought it was "highly important at this Juncture to restrain the Authority of the said Governor, Council, and Assembly, within the Bounds of their Charter." That at least was the ostensible reason. The deeper reason was political, for Bedford clearly wanted to embarrass the ministry for not acting more expeditiously on the issue. Mansfield was the most impressive speaker to join in Bedford's attempt. According to Newcastle's report, "my Lord *Mansfield* spoke most astonishing well"; the diary of George Grenville's wife reads, "Lord *Mansfield* distinguished himself extremely"; Walpole added, "Lord *Mansfield* spoke finely for the motion."[6]

According to the report filed by Connecticut's Agent the ministry and its friends thoroughly agreed that the Massachusetts Indemnity Act was "wrong in its principle and very exceptionable in its form." While substance was not involved in this controversy, what the ministry found distasteful in the Opposition's motion was how it "would carry with it an implied censure upon the administration." It suggested that the ministry had been "inattentive to so important a subject, and so negligent of their duty as to demand *the interposition of Parliament*" (my emphasis). Positively put, the ministry maintained that the Massachusetts Indemnity Act would certainly be "disannulled by the King-in-Council, to whom in course of office it properly belonged to vacate any improper Act passed in the plantations." Mansfield, in any event, would have none of it. He "declared it as his opinion that there was no room to consult charters upon the subject, because this was a prerogative of the Crown, which the King could not grant away nor divest himself of, even by the most express words."

Although the Chatham Administration carried the vote 63 to 36, the issue did not go away. On 6 May 1767 the House of Lords revisited the issue on a motion by Lord Gower to have all the relevant papers to the Massachusetts Act laid before the House.[7] That motion was also defeated 52 to 43 (with the significant help of proxies), but Lord Gower persisted and on 22 May moved that the question "on the nullity or validity of the Massachusetts Act" be put to the judges, a motion strongly supported Mansfield. According to Walpole, "Lord *Mansfield*, to interpose solemnity, proposed, as his way was, that the judges should be consulted, and spoke with singular art and subtlety, disclaiming a spirit of opposition." Both Lord Chancellor Camden and Lord President Northington, however, treated him "most severely," Camden "taxing him directly with faction, and telling him the motion was complicated, involved, irregular, and yet betraying the marks of a lawyer."[8] And Mansfield lost 62 to 56.

Four days later Lord Gower again moved—after "the Opposition had brought down 9 new men"—to have the issue considered in committee. According to Walpole, "Lord *Denbigh* treated Lord Mansfield in still harsher terms than he had experienced the last day." The Duke of Bedford's *Journal* has a more detailed account of how the Earl of Denbigh addressed "himself in a very unbecoming manner, and personally to Lord Mansfield." After "averring a fact which his lordship absolutely denied, the Earl was again taken down to order" by Bedford himself. Many in the House "cried out Bar! Bar! intending to bring him there on his knees, to ask pardon of the

House." After Lord Denbigh asked "pardon in his place [Mansfield] with great candour, desired the affair might pass over, without having the Earl's words taken down by the clerk." But the motion was still defeated 65 to 62.[9]

One can only speculate on what decision Mansfield might have handed down in the Court of King's Bench had these motions not been repeatedly voted down. That the judges would have declared it unconstitutional is a given, for it was universally acknowledged that the Crown alone could exercise the right to pardon. What would have been up for action were *charter rights*. That is what Mansfield wanted to have clarified in an authoritative ruling. According to Walpole's *Memoirs*, "Lord *Mansfield* maintained that ... [the Massachusetts Act] ought to have been declared null *ab initio*; and demanded that the opinions of the judges might be taken." The preponderance of the evidence suggests that in Mansfield's reading of the Constitution of the British Empire, any colonial charter right would be null and void *ab initio* if or when it was found to be incompatible with the evolving British Constitution itself. He apparently wanted the judges to rule directly and unequivocally on that essential principle at the core of his reading of the doctrine of Parliamentary Supremacy.[10]

WHILE Mansfield and Camden were quarrelling over these rather abstract constitutional contentions, the Chatham Administration was fast falling into disarray because the ministry had been left with precious little guidance from the Earl of Chatham since the opening of 1767. Walpole's indictment of the Chatham Administration was this scathing: "Like oracles and groves whose sanctity depended on the fears of the devout, and whose mysterious and holy glory vanished as soon as men dared to think and walk through them, Lord Chatham's authority ceased with his popularity; and his godhead, when he had affronted his priests." For presumptive health reasons the Prime Minister had become "as inactive as the gods of Epicurus," and given this vacuum, "The Duke of Grafton was charmed to be idle; Conway was disgusted; Townshend delighted in the prospect of confusion."[11]

ACTIVE leadership within the Chatham Administration devolved upon the one person in the ministry who most thoroughly shared Lord Mansfield's understanding of the Constitution of the British Empire—the Chancellor of the Exchequer, Charles Townshend (1725-1767).[12] Regardless of whatever else might need to be said, his contemporaries thought he was a charmer with a gift for words as well as a taste for the high life. At a critical moment, for example, he returned to the House of Commons "about eight in the evening half drunk with champagne, and more intoxicated with spirit" to address the ministry's negotiations with the East India Company. Capturing "the amazing powers of his capacity, and the no less amazing incongruities of his character" tasked even Walpole's linguistic powers of expression.

Walpole's attempt reads: "before he sat down," after his off the cuff performance in the House of Commons, "he had poured forth such a torrent of wit, parts, humour, knowledge, absurdity, vanity and fiction, heightened by all the graces of comedy, the happiness of allusion and quotation, and the buffoonery of farce. To the purpose of the question he said not a syllable." Although people in a position to know realized full well that his denial of any involvement in the issue at hand was "absolutely false," his prevarications were but half his charm. Indeed, "The bacchanalian enthusiasm of Pindar flowed in torrents less rapid and less eloquent, and inspires less delight than Townshend's imagery, which conveyed meaning in every sentence." His champagne speech "excited such murmurs of wonder, admiration, applause, laughter, pity and scorn, that nothing was so true as the sentence with which he concluded, when speaking of government, he said, it was become what he himself had often been called, a weathercock."[13]

Townshend's legal education in the Netherlands had been limited to the Roman Civil Law Tradition. While a junior member of the Board of Trade he sent a 1753 circular letter to several colonial governors that, in Walpole's judgment, was "better calculated for the latitude of Mexico and for a Spanish tribunal, than for a free, rich British settlement." While on the Admiralty Board in 1754 he favored immediate taxation of the colonies. Before the Stamp Act he spoke openly in favor of a tax on the Americans. In the debate over the Stamp Act he "heard with great pleasure the right of taxing America asserted and not disputed." As the Paymaster General in the Rockingham Administration he even supported Northington's October 1765 motion to enforce the Stamp Act. Although he voted for the Repeal of the Stamp Act on expediential grounds, he made it abundantly clear that he championed the right of Parliament to tax the Americans in principle. The Ryder Diary contains this report on his mentality in the critical 17 January 1766 debate: *"Charles Townshend* well observed that we should not blend matters, but carefully distinguish between the repeal of the Stamp Act, the restrictions said to have been laid on American trade, and the right of the British Commons to lay an internal tax in America. For this last right he declared himself an advocate."[14] So far as the Chancellor of the Exchequer was concerned, the question in 1767 was not whether to tax the Americans but how.

From the moment Townshend joined the Chatham Administration, he was faced with the question of how to fund the Army in America, an expense that had been estimated in 1763 to be £225,000 per year. In January 1767 the Secretary at War raised that figure to £405,607. It was in this context that he informed the House of Commons that he "Much approved the general idea of taxing America" and even "pledged himself that something should be done this session [of Parliament] to give relief to Great Britain from bearing the whole of the expense of securing, defending and protecting America and the West India Islands."[15]

Townshend did not pretend that his plan would even begin to raise funds sufficient for the intended purpose—it would simply be a crucial first step toward forming "a revenue in time to bear the whole" expense. Although he did not explain how he would proceed in this matter of "Great delicacy," he did say that the given distinction between "internal taxation and external was *perfect nonsense.*"[16] On 18 February 1767 Townshend dropped a further hint on how he planned to begin paying for the British Army in North America.

According to the Ryder Diary, he "Spoke of the distinction between internal and external taxes as *not founded in reason but proper to be adopted in policy*" (my emphasis).[17] And given time it would become transparent what his fertile mind had hatched.

Since the Americans had said they were opposed to *internal taxes* but not to *external regulations*, he would accommodate their mindless distinction by foregoing *internal taxation* patterned on the Stamp Act. No, he would place the entire burden of raising revenue upon *external taxes* patterned on the traditional Navigation Acts that the Americans acknowledged to be within the jurisdiction of Parliament. What he apparently did not realize—or chose to glide over—was the fact that what had been considered *external* in the earlier debates over the Repeal of the Stamp Act were *regulations designed to control the colonial trade, not raise revenue.* If some little revenue was *incidentally* raised, that was perfectly acceptable to the Americans. Townshend's avowed intention dropped that *incidentally* so as to *raise revenue for the British Exchequer.*

Townshend had already settled upon his plan to tax the Americans long before 27 February when the ministry suffered an unexpected defeat of 206 to 188 on the British land tax, a defeat that reduced this crucial tax from 4 shillings on the pound to 3, thereby forfeiting a projected £500,000. Although Walpole was convinced that "the loss of the question of one shilling more on land hurried Townshend into new taxes on America," Peter D. G. Thomas explicitly denied Walpole's thesis in *The Townshend Duties Crisis*: "It is now apparent that there was no connection, as was long thought, between this event and Townshend's decision to tax America." The proof? On the most optimistic projections, Townshend's plan would not cover even a tenth of the forfeited revenue. Furthermore, Thomas correctly observed that his "aims were political rather than financial."[18] And his larger political objective still remained hidden from view.

One of the adroit things Townshend did was consult with the relevant players on the impact of particular custom duties without disclosing the full scope of his plan. For example, he floated with John Huske the idea of imposing "a duty of Six pense per Bushel upon Salt imported into America with a Bounty upon Fish and upon salt meat exported, in proportion to that Duty." After conferring with Benjamin Franklin, Huske informed Townshend that "a more fatal imposition to both Great Britain and her colonies could not be devised." So, salt was promptly dropped from the list. There were also extensive negotiations with the East India Company concerning tea. Accommodations were made. The possibility of direct trade between Portugal or Spain and America was actively considered. Although Franklin was eager to accept import duties on "Wine, Fruit and Oil from those Countries to America," he abandoned that option, too, because the British merchants objected to the loss of their monopoly. By the time he had finished the consultative process the Townshend Duties were projected to raise only £40,000 per year for the British Exchequer.[19]

In contrast to Grenville's unilateral approach in 1765, Townshend pieced together a considerable package by listening to the conflicting concerns and accommodating the various interests during the early months of 1767. What his plan failed to do, however, was transparent for all to see, especially Grenville—it would not even begin to cover the rising expenses of the British Army in America now projected to cost £570,000 per year. Townshend was much more interested in exercising the authority of Parliament to tax the colonies than in raising the maximum amount of money to cover the British Army. Indeed, covering the British Army was no longer even his primary end-in-view, as became clear when the Resolutions on New York were taken up in committee on 13 May 1767.[20]

Although many of the colonies had complied with their obligations for quartering the British Army (now being relocated from the distant frontier posts to the major cities) they had done so in such a way as to make it appear that the Act originated in their own Assemblies without acknowledging that it was in obedience to an Act of Parliament. But Townshend put their actions in the best possible light, pointing out, for example, "Pennsylvania and Connecticut had done meritoriously." New Jersey "had in part obeyed it but not completely"; nevertheless, its Governor had deemed that to be "sufficient."

What could not be allowed to stand was the response of New York, for it had "boldly and insolently bid defiance ... and threatened the whole legislative power of this country, obstinately, wickedly and almost traitorously in an absolute denial" of Parliament's authority. So egregious were New York's actions that "the present attention and interposition of Parliament" was called for in order to show "the Americans that this country would not tamely suffer her sovereignty to be wrested out of her hands." New York was singled out so as to "strike an awe into the factious and turbulent." To accomplish this objective he proposed "a law to prevent the Governor, Council or Assembly of New York from passing any Act till they had complied with the Act of Parliament." Walpole pointed out the obvious: "This step would in effect have been a dissolution of their government; and not less violent than the seizure of charters by Charles II" before the Glorious Revolution.

Townshend was convinced that the ongoing quarrel between Great Britain and her colonies "must soon come to an issue." Indeed, "the superiority of the mother country can at no time be better exerted than now." New York's rebellious actions presented a splendid occasion to respond to the larger situation confronting the imperial government. This was the immediate context in which he finally revealed the primary objective of his plan, namely, (1) to provide for "the judges and magistrates who are now in many colonies dependent every year for their salary or at least a part of it on the Assembly"; (2) to establish a "custom house" in North America; and (3) "to lay taxes upon America."

Although Townshend was not quite ready to disclose the full scope of his taxation plans—he was still negotiating the details—he wanted what he considered "external taxes" to be "moderate and prudent." Alas, anything like sufficient financing for the British Army simply disappeared from his view. According to the report Charles Garth sent to South Carolina, "out of the fund arising from the American duties now, or to be imposed, His Majesty should be enabled to establish salaries that might be better suited to support the dignity of the respective Officers, and for which to be no longer dependent upon the pleasure of any Assembly."[21] So, the Townshend Duties, in fact, were primarily designed *to liberate the colonial civil governments from their dependence upon the colonial assemblies.* An erratic weathercock though he might be, it simply remains the case that Charles Townshend had consistently pursued that institutional objective since he had been a Junior Member of the Board of Trade in 1753.

FROM a variety of points of view a series of attempts were made to have the resolutions of the committee recommitted when the House of Commons took them up two days later. Some wanted them to be recommitted "as not being well founded in fact, the disobedience of New York not being *direct,* as the resolution expresses it, but *constructive* only." George Grenville, from the opposite end of the spectrum, wanted "all American Governors and all members of either House of Assembly" to be "obliged to sign a declaration ... that the King, Lords and Commons in Parliament assembled have full power and authority to pass and enact laws whereby to bind the colonies in all cases whatsoever." But the decision to recommit failed 141 to 42.

It also did not go unnoticed that Rockingham's friends voted against Grenville's motion. They were for recommitting on a radically different principle. Their spokesman in Commons "lamented that whatever was proper to be done had come before Parliament, for *it ought to have been settled by the King and Council* with unanimity, firmness, secrecy and dispatch," but this motion was also rejected (my emphasis).

Perhaps the most extraordinary oration of the day was from someone who had extensive experience at the highest levels in colonial America, Thomas Pownall (1722-1805). From 1753 to 1760 he had served in British North America, first as a secretary to the Governor of New York, Sir Danvers Osborn, then as the Lieutenant Governor of New Jersey; in 1757 he was appointed the Royal Governor of Massachusetts, only to be transferred two years later to the governorship of South Carolina. From 1761 to 1763 he served as the director of supply for the British forces in Germany. His lived experience throughout the French and Indian War in America—and his critical position in the Seven Years War on the European Continent—informed his thoughtful treatise, *The Administration of the Colonies*, initially published in 1764. No member of the House of Commons could match Pownall's intimate knowledge of American affairs when he rose to speak for the first time in the House of Commons. (One suspects that he handed over a copy of his 15 May 1767 oration to be printed in the *Almon Debates*, which records 30 full paragraphs.)

Pownall began by saying that the "Act for punishing Mutiny and Desertion, and for the better Payment of the Army and their Quarters" was filled with "errors and defects" so grievous that it "perverted every means of carrying the measure into execution." The impracticality of the Act was explained: "It endeavours to lay down general rules, which can never be applied to numberless particular cases that must arise; and, under the spirit of impracticality, it allows no latitude in the execution thereof." But his critique cut much deeper than the sheer impracticality of the Act. He was convinced that it "has, from the tenor of it, been the natural occasion of all the confusion and misconduct which government now complains of" precisely because it was "so contrary and discordant to the constitution."

In the midst of a veritable cascade of rhetorical questions, Pownall called attention to the fact that "the people of the colonies, from one end of the continent to the other, do invariably consider the clause in the Act of Parliament, directing how that charge shall be supplied, as an *internal tax* imposed upon them" (my emphasis). Townshend's idea of making an example out of New York, furthermore, would not work:

> Those whom you are willing to understand as having obeyed your Act, have contrived to do it *in a mode* which neither recognized the Act of Parliament, nor submits to the taxation as such.

197

LORD CHIEF JUSTICE MANSFIELD: CHIEF AUTHOR OF THE AMERICAN REVOLUTION

And although you represent the Assembly of the province of *New York alone*, as having revolted against this power—believe me, there is not a province, a colony, or a plantation, that will submit to a tax thus imposed ..., not one single Assembly has or ever will, act under the powers and provisions of this Act, as acknowledging, and, in consequence thereof apportioning, assessing, and levying, the supply, as a tax imposed by Parliament. They have either acted without taking notice at all of this Act of Parliament, or have contrived some way or other to vary in some particulars, sufficient to make the execution of the tax an act of their own.

Pownall knew what he was talking about when he cautioned, "Don't fancy that you can divide the people upon this point, and that you need only divide to govern—you will by this conduct only unite them the more inseparably—you will make the cause of *New York* a common cause."

Whereas Townshend pretended that the American agitation was the work of just a few extremists and malcontents that needed to be disciplined, Pownall openly proclaimed that he was misinformed, for the American opposition to the Quartering Act was not the work of "party leaders and demagogues" or "speculative enthusiasts" or "the mere ebullition of a faction." No, the responses from the American colonies proceeded from "the cool, deliberate, principled maxim of every man in business in the country." And "the people of *America*, universally, unitedly, and unalterably, are resolved not to submit to any *internal tax* imposed upon them by any legislature, in which they have not a share by representatives of their own election" (my emphasis).

Pownall then lined out the American understanding of the proper mode for taxing the colonies: "They say, that supplies are *of good will*, and *not of duty*; are the *free and voluntary act of the giver*, having *a right to give*, not obligations and services to be complied with, which the subject cannot in right refuse—they therefore maintain, claim, and insist upon, that whatever is given out of the lands or property of the people of the colonies, should be given and granted *by their own act.*" That always had been the way taxes had been raised "before some *late innovations* in our system shook that basis." Simply put, Pownall did not share Townshend's understanding of *external taxes.* Notice how he uses the category in this sentence: "What remains, but that we act, as to *external taxes,* with that commercial spirit and prudence, which the wisdom of parliament hath always exercised towards the colonies, since their first establishment" (my emphases). In his universe of discourse *external taxes* denoted those *regulations of the colonial trade* for the benefit of the whole British Empire, regulations that the colonies acknowledged were under the control of Parliament. When colonial supplies were necessary, Pownall again evoked the Old Colonial System by stating directly that the colonies should be "properly applied to by requisitions in the old accustomed, known mode, which hath always succeeded and been found effectual."

Pownall was deeply concerned with the future of the British Empire. Indeed, from the time he published *The Administration of the Colonies* he was on record as a proponent of a transformed system that would unite the whole into a new governmental entity. Nevertheless, at this juncture "Matters are not yet gone far enough to point out the practicality and necessity of such political union." What he could not fathom in 1767 was why Townshend was pursuing a *"mode of policy"* that was "somewhat eccentric to the system of *our happy constitution*" (my emphases). So far as he could determine Townshend's line of reasoning ignored the fact that a colonial assembly was "a legislative, deliberative body," and treated it "merely as commissioners of taxes, appointed in such case to receive and register the Act, to apportion and assess the tax." Townshend's approach came "too near to the course taken by the arbitrary and despotic spirit of a neighbouring government" across the English Channel where the provincial parlements were not deliberative bodies at all.

Hardly anybody, however, was paying much attention to Pownall's critique or his proposals. That at least is all one can surmise from the fact that his name does not appear in the reports on this debate in either the Ryder or Harris Diaries. The summary statement ignores him altogether. The American agents Garth and Johnson did not find his 15 May oration worth mentioning. Supporting evidence for the lengthy Almon statement can be found only in West's letters to the Duke of Newcastle where one reads that Pownall "knew that from one end of America to the other every wise, honest, able man was from conscience and principle determined to resist every *Internal Tax* or attempt by Great Britain to lay it" (my emphasis).[22]

Although Townshend thought the distinction between *internal and external taxes* was utter nonsense, he sincerely believed his proposed duties fell on the *external* side because they were patterned upon the traditional regulations of the colonial trade. Pownall was not alone, however, in believing him wrong, for his distinction was consciously designed to raise money for the British Exchequer without the consent of the Americans. Given Townshend's misreading of the meaning of *external*—and many in Parliament shared this misreading—it is no wonder that the imperial government carelessly stumbled into a web of confusion.

BENJAMIN Franklin became aware of Townshend's novel political objective only a few weeks before it was announced in the House of Commons. On 11 April he reported, "a Project is on Foot, to render all the Governors and Magistrates in America independent of the annual Support they receive of their several Assemblies." The implication was spelled out in his 13 June 1767 letter to Speaker of the Pennsylvania Assembly: "It seems to me a very extraordinary Act, equally restrictive on the Prerogative of the Crown as on the Privileges of the People: For if the King should in some future War want Aids of those Provinces, he cannot obtain them, till the Act is repeal'd that forbids his acting in Legislation with them." Franklin was speaking for many Americans when he claimed—directly contrary to Townshend's understanding—that America's seventeenth-century charters were with the King alone. Parliament had nothing to do with their governmental polity whatsoever. Parliament's role was limited to the regulation of trade within the Empire.[23]

Regardless of what Benjamin Franklin said, at the opening the Townshend Duties Crisis, the doctrine of Parliamentary Supremacy over America was not under dispute within the British political nation.[24] Even Lord Chancellor Camden himself had surrendered his principled opposition. Because of his own reading of the Declaratory Act, he found himself incapable of acting on his prior opinion. In an earlier Lords Debate, Camden had openly stated that "perhaps this might be the last time when it would be lawful for him freely to deliver his sentiments" on the issue of colonial taxation, "since, when once the [Declaratory] Bill should have passed into a law, he should think himself obliged to acquiesce in the same manner as he should believe himself bound to draw his sword in his country's cause, even though the quarrel might appear to him unjust." And Camden was more than serious, too. For example, he "held stout language" against the Americans during the Lords Debate on 30 March 1767.[25]

Rockingham's report to his wife is instructive: "We had a curious day today in the House of Lords, mere conversation and mere taking opportunities of abusing Lord Chatham, Lord Camden and Administration." "The five Lords who were against this country's having the Right over North America last year were well dressed." Apparently Camden got dressed so well because he dropped his principled position altogether. Indeed, Lord Talbot observed "that he was not surprised to find Lord Camden's language so much altered, as it was a known maxim that new converts were always the most zealous."[26] Regardless of his earlier opinion, Lord Chancellor Camden found the Declaratory Act to be binding throughout the opening years of the Townshend Duties Crisis. Only later would he again reverse course.

Curiously, one finds in the memoirs of Sir George Colebrooke the claim that in 1767 Mansfield "had declared himself explicitly against the absurd and dangerous measure of imposing duties [on America], in which he was followed by three cabinet ministers."[27]

Colebrooke did not trouble to say who these three cabinet ministers were, but surely one was the Leader in the House of Commons, Henry Seymour Conway, who openly disagreed with Townshend's plans. Shelburne, it is reasonable to suppose, was the second. Perhaps the third was Grafton. The major thrust of Colebrooke's statement, however, concerns the judgment of the Lord Chief Justice of King's Bench. The issue deserves a careful review.

On the face of it, Colebrooke's claim would indicate that from the outset Mansfield saw that the duties were absurd because Townshend's approach violated commercial principles and, therefore, would hamper trade, but he also thought it was dangerous simply because it tacitly conceded that Parliament should not impose *internal taxes* upon the colonies, even though Townshend claimed he could not see the slightest difference in the distinction whatsoever. Once Townshend gave up on internal taxes, however, Mansfield believed the colonies would quickly advance to a denial of Parliament's jurisdiction over trade as well. Positively put, Mansfield's promotion of internal taxes rested upon this obvious principle—they cut to the heart of colonial life as such. Revenue should flow from whatever the colonies managed to do. In brief, he wanted a restoration of something like the Stamp Act whereby the Americans would be directly and unequivocally taxed.

It was late in the season and most members had already gone home by the time Townshend laid out his plan to impose duties on several items, such as paper, glass, lead paints, and especially tea. At the report stage, James West informed Newcastle, "there has nothing happened material in the House of Commons today." Then he added: "There were not above fifty members in the House at any one time."

Exactly what happened is impossible to reconstruct with any confidence, but Peter D. G. Thomas surely could not be far wrong when he writes: "That no Parliamentary opposition to the American Revenue Bill was voiced is virtually certain from the complete absence of any information on either debates or divisions in Commons or Lords." In any event, "The bill received the royal assent on 29 June. Never could a fateful measure have had a more quiet passage."[28]

LORD Mansfield had been in something of a foul mood at the time. His enduring hostility against the Chatham Administration was radically intensified by the unpleasant exchange he had with Lord Denbigh on 26 May in the controversy over the Massachusetts Indemnity Act and the rejection of his demand that the judges review the case. When the debate on the "Civil Government and Religious Establishment" of Quebec opened on 2 June (according to Walpole's narrative) "Lord Mansfield did not appear in the debate, so deeply had he felt his late treatment." The Duke of Newcastle informed him in a letter, "We were beat the other day, 61 to 73. The Court fetched up Lords who had scarce ever been in the House or had been absent many years."[29] The Lord Chief Justice of King's Bench was nursing more than his wounded pride as this session of Parliament came to so inauspicious a conclusion.

AS early as 8 August 1767 Benjamin Franklin wrote a long letter to Joseph Galloway describing the unfolding disarray plaguing the imperial government: "The Confusion among our Great Men still continues as great as ever, and a melancholy thing it is to consider, that instead of employing the present Leisure of Peace in such Measures as might extend our Commerce, pay off our Debts, secure Allies, and encrease the Strength and Ability of the Nation to support a future War, the whole Time seems wasted in Party Contentions about Power and Profit, in Court Intrigues and Cabals, and in abusing one another." Ominous party distinctions furthermore had now arisen, with those who "have shown a Disposition to favour us, being called by Way of Reproach *Americans*," while the "Adherents to Grenville and Bedford" are referred to as "Adversaries to America." And these adversaries "value themselves on being true to the Interest of Britain, and zealous for maintaining its Dignity and Sovereignty over the Colonies." Indeed, "Every Step is taken to render the Taxing of America a popular Measure." And the situation had grown so perilous that Franklin advised "that we should all do our Endeavours on both sides the Water, to lessen the present Unpopularity of the

American Cause" before the forthcoming General Election scheduled for early 1768.[30]

What added to the chaos was the sudden death of Charles Townshend on 4 September 1767. He had been the guiding light within the Chatham Administration. Now that burden was shifted to the lackluster Duke of Grafton. George III turned to Grafton to reorganize the ministry, primarily in Walpole's opinion, because the Duke was "a man totally unconnected, and detached from all factions, the favourite qualification in the present reign!" Because the office of the Chancellor of the Exchequer never lies empty, Lord Mansfield automatically filled the office. "As soon as [Townshend] was dead, Lord Mansfield owned that Townshend had assured him he would blow up the newly resettled administration," meaning, apparently, the transformation of the ministry the Duke of Grafton had been actively pursuing without success during the summer of 1767.[31]

WHILE the Chatham Administration was drifting about in late 1767, the Americans were getting organized, and some were in no mood to follow Benjamin Franklin's advice "to lessen the present Unpopularity of the American Cause." Beginning in late 1767 the weekly *Pennsylvania Chronicle and Universal Advertiser* began publishing the anonymous *Letters from a Farmer in Pennsylvania* written by John Dickinson.[32] Educated at the Middle Temple in London, he was one of the most influential constitutional lawyers to grace the American scene. His *Letters* published over the next twelve weeks were the most influential articulation of the American understanding of the Constitution of the British Empire during the later half of the 1760s. (The initial letter was predated "Nov. 5.*" to indicate "The day of King WILLIAM the Third's landing" in 1688.)

In these *Letters* Dickinson never mentioned Mansfield by name, but he clearly had the Lord Chief Justice clearly in mind when he made this observation in Letter X: "If the late act of parliament takes effect, these colonies must dwindle down into 'COMMON CORPORATIONS,' as their enemies, in the debates concerning the repeal of the *Stamp Act, strenuously insisted they were*." Mansfield was publicly known to be the most prominent of these enemies because he openly advanced the opinion that the colonies should be considered as joint-stock trading corporations, not separate governments.[33] While Dickinson rejected that opinion, he readily acknowledged that Parliament "unquestionably possesses a legal authority to *regulate* the trade of *Great Britain*, and all her colonies." Indeed, he spoke for most Americans when he announced in Letter II, "there must exist a power somewhere, to preside, and preserve the connection" between the colonies and the mother country. Needless to say, "This power is lodged in the Parliament."

Having established the constitutional point that Parliament alone was in a position to regulate the imperial trade, Dickinson laid out in learned detail the documentary evidence that all acts prior to 1763 were "calculated to regulate trade, and preserve or promote a mutually beneficial intercourse between the several constituent parts of the empire." Traditionally, the end-in-view had been "to promote the general welfare" of the British Empire as a whole. The corollary was explicitly spelled out: "Never did the *British* parliament ... think of imposing duties in *America* FOR THE PURPOSE OF RAISING A REVENUE"—until the novel imperial policy was put into motion by Prime Minister George Grenville.[34]

Structurally, Dickinson distinguished between (1) regulations of trade and (2) taxes to raise revenue, regardless of whether they are collected in Great Britain or in America. And he correctly pointed out that the sixth declaration of the Stamp Act Congress rejected "ALL" taxes, adding: "Here is no distinction made between *internal* and *external* taxes."[35] The upshot? While Parliament did have the right to regulate the colonial trade for the general good of the Empire as a whole, the authority to levy any type of tax upon the Americans was exclusively within the purview of the various colonial governments.

Dickinson was not content with simply lining out the historical evidence that documented that the parliamentary laws had been designed to regulate trade and not raise revenue for the British Exchequer. He pressed on to argue in Letter III: "If at length it becomes UNDOUBTED that an inveterate resolution is formed to annihilate the liberties of the governed, the *English* history affords frequent examples of resistance by force." Within moments he referred to the violent resistance that so troubled "the reigns of the *Stuarts*" during the seventeenth century.[36]

In his *Letters from a Farmer in Pennsylvania*, John Dickinson repeatedly cited evidence from the seventeenth century. For example, "It is a worthy observation how quietly subsidies, granted in forms *usual* and *accustomable* (though heavy) are borne; such a power hath use and custom. On the other side, what discontentments and disturbances subsidies *framed in a new mold* do raise (SUCH AN INBRED HATRED NOVELTY DOTH HATCH) is evident by examples of former times." Just as the early Stuarts had introduced innovations that resulted in resistance and civil discord, so George Grenville and now Charles Townshend had embraced "a most dangerous innovation."[37]

While some would argue that the new duties were "so *small*" that they should not be resisted, Dickinson was convinced that "the authors of this law would never have obtained an act to raise so trifling a sum as it must do had they not intended by *it* to establish a *precedent* for future use." Not the price but the principle was what should matter to "A FREE PEOPLE." The Townshend Duties were "*expressly laid* FOR THE SOLE PURPOSE OF TAKING MONEY." With rising anger he laid out the American position: "This money is to be taken from *us*. *We* are therefore taxed. *Those* who are *taxed* without their own consent, expressed by themselves or their representatives, are *slaves*. *We are taxed* without our consent, expressed by ourselves or our representatives. *We* are therefore—SLAVES." Before he laid down his pen, Dickinson reminded his fellow Americans of a pregnant quotation from Montesquieu's *Spirit of the Laws*: "SLAVERY IS EVER PRECEDED BY SLEEP."[38]

In Dickinson's understanding of the Constitution of the British Empire, Parliament held supremacy over the trade policies of the whole system, but it had no jurisdiction over the internal affairs of the colonies, and it could not lawfully levy taxes of any kind on the Americans. In brief, he wanted to preserve the Old Colonial System prior to 1763.

REALIZING the need for more support, the Duke of Grafton had opened negotiations with the Rockingham party during the summer of 1767, but this gambit showed no promise of success. So, on 24 November 1767 he reached out to the Bedfords. As a lure he dropped the hint that he anticipated the resignation of Lord Shelburne as the Secretary of State for the Southern Department, which had oversight of the American colonies. And the Bedfords were also left with the understanding that Henry Seymour Conway would surrender the seals of the Secretary of State for the Northern Department as well.

Lord Mansfield was not a passive observer of these negotiations. According to Walpole's *Memoirs*, "Many persons ascribed the suggestion of the treaty [with the Bedfords] to Lord Mansfield, and to his weariness of opposition, which was not his turn, and in which his aversion to Lord Chatham had solely embarked him." He even "wished to obtain a seat among the sixteen Scotch peers in the new Parliament for his nephew, Lord Stormont." As events turned out, by reaching out to the Bedfords, Grafton would "give the finishing blow to Lord Chatham's Administration."[39]

THE GRAFTON
ADMINISTRATION

BY THE OPENING OF 1768 A TRANSFORMED MINISTRY HAD TAKEN SHAPE UNDER THE guidance of the Duke of Grafton. While it took time for him to solidify the new regime, it would seem fair to say that this in effect was the beginning of the Grafton Administration. The Duke of Grafton retained powerful persons selected by the Earl of Chatham. The Chathamites included the Duke of Grafton himself, Lord Chancellor Camden, Lord Shelburne, Sir Edward Hawke at the Admiralty, and Lord Granby of the Army. Henry Seymour Conway of the Rockingham party remained in the Cabinet as a minister without portfolio. Prominent in the Cabinet, however, were what Benjamin Franklin called "Adversaries to America." The Bedfordite, Lord Gower, became the Lord President of the Council, replacing Lord Northington. Another Bedfordite, Lord Weymouth, replaced Henry Seymour Conway as the Secretary of State for the Northern Department. Lord Hillsborough, who had been President of the Board of Trade during the Grenville Administration, was appointed to the new office of Secretary of State for America. And the Chancellor of the Exchequer, Lord North, replaced Conway as the Leader of the House of Commons. Gower,

Weymouth, Hillsborough and North all shared Lord Chief Justice Mansfield's maximal understanding of Parliamentary Supremacy. Given the conflicted composition of the ministry, it should not come as a surprise to discover, in the words of Peter D. G. Thomas, that from the outset the new regime was divided on "whether to adopt coercive or conciliatory measures" in response to the growing American opposition to the Townshend Duties.[1]

Before this resettled and split ministry had time to get up and running, it had to prepare for the General Election of March 1768. And what made the task all the harder was the return from exile in France of the notorious outlaw, John Wilkes. Although the Stamp Act Crisis and the opening of the Townshend Duties Crisis had passed without this professional agitator, even before his return to London he was a valiant defender of English Liberties in the eyes of many on both sides of the Atlantic. Needless to say, not many weeks would pass before the person Mansfield had declared an outlaw in 1764 would become a major distraction for the Grafton Administration in general and the Lord Chief Justice of King's Bench in particular.

On 4 March 1768 Wilkes directly petitioned George III for a pardon. Receiving no reply, the moment Parliament was dissolved he dropped his disguise—for over a month he had lived clandestinely in London under the name of "Osborn"—and announced that he was standing for one of the four seats in the House of Commons held by the City of London. Of the seven candidates running for these four seats, Wilkes came in dead last. This miserable showing on 23 March, however, did not discourage him in the least, for he blamed his poor showing on his late entry. He then turned around and immediately announced that he was standing for "the county of Middlesex," which had two seats. That election was scheduled for 28 March—and Wilkes won quite handsomely through careful organization, clever propaganda, and outright intimidation of his opponents. Because he ran as the champion of the "civil and religious rights" of his constituents, the libertine became (in Walpole's ironic reading) "the new Defender of the Faith."[2]

The ministry was shocked. Even Lord Chancellor Camden was appalled: "A criminal flying his country to escape justice—a convict and an outlaw—that such a person should in open daylight thrust himself on the country as a candidate, his crime unexpiated, is audacious beyond description." After more than a little prodding by George III, the ministry decided that the newly elected MP for Middlesex was not fit to participate in Parliament. To complicate matters even further, our audacious convict and outrageous outlaw—and now elected MP for the county of Middlesex—announced that he would surrender himself to the Court of King's Bench on 20 April.[3] Mansfield, however, was none too eager to see Wilkes in his court again. If Walpole's *Memoirs* can be credited, "Lord Mansfield, equally revengeful, timorous and subtle, pretended that it was the office of the Chancellor to bring this outlaw to justice." But neither Camden nor Grafton was willing "to increase their unpopularity by adding persecution to the complaints Wilkes had already made of their giving him up." Only then did Walpole add this acid comment: "Still less was Lord Camden solicitous to save Lord Mansfield from danger and odium." Although "Lord Mansfield tried every subterfuge of the law, not so much to crush Wilkes as to shift the odium of the prosecution on any other shoulders," he could not escape having to deal with the consequences of his own ruling four years earlier. He alone had declared Wilkes an outlaw, and he alone was in a position to resolve the issue.

At the hearing on 20 April Wilkes requested bail, while the Attorney General demanded his commitment in prison awaiting trial. The Lord Chief Justice, however, confounded everybody by declaring that Wilkes was free to go on his own recognizance without bail precisely because he had appeared on his own volition without any legal process—and had no legal standing! Technically, our Scottish Law Lord ruled that the Attorney General was at fault because he should have had Wilkes arrested on a warrant of *capias ut legatum* the moment he had arrived in England.[4] Such a warrant was issued the next day, but for a week Wilkes remained free—because he had departed from the county and this type of warrant was valid in Middlesex alone! On 27 April—after notifying the ministry of his decision—Wilkes surrendered himself again to the tender mercies of Lord Mansfield. This time the Chief Justice ruled that Wilkes could appeal his outlawry, but to prison he must go awaiting formal sentencing on account of his having been found guilty in 1764 for republishing *North Briton, Number Forty-Five* and *Essay on Woman*.

The London mob, however, had other plans for the day. As the coach carrying their hero crossed Westminster Bridge, a crowd of men intercepted it. The three officers taking him to the King's Bench Prison were urged by Wilkes to flee for their lives, sound advice they willingly took, after he promised to turn himself in at the first opportunity. The mob removed the horses and pulled the carriage in triumph to Three Tuns Tavern in Spitalfields. After much drinking the party dissipated to such an extent that Wilkes somehow managed to slip away in disguise and make his own way to King's Bench Prison, much to the amusement of the public and the embarrassment of the government.[5]

Crowds immediately began forming in St. George's Fields to show their support as Wilkes saluted them from his prison window. When the new Parliament met two weeks later, an enormous crowd—estimated to be somewhere between 15,000 and 40,000—shouted defiance: "Wilkes and Liberty! No Liberty, No King! Damn the King! Damn the Government! Damn the Justices!" The protest intensified to the point that open hostilities soon broke out. The Scottish infantry regiment on duty that day fired their weapons and killed seven "martyrs" in what became known as "the Massacre of St. George's Fields" on 10 May 1768.

As rumors spread, riots broke out within greater London. The next day a massive mob appeared before Parliament. According to Walpole's *Memoirs*, "Lord Mansfield sitting by the Duke of Bedford in the House of Lords, said, if something vigorous was not done immediately, there would be a revolution in ten days and the government overturned—yet when a motion was made against the riot, that dastardly magistrate sat still and did not utter a syllable!" The agitation continued for days, leading Newcastle to comment to

Rockingham, "we must be either governed by a mad, lawless Mob, or the peace be preserved only by a military force; both of which are unknown to our constitution."[6]

With the populace so worked up, Mansfield knew that he was in a rather delicate situation. Before he ruled on whether Wilkes was still an outlaw, he prepared a speech in which he acknowledged that his life was in eminent danger "but he was past sixty, and valued not the remnant of being." He would stand firm at all costs. "He would act boldly; *fiat justitia, et ruat coelum.*" After this brave front, Mansfield proceeded to dutifully reject all the arguments advanced by the lawyers and ruled that Wilkes's outlawry was void because of a *flaw* in the original writ. The reader might need to read Walpole's exposition of this farcical show rather slowly several times to detect the flaw: "This curious error was, that the proceedings were stated *at the county court for the county of Middlesex*, when lo! the form ought to have been *at the county court of Middlesex for the county of Middlesex*—a form of words, said that oracle of law, absolutely necessary." Yes, because of this technical error in the original warrant, Wilkes was deemed no longer an outlaw! But because he remained a convicted felon, to King's Bench Prison he must go awaiting formal sentencing.[7]

Sir Joseph Yates was handed the honor of lecturing the convict upon the enormity of his crimes. As Yates was "animadverting upon the nature of his crimes," Wilkes "affected ease and indifference by picking his teeth and talking to those near him." The judge then sentenced him to 10 more months for republishing *North Briton, Number Forty-Five*, plus 12 months for his *Essay on Woman*, with fines of £500 for each performance.

A few days before our notorious prisoner was sentenced to another twenty-two months in prison, Walpole was moved to confess: "it is most indifferent to me who is in or who is out, nor which is set in the pillory, Mr Wilkes or my Lord Mansfield. I see the country going to ruin, and no man with brains enough to save it." But he was surprised when the sentence lacked its usual severity: "the pillory was for the first time omitted in a case of libel and blasphemy," even though in the blasphemy case a few years earlier, "Lord Mansfield had willingly executed the inquisitorial power."[8] Walpole's depression was intensified by the way the ministry was responding to the protests that for months had been pouring in from across the Atlantic.

THE anonymous *Letters from a Farmer in Pennsylvania* arrived in London about the time John Wilkes exploded upon the political scene. Then the ministry received a copy of the Massachusetts Circular Letter that Samuel Adams and James Otis, Jr. had persuaded the Assembly to adopt in a thin house on 11 February. While it acknowledged that Parliament was "*the supreme legislative power over the whole empire,*" that supremacy was limited to the governance of the acts of trade (my emphasis). Because the Townshend Duties sought to raise revenue, the Massachusetts Assembly thought these duties were taxes and, therefore, ought to be repealed because they were unconstitutional. In brief, the Massachusetts Assembly lined up solidly behind Dickinson's traditional understanding of the Constitution of the British Empire.[9]

Not many days passed before the Secretary of State for America, Lord Hillsborough, brought this constitutional challenge before the Cabinet and was authorized to address it explicitly. In his circular letter to all the colonial governors, the American Secretary denounced the Massachusetts Circular Letter for its "open opposition to and denial of the authority of Parliament." The instructions were severe—if any of the lower houses attempted to follow the example of Massachusetts, the governors were to prorogue them. But before Hillsborough's instructions reached America, a furious round of violence had been set off in Boston when the custom officials impounded John Hancock's sloop appropriately named *Liberty*. When Governor Bernard attempted to carry out Hillsborough's demand that the Assembly rescind the Massachusetts Circular Letter, the motion was rejected 92 to 17.

Because it took weeks for communications to cross the Atlantic, Hillsborough did not realize the extent of the opposition to the

Duties in general, or the disorder pulsating through Massachusetts in particular, when on 8 June he ordered the Commander-in-Chief of the British Army in America, General Thomas Gage, to move troops to Boston "to be quartered in that town, and to give every legal assistance to the civil magistrate in the preservation of the public peace." The Admiralty was also instructed to intensify its patrol of the Boston harbor. Scarcely a month had passed since the St. George's Field Massacre, and the very day Lord Mansfield reversed Wilkes's outlawry.

While the Grafton Administration feared that this action could result in an armed confrontation, to its transparent relief Boston sullenly but quietly witnessed the arrival without incident of two regiments of Red Coats—derisively called "Lobsterbacks"—on 1 October 1768. That date decisively marks the commencement of the occupation of Boston by a standing army without the consent of the elected representatives of the people of Massachusetts.[10]

WITHIN a matter of weeks, the Earl of Chatham formally resigned, thereby officially ending the Chatham Administration. Lord Shelburne followed Chatham, thereby opening his position as the Secretary for the Southern Department to Weymouth, thereby opening his position as the Northern Secretary to Rochford. Although the Duke of Grafton was now officially designated the Prime Minister, he had actually functioned as such at least since the Bedfordites and Hillsborough joined the ministry.[11] The other moderates, moreover, remained in place. Therefore, the ministry remained split over how to address the growing problem with America because of the Townshend Duties. Lord Chancellor Camden felt particularly vexed by the unfolding situation because he had fallen into a conceptual quandary after he abandoned his principled stance against taxing the Americans and embraced the Declaratory Act. In a 4 October letter he informed Grafton, "the issue is now joined upon the right, which in my apprehension, is the most untoward ground of dispute that could have been started, fatal to Great Britain, if she miscarries; unprofitable if she succeeds." In despair he concluded, "I do not know what is best to advise."[12]

American challenges to the Townshend Duties put the ministry in a rather acute bind, for (1) it was transparently the case that the plan was a complete bust in terms of raising more than a trifling amount of money for the British Exchequer, but (2) the ministry could not even consider altering the 1767 Act without appearing to compromise the supremacy of Parliament by backing down under pressure. In this rather awkward situation, the decision was made to talk tough for now and then adopt conciliatory measures when things settled down to such an extent that a sensible retreat could be made without loss of dignity. According to the detailed analysis of this two-stage policy by Peter D. G. Thomas, this amounted to "the application of the big stick before the offer of the olive branch."[13]

The big stick was prominently exhibited when Parliament opened on 8 November 1768: "we shall always consider it as one of our most important Duties, to maintain entire and inviolate, *the Supreme Authority of the Legislature of Great Britain over every Part of the British Empire*" (my emphasis). In seconding the Address, Hans Stanley acknowledged, "There never was a more delicate crisis, nor a time in which our first steps may be more decisive." But he welcomed the fact that "we have put the obedience of the Americans to the test," for he did not entertain the slightest doubt "that the colonies, and plantations are, and of right ought to be dependent upon the Crown of Great Britain."

For the first time since the passage of the Townshend Duties Act the House of Commons engaged in a full-scale debate over colonial policy. William Dowdeswell, speaking for the Rockingham party, argued that while Parliament did have the right to tax the colonies, it should not exercise so unprecedented a right. He even questioned the wisdom of Hillsborough's demand that the Massachusetts Circular Letter be rescinded, stating that it had not been illegal, and insisting that Parliament should have been consulted on such important policies as closing down colonial assemblies if they did not comply.

More dramatically, his fellow Rockinghamite, Edmund Burke, did not attempt to hide his profound astonishment over the fact that "Two of the greatest authorities: the one a stateman [i.e., Lord Chatham], the other a lawyer [i.e., Lord Chancellor Camden] ... pleaded the cause of the Americans [during the Stamp Act Crisis], but they have changed their opinions." He then pressed the point: "When the Stamp Act was repealed [in 1766] there was peace in America, and trade flowed in its usual channels. The very next year, such was the fashion of throwing our own burdens upon the shoulders of others, we began to hanker after an American revenue." Incomprehensibly, these two authorities had permitted Charles Townshend—"A person of the first abilities, of ten thousand talents"—to shepherd the 1767 Act through Parliament on their watch. Burke shared with numerous others members this overarching belief: "Nothing can tend to estrange America more from us than an opinion, that there is no person in Great Britain steady." So radical a reversal by two such prominent but unsteady leaders "must throw America into despair."

Without entering into the question of right, Alderman Beckford was for repealing the Townshend Duties precisely because they violated commercial principles. After openly saying that "taxing America for the sake of raising a revenue would never do," he passionately asked, "Why would you stir those waters? Let the Nation return to its old good nature, and its old good humour."

Colonel Barré, the spokesman for Lord Shelburne, took a more principled stand: "It is time to hold one doctrine. You have no right to tax the Americans." And he pressed the point that if "you wish to have their money," the way to proceed would be through requisitions by the Crown. While that cryptically but fairly represented the American understanding of the Constitution of the British Empire, Barré entertained no illusions about the impact his argument would make on the House of Commons.

George Grenville was perplexed but still disagreed. As the proud author of the Stamp Act, he opposed any concessions of Parliament's authority in principle. He was also suspicious of the ministry's policy of talking tough while hinting at future conciliation. An accommodation on expedient grounds, as Beckford maintained, would only encourage the Americans to go even further and challenge the laws of trade. And he even called the *Farmer's Letters* "libelous throughout," directly dismissing John Dickinson's understanding of the Old Colonial System by claiming, "There were laws for raising a revenue before the Stamp Act." (Grenville left many confused by his convoluted performance.)

As the Leader in the House of Commons, Lord North articulated the tough stance of the first stage of the policy, which called for a return to obedience by Massachusetts before any concessions would be even entertained. According to the Cavendish Diary, North declared, "I am against repealing the last Act of parliament [i.e., the 1767 Townshend Duties]. There has been no proof of any return of friendship. In America they will give you no credit for affection, no credit for commercial interest. Taxation, and regulation. If America is to be the judge, you may tax in no instance, you may regulate in no instance." In response to Alderman Beckford's proposal to "conciliate the colonies by moderation and kindness," North responded, "he would never think of repealing [the Townshend Duties] *until he saw America prostrate at his feet.*"[14]

SOON the ministry wanted a formal rejection of the votes of the Massachusetts Assembly, plus a condemnation of Boston's riots over the impoundment of John Hancock's *Liberty*. To put some teeth into these pronouncements, the ministry adopted Hillsborough's idea of having those Americans responsible for the riots arrested and tried for treason, according to a statute in effect since the reign of Henry VIII. Nothing of consequence, however, was in the offing, as became transparent as soon as Hillsborough addressed the colonial agents on 6 December. After saying that "the authority of the legislature of Great Britain" would be enforced, he proceeded to add this qualification: "with all the moderation and lenity that the nature of the thing would admit of." And then he openly confessed that the ministry "had no particular fondness" for those Townshend Duties. Indeed, "the late Duty Act is so anti-commercial that he wished it had never existed, and it would certainly have been repealed had the colonies said nothing about it."[15]

Simply put, Hillsborough maintained that the Americans were to blame for the Grafton Administration's refusal to forthrightly repeal the Townshend Duties, because the colonies should have pointed out the *anti-commercial* nature of the Act instead of openly challenging its *constitutionality*. If the Americans would only see that it was in their interest to keep quiet long enough to satisfy British sensitivities, then the ministry would graciously repeal the Duties on the grounds that they were inexpedient. The message—on commercial principles Parliament was eager to deal; on constitutional principles Parliament would never yield.

As North would insist the next day in the House of Commons, "Parliament themselves are the only persons to judge of the propriety of their measures." The Americans were simply wrong, and their error was grounded in "the false apprehensions of their rights." In his vision, the British Empire was "united into one Government full of men, full of money." After reducing the Constitution of the British Empire to the Constitution of Great Britain, North informed the House of Commons, "I think no line can ever be drawn; you must possess the whole of your authority, or none." In terms of Parliament's right, it was everything or nothing. Sovereignty was indivisible.[16]

Lord Hillsborough rolled out the Grafton Administration's colonial policy on 15 December 1768.[17] According to Agent Johnson's report to Connecticut, he "opened the subject with a very long speech," but in his rehearsal of the last few years, he candidly admitted that "he thought the Stamp Act was inexpedient, had advised against it when first proposed, and voted for its repeal upon that principle, as he believed almost everybody else had done." Nevertheless, it simply was the case that "nothing was more clear than the right of Parliament to tax the colonies." He then labored the point that the Townshend Duties were projected to bring in very little revenue, say, somewhere between £8,000 and £10,000 per annum.[18]

Hillsborough noted that "the amount of the duties" was not a problem, for the Americans centered their objections squarely on "the principle" involved. They refused to acknowledge "the supremacy and legislative authority of Parliament." Because he agreed thoroughly with Mansfield's claim that "legislation and taxation were essentially connected, and would stand and fall together," he was persuaded that the "notions the Americans entertained" were not only "the most absurd that could be imagined," they were based upon what he called "*a polytheism in politics*" (my emphasis). Because America's polytheistic faith had divided loyalty among so many different assemblies, those minor deities would be "fatal to the constitution, and must never be admitted here." In his political theology, the legislative supremacy of Parliament over the whole was "a principle essential to the existence of the empire." His creed? Within the British Empire there was only one god, and Parliament was his prophet.

Hillsborough had hoped that the Repeal of the Stamp Act "would have established the right, at the same time that it gave peace to both countries." Although he soon discovered that his fond hope had been in vain, he still thought that the Americans might come to "see their error and quietly submit" to Parliament's authority. If yes, "it would be right to give them every relief and encouragement that they could reasonably desire." If no, then it followed necessarily that this ultimate either/or would have to be faced: "Parliament must now give up its authority over the colonies, or they be brought to effectual submission to its laws." Giving up was nothing more than a rhetorical option; therefore, "he thought their Lordships would see it absolutely necessary to stand firm, and not recede an ace." The House of Lords stood firm and without a division forwarded the Resolutions and the Address to the House of Commons.[19]

SO that it could engage in an extensive debate on the Resolutions and Address passed by the House of Lords, the House of Commons resolved itself into the Committee on America. The Solicitor General, John Dunning, laid out the legal situation, as the Grafton Administration understood it. While the Stamp Act and the Declaratory Act were under consideration in 1766, "it was the duty of every man to declare an opinion" on whether Parliament had the right to tax America. After that question had been decided affirmatively, what once had been an "innocent" opinion now became "criminal." There could be no going back, for "no good can result by keeping alive the memory" of that prior debate. Parliament had spoken.

As would be expected, George Grenville took the ministry to task for not having any real plan of action. All this tough talk was nothing but "waste paper" he thought. "In truth you don't mean to send for anybody" to be tried here in England. "This way we hold out angry words on the one hand, and give no remedy on the other." What the ministry was proposing was "a sort of wisdom which fools put on, and think are wondrous wise." The only way to cut through the ambivalence was to be steady and enforce the Townshend Duties, inadequate though the plan most certainly had proven to be.

Colonel Isaac Barré spoke from the opposite end of the spectrum of opinion. After noting that "every man in this House allows [the Townshend Duties] to be contrary to all commercial principles," he proceeded to his real message derived from his extensive knowledge of America: "My opinion from all I have heard, from all I have seen is, that they will not submit to any law imposed upon them for the purpose of revenue." If Parliament persisted in "imposing a tax upon" the colonies, the House should understand, "you must enforce it by arms." But Barré was not through. In agent Johnson's report to Connecticut, one finds this extensive passage in quotation marks, plus brackets:

> Before I sit down I cannot forbear a word upon what fell upon another occasion [meaning the first day of the session] from a noble lord over against me [pointing to Lord North], who said, if I did not mistake him, that he would listen to no propositions for repealing the offensive acts until he saw American prostate at your feet! I have, upon a

former occasion, told you my opinion, that it is not
so easy, as some imagine, to effect it. The Americans
are a numerous, a respectable, a hardy, a free people.

America would not give up without a fight, or so Barré thought, but
war would be devastating: "America thus humbled, ruined, undone"
would "serve only as a monument equally of your vengeance and of
your folly, and would remain your everlasting reproach." He then
laid out his own vision:

> For my part, the America I wish to see is America
> increasing, flourishing, prosperous, rising in
> graceful dignity, and with becoming freedom and
> firmness asserting at your Bar her rights, supporting
> upon all proper occasions her own importance,
> and vindicating her and your liberties. This is the
> America I wish to see—that every friend to his
> country should wish to see. This is the America
> that will be able to fight your battles with you and
> for you, to sustain and strengthen you when perhaps
> hard pushed by some proud prevailing foreign foe;
> and by her industry and increase to consume your
> manufactures, support your trade, and pour wealth
> and splendor into your towns and cities.

The Cavendish Diary has Barré concluding, "I say without repealing
this law, you run the risk of losing America."[20] The House Committee
on America, however, was not moved by Barré's vision. Tough talk,
coupled with postponing action, plus hints of accommodation upon
good behavior, was the winning ticket. When votes were counted,
the Administration prevailed 213 to 80 on the Resolutions and 155
to 89 on the Address.[21]

SO long as the Duke of Grafton remained Prime Minister, John
Wilkes remained locked up in King's Bench Prison, and on balance
it would seem that Wilkes had a much better time of it in prison than

Grafton did in politics. Our inmate's confinement was anything but dull. He apparently lived a rather charmed life, for he had lots of good food and drink, a steady stream of visitors of the highest quality, even Americans, and frequent visits of a more intimate kind with a former lover now unhappily married to one of his devoted followers. When her naïve husband brought her along on a visit to show his undying support, Wilkes passed her a little love note and she embraced the opportunity with gusto over the coming months. While enjoying his enforced leisure in the comfortable quarters of prison, Wilkes had plenty of time to make life miserable for the ministry.[22]

Shortly after Parliament opened in November 1768 Sir Joseph Mawbey presented Wilkes's petition that directly charged that Lord Chief Justice Mansfield had altered some legal records before his trial *in absentia* on 21 February 1764. Arthur H. Cash's exposition of Mansfield's alteration shows how the legal system can turn upon rather technical points:

> The day before the trials, at eight o'clock in the morning, Lord Mansfield summoned to his house in Bloomsbury Square the clerks of the court and the lawyers for the defense and announced that he intended to alter the informations (indictments), changing the phrase "purport and effect" to "tenor and effect." Francis Barlow and William Hughes of the Crown Office said they "could not consent," but Mansfield replied that he did not ask for consent, but for objections. He then cited a long list of precedents and proceeded to change the words.

Whereas *purport* "included the idea of the writer's intention," *tenor* omitted any suggestion of something so subjective and focused on what actually transpired, thereby significantly lowering the burden of proof.[23]

The relevant papers from the 1764 trial were brought forward on 23 November. Because so many witnesses would have to be called—the list continued to expand until it grew to over forty—the hearing on Wilkes's petition was postponed. In the meantime, the Grafton Administration thought it could easily pick up another seat in the House of Commons. Two seats had been up for action in the recent Middlesex Election. While John Wilkes had won one seat and George Cooke had won the other, unfortunately Cooke soon died. The ministry wanted that second seat for Sir William Beauchamp Proctor, the MP who had been forced out by Wilkes's victory. Locked away in King's Bench Prison, our inmate had a different idea. He persuaded the lawyer who had defended him before the Lord Chief Justice to run against Proctor. Everybody knew that John Glynn was a stand-in for John Wilkes.[24]

Arthur H. Cash's version of this by-election—coupled with a print of the action on this day—captures the turbulent nature of eighteenth-century voting practices:

> Polling began on 8 December 1768 at Brentford. Proctor ... showed the true color of a ministerial candidate: he purchased the services of a notorious organizer of mobs-for-hire, Edward MacQuirk, called "the Infant" because of his enormous size. At the head of a crowd of Irish chairmen armed with clubs, MacQuick made a vicious attack upon the voters and even mounted the hustings wielding his club. A lawyer named George Clarke was clubbed to death. The sheriffs closed the polls and declared the election void.

Of the thirty-three poll books, eight also had gone missing. Only after these eight books could be found would the poll reopen, as it did on 14 December. And John Glynn defeated the ministerial candidate, thereby exhibiting the power that John Wilkes exercised over the populace of Greater London.[25]

In the midst of this combustible mix, Wilkes got tired of waiting for the Administration to take up his complaint against

Lord Mansfield. With malice aforethought he set things on fire by writing a "Preface" to Secretary of State Weymouth's letter, one that alerted the neighboring counties that further military support might be needed to keep order when Wilkes had been sent to prison. On 10 December the *St. James's Chronicle* published this Preface that pointedly stated that Weymouth's letter documented "how long the horrid massacre in St. George's Fields had been planned ... and how long a hellish project can be brooded over by some infernal spirits without one moment's remorse."

Early in January the City of London elected John Wilkes to be the Alderman for the Ward of Farringdon Without, only to have the election overturned by the Court of Aldermen. After he won a second election, five of eight on the Court of Aldermen ruled in his favor, even though he was still "a criminal of State and a prisoner."[26]

Wilkes did not fare so well, however, with the Grafton Administration, even though it was split on whether there were sufficient grounds to keep the duly elected MP for Middlesex from taking his seat in Parliament. The moderates in the council—Lord Chancellor Camden, Sir Edward Hawke at the Admiralty, Lord Granby of the Army, and Henry Seymour Conway without portfolio—were opposed to the expulsion of Wilkes on *political grounds*. As Camden informed Grafton, the "Wilkes's business ... is a hydra multiplying by resistance and gathering strength by every attempt to subdue it. As the times are, I had rather pardon Wilkes than punish him. This is a political opinion independent of the merit of the case."

The Duke of Grafton was more than displeased. Although he had tried for months to keep the John Wilkes Affair on the back burner, he was so upset that he introduced a resolution that this Preface was "an insolent, scandalous and seditious libel, tending to inflame and stir up the minds of his Majesty's subject to sedition."[27] Grafton soon abandoned the four moderates and switched sides to the hardliners—Lord Weymouth, Lord Gower, and Lord Hillsborough, plus Lord North. At a meeting of the Cabinet on 22 January 1769, it was decided five to four that as a seditious libeler Wilkes should not be allowed to represent the county of Middlesex in Parliament.[28]

This was the context when the House of Commons decided to take up Wilkes's complaint against Lord Mansfield for substituting "tenor and effect" for "purport and effect" in the original indictment. According to Walpole's *Memoirs*, "Dr Blackstone moved a long obscure question, setting forth that Wilkes's complaint against Lord Mansfield was frivolous and trifling; and as the courts below had pronounced that alteration of writs was not unusual, the charge was scandalous, as tending to calumniate the Chief Justice, and lessen the respect of the people for the law and the judges." After Wilkes's complaint was deemed frivolous and trifling—and his charge that the government had bribed a witness failed for lack of proof—he realized that his petition was a lost cause.

When Wilkes was brought before the Bar on 2 February to answer for his libel against Weymouth's letter, he defiantly acknowledged that he had written the Preface to "so bloody a scroll." The Attorney General then moved the same resolution that had passed the House of Lords, namely, that his Preface was "an insolent, scandalous and seditious libel." The resolution passed 239 to 136. After the debate on his fate in the House of Commons, John Wilkes was formally expelled from Parliament on 3 February 1769.[29]

IN the Hardwicke Papers one finds a curious comment on 15 December 1768: "Lord Lyttelton and Lord Mansfield were not there; the Lord Chancellor was silent." Surprisingly, Mansfield was absent that day, while Camden said not a word. But it does seem quite odd that these two antagonists failed to engage in the one Lords Debate on American Affairs during the Grafton Administration. And that oddity did not go unnoticed.

From the moment Camden entered the House of Lords, the longstanding personal antipathy between him and Mansfield had steadily intensified. At times their quarrels even went beyond the ordinary rough and tumble of eighteenth-century parliamentary debate. In Lord Campbell's telling, the two most prominent legal authorities within the realm at one point "attacked each other in debate so sharply" that a resolution was considered in the House of Lords that "they should be required to give an assurance that *the matter should not go further*, or that they would be taken into the custody of the Black Rod."[30] For political theater few events could rival the spectacle of the Lord Chancellor and the Lord Chief Justice of King's Bench so viciously quarreling on the floor of the House of Lords.

With this enduring enmity in mind, consider what happened when the House of Lords heard "the great cause between the houses of Douglas and Hamilton" from 19 January to 27 February 1769. At a critical moment in this bitter dispute over an estate issue between these two powerful Scottish families, Lord Chancellor Camden "rose, and with becoming authority and infinite applause told the Lords that he must now declare he thought the whole plea of the Hamiltons a tissue of perjury." According to Walpole, "He then went through the heads of the whole case, and without notes recapitulated even the dates of so involved a story." Lord Chief Justice Mansfield then rose and "spoke till he fainted with the heat and fatigue." In this rhetorical contest, Camden's "speech, in which it was allowed he outshone Lord Mansfield, had the most decisive effect." Douglas won, but unless one were paying close attention while reading Walpole's narrative, one would not have notice that both the Lord Chancellor and the Lord Chief Justice were actually arguing on the same side in this particular case.[31]

AFTER expelling John Wilkes, the House of Commons debated the Committee's Report on the Resolutions and Address. Barlow Trecothick brought forward the complaint of the merchants that these duties violated all known commercial principles and encouraged the Americans to engage in manufacturing for themselves. In an earlier debate he had reminded the House that he spoke "from knowledge, from facts, from belief." With his personal awareness of American affairs derived from years of experience he could say, "The general complexion of the country [i.e., America] was submissive to Great

Britain for the regulation of trade." They had consented when they were "obliged … to come to our market for her supplies." "Experience will show without exception that in all cases of requisitions, they have gone to the utmost extent of their abilities." He then brought up how he had negotiated with Townshend after he "wantonly threw out that he would tax America" in 1767. Trecothick was explicit: "After beating about for taxes upon salt, and such taxes, after consulting with the merchants, the merchants offered to pay the taxes here. We remonstrated against the taxes as likely to involve America in disputes." And he directly added that Townshend believed that his plan had run "against his own judgment." Nevertheless, he had given his word. Consequently, "America was to be taxed at the expense of the commerce of Great Britain," regardless of the wisdom of the policy.

Grenville held a radically different opinion, for he was convinced that the Administration was going to surrender to the Americans— after they paid some lip service to Parliament's supremacy. Such a policy would be completely inadequate—it lacked "the shape of anything like a remedy." For all the tough talk, "It is only a delusion to the people of England, an offence to the people of America; it is false logic, a consequence not deducible from any of the premises." Grenville minced no words in spelling out the alternative: "You must give up the whole, or stand for the whole." "If you mean to give up the proposition that you have no right to tax, do it like men." If you mean to enforce our right, "take some proper measure to show your mind." By "standing between both, you will plunge that country as well as this into confusion."

Finally, Thomas Pownall, the former Royal Governor of Massachusetts during the reign of George II, gave a thoughtful oration based upon his lived experience in America. He wanted the House to realize the power of what they were really up against. One can call it *enthusiasm* or *fanaticism*, if you like, but you need to know that *the spirit of the people* is not dead. This was the same spirit that led the founders of New England "to break off from every thing which is near and dear to the human heart—from every connection which friendship, relation, blood could give—which led them to quit every comfort that a settled and civilized country (their own native country) could afford; and to encounter every difficulty and distress, which a wild wilderness of savages could oppose to them, to struggle even for their existence." But their situation has now changed, radically, for "that spirit, equally strong and equally inflamed, has but a slight and trifling sacrifice to make at this time—they have not to quit their native land, but to defend it—they have not to forsake their friends and relations, but to unite with and to stand by them, in one common union."

Pownall then evoked Benjamin Franklin's testimony during the debate over the Repeal of the Stamp Act by saying, "those people whom *Great Britain* hath to this hour drawn as it were with a thread—and whom it has governed … with a little paper and packthread," could easily be provoked, their spirit aroused. "If this spirit should once take fire—and believe me, Sir, it is in such a state of inflammability that the smallest spark would give it fire—it will break out into a flame, which no reason, no prudence, no force can restrain." Once this spirit was fully in motion, "the people (to use their own phrase) will be led by Moses and Aaron, by the civil and religious, under a bond of unity that no factions will divide, no force can break."

After this prologue Pownall offered this "plain and simple advice" to the House of Commons: "that you should not stir up, but waive, all questions which become mere articles of faith—that you should make no innovations in practice, nor suffer any encroachments to be made on government—that you should take the ground that you now actually stand upon—and that government should act upon that ground, as it hath done invariably for 160 years past, from that first establishment of the colonies." If you would do that, "This would heal that union between the mother country and her colonies, which hath been vitiated." Such a policy "would restore that communication of commerce which otherwise will be cut off—would revive again the spirit of obedience—and re-establish the power of government."

According to the Cavendish Diary, Pownall argued, "When these colonies were first established, the government did stipulate by a condition that they should pay port duties," which he accurately claimed were designed to govern trade, not raise revenue. And he insisted, the Americans "have never objected to the principle, they have never objected to the exercise of the jurisdiction. They have never objected to the manner in which these duties were laid. They never objected to the moderation with which government has laid them." In Pownall's longstanding opinion, "if you will proceed as you have done for one hundred and sixty years back, ... you may quiet these people, you may recover their obedience, you may reestablish ... the authority of government." On the other hand, "if you attempt to force *taxes* against the spirit of the people there, you will find, when perhaps it is too late, that *they are* of a spirit which will resist all force—which will grow *stronger* by being *forced*—will prove superior to all force—and ever has been unconquerable."

Pownall's final piece of advice, according to the Almon Debates, reads: "Let the matter of right rest upon the declaratory law [of 1766], and say no more about it. It may be understood (as it is in the same words as that respecting Ireland) that it shall stand in the same line of administration—I say it may be so understood, and will be better understood by being never explained." What needed no explanation was the sheer fact that Parliament had never tried to tax Ireland.

Agent Johnson filed a glowing report on how Pownall "expatiated well upon the ill conduct of this country towards the colonies for several years past, and pointed out, with great force, the fatal consequences which must inevitably follow, and which they would very soon feel, from such preposterous conduct." Pownall's oration, however, fell on deaf ears, as had Trecothick's argument.[32]

According to Peter D. G. Thomas, "The ministry did not challenge the contention that Townshend's taxes were unenforceable and harmful to British exports." The crux of the issue was this simple: "the American denial of the right of taxation made repeal impossible." Although the Grafton Administration "carried the Address by 169 votes to 65," this result probably masked the underlying understanding, for a few days later the Secretary at War, Lord Barrington, confided in a letter to the Governor of Massachusetts that he believed that the Address was "not approved by five men" in either House of Parliament, "some thinking it too much and others too little in the present crisis."[33]

DISTRACTED though the ministry may have been at this juncture in regard to America, John Wilkes made sure the ministry did not have the luxury of fiddling with the crisis on the home front. The expulsion of the elected MP for Middlesex required a writ for a new by-election to replace our resourceful convict happily ensconced in King's Bench Prison. As many had predicted he lost no time in announcing that he would stand in the upcoming Middlesex by-election on 16 February 1769.

While his high life in prison was quite expensive for a person of quality, Wilkes desperately needed additional funds to run for office while still in jail. In this rather awkward situation his supporters rallied to supply him with some much-needed cash. Drawing from the calculations of a close ally of Wilkes at the time, Peter D. G. Thomas states, "Wilkes's debts had swollen from £6,000 in March 1768, when a public subscription to pay them off raised only £1,116, to £14,000 in February 1769." That was the month when "a meeting of his supporters at the London Tavern … promptly subscribed £3,340" to begin paying off his debts. Then on 25 February 1769 the "Society of Gentlemen Supporters of the Bill of Rights" was founded to make sure that on his release from King's Bench Prison he would not be transferred directly to the debtor's prison.[34]

In the meantime Wilkes won the 16 February by-election without opposition, only to have the vote declared void. Another by-election was scheduled for 16 March—and he won yet again, only to have this vote also declared void. On the third round Colonel Henry Luttrell and Sarjeant Whitaker ran against Wilkes. Before that vote he laid out the constitutional point at stake: "The question is whether the people have an inherent right to be represented in Parliament by the man of their free choice, not disqualified by the law of the land." And

Wilkes and his followers firmly believe that he was "not disqualified by the law of the land." When the votes were counted on 13 April, Wilkes defeated Luttrell 1,143 to 296, with Whitaker receiving only 5. The House of Commons, however, declared Luttrell the winner on the legalistic ground that all of the votes for Wilkes should not be counted. Luttrell's triumph, however, did not go over so well out of doors—he was "assaulted by persons unknown as he quitted the House, and for some months did not dare to appear in the streets, or scarce quit his lodging."[35]

THE ministry had been searching for a convenient way to offer concessions to the colonies without appearing to be responding to pressure. Agent Johnson captured the essence of the situation when he reported to Connecticut that the colonies "are left with only a kind of *ministerial encouragement* that, if they are *very quiet* and *quite silent upon the right*, and will *humbly ask it as a favour, perhaps* the offensive acts shall be repealed *next winter.*"[36]

During the 19 April 1769 Commons Debate the issue was joined.[37] Pownall led off with the observation, "You will never be able to raise the power of this country higher that it is at present." Because the various participants seemed to agree on Parliament's right, he believed now was the propitious moment—"All is peace"—to declare victory and withdraw all those taxes in so impolitic an Act. Barlow Trecothick weighed in: "Every measure of severity, Sir, adopted by Great Britain against her colonies recoils upon ourselves. Sound policy respecting America seems to have forsaken our councils." Edmund Burke cut to the heart of the matter: "Absurdity itself never did concert such a plan of taxation" as Townshend cooked up. Then he eloquently concluded, "The Americans have made a discovery, or think they have made one, that we mean to oppress them. We have made a discovery, or think we have made one, that they intend to rise in rebellion. Our severity has increased their ill behaviour. We know not how to advance, they know not how to retreat." Before the debate was over, as one participate expressed it, "not one word had been said in favour of the Act of Parliament."[38]

Because there was such widespread agreement on the inutility of the Townshend Duties—and because on 10 March Pennsylvania had finally decided to join the boycott—the ministry realized that it was a fitting moment to move to the conciliation stage of its policy. On 1 May the Cabinet met to decide upon what concessions would be held out to the Americans during the next session of Parliament. The critical choice lay between a *total* repeal of the Townshend Duties, and a *partial* repeal of all *except the duty on tea.*

In retrospect this meeting proved to be the critical turning point in imperial affairs. The minority championing a total repeal of all the Townshend Duties was composed by Prime Minister Grafton, Lord Chancellor Camden, Lord Granby of the Army, and Henry Seymour Conway, minister without portfolio. Had Sir Edward Hawke of the Admiralty been present it is reasonable to suppose that this Chathamite would have voted with Grafton. If yes, the vote would have been five to five. On a tie vote the Prime Minister's opinion would have prevailed—and the Townshend Duties would have been totally repelled. But the majority in this fateful five to four vote was composed by the Leader of the House, Lord North, American Secretary Hillsborough, Lord President Gower, Southern Secretary Weymouth, and Northern Secretary Rochford. With the British Empire hanging in the balance, the ministry voted for only a partial repeal. The tax on tea was preserved, narrowly.[39]

When the decision was communicated to the Americans in a circular letter, the American Secretary announced these three important policy decisions: (1) "no measure ought to be taken which can in any way derogate from the legislative authority of Great Britain over the colonies"; (2) "His Majesty's present administration have at no time entertained a design to propose to Parliament to lay any further taxes upon America for the purpose of raising a revenue"; and (3) "it is at present their intention to propose in the next session of Parliament to take off the duties upon glass, paper, and colours upon consideration of such duties having been laid contrary to the true principles of commerce." In his mind, these decisions did not represent a change in colonial policy, only an adjustment in certain items. Tea, needless to say, was conspicuously absent from the list.[40]

WHEN Parliament wound up its business on 9 May 1769, the Grafton Administration thought it had successfully dealt with the ongoing colonial crisis not only by promising deep concessions during the next session but by also promising that there would not be any new taxes levied. The political nation, however, was not focused on America. The center of attention was on another constitutional question much closer to home. By denying John Wilkes his seat as the properly elected MP for Middlesex, the ministry temporarily united the different wings of the Opposition under a banner that read, "Freedom of Debate within doors and freedom of Election without," to quote a toast during a dinner at the Thatched House Tavern on the very day that Parliament ended. No less than 72 MPs were present at this dinner, where plans were laid for bringing down the Grafton Administration. During the summer the Opposition launched an extensive campaign to petition George III over the John Wilkes Affair. Soon Lord Chatham regained sufficient health to attend the King's levy and he was *strongly against the measure of expelling Mr Wilkes.* As the Opposition intensified the pressure from without, the split within the administration grew.[41]

Wilkes himself pursued his suit against Halifax, who had initially signed the general warrant in 1763 that led to the arrests of so many printers and associates, to the great cost and embarrassment of the government. So long as he remained an outlaw he lacked legal standing, but as soon as Mansfield declared that our convict was no longer an outlaw, he reactivated his suit. When the trial was finally held in the Court of Common Pleas on 11 November 1769, the presiding judge instructed the jury to give "liberal and exemplary not excessive damages."

While Wilkes had sought £10,000 in damages for the invasion of his private property—Walpole put the figure at £20,000—he had to settle for £4,000. Not too bad a settlement for an inmate in King's Bench Prison with a serious cash flow problem, but Walpole still reported, "The jury having disappointed the expectations of the populace by so moderate at fine, were hissed, and forced to escape by a back way."[42]

Prime Minister Grafton, furthermore, was so completely negligent that he simply ignored the gathering storm and "diverted himself in the country, coming to town but once a week or once a fortnight to sign papers at the Treasury." Walpole then added, "and as seldom to the King." When he did seek the counsel of Lord Chancellor Camden on one occasion, he was told in no uncertain terms "that his grace had consulted him but twice last session, and then had acted directly contrary to his advice." During the fall of 1769 Grafton simply avoided taking any actions whatsoever, and even postponed the opening of Parliament until after Christmas.[43]

BEFORE Parliament opened in January 1770 "at least fourteen counties and twelve boroughs had presented petitions to George III, signed altogether by some 60,000 Parliamentary voters." That represented "about 20 per cent to 25 per cent of the English electorate" and indicated that "an organized nationwide political movement" had finally surfaced in the British political nation, according to Peter D. G. Thomas.[44] Walpole even opened his *Memoirs* for the year 1770 with this truly alarming sentence: "As a question of greater magnitude had seldom been agitated than the demanded dissolution of the Parliament, the expectation of the public rose in proportion as the session approached."[45] With the situation deteriorating so rapidly, he reached for a line from *The Campaign* by Addison: "Ride in the whirlwind and direct the storm."[46]

The petitioning campaign, however, paled in significance compared to what happened when Parliament took up the King's Address on 9 January. Having returned to vigor and transparently in a fighting mood, Chatham proposed this amendment in the House of Lords: "that this House would take into consideration the proceedings of the House of Commons touching the incapacity of John Wilkes, Esq., whereby the electors of Middlesex were deprived of their free choice of a representative."

Mansfield responded to the motion by pronouncing it "of a nature so extraordinary and alarming as to preclude the possibility of my remaining silent." He opened on an abstract level by making a general point: "Declarations of law made by either House of Parliament are always attended with bad effects. I constantly oppose them when I have an opportunity; and never, in my judicial capacity, think myself bound to honor them with the slightest regard." That is the way he addressed—or rather, dismissed—the claim that the expulsion of Wilkes had violated constitutional norms. And that is why, as a matter of course as a judge, he refused to reveal his hand "on the legality of the proceedings of the House of Commons on the Middlesex election."

In Mansfield's frame of reference, the constitutional context was simply irrelevant to the issue at hand. What needed to be understood was that "particular decisions ... on a case regularly submitted to their discussion and properly the subject of their jurisdiction ... may judicially be pronounced by either House." "Wherever a court of justice is supreme, as the House of Commons in matters of election, the determination of that court must be received and submitted to as the law of the land." The House of Lords had "no right to inquire" about any decision made by the House of Commons, for in its own sphere, it remained supreme and uncontrollable. Chatham was simply wrong, for his "amendment threatens the most pernicious consequences, as it manifestly violates every form and law of parliament, must stir up a quarrel between the two Houses, and may entirely destroy the balance of the constitution." Walpole's report has Mansfield saying that "though the House of Commons should have done wrong, a breach between the two Houses would be much more fatal."[47]

In his rebuttal Chatham reminded his Lordships, "I have had the pleasure of sitting with [Mansfield] in the other House of Parliament, and I have often felt his power." In a brutal 1755 debate he had castigated Mansfield's approach by remarking, "When master principles are concerned, he dreaded accuracy of distinction: he feared that sort of reasoning; if you class everything, you will soon reduce everything into a particular; you will then lose great general maxims."[48] And now fifteen years later, he was convinced that by reducing the issue to "a particular" the Lord Chief Justice had lost sight of "general maxims" of a most important nature. Chatham wanted it to be understood, "The constitution has already been openly invaded, and I have heard, with horror and astonishment, that invasion defended upon principle. What is this mysterious power, undefined by law, which we must not approach without leave, nor speak of without reverence, which no man may question, and to which all men must submit?" "Instead of the arbitrary power of a King," would the Lord Chief Justice have us "submit to the arbitrary power of a House of Commons?" After exalting the ancient sources of the constitution and condemning the refinements of the lawyers, he cast "a scornful glance at Lord Mansfield." One report claimed, Chatham "endeavoured with all his might, (but without success,) to browbeat Lord Mansfield, and to turn his speech into ridicule, as if it had consisted only of the niceties of the law."[49]

Although Chatham's amendment lost 100 to 36, this attack made it utterly transparent from the opening day of Parliament that his principal followers—Camden, Temple, Lyttelton and Shelburne—would support a steady attempt to bring down the Grafton Administration. This left the ministry with no choice but to dismiss Lord Chancellor Camden from his lucrative office on 17 January 1770.[50]

NEVER content with serving as an opposition spokesman, since at least early May Lord Chief Justice Mansfield had seized upon an opening into the heart of the Grafton Administration. The divided vote to preserve the tax on tea, while rescinding the tax on all the other items in the Townshend Duties, convinced him that the time was fast becoming ripe for, say, a palace revolution. So, he began to plot, secretly from behind the curtain, until Camden was turned out of office. Immediately George III offered him the Great Seal, only to have him refuse to accept it. But he "boasted of the offer," and of course it did not take long before "the secret" was trumpeted around town. While refusing the Great Seal for himself, he recommended Charles Yorke, the son of the former Lord Chancellor Hardwicke and one known to deeply desire the office. But after taking "three days to consider"—and confidential conversations with Rockingham and his political connections—Yorke also "refused to accept the seals of Chancellor." Walpole's description of the chaotic situation engulfing Prime Minister Grafton is compelling:

> Not a lawyer could be found able enough [to be Lord Chancellor]; or if able, bold enough; or if bold, decent enough, to fill the employment. [Sir Fletcher] Norton had all the requisites of knowledge and capacity, but wanted even the semblance of integrity, though for that reason was probably the secret wish of the court. He was enraged at the preference given to [Charles] Yorke—yet nobody dared to propose him, even when Yorke had refused. Sir Eardley Wilmot had character and abilities, but wanted health. The Attorney-General De Grey wanted health and weight, and yet asked too extravagant terms. [John] Dunning the Solicitor-General had taken the same part as his friends Lord Camden and Lord Shelburne. [Richard] Hussey, so far from being inclined to accept the office, determined to resign with his friend Lord Camden.[51]

And the situation grew even more desperate as the week unfolded. Nevertheless, before long Yorke reversed himself and accepted the position—because the King "so overwhelmed him with flatteries, entreaties, prayers, and last with commands, and threats of never giving him the post if not accepted now, that the poor man sunk under the importunity." After kissing the King's hand—and after being deliberately shunned by Rockingham and his older brother for breaking his promise not to accept the Great Seal—"it was whispered that the agitation of his mind working on a most sanguine habit of body, inflamed of late by excessive indulgence in meats and wine, had occasioned the bursting of a blood vessel." The surgeons were called in on Friday. By Saturday afternoon the new Lord Chancellor was pronounced dead. Whether his death was by natural causes or "by his own hand" remains unresolved.

With no viable options left, Mansfield was pressed to accept the office yet once again. While he refused the offer this second time, he did agree to repeat what happened in late 1756 when Yorke's father had resigned, namely, to put the Great Seal into commission. And he "named three commissioners, over whom he was supposed to exercise unbounded influence, and whose decrees he was afterwards said to dictate."[52] For all intents and purposes Lord Chief Justice Mansfield was now also the Acting Lord Chancellor, collecting the salaries of the two most prestigious legal positions within the realm. Nice work, that.

THE Marquis of Rockingham added to the volatile mix when he addressed "the state of the nation" in the House of Lords on 21 January 1770. "The object of his lordship's speech was to show that the present unhappy condition of affairs, and the universal discontent of the people, did not arise from any immediate temporary cause, but had grown upon us by degrees, from the moment of his Majesty's accession to the throne."[53] From 1760 forward nothing had happened but increasing chaos. Something was wrong, systematically.

In the House of Commons Edmund Burke pursued Rockingham's thesis in *Thought on the Cause of the Present Discontents*.[54] Burke's extended analysis of the chronic instability in governance during the first decade of the reign of George III opened with the assertion that "hardly a man in or out of power" would disagree with the claim "that there is something particularly alarming in the present conjuncture." Indeed, he confessed, "There is ... a peculiar venom and malignity in this political distemper beyond any that I have heard or read of." In his reading of the unfolding development of the unwritten constitution, he located the source of this "malignity" in "the distempers of Parliament," a situation that he explicitly juxtaposed to "the distempers of Monarchy" that had so vexed the seventeenth century.[55]

The people had lost confidence in the government, in the first instance, because of a transformation in the very nature of the House of Commons. Whereas "the virtue, spirit, and essence of the House of Commons" had traditionally consisted "in its being the express image of the feelings of the nation," it now had mysteriously lost its footing as "a middle nature between subject and Government." Instead of serving as the people's *"corrective and controul* of the active powers of the State," it had been absorbed into "the offices of executive Government," thereby forfeiting "all the confidence, love, and veneration" of the people.[56]

Although Burke did not explicitly say so, it is reasonable to assume that the development he had in mind originated during the long and stable ministries of Sir Robert Walpole and Henry Pelham. They at least were largely responsible for drawing "the House of Commons towards the character of a standing Senate." That, however, was but a first step. The decisive transition had come "in our time" when "a new plan" of governance was adopted. He saw the lineaments of this "great scheme of power" in a novel *system* that had "totally abandoned the shattered and old-fashioned fortress of prerogative, and made a lodgement in the strong hold of Parliament itself." "In Parliament the whole is executed from beginning to end. In Parliament the power of obtaining their object is absolute." When something was needed, ministers would simply call down "the god in the machine"—"the wonder-working *Law of Parliament.*" The implication: "Thus the controul of Parliament upon the executory power is lost; because Parliament is made to partake in every considerable act of Government."[57]

At this point an advanced paradox swung into view. From the moment the active powers of the state were lodged "in the stronghold of Parliament itself," the public "exterior" ministries of the 1760s were undercut—because operational power was actually located in the hands of an "interior" Cabinet. As Burke put it, "The whole system, comprehending the exterior and interior Administrations, is commonly called, in the technical language of the Court, *Double Cabinet.*" And this interior cabinet—call it a Cabal, Rota, Junto or Faction as you will—managed affairs through "the King's Friends." Indeed, because the "cabal of the closet and back-stairs was substituted in the place of a national Administration," the public "exterior" ministries of the 1760s lacked respect, consistency, and endurance.[58]

Burke also labored the point that "a great spirit of innovation" was moving through "this new scheme of government"—"this new project"—this *"system of Favouritism."* So readers would not make the mistake of thinking that he was basing his analysis of this Double Cabinet upon the sinister influence of the thoroughly despised Scottish Earl of Bute, he directly rejected this popular prejudice. Indeed, he correctly stated that Bute "communicates very little in a direct manner with the greater part of our men of business." He was even convinced that this novel *system* would have taken hold "if the Earl of Bute had never existed."[59] And he could have added that Bute believed that it was a capital error for George III to abandon "the shattered and old-fashioned fortress of prerogative."

In justification for his analysis he appealed to the lived experience of those who served in the various ministries during the chaotic 1760s. And he was quite sure that "there is not a single public man, in or out of office, who has not, at some time or other born testimony to the truth" of what he had said about the Double Cabinet. Even more convincing would be the testimony of "those who compose all the exterior part of the present Administration," namely, according to his marginalia, "Duke of Grafton, Lord Weymouth, Lord Gower, Rigby, etc."

Although Mansfield was never mentioned by name, Burke most certainly realized that our Scottish Law Lord was deeply involved in the creation of this new system. Notice his claim that by "carrying offences, real or supposed, into the legislative bodies"—the John Wilkes Affair comes readily to mind—one ran the risk of reviving "all the evils of the *Star Chamber.*" The next sentence succinctly captured the spirit of the laws moving through Mansfield's jurisprudential reform project: "A large and liberal construction in ascertaining offences, and a discretionary power in punishing them, is the idea of *criminal equity*; which is in truth a monster in Jurisprudence." A few paragraphs later he grouped up "a dependent House of Commons" with "a dependent court of *Star Chamber*" and "a dependent court of King's Bench."[60] And early on he observed that "those who have been of the most known devotion to the will and pleasure of a Court, have at the same time been most forward in asserting an high authority in the House of Commons."[61] That describes quite nicely the mentality of Lord Chief Justice Mansfield.

THE Duke of Grafton was sorely tired of his increasingly untenable position. When he informed George III that he was thinking of resigning, his Majesty dropped the hint that the ministry might "go on, if Lord North would put himself at the head of the Treasury." In point of fact, George III had already made up his mind to replace Grafton, for the next day "Lord North owned to Conway that the King had pressed him to accept the Treasury."[62] Two days later, however, Grafton still "talked of going on" in a confidential conversation with Conway, a conversation that convinced Conway that Grafton's "wayward fit" about resigning had past. That conviction did not last more than a day, for after a debate in the House of Commons on this Thursday the ministry's amendment carried by only "224 to 180—a threatening diminution to the administration, who saw their majority on the first day of the session sunk from 116 to 44." According to Walpole, "If the Duke of Grafton was alarmed before, his panic was augmented by this decrease of fortune. He again declared to the King he would resign, yet still desired his friends to keep the secret." On Friday he informed a startled Conway, "I will go to Lord North, and press him to accept directly." By Saturday evening the political career of the Prime Minister was finished. "Whether betrayed by his fears or his friends," in Walpole's opinion the fickle Duke of Grafton "had certainly been the Chief Author of his own disgrace" (my capitalizations).[63]

XV

THE OPENING YEARS
OF THE NORTH
ADMINISTRATION

THE POLITICAL LANDSCAPE LOOKED MORE THAN PROMISING TO LORD MANSFIELD IN January 1770. He had emerged as the Acting Lord Chancellor in the North Administration, a situation that lasted "for a longer time than had been known since the reign of William III." And when he resigned that position a full year later he made sure that the least competent of the three commissioners who had served was appointed, a shift that left him in control of considerable power.[1] The configuration of the North Administration pleased him even more, for it left out of office Lord Chancellor Camden, Lord Granby of the Army, Henry Seymour Conway, and the Duke of Grafton—and *they were not replaced.* Those who sided with Lord North in that critical five to four vote *to retain the trifling tax on tea*—Lord President Gower, Southern Secretary Weymouth, Northern Secretary Rochford, and American Secretary Hillsborough—remained at their posts.

Before becoming the Lord of the Treasury, North had secured a reputation as a seasoned politician with extensive experience in

Parliament and intimate knowledge of the financial machinery of the imperial government. He had served in the House of Commons since the watershed General Election of 1754. Although he had voted against the Repeal of the Stamp Act, the Chatham Administration appointed him joint Paymaster-General of the Army. And soon after the sudden death of Charles Townshend in 1767, he was appointed Chancellor of the Exchequer. Then at the beginning of 1768 he replaced Henry Seymour Conway as the Leader of the House of Commons. A considerable amount of his enduring power derived from the fact that he retained the office of Chancellor of the Exchequer and remained the Leader of the House of Commons. As such, he could speak with commanding authority in the Commons Debates. (While he has come down in history as *Lord North*, he remained a commoner with this courtesy title.)[2]

When the distracted and divided Grafton Administration came to an ignominious end, North was left to pick up the pieces, which he did "in a manly style" as the ministry faced a vote of confidence in the House of Commons. Walpole's narrative is gripping: "A more critical day had seldom dawned. If the court should be beaten, the King would be at the mercy of the opposition, or driven to have recourse to the Lords—possibly to the sword. All the resolutions on the Middlesex election would be rescinded, the Parliament dissolved, or the contest reduced to the sole question of prerogative." With only a day or two to prepare, the new Prime Minister displayed remarkable energy and skill in organizing support. And the reconfigured ministry prevailed when the votes were counted with "a majority of 40," which was "greater by fifteen or twenty, than was expected by the most sanguine, the numbers being 226 to 186."[3]

This victory proved to be a pivotal turning point, for the Prime Minister steadily increased his majorities in the House of Commons. It did not take long before the political nation came to the realization that the endemic fluctuations in colonial policy that had so vexed the 1760s had become a thing of the past, for the King had at last secured a reliable Prime Minister. The North Administration was destined to last for twelve years.

LORD North wasted no time in letting the House know that the reorganized Cabinet was committed to carrying through the maximal form of the doctrine of Parliamentary Supremacy championed by Mansfield. Nevertheless, the North Administration was also intent upon promoting the conciliatory measures already promised the previous year.

The Commons Debate on the Partial Repeal of the Townshend Duties opened on 5 March 1770. North began with tough words against the American boycott of British goods, but after castigating those "illegal combinations" he proceeded to lay out the overarching aim of the conciliatory policy by reviewing the earlier decision by the Grafton Administration and the subsequent letter sent by Hillsborough "to several of the governors in America."

Although the "flame" of opposition still burned, North wanted to accommodate some of the grievances so as "to promote a reconciliation between the colonies and Great Britain." With that end-in-view, he disclosed (1) that the intention of the ministry was never "to lay any further tax upon America"; (2) that most of the Townshend Duties would be repealed; but (3) "the duty on tea must be retained" because it would stand "as a mark of the supremacy of Parliament, and an efficient declaration of their right to govern the colonies." Not only was the duty on tea "light," it was "not the manufacture of British commodities." And as "an object of luxury" it would produced only a trifling £11,000 per year. In brief, what today would be called "peanuts" in the eighteenth century was called "a peppercorn."

In making the case for retaining this tax on tea, North explicitly rejected the distinction the Americans were drawing between port duties for regulating trade and taxes for raising any revenue for the British Exchequer. In his opinion, if once so vague a distinction gained a footing in the ongoing argument, the Americans would claim that all duties were "for the purpose of a revenue" while the British would insist that all duties were "for the purpose of trade." Not a single item under dispute, therefore, could ever be settled.

So, in direct continuity with the stated objective in the Preamble to the Townshend Duties Act—and with his own longstanding position on colonial matters—North emphatically insisted that this light duty on tea was designed to show the Americans that the ministry would never "consent to any measures which could any way derogate from the legislative authority of Great Britain over the colonies." On that overarching principle—contrary to regrettable "variations" in policy since the Stamp Act Crisis—the North Administration would hold to a steady course, for on the great question of "whether Great Britain has or has not a right to tax America for the purpose of a revenue" North would never yield an inch, especially in the face of "the most illegal and unwarrantable steps" taken by the Americans.

The ensuing Commons Debate was basically nothing more than a rehearsal of the polarized positions marked out over the last three years. After the Lord Mayor of London, speaking for the merchants, testified against the tea tax on commercial grounds, Thomas Pownall introduced an amendment to add tea to the list of duties to be repealed, thereby transforming the motion for a partial repeal into a total one. Pownall wanted the House to realize that "the reasoning of the better part in [America] goes against the preamble" because "by raising a revenue for the support of the civil government, you destroy the utility of their Assemblies." And the major grievance "rankling in their bosoms" was dreadfully serious. Indeed, the Americans were asking "whether they have courts or not. Whether they have a Bill of Rights. Whether the Habeas Corpus Act extends to that country."

Colonel Mackay, recently returned from his command in the British Army in Boston, reported accurately that the Americans "allow that you have a right to regulate their commerce, but as far as regards taxing them," they hold to the conviction "that you really have no right to tax them." Then he pointedly pressed on to say, "it is not the duty," which was acknowledged to be trifling, but the principles exhibited in the preamble that the Americans found so objectionable.

Henry Seymour Conway avoided the issue of Parliament's "right" and focused on "the practical idea," for he was persuaded that "a system of force over the minds of free people can never be a successful system." The only practical way of "drawing a revenue" from the Americans was to revert to the traditional system of requisitions from the Crown and give up on taxes levied by Parliament.

Sir William Meredith then evoked the pleasant harmony during the reigns of George I and George II, when America "exhausted herself" in defense of the Empire. After Parliament had richly indemnified the colonies with cash for all their efforts, he came to a crucial plank in the Rockingham position, namely, the conviction that "there is a distinction between the right and the exercise of the right." How Parliament lost sight of that critical distinction was something of a mystery to him. He even openly confessed, "Who advised that fatal plan of government, I know not." But he was convinced that "all the confusion, all the violations of our liberty, all the contempt that has fallen upon this country" flowed from "that rash system" which put into practice a theoretical right best left in the realm of speculation. "Like Apollo" in "a Grecian camp," this error of judgment has been controlling events from "behind a cloud of darkness." Indeed, it has "hung over every administration" and "perplexed everybody" ever since. Now the North Administration was so caught up in dialectical contradictions of its own making that it would appear to be "disposed neither to tax America nor to restore peace to America."

At the opposite end of the political spectrum, George Grenville weighed in with a lengthy review of the alterations in policy over the last few years. He then even openly confessed, "If I had imagined, that great bodies of people would in the space of a few months have changed their opinions, I would not have proposed" the Stamp Act in the first place. Although he had not foreseen how events had played out, this new initiative was appalling to him. The policy amounted to "throwing out angry expressions" while the government had "given way from one step to another, from one idea to another, till we know not upon what ground we stand." So, instead of partially repealing the Townshend Duties, what needed to be done now was to cut through the endless vacillations and bring down upon the

Americans the full weight of "the King, Lords, and Commons." Parliament's voice should be enforced, not modified.

Mr. Ellis thoroughly shared Grenville's posture, saying, "I think, that all the confusion is totally owing to the repeal of the Stamp Act." "The uncertainty and fluctuations of our councils" had "set up those pretensions, and … put this country under an interdict of commerce." In his gloomy opinion, "It is no sound policy to take a measure inconsistent with dignity, honour and authority." To even think of reversing policy "upon anti-commercial principles" when the Americans were "using means of violence" was to become a laughingstock in the eyes of the world.

Counsellor Wedderburn thought the announced policy would be yet another dangerous step down the slippery slope set up by "that repeated contradiction which has obtained with regard to America since 1766." Lord Barrington boldly declared, "There can be no plan to put America upon a right footing, till the Americans obey the legislature of this country."

Colonel Barré got in one last word in this Commons Debate from, say, the American perspective: "For three years we have seen nothing but the folly, the absurdity of succeeding administrations." Alas, "We now come to what is no system at all, but [a policy that] carries nothing with it but monuments of our tyranny, monuments of our folly."[4]

After Pownall's amendment to add tea to the list of duties to be repealed was rejected 204 to 142, North's original motion was sent to the House of Lords. When the Opposition failed to come together, the Marquis of Rockingham sought to postpone the debate, only to have his motion rejected. On 12 April the Bill to Repeal the Townshend Duties, Except on Tea received the royal assent.[5]

WHEN the House of Commons began debating the Repeal of the Townshend Duties on 5 March 1770, it was widely known that the tensions between Boston and the British standing army that had been on parade since the beginning of October 1768 were reaching a boiling point. What could not be known was that on the same day that Parliament passed this legislation, British soldiers killed five civilians and wounded several more.[6]

In a report on the Boston Massacre, Acting Governor Thomas Hutchinson explained why the Regiments of the British Army had been removed to Castle William. He clearly believed that the Army was facing an uprising of alarming proportions. He also knew that the military commander alone could rightfully make the critical decision on what to do with the soldiers in such an explosive situation. But the officer in charge, Colonel Dalrymple, shifted the burden of the decision by agreeing to remove the troops *if* the civil magistrate would merely express the *desire* that they be removed, which, of course, put the Acting Governor in an acute bind, for he lacked the authority to make so serious a decision. But a desire was not a command, right? So, pressed on all sides, and after seeking the advice of the Council, with great reluctance and transparent anxiety Hutchinson expressed the desire and the troops were removed.[7]

Hutchinson's report on the Boston Massacre did not reach the imperial capital until 21 April, that is, a week after Hillsborough had forwarded to America copies of the Partial Repeal of the Townshend Duties. Although Hillsborough promptly assured Hutchinson that his actions were highly commendable, Hutchinson had to wait weeks before receiving this news, plus the fact that he had been officially elevated to the post of Royal Governor of Massachusetts, a position he reluctantly accepted only after much soul searching and deep reflection on the unfolding political situation.

As Hutchinson anxiously waited, the House of Commons began its debate on the Boston Massacre. Barlow Trecothick opened the debate on 26 April by moving for the relevant papers leading into the conflict between the soldiers and the citizens of Boston. He then proceeded to castigate the ministry: "We have shown the Americans, that we are not incapable of adopting ideas, and even systems of despotism." For the past few years "We have taken every step to destroy the advantages put in our hands by Providence," namely, "wealth, grandeur, happiness to the mother country." Instead of governing by reason, "We choose rather to govern by will." Convinced that it was "absurd to think of raising a revenue upon America," he advocated "going back to the time, and circumstance, in which happiness and good order took place," that is, to the Old Colonial System. William Beckford and Isaac Barré amplified this line of attack by comparing the military action in Boston to the violence against the London mob chanting "Wilkes and Liberty," thereby linking the Boston Massacre to the earlier Massacre of St. George's Fields outside the King's Bench Prison.[8]

A few weeks later the House engaged in a debate on "the power of the civil and military authorities in North America." While the way the Army had been removed after the Boston Massacre surely intensified this debate, the proper lines of authority had been a longstanding issue. Indeed, Thomas Pownall, the former Royal Governor of Massachusetts, had given notice several months before that he would examine this very issue.

Pownall began by saying, "we, his Majesty's subjects, here *within the realm*, are not called upon as parts of a collective sovereign, to exercise the sovereignty of this kingdom over our fellow subjects in other parts of the empire *without the realm*" (my emphases). He reminded the House that traditionally it had been "the sole right, the sole power of the Crown" to "form establishments of government" for the colonies. He told the House of Commons, "we must not take it up as though we were called upon to make laws for the interior conduct of the executive power in these colonies." And he emphasized this fact: "The Assembly of each is, within their respective jurisdiction, competent to this purpose; and has in its hands the full power of all the means to this end."

After so carefully lining out his understanding of the limited, advisory role of Parliament, Pownall turned to what he considered to be the constitutional issues at the heart of the unfolding dispute: (1) "what powers of government the Crown can and ought to grant, to the dependencies of the realm"; (2) "what form and power of government the British subjects in those parts ought to be governed by"; (3) "what powers are granted, both civil and military"; and (4) "what have been the arrangements made … for administering and executing those powers."

Pownall clearly thought the interior affairs of the American colonies stood outside of the jurisdiction of Parliament. He also thought the Governor of a given colony was the superior officer who could direct the military authorities within the colony. After evoking the loyalty of "the people of New England" when he served as the Royal Governor of Massachusetts, Pownall insisted that prior to the structural transformation that resulted in the Stamp Act Crisis, they "had no other ideas of England but that of *home*" (my emphasis). Given this pervasive sentiment, he thought the House of Commons "ought to inquire, what strange cause could have produced so strange an effect."

After rehearsing the recent history Pownall cut to the crux of the constitutional conflict. The Cavendish Diary reads:

> The Revenue Act has a tendency to render their Assemblies useless. Not only their doubts, but they believe, they feel, that you not only mean to alter their constitution, but to establish a military government, that you mean to draw a military net over them. This is what they feel. This is what they apprehend, this is the way that every free government upon the continent of Europe has lost its liberty. Their apprehensions are well-founded. The constitution of the *états de Pays* in France, the constitution of Hanover was as free as the constitution of Great Britain at this day. Nor a farthing was raised but at the requisition of the King. But the separation of the supreme military from the supreme civil power has ruined liberty in all these countries.

In Pownall's opinion, "If you attempt to force troops upon them, … you may drive the people to rebellion." In fact, "every inhabitant to a man" believed that the novel parliamentary doctrine tends toward "an absolute disfranchisement of his personal liberty." That is why "every Assembly, without exception, has come to resolutions directly contrary" to the trajectory exhibited in the recent revenue acts passed by Parliament. That is why "the continuance of the structure of the empire, in its several parts" was now hanging in the balance.

The Secretary at War, Lord Barrington, responded to Pownall's argument by saying that he had already asked for the legal opinion of the Attorney General and the Solicitor General on whether the military or the civil officers in a colony held the final authority. Although they had not yet handed in their opinion, Barrington made it clear that he himself entertained no doubt that the supreme power was held by the military. Furthermore, he called attention to the fact that at the opening of the Seven Years War Lord Chancellor Hardwicke had prepared "the first commission of Commander in Chief" for the Earl of Loudon "with great deliberation." In Charles Garth's report to South Carolina, he noted that Barrington maintained "that it became necessary for the service that some measure should be taken to prevent the military from being subject to the control of Governors." And according to the Cavendish Diary, he said that this commission "expressly intended that the civil Governor should have no command" over the King's forces.

What Barrington failed to mention, however, was the fact that Mansfield was the closest advisor to Lord Chancellor Hardwicke at that moment. And it should not be forgotten that after Hardwicke promptly resigned in October 1756 Mansfield exercised the powers of that office while the Great Seal was placed in commission. Now fourteen years later the Attorney General and the Solicitor General would surely have conferred with the Acting Lord Chancellor before they finally handed in their opinion that while the authority of colonial governors extended over the provincial militias, the civil magistrates held no authority whatsoever over the King's Army in America.[9]

The next day the House of Commons opened its debate on "the conduct of administration with regard to America." Edmund Burke led off with a two-hour speech on the "confusion" pulsating through every corner of the polycentric empire, with "one part tottering, another tumbling," but all "crumbling I know not how." Speaking for the Rockingham party, Burke claimed "the declaratory law [of 1766] did sufficiently establish the sovereignty of this country over its plantations and colonies." And "the prevailing sense of this House" at the Repeal of the Stamp Act indicated "the true policy was not to exercise that right in the taxation of America." Nevertheless, the Townshend Duties Act of 1767 was designed as "a test" so as to "make the Americans show themselves to the House, and the House to show themselves to the Americans, to discover the true character of each, which could hold out longest." When it was suggested that the Townshend Duties Act should be repealed, Burke noticed that the response was "never"—sometimes not give "an iota"—once "We shall have them at our feet." The plan—"if such could be so called"—remained "to overrule all the constitutional power of America, and set up in its place a standing army." On the face of it, the ministry's pursuit of what Burke tagged "a peppercorn" amounted to "a strong mixture of ancient ferociousness and modern effeminacy."[10]

The House of Lords soon took up the argument. Rockingham called attention to the fact that "we ourselves are exceedingly divided, with regard to the necessary measures of effecting a reconciliation between [the Americans] and the mother country." While "many of the ablest members in both Houses think that we have no right whatever to tax them," Rockingham spoke for those who "contend for the right, but exclaim against the exercise." Earl Temple in abject frustration castigated the ministry—"so lost to all sense of shame, so eminently above the mere pretence of regard for justice"—and lamented the fact that the parliamentary session was coming to an end with "everything consigned to the minister of that department, who breathes nothing but sanguinary measures." Lord Shelburne even bemoaned the fact that the present ministers had "adopted *the principle of the Roman tyrant* as far as they were able" (my emphasis).

Regardless of what the Opposition might argue or the Americans plea, the conciliatory policy of the North Administration would never include anything like surrendering the right to tax the Americans. North made that absolutely clear when he openly stated that the

Americans maintained they were "subjects of the King" and "have nothing to do with" Parliament. He even added, "we should have been perfectly quiet, if this government at any time had been able or willing by such a wicked act to come into that idea." Within his understanding of the Constitution, the "whole ground" was covered by "the claim of Parliament."[11]

Lord Chief Justice Mansfield was more than pleased with the new regime. When this session of Parliament came to an end on 19 May 1770, the political nation thoroughly understood that the temporary union of Chatham and Rockingham—never a coherent alliance—had completely collapsed. With the North Administration now firmly in control and remarkably unified, it was easy for the ministry to decide to wait and see how the Americans would respond to the Repeal of the Townshend's Duties, Except on Tea.[12]

WHAT agitated the political world during the recess of Parliament was a series of libel suits that arose from a letter that *Junius* addressed to the King, a letter that (in Lord Campbell's telling) "contained insinuations and charges against his Majesty's conduct and personal honor." After this letter appeared in Henry Sampson Woodfall's *Public Advertiser*, John Almon and John Miller quickly republished it in their newspapers as well. Although separate libel cases were promptly filed against these different publishers, the trials did not commence in the Court of King's Bench until the summer of 1770.

The attention of the reading public was captured by how the Lord Chief Justice understood the role of juries in these libel cases. When the case against John Almon was brought before the Court of King's Bench in June, the question of whether the published letter was libelous never even came up—it was simply assumed. The government had sent an agent to Almon's shop and bought a copy from a clerk. Although it was argued that Almon should not be found guilty for an act performed by a clerk who had sold this copy, Mansfield ruled, "a sale by the servant was *prima facie* evidence of a publication by the master." The jury was instructed to rule on the narrow ground of whether Almon had published a letter by *Junius* already in circulation. Since his name was clearly on the title page as the publisher, the jury returned a verdict of guilty. This result, however, ran into vigorous opposition from the public clamoring for the freedom of the press.

When the case against Henry Sampson Woodfall was tried a few weeks later, Mansfield's opinion on the role of juries was immediately challenged. As the publisher of the original letter Woodfall was clearly as liable as Almon for the fact of printing, but whether the letter itself was libelous was now raised for the first time. Mansfield ruled that it was not the position of a jury to decide so delicate a question. While the jury could determine the import of "the *innuendoes*" such as whether "the K___" referred to King George III, it could not enter into the law itself, only the fact. After hours of deliberation the jury returned a verdict of "GUILTY of the printing and publishing ONLY."

That qualification of a guilty verdict signaled a significant shift in public opinion, a fact not wasted upon Mansfield, for when the case against John Miller was tried he adjusted his final instructions to the jury. His opening statement was consistent with his longstanding directions: "I inform you that the question for your determination is whether the defendant printed and published a paper of such tenor and meaning as is charged by the information." He even told the jury that it had nothing whatsoever to do with whether the paper was "legal or illegal." But then he surprisingly added, "If you choose to determine the point of law, you should be very sure, for your conscience' sake, that your determination is law; but if the law was in every case to be determined by juries, we should be in a miserable condition, as nothing could be more uncertain, from the different opinions of mankind."

To Mansfield's chagrin, the jury did take the second half of his instructions to heart and ruled on whether the letter was libelous. And this is what happened, according to Lord Campbell's narrative:

> Half the population of London was assembled in the streets surrounding Guildhall, and remained

several hours impatiently expecting the result. Lord Mansfield had retired to his house [on the fashionable Bloomsbury Square], and many thousands proceeded thither in grand procession when it was announced that the jury had agreed. At last a shout, proceeding from Bloomsbury Square and reverberated from the remotest quarters of the metropolis, proclaimed a verdict of NOT GUILTY.

To his sorrow, Mansfield realized that the ground had shifted more than significantly in the public's understanding of the liberty of the press. For the same offence three juries had returned three incompatible verdicts.

When the Woodfall case came up for review—after the verdict in the Miller case had been given—the lawyers pressed diametrically opposing interpretations of "ONLY" in the original Woodfall verdict. After much wrangling (according to Walpole's version) Mansfield "in the coldest fit of his panic" declared the qualification had introduced "discordance." Therefore, he ordered "the verdict to be set aside and that there should be a new trial," which meant (in Lord Campbell's telling) that "Woodfall was henceforth secure, for it was well known that no jury in the city of London would find a verdict against the publisher of JUNIUS, what ever they might be told from the bench as to their functions or their duties."[13]

LORD Chief Justice Mansfield could take some comfort in the way his fellow judges all agreed with his interpretation of the libel law. Before sentencing John Almon in November, Judge Richard Aston openly stated that *he should pay very little regard to any affidavit* presented in support of Almon's innocence, especially one from Robert Morris, even though he was "a gentleman of unquestionable honour and integrity." And, according to *Junius*, Morris had presented "his evidence on oath."[14]

As a "Barrister at Law and late Secretary to the Supporters of the Bill of Rights," Morris retaliated by publishing an open letter to Sir

Richard Aston that called attention to the remarkable unanimity on the Court of King's Bench ever since Lord Chief Justice Mansfield was appointed in 1756. When John Adams read Morris's letter a few months later, he entered this lengthy reflection in his Diary:

> This mettlesome Barrister gives us the best Account of the Unanimity of the Kings Bench that I have ever heard or read. According to him, it is not uncommon abilities, Integrity and Temper as Mr. Burrows would perswade us, but sheer fear of Lord M[ansfiel]d, the Scottish Chief which produces this Miracle in the moral and intellectual World—i.e. of 4 Judges, agreeing perfectly in every Rule, order and Judgment for 14 Years together. 4 Men never agreed so perfectly in Sentiment, for so long a Time, before. 4 Clocks never struck together, a thousandth Part of the Time, 4 Minds never thought, reasoned, and judged alike, before for a ten thousandth Part.

While it cannot be determined with confidence exactly when Adams began tracking Mansfield's innovations, this entry is the first significant entry in his Diary on the overarching influence of our Scottish Law Lord.[15]

THE arguments over the libel laws reached something of a climax when *Junius* addressed "THE RIGHT HONOURABLE LORD MANSFIELD" on 14 November 1770. When *Junius* submitted this letter the day after Parliament reopened, he informed Woodfall, "We have got the Rascal down. Let us strangle him if it be possible." Writing to Horace Mann, Walpole pronounced this letter to be "the most outrageous, I suppose, ever published against so high a magistrate by name."

For some months *Junius* had been attacking the "new principles of government" that he thought were destroying "the substance of our civil and political liberties." In his judgment, "A new system has not only been adopted in fact, but professed upon principle. Ministers are no longer the public servants of the state, but the private domestics of the Sovereign." That ongoing transformation had been engineered by *the King's friends*, a "particular class of men" that *Junius* defined in a footnote by citing this statement by Davenant: "An ignorant, mercenary, and servile crew; unanimous in evil, diligent in mischief, variable in principles, constant in flattery, talkers of liberty, but slaves to power."[16]

The opening salvo in this 14 November letter was this nasty: "Our language has no term of reproach, the mind has no idea of detestation which has not already been happily applied to you, and exhausted." As *Junius* cast his eye over our Scottish Law Lord's political career, he entertained no doubt that Mansfield was intent upon "reviving and establishing the maxims of government" championed by "the banished house of Stuart." So far as *Junius* was concerned, Mansfield had always been "a rank Jacobite." He called attention to the fact that his older brother had served as "CONFIDENTIAL Secretary to the late Pretender." He even dragged up how "Lord Ravensworth produced the most satisfactory Evidence of his having frequently drank the Pretender's health upon his knees." Given this Jacobite background, *Junius* had no difficulty in discovering "one uniform plan to enlarge the power of the crown, at the expence of the liberty of the subject. To this object, your thoughts, words and actions have been constantly directed."[17]

In this frontal assault *Junius* labored how Lord Mansfield would "meanly skulk into the closet and give your Sovereign such advice, as you have not spirit to avow or defend." So far as *Junius* could tell, for all his attempts to pretend that he took "no share in government," it remained the case that he was "the main spring of the machine."[18]

Mansfield's jurisprudential reform project then came in for a savage attack that fairly well summarizes the critique *Junius* was intent upon advancing:

> In contempt or ignorance of the common law of England, you have made it your study to introduce into the court where you preside, maxims of

jurisprudence unknown to Englishmen. The
Roman code, the laws of nations, and the opinion
of foreign civilians, are your perpetual theme—but
whoever heard you mention Magna Charta or the
Bill of Rights with approbation or respect? By such
treacherous arts the noble simplicity and free spirit
of our Saxon laws were first corrupted. The Norman
conquest was not complete, until the Norman
lawyers had introduced their laws, and reduced
slavery to a system.

To document his charge *Junius* then reviewed a variety of cases in
order to expose *the pattern* exhibited in the rulings handed down
in the Court of King's Bench, a pattern that had transformed this
court into "a court of equity" governed by the rules appropriate
to the Chancery Court. And he concluded this letter by casting
coals of liquid fire upon the cobwebs this spider of the law was
weaving in Westminster Hall: "No learned man, even among your
own tribe, thinks you qualified to preside in a court of common law.
Yet it is confessed, that under *Justinian*, you might have made an
incomparable *Praetor*."[19]

ALTHOUGH it had been assumed that Parliament would not
reconvene until after Christmas, Spanish naval forces had expelled
the British military from the Falkland Islands off the coast of
Argentina during the summer recess, thereby forcing an earlier
meeting of Parliament. With attention focused on Argentina—and
because it had become clear that the Non -Importation Agreement
was beginning to collapse in the wake of the decision by New York to
open its port to all British goods except tea—North "chose to waive
entirely for the present … the subject of America."[20]

Besides wrangling over the conflict with Spain, Parliament took
up Mansfield's recent rulings on the libel law. On 6 December 1770
John Glynn moved for "a committee to inquire into the proceedings
of the judges in Westminster Hall, particularly in cases relating to the

liberty of the press." Soon John Dunning took up the cause. Finally, Edmund Burke weighed in on the proceedings in the Court of King's Bench. According to Walpole, "The House sat till near one in the morning, but the question was lost by 75 against 180."[21]

That same day Chatham brought up in the House of Lords yet once again the issue of the Middlesex Election, but in a digression he alluded to "the modern manner of directing a jury from the bench, and giving judgment upon prosecutions for libels." Mansfield responded sharply: "the directions now given to juries are the same that they have ever been." He even claimed that Chatham had so thoroughly exhibited his "*ignorance*" that "the highest authorities will not extend his ideas of jurisprudence nor entitle him to a patient hearing upon a legal question in this assembly." Before finishing he informed the House, with *Junius* in mind, "The scurrility of a newspaper may be good information for a coffee-house politician; but a peer of parliament should always speak from higher authority."

Mansfield carried the day, even though both Chatham and Camden responded with vigor. With his spirits elevated by this triumph, the next day he "intimated that he had something of importance to bring to the notice of the House." According to Lord Campbell, "It was generally believed that the Lord Chief Justice was going to move a vote of censure on Lord Chatham and Lord Camden for calumniating the Judges, and the coming passage of arms between them was expected to be more dazzling than any ever before witnessed." But at the decisive moment Mansfield simply rose and announced calmly, "My Lords, I have left a paper with the clerk-assistant of this House, containing the judgment of the Court of King's Bench in the case of *The King against Woodfall*, and any of your Lordships who may be so inclined may read it and take copies of it." When he sat down, Camden asked whether "the noble and learned Lord on the woolsack" intended to make a motion. Mansfield replied, "No, no! Only to leave it with the clerk."

Those looking for some dazzle were deeply disappointed by this turn of events, but after studying Mansfield's paper Camden declared the following day that it was "a challenge directed personally to me, and I accept it; he has thrown down the gauntlet, and I take it up. In direct contradiction to him I maintain that his doctrine is not the law of England." Indeed, he thought Mansfield's instructions to the jury were not only "illegal and unconstitutional" but not very intelligible as well. He then posed several technical questions that he wanted Mansfield to answer categorically.

After paying Camden "the highest compliments" in the polite language so fashionable in the etiquette of the House, Mansfield reached this climax: "I will not answer interrogatories!" At that point Chatham shouted, *"Interrogatories!"* And he proceeded to browbeat Mansfield by pointing out that the Lord Chief Justice had "so recently imprisoned a man (Brindley) for a year or two, for refusing to submit" to his own interrogations. According to Walpole's *Memoirs*, "The dismay and confusion of Lord Mansfield was obvious to the whole audience; nor did one peer interpose a syllable in his behalf; even the court ... despised his pusillanimity and meanness."[22]

PARLIAMENT adjourned for the Christmas holidays, and before it reconvened in late January 1771 the war scare over the Falkland Island had largely dissolved. Even though the question of sovereignty was left in limbo, the King of Spain promised to allow the British to return, and the North Administration eagerly embraced so ambiguous a resolution of the crisis.

For some months Mansfield had also been signaling that he no longer wanted to continue as the Acting Lord Chancellor. So, when Parliament reconvened the least competent of the three Commissioners holding the Great Seal over the past year would be sitting on the woolsack as the Lord Chancellor and Speaker of the House of Lords with the title of Lord Apsley. Walpole sarcastically noted that the legal profession punned on his title by "calling him Lord Absque," which the editors of his *Memoirs* explained as "a Latinism roughly translatable as 'Lord Absent' or 'Lord Not With Us'." The appointment of Apsley, it should be mentioned, did not change the situation to any significant extent, for the new Lord Chancellor was (in Walpole's words) "too poor a creature to have any weight," while the Lord Chief Justice "had more weight with the King than Lord North himself."[23]

Prime Minister North's grip on power had been solidified by recent events, too. After the death of George Grenville, he gained a significant portion of his followers. Alexander Wedderburn now became Solicitor General. When Southern Secretary Weymouth resigned, Rochford was transferred to the Southern department, thereby opening the way for Lord Suffolk to become the Secretary of State for the Northern department. When Edward Hawke resigned, Lord Sandwich returned as First Lord of the Admiralty. And Thomas Whately—the prime architect of the doctrine of virtual representation—returned to the Board of Trade. In brief, persons directly identified with the Stamp Act were now completely in charge of the imperial government.[24]

IN February the political nation became embroiled in the Printers' Case. Since 1729 there had been a standing order prohibiting the publication of the parliamentary debates, but for some time John Almon had been printing in the *London Evening Post* three times a week what he called "a sketch of every day's debate" and it did not take long before other newspapers followed in his steps. When the North Administration tried to stop these publications, it played into the hands of John Wilkes, who conspired with John Almon, John Miller, and Robert Morris to trap the government into yet another confrontation.[25]

After being summoned for violating a standing order against publishing parliamentary debates, John Miller deliberately refused to attend the House of Commons. The next day the Speaker of the House, Sir Fletcher Norton, issued a warrant for his arrest, but when the messenger attempted to arrest him, a constable of the City charged the messenger with assault and false arrest. The constable then escorted Miller and the messenger, plus witnesses, to the Mansion House, where they found Lord Mayor Crosby sick in bed with the gout. When the hearing finally got under way, Robert Morris served as Miller's counsel before Crosby and two Aldermen,

Richard Oliver and John Wilkes. They ruled, after much haggling, that Miller had been illegally arrested because the messenger was not a constable of the City and no City magistrate had issued a warrant for his arrest. The messenger was ordered to appear at the next session of the court to answer the complaint filed against him. Of course, the populace fully supported the chartered privileges of the City. Hats started showing up carrying the banner "Crosby, Wilkes, Oliver, and the Liberty of the Press." The mob grew violent; members of the House of Commons were harassed; North's carriage was trashed on 27 March 1771.[26]

After Alderman Oliver refused to defend himself before the House of Commons, he announced with deliberation, "I know the punishment I am to receive is determined upon. I have nothing to say, … I defy you." To the Tower he went. Next to go was Lord Mayor Crosby. At the end of the parliamentary session, when Oliver and Crosby finally walked out of the Tower, they were escorted in triumph to the Mansion House by fifty-three carriages.

The ministry's attempt to stop the London press from reporting on the debates in the House of Commons was a dismal failure, for (as Peter D. G. Thomas writes), "Long before the release of Crosby and Oliver reporting was in progress as if there had never been any interruption." The liberty of the press was officially celebrated on 24 January 1772 when silver cups were given not only to Crosby and Oliver but also to Wilkes "for the noble stand they made in the business of the printer." (Publication of the debates in the House of Lords, however, did not resume until January 1775.)[27]

THE *Somerset* case that came up in early February 1772 posed the critical question on whether a Negro slave could be kept in bondage after he landed in England. Legal opinion was none too clear on that question. The person determined to force Mansfield to render his authoritative judgment on the question was Granville Sharp, a gifted flutist in an extended musical family of some renown that performed on a barge along the Thames on Sunday afternoons. (G. Sharp was given to signing his name "G#" on occasions.)[28]

Sharp earned his living by working in the Ordnance Office, a rather minor government position that left this talented amateur musician with plenty of time on his hands to cultivate his own wide-ranging interests. The organizing passion that captured his attention in the late 1760s was the legal status of slavery in the English Common Law Heritage. What provoked this passion was the dreadful appearance of a slave who showed up barely alive at the medical office of his older brother. It did not take long before he became a prominent leader within the nascent anti-slavery movement.

Sharp soon came to the conclusion that many of those learned in the law had embraced a 1729 opinion by Solicitor General Talbot and Attorney General Yorke that slaves brought into England still remained slaves even if they had been baptized as Christians. That opinion, however, had not been handed down in a court of law dealing with an actual case. According to Simon Schama in *Rough Crossings*, it was "merely an informal opinion voiced after dinner at Lincoln's Inn when the gentlemen were at their ease with pipes and wine."[29] (The future Lord Mansfield was a student of the law when this opinion was aired.) After Philip Yorke became Lord Chancellor Hardwicke, he reaffirmed that informal opinion. (The future Lord Mansfield was Hardwicke's closest advisor when this reaffirmation occurred.)

Without the slightest preparation in legal studies, our inquiring flutist plunged into an historical investigation of the issue in order to correct what he considered to be a carefully orchestrated subversion of ancient rights, Christian principles, and English sensibilities. He quickly found some arresting cases:

> In 1569, according to Rushworth's *Historical Collections*, a certain Captain Cartwright had brought a Russian serf-slave to England and, when he had "scourged" the slave without cause and been brought to book for it, had been told by the justice ruling on the case "that England was too pure an air for Slaves to breathe."

That was not all that Sharp uncovered, according to Schama's exposition:

> In 1679, during the reign of Charles II, for example, a law enacted for "the better securing of the Liberty of the Subject" had plainly stated that property in a black could only be upheld if proprietors could prove that the slave "is neither man, woman nor child." The reduction of a man to a beast, it was further said, was "unnatural and unjust." Faithful to that tradition, in 1706 Lord Chief Justice Holt had ruled that "as soon as a Negro comes into England he becomes free," and as recently as 1762 the Lord Chancellor Henley, had invoked ... the Cartwright case in dismissing a claim to a negro as an item of property in a contested inheritance.

Furthermore, Sharp was encouraged in his historical pursuit by a statement he found in the first edition of *Commentaries on the Law of England* by Sir William Blackstone: "The spirit of liberty is so deeply implicated in our constitution and rooted even in our very soil that a slave or negro, the moment he lands in England, falls under the protection of the laws and in regard to all natural rights becomes *eo instanti* [from that moment] a freeman." Armed with these precedents—and Blackstone's *Commentaries*—our gifted musician quickly came to the conclusion that the "informal opinion" of 1729 could be easily refuted.

Alas, the Vinerian Professor of Common Law at Oxford University promptly informed him, ever so politely in a letter, that this statement had been dropped from the later editions of his *Commentaries* because of those informal opinions championed by Solicitor General Talbot and Lord Chancellor Hardwicke.[30] Sharp, however, was not given to bowing before academic authority. With a healthy dose of self-assurance he proceeded to publish *A Representation of the Injustice and dangerous Tendency of tolerating*

Slavery or even Admitting the Least Claim of private Property in the Persons of Men in England.[31]

The relevance of this 1769 tract was initially tested in the Court of King's Bench on 21 February 1771 when Thomas Lewis accused Robert Stapylton and associates of kidnapping him in London. Although the prosecutor quoted extensively from Sharp's *Representation*, he made the tactical mistake of arguing that the black man had been born free, lived as Stapylton's paid servant for years, and had never been Stapylton's slave at any time.

The prosecutor's argument provided Mansfield with an opening to avoid the larger issue. He instructed the jury to ignore the argument on "whether or not there could *ever* be property in persons in England" and to rule narrowly on "whether Lewis, *in particular* could be proved, at the time of his abduction, to have been Stapylton's possession." After being instructed to sidestep the issue of slavery itself, the jury declared Lewis to be a free man because of the particular circumstances of the case. And while the jury found Stapylton guilty of assault, he escaped from any penalty for so minor an offence. Mansfield even let it be known that he was none too pleased with how the larger issue had been pressed.

Sharp, however, was none too pleased with the way the high and mighty Lord Chief Justice had managed to avoid ruling on the legality of slavery. According to Schama,

> In his private notebook he commented, with much indignant underlining, that "the refusal of a proper judgment in this case is so far from being a proper precedent that it ought to be esteemed an open contempt to the legislature and <u>a notorious breach and perversion of the laws</u>."

Sharp furiously continued in the privacy of his notebook,

> I am the more solicitous to protest against this precedent because I had the mortification to hear the <u>same judge</u> upon <u>the same trial quote some</u>

precedents of his own making which are equally
contradictory to the Spirit and meaning of the
English Laws.[32]

Before the *Somerset* case came before the Court of King's Bench, the contest between our gifted musician and our Scottish Law Lord had become deeply personal.

Whereas Thomas Lewis had remained free precisely because he had never been a slave, it was beyond dispute that James Somerset was a certified slave of Charles Stewart, for he had been purchased on the Virginia slave market in 1749, carried to Massachusetts, and brought to London in 1769. After he escaped in September 1771, Stewart and his associates recaptured him. Witnessing the kidnapping, however, was Elizabeth Cade, and she proceeded to secure a writ of Habeas Corpus. To complicate matters, when Somerset was brought before a magistrate, Stewart as well as the captain of the *Ann and Mary*, where he was held below deck, exercised their right to "return to the writ," a technical phrase that permitted a reversal of the charge, a clever tactic encouraged by Mansfield himself. Since Stewart had complained that Somerset had defrauded him of his property, Somerset—not the slave master or the ship captain—stood as the accused in the clutches of the law machine. Even more surprisingly, the prosecutor presenting the case against Somerset was the legal luminary who had argued so eloquently from Sharp's *Representation* in the Lewis trial the previous year.[33]

On hearing about the unfolding situation Sharp sprang into action. Not only did he promote the trial through the network coalescing around the anti-slavery cause, he retained a team of competent lawyers to defend Somerset. Serjeant-at-Law William Davy (known as "Bull" Davy) was the leading lawyer. He also retained Serjeant-at-Law John Glynn, who had been closely associated with John Wilkes since the *North Briton, Number 45* affair in 1763. Then as a stand-in for the imprisoned Wilkes, he had won the December 1768 Middlesex Election, had served as John Almon's counsel in the case of reprinting a libelous letter of *Junius*, and had introduced the 6 December 1770 motion for an inquiry into Lord Mansfield's instructions to juries in libel cases. Then on 5 April 1771 he and another lawyer unsuccessfully pleaded in the Court of King's Bench for a writ of Habeas Corpus to liberate the Lord Mayor of London, Brass Crosby, and Alderman Richard Oliver from the Tower of London. In addition to Davy and Glynn, the defense team included Francis Hargrave (an antiquarian expert), John Alleyne (an upcoming young volunteer in the cause), plus another confidante of John Wilkes, James Mansfield (no relation to the Chief Justice). With such high-powered legal talent in play, the London press, coming off its triumph in the Printers' Case, eagerly prepared to cover the action in the Court of King's Bench.[34]

One suspects that Mansfield realized that he could no longer skirt the issue of slavery itself as he had in the Lewis trial, for he tried to persuade Elizabeth Cade to avoid the trial by purchasing Somerset from Stewart and setting him free! Her response? She let it be known that his suggestion would amount to "an acknowledgement that the plaintiff had a right to assault and imprison a poor innocent man in this kingdom and that she would never be guilty of setting so bad an example."

Serjeant Davy opened the argument in defense of Somerset by referring to the ruling in the Cartwright case during Queen Elizabeth's reign when "it was resolved that England was too pure an air for Slaves to breathe in," then he pointedly continued, "I hope, My Lord, the Air does not blow worse since." During a lengthy rehearsal of all the historical record Davy also labored the point that regardless of what may have been legal in the British colonies, their laws should have no more "influence, power or authority in *this* country than the laws of Japan." Although Glynn was much briefer than Davy, Mansfield decided that the argumentation would be so extensive that it could not be finished during this February term. So, the parties had a three-month recess to prepare for the next round in the *Somerset* case, which opened in May 1772.[35]

When the case resumed, James Mansfield, Francis Hargrave, and John Alleyne defended Somerset admirably by pressing the terrible plight of slaves in America and emphasizing the centrality of liberty in the English Common Law Heritage. So powerful were these lines of argument that Mansfield "began to wonder out loud about the social and economic consequences were every enslaved black in Britain to suppose he had got his freedom along with Somerset." (There were somewhere in the neighborhood of 15,000 slaves in England at the time. Valued at, say, £50 per person—the standard price for a stout Negro on the open market—that would add up to £750,000. The Townshend Duties, in comparison, were netting around a miserly £11,000 per annum.)

The climax of the argumentation came during Davy's review of the case history that documented just how repugnant slavery actually was in the English Common Law Heritage. Lord Chief Justice Mansfield was taken aback, interrupting Davy at one point with this observation: "If what you say is true then I had better burn all my law books." Davy had the address to respond: "My Lord had better read them first."[36]

For a full month the Lord Chief Justice pondered the case before handing down his judgment. As usual he maneuvered around the general issue and focused narrowly on the particular circumstances in this case. His convoluted reasoning turned on the technical question of whether those prosecuting Somerset had proven that they were the victims because Somerset had violated their lawful claims by trying to escape. Had the charge against Somerset been adequately sustained? That was the question. A hush fell over Westminster Hall before our Scottish Law Lord finally announced: "we cannot say the Cause set forth by this Return [to the writ] is allowed or approved of by the Laws of this Kingdom; therefore, the Man must be discharged."[37]

That Mansfield himself did not entertain the belief that his ruling made slavery illegal in England is most convincingly documented by his attachment to Dido Elizabeth Belle Lindsay, the mulatto daughter of one of his nephews and a West Indies black female. Dido lived at Kenwood for about thirty years, and apparently Mansfield was quite fond of her. According to Julius Bryant in *The Iveagh Bequest:*

Kenwood, "At Lord Mansfield's death in 1793 she was left £500 and an annuity of £100 for life." Then Bryant troubled to add this decisive clarification: "He also took the precaution of confirming her freedom from slavery in his will."[38] (Slavery was not officially ruled to be illegal in England until much later.)

Why Mansfield set James Somerset free on 22 June 1772 may never be known with confidence. Nevertheless, it was widely assumed that the case of *Somerset* did mark a critical turning point in the history of the anti-slavery cause. And it is reasonable to assume that he did not want to provide *Junius* with a ruling that could be construed as being repugnant to the English Common Law Heritage.[39]

IN late 1771 *Junius* reopened his claim that the Lord Chief Justice of King's Bench had not only introduced "*new law*" but had also "removed the landmarks established by former decisions." Because Mansfield's organizing intention was "to bring every thing within the *arbitrium* of a *praetorian* court"—"changing a court of *common law* to a court of *equity*"—*Junius* thought "he will have it in his power to do injustice, *whenever he thinks proper.*" He even intensified his blistering critique by asking a long series of pointed questions:

> Who attacks the liberty of the press? Lord Mansfield. Who invades the constitutional power of juries? Lord Mansfield. Who is it makes commissioners of the great seal? Lord Mansfield. Who is he, that has made it the study and practice of his life, to undermine and alter the whole system of jurisprudence in the court of King's Bench? Lord Mansfield.

Then he added this stinger: "Compared to these enormities, his original attachment to the Pretender ... is a virtue of the first magnitude. But the hour of impeachment *will* come, and neither he nor Grafton shall escape me."[40]

This call for the impeachment of the Lord Chief Justice of King's Bench was occasioned by the arrest of John Eyre for stealing paper from Guildhall, a "piddling" affair that Walpole thought noteworthy only for providing an opportunity to revive the proverbial abuse of Scotland in general and Mansfield in particular.[41] Whereas the local magistrates had refused to grant Eyre bail on the grounds that he had been caught red-handed in the act (or in the technical language of the law, with the thing stolen upon him, *in manu*), Mansfield proceeded to grant him bail on 19 October.

Soon *Junius* charmed the public with this announcement in Letter LXV: "I affirm, in contradiction to YOU, LORD CHIEF JUSTICE MANSFIELD, that, by the laws of England, he was *not bailable*. If ever *Mr. Eyre* should be brought to trial, we shall hear what You have to say for Yourself; and I pledge myself, before God and my country, in proper time and place to make good my charge against you." Finally, in a letter addressed to Mansfield, *Junius* made this grand pronouncement: "you stand degraded from the respect and authority of your office, and are no longer, *de jure*, Lord Chief Justice of England." Attached to this letter was this parting shot: "Considering the situation and abilities of Lord Mansfield, I do not scruple to affirm, with the most solemn appeal to God for my sincerity, that in *my* judgment, he is the very worst and most dangerous man in the kingdom."[42]

From the outset of his quarrel with Mansfield, *Junius* had castigated him for abandoning the Common Law in favor of the Roman Civil Law. Indeed, his initial letter contained this prescient remark: "It is remarkable enough, but I hope not ominous, that the laws you understand best, and the judges you affect to admire most, flourished in the decline of a great empire, and are supposed to have contributed to its fall."[43]

American affairs were quite incidental to the concerns *Junius* was intent upon addressing, but at one point he pointedly suggested, "The spirit of the Americans may be a useful example to us. Our dogs and horses are only English upon English grounds; but patriotism, it seems, may be improved by transplanting" to America.[44] In yet another letter, written in the third person: "*Junius* considers the right of taxing the colonies, by an act of the British Legislature, as a *speculative* right merely, never to be *exerted*, nor ever to be *renounced.*"[45] On this pivotal issue he agreed with Rockingham over against Chatham.

If all the different people accused of being this Epistolary Sphinx were gathered together in a group, such a crowd of witnesses could march in a rather impressive parade in front of Westminster Hall to exhibit their opposition by burning in effigy the Lord Chief Justice of King's Bench, with a sign hanging around his neck taken directly from the *Letters of Junius*: "the CHIEF JUGGLER behind the curtain."[46]

THOMAS HUTCHINSON:
LORD MANSFIELD'S
FOREMOST AMERICAN
DISCIPLE

OLLOWING THE REPEAL OF THE TOWNSHEND DUTIES,
EXCEPT ON TEA, THE BRITISH government adopted a prudent
wait and see attitude—and was encouraged by what it saw. After
the port of New York reopened for business (on everything but tea
from the British Isles) the other colonies soon followed suit. Even
Massachusetts appeared to settle down several months after the
Boston Massacre. "There seems now to be a pause in politics," the
Rev. Samuel Cooper wrote in a letter to Benjamin Franklin, adding,
"The agreement of the merchants is broken. Administration has a
fair opportunity of adopting the mildest and most prudent measure
respecting the colonies without the appearance of being threatened
or drove."[1] But the North Administration blithely ignored this fair
opportunity and let the trifling tax on tea stand.

About the time Mansfield declared James Somerset a free man
in Westminster Hall, disturbing news arrived in London that on
10 June 1772 the *Gaspée* had been burned after it ran aground off

the coast of Pawtuxet, Rhode Island. Governor Hutchinson of the Bay Colony told the ministry directly, "If some measures are not taken in England in consequence of so flagrant an insult upon the King's authority, I fear it will encourage the neighbouring colonies to persevere in their opposition to the laws of trade and to be guilty of the like and greater acts of violence."[2] For a schooner in the Royal Navy to be torched and its commander seriously wounded spelled the end to the wait and see stance so carefully cultivated by the North Administration.

Two weeks after the report on the *Gaspée* affair arrived in London the cabinet took up "the Rhode Island business." Because it was not clear exactly what crime had been committed, American Secretary Hillsborough was ordered to consult with Solicitor General Wedderburn and Attorney General Thurlow. Given that the burning of one of His Majesty's warships registered on the Attorney General's scale at "five times the magnitude of the Stamp Act," it was not at all surprising that the law officers put the worst possible interpretation on the assault, declaring it to be "an act of high treason."[3]

In the midst of this struggle the hard charging Hillsborough was replaced by the mild mannered Lord Dartmouth. Although it was assumed that this change in the ministry signaled a turning even further away from a hard line in colonial policy, in one of his first official acts as the new American Secretary, Dartmouth sent formal instructions to Governor Wanton of Rhode Island: "It is His Majesty's intention that the persons concerned in the burning the *Gaspée* schooner, and in the other violences which attended that daring insult, should be brought to England to be tried." And the trial would be conducted under the Treason Act of Henry VIII.[4]

While it is reasonable to suppose that Wedderburn and Thurlow consulted Mansfield before handing down their decision, his role in this cabinet decision remains obscure. What does remain clear is that his foremost American disciple—the Governor of Massachusetts, Thomas Hutchinson—radically impacted the escalating controversy over the Constitution of the British Empire.

THOMAS Hutchinson had a thorough command of the institutional development of colonial New England. He had served as the Lieutenant Governor of Massachusetts since 1758, and the Acting Governor from the moment Sir Francis Bernard left for England in 1769. With great reluctance and transparent anxiety he had consented to become the Royal Governor, formally taking the oath of office on 14 March 1771.[5]

Hutchinson adored Lord Chief Justice Mansfield, carefully noting his every move at least since, say, the late 1750s. And for years this learned historian and political leader had pleaded with correspondents in London to prod the government to adopt a sensible colonial plan and pursue it with a steady hand. He had also attempted for years to persuade those in leadership positions throughout Massachusetts that it was in their self-interest to settle down and obey the laws, as Parliament in its wisdom saw fit to enact them. With merely a touch of sweet reasonableness on both sides, he was convinced everything would be just fine. What he could not fathom was why his arguments fell increasingly upon deaf ears. Immediately after the burning of the *Gaspée* in neighboring Rhode Island, for example, he asked some sober members of the House of Representatives, "what good can come from such rash, intemperate measures?" They assured him that he was not at all the problem. They admired his efforts—reconciliation with Great Britain was greatly to be desired. The problem was that the House supposed "a design" had been "formed to enslave them by degrees." And so long as that suspicion endured, these colonial leaders were determined to "make a stand against the measures which the ministry are taking to enslave them."[6]

Maddening though that line of oppositional thought was to the frustrated and anxious Governor, it only intensified when it was finally confirmed in July 1772—after a year of vigorous agitation—that he had been granted a crown salary of £1,500 per annum. Immediately a House committee attacked this "dangerous innovation" because it destroyed an essential "check" and "balance" in the constitution. Within moments it was also rumored that from now on crown salaries—partially funded by the trifling tax on tea—would be provided for the judges on the Superior Court of Massachusetts. "Indignation, fear, and rage roared like a sheet of flame across the troubled community," according to Bernard Bailyn's narrative in *The Ordeal of Thomas Hutchinson*.[7] Desperate to dampen the conflagration Hutchinson prorogued the General Court.[8]

At a town meeting on 28 October 1772 Boston took up the issue by voting to inform the Governor that the town was "apprehensive" that this novel mode of paying the salaries of such high officers in the civil government would be "attended with the most fatal consequences." His response? "It is by no means proper for me to lay before the inhabitants of any town whatsoever ... any part of my correspondence as Governor of this Province." And so it went until finally Samuel Adams moved on 2 November that "a Committee of Correspondence be appointed, to consist of twenty-one persons, to state the Rights of the Colonists and of this Province in particular, *as men, as Christians, and as subjects*" (my emphasis).[9]

The deep background for this initiative was laid in the preamble to the 1641 Massachusetts Body of Liberties:

> The free fruition of such liberties Immunities and priveledges as *humanitie, Civilitie, and Christianitie* call for as due to every man in his place and proportion without impeachment and Infringement hath ever bene and ever will be the tranquilitie and Stabilitie of Churches and Commonwealths. And the deniall or deprivall thereof, the disturbance if not the ruine of both [my emphasis].[10]

"Humanity, Civility, Christianity"—that hierarchy of meaning and value exhibits the traditional frame of reference in the New England Mind. As participants in humanity, the people held *human rights*. As participants in civility, the people held *civil rights*. And as participants in Christianity, the people held *religious rights*.

The people's *religious rights* were initially threatened in the early 1760s by an attempt "to establish an American Episcopate." The Stamp Act Crisis that immediately followed that paper quarrel opened what the Americans called "the pernicious Project" that directly assaulted their *civil rights*. As the conflict deepened, the Americans increasingly took their stand on their *human rights*. While the organizing focus of the contest at this juncture fell on *the civil rights of the American subjects of the King*, all three dimensions interpenetrated throughout the struggle.

On 20 November 1772 the Committee of Correspondence filed its report on *The State of the Rights of the Colonists*, plus a twelve item *List of Infringements and Violations of Rights*. This expansive list covered a plethora of grievances, but the occasional cause was the sixth, which unequivocally stated that Massachusetts could no longer be a "free state" if "an equilibrium" that is "absolutely necessary in a mixt government" was not preserved. What was subverting Massachusetts as a free state was spelled out in detail:

> In particular it has always been held that the dependence of the Governor of this Province upon the General Assembly for his support, was necessary for the preservation of this equilibrium; nevertheless His Majesty has been pleased to apply fifteen hundred pounds sterling annually out of the American revenue, for the support of the Governor of this Province independent of the Assembly, whereby the ancient connection between him and this people is weakened, the confidence in the Governor lessened and the equilibrium destroyed, and the constitution essentially altered.

After adding that the other principal officers in the civil government would also be supported in the same way—"from the best intelligence we have been able to obtain"—grievance six concluded, "This will if accomplished compleat our slavery."[11]

IN the midst of this controversy Great Britain took up the new Tea Act. While the Tea Act would radically alter the way a cup of tea was supposed to be taxed in America, the colonies were not the primary focus. That concerned the ways and means of relieving the embarrassing financial situation of the East India Company, a venerable corporation established during the Reign of Queen Elizabeth. Since 1698 the Company had held a monopoly on imports into England from Asia, but it had to auction its goods on the open market to merchants, who then sold the goods to customers. While these imports into England were ordinarily charged a 25% *ad valorem* custom duty, in 1721 all East Indian exports to America were granted a drawback of three-fifths of that 25% tax so that the Americans paid only a 10% custom duty. That at least was the standard operating procedure during the period leading up to the Indemnity Act of 1767, an Act that allowed *as a five-year experiment* a full 100% drawback of this traditional customs duty on all the many items exported to America from Great Britain.[12]

According to the calculations of Benjamin Woods Labaree in his splendid study, *The Boston Tea Party*, "English merchants trading with America waited until the [Indemnity] Act took effect in July 1767, when the actual price of Bohea [tea] was dropped by the drawback from 2s. 9d. to 2s. 1d., and then shipped out enough tea to bring the year's total to about 500,000 pounds. In the year following 869,000 pounds were exported to the colonies, the largest amount yet."[13]

Although the price of tea varied according to quality and type, the Indemnity Act of 1767 *reduced* the price of tea by around eight pence per pound during the time of this five-year experiment. The Townshend Duties Act that shortly followed in 1767, however, imposed a three-pence per pound tax on tea. Consequently, the reduction turned out to be around 5 pence per pound.

Whereas the traditional custom duty and in turn the drawback were understood to be regulations of trade, the Townshend Duties were explicitly designed to raise revenue in America "for defraying the charge of the administration of justice, and the support of civil government." And that openly stated difference is precisely what triggered the Non-Importation Agreement that lasted from late 1768 to late 1770.

In 1770 Parliament repealed the Townshend Duties—*except on tea*. While that effectively ended the Non-Importation Agreement, the boycott on English tea remained in effect, though it was honored more faithfully in Philadelphia and New York than in Boston. In Philadelphia the legal sale of tea fell between 1768 and 1772 from 174,883 pounds a year to 128 pounds. In New York it fell from 320,214 to 530 over the same period. But the quantity of legal tea sold in Boston told a remarkably different story. Over against New York's 269 pounds and Philadelphia's zero in 1770, New England imported 85,935 pounds, only to see that figure rise to a grand 282,857 pounds of English tea dutifully taxed at three pence per pound in 1771.[14] To labor the obvious, Boston relied vastly more upon legally imported English tea than its neighbors to the south, who were happily enjoying their smuggled Dutch brew and looking askance at their less faithful merchants to the north.

Calculating the amount of smuggled tea is transparently something of a guessing game, but there is a working consensus among historians that around three-fourths of the tea consumed in America during this period was illegally imported, mostly from Holland through New York and Philadelphia. Thomas Hutchinson put American consumption of tea at above six million pounds a year; Samuel Wharton of Philadelphia guessed five million; a London merchant suggested three million.[15] In any event, in 1772 the expiration of the five-year experiment under the Indemnity Act automatically revived the 10% *ad valorem* custom duty on legally imported tea, thereby raising the price of English tea by, say, five pence per pound, which, of course, enhanced the position of the numerous smugglers of illegal tea in the American market.[16] It should not go unnoticed that the Americans did not protest this rise in the price of tea in 1772.

For a variety of reasons—not all related to the American boycott—the East India Company had amassed a good three years supply of tea in its warehouses in Great Britain. With so much excess tea molding away at enormous expense, the Company turned to the government for relief. What it got (in the words of Labaree) was "a drastic reorganization" that placed the Company under firmer governmental control.

To cope with the growing financial emergency, one of the various options under consideration was a plan to dump the excess tea on continental Europe at a reduced price, but that was soon scratched when it was pointed out that the tea would be instantly smuggled back into Great Britain, thereby further undercutting tea in the home market. That gambit failing, attention turned to America. The task at hand was to devise a way to squeeze the smugglers out of their lucrative market. According to Labaree's account, the plan was this simple: "if the East India Company were to export its surplus directly to the colonies free of all English custom duties and at rock-bottom prices, perhaps Dutch tea could be undersold there." With that strategy in mind, the Company petitioned Parliament "that leave may be given to export teas *duty free* to America" (my emphasis).[17]

PRIME Minister North opened the debate in the House of Commons with this observation: "it appears that the East India Company have now actually in their warehouses very near seventeen million pounds of tea, which the Company report near three years' consumption." Given that disastrous situation, the Company "shall now be empowered to pursue the export of tea, *free from all duties, both importation duties and taxes*" directly to America (my emphasis). That meant that the Company would no longer have to process tea through English middleman merchants. It also meant that the 10% *ad valorem* tax that had been reintroduced in 1772 would be cancelled for yet another five-year experiment.

William Dowdeswell, spokesman for the Rockingham party, immediately pointed out an ambiguity in North's announcement: "I observe that the Noble Lord has made no proposition with regard to the duty laid upon teas imported into America." North responded to Dowdeswell observation with force: "I am unwilling to give up that duty upon America upon which the [colonial salaries] are charged. If the East India Company will export tea to America, they will very much increase that duty, and consequently very much facilitate carrying on government in that part. I see no reason for taking it off. I must see very substantial reasons before I part with a fund so applicable to the support of civil" government in America.

So, North's "*free from all duties, both importation duties and taxes*" covered only those *ad valorem* custom duties and other taxes collected in Great Britain, not the Townshend Duty of three pence per pound on tea collected in America. Later in the debate North made it perfectly clear that his refusal to budge on the constitutional issue was due to "political reasons," for he said, "I know the temper of the people there is so little deserving favour from hence." But his organizing intention remained the funding of the civil government in America, especially in Massachusetts where the ministry had already made the most significant commitment. That commitment was considerable, too, with £1,500 for Governor Hutchinson, £400 for the Chief Justice Peter Oliver, £200 for each of the four Associate Justices, £150 for the Attorney General, and £50 for the Solicitor General.[18]

While North entertained visions of around £7,000 flowing into the Exchequer from the new arrangement, according to Dowdeswell's calculations expressed during the debate, the duty would net only "about £400 ... after the charges are all paid." For so measly a "peppercorn"—that was Dowdeswell's word for the supposed advantage—he thought it was simply preposterous for the ministry to be willing to "risk the export of £2,000,000 to America." "I tell the Noble Lord now," he concluded, "if he don't take off the duty they won't take the tea."

Instead of the three pence collected in America, it would make much more sense, or so he and several others thought, to retain a small duty in Great Britain in place of the complete drawback of the 10% *ad valorem* duty. That would leave some much-needed cash in American hands so they could buy other English goods, and the constitutional contention would be conveniently circumvented.

But North would not consider so obvious an alteration in the plan precisely because he wanted to secure an acknowledgment of Parliament's right to tax the colonies.[19] And given the commanding position of the North Administration, the Opposition did not think it was promising to pursue the debate. Without a division, the House passed the Tea Act. Without a debate, the House of Lords casually adopted it two days later. Without a second thought, George III gave his royal assent on 10 May 1773.

WHILE the Tea Act of 1773 was under consideration in London, Boston was caught up in a most serious controversy over the principles governing the Empire. Governor Hutchinson drew up a review of the position advanced by his opponents. With precision he presented to the different towns of Massachusetts the "Principles" of that stance:

> [1] That the sole Power of making Laws is granted by Charter to a Legislature established in the Province, consisting of the King by his Representative the Governor, the Council and the House of Representatives.

> [2] That by this Charter there are likewise granted or assured to the Inhabitants of the Province all the Liberties and Immunities of free and natural Subjects, to all Intents Constructions and Purposes whatsoever, as if they had been born within the Realm of England.

> [3] That it is a Part of the Liberties of English Subjects, which has its Foundation in Nature, to be governed by Laws made by their Consent in Person or by their Representative.

> [4] That the Subjects in this Province, are not and cannot be Represented in the Parliament

of Great-Britain and, consequently, the Act of Parliament cannot be binding upon them.[20]

Samuel Adams himself could not have expressed more accurately the constitutional position of those now disturbing the peace of the Province. Needless to say, Hutchinson pronounced them to be dangerously irrational: "I know of no Arguments, founded in Reason, which will be sufficient to Support these Principles or to justify the Measures taken in Consequence of them."

Over against these four unjustifiable principles, the Governor juxtaposed "a few plain fundamental Principles of Government which carry within themselves such Evidence as cannot be resisted, and are no sooner proposed than assented to." His own self-evident, rationally supported "Principles of Government" were also condensed into four propositions:

[1] That in every Government there must be somewhere a supreme uncontroulable Power, an absolute Authority to decide and determine.

[2] That two such Powers cannot coexist, but necessarily will make two distinct States.

[3] That in a State of Society we give up Part of our natural Liberty in order to secure that legal Freedom which it is the great End of Government to maintain and preserve.

[4] That a Right in Individuals or Parts of a Government to judge of the Decisions of the Supreme Authority and to submit or not submit as they think proper cannot consist with a State of Government and must work the Dissolution of it.[21]

The disagreement could not have been proposed in a more extreme formulation. It cut to the bone. And Hutchinson candidly admitted, "this Disagreement in our Principles will have its Influence upon all the Deductions which are made from them." Given this situation, the die was cast for an extended disputation over what he called "the Fundamentals of our Government."[22]

GOVERNOR Hutchinson called the General Assembly of the Province of Massachusetts into a special session that lasted from early January to early March 1773 in order to probe the two incompatible interpretations of "the Constitution of the Kingdom and of the Province so far as relates to the Dependence" of Massachusetts upon the King and Parliament.[23] The resulting papers were widely reprinted throughout British North America, and Benjamin Franklin made sure they were available in the London press.

After declaring that "the Government is at present in a disturbed and disordered State," Hutchinson laid out what he considered to be the true Principles of the Constitution in a seventeen-paragraph Address. The Council responded with an Answer half again as long as the Governor's Address, followed by the Answer of the House which was almost three times its length. Hutchinson's extensive Replication on 16 February matched those two Answers. The Rejoinder of the Council on 2 March was short, but the Rejoinder of the House the same day was almost as long as Hutchinson's Replication. The Governor then made a final Surrejoinder and adjourned the special session on 6 March 1773.[24]

A critical edition of the seven distinct but interlocking papers, plus some relevant documents, was edited by John Phillip Reid and published in 1981 under the title, *The Briefs of the American Revolution*. To track the salient points through these *Briefs* is to grasp with conceptual clarity the conflicting Principles involved in the rapidly escalating dispute.

HUTCHINSON wasted no time in tracking down "the Cause" of this "disturbed and disordered State" to the refusal by so many towns in the Province to acknowledge "the Supreme Authority of Parliament." This challenge, so far as he could discover, sprang into life during the Stamp Act Crisis. Although "at first" it was "whispered with

Caution," it "was soon after openly asserted in Print" and now had become pervasive throughout Massachusetts.[25]

The Answer of the Council politely informed him, "If your Excellency meant only that the Province is discontented, and in a State of Uneasiness, we should entirely agree with you." But they hastened to add that what he thought was "the Cause" they thought was "an Effect" that flowed from "some preceding and succeeding Acts of Parliament, subjecting the Colonies to Taxes without their Consent." That was, according to the Council, "the original Cause of all the Uneasiness."[26]

The Answer of the House agreed with the Governor's claim that "the Government at present is in a very disturbed State." That disturbance, however, was not due to "the People's having adopted unconstitutional Principles," but rather it was triggered "by the British House of Commons assuming and exercising a Power inconsistent with the Freedom of the Constitution to give and grant the Property of the Colonists, and appropriate the same without their Consent." In the judgment of the House, what had plunged the Province into so dreadful a condition was "the Principles that induced the Councils of the Nation to so new and unprecedented a Measure" as taxing the American colonies in the Stamp and Townshend Acts.[27]

When he addressed the Answer of the House in his Replication, Hutchinson refused to take notice of its claim that "the Disorders of the Province" resulted from "an undue Exercise of the Power of Parliament" simply because the House had taken "for granted, what can by no Means be admitted, that Parliament had exercised its Power without just Authority."[28] His entire legal orientation would not permit him to even consider the corner stone of the House's Answer.

The Governor never mentioned Lord Chief Justice Mansfield by name, but when Hutchinson evoked "a very great Authority" to back up his constitutional claim that the colonies were "holden as feudatory of the Imperial Crown of England," he was citing the 1759 ruling in the Court of King's Bench.[29] The House in its Rejoinder called attention to the fact that he had not named this "very great

Authority."[30] So, in his Surrejoinder Hutchinson answered, "The Case I refer to is the King against Crowle [*sic*.], in the 2d. Vol Burrow's Reports, and for the Authority, which you will find mentioned there, I am not able to name a greater."[31] He not only shared the conviction that Mansfield was the leading luminary of the law in eighteenth-century British public life; in a letter to his friend Charles Paxton he expressed a profound wish that he could begin his career over again and "rise in the world under [Mansfield's] protection."[32]

HUTCHINSON never deviated from what he considered it to be *a self-evident, fundamental maxim* that "from the Nature of Government there must be one supreme Authority over the whole," and that Authority by definition must be "a supreme uncontroulable Power."[33] He applied that principle to the two radically different types of governments operative in the founding of the New World. First, "in absolute Monarchies the Legislative and executive Powers are united in the Prince or Monarch." Louis XIII of France was mentioned as a perfect model of such an absolute monarch. Second, England thoroughly rejected that model in favor of a mixed form of government: "in the English Constitution there is, and always has been, a Legislative Power distinct from the regal or executive Power."[34] The legislative authority in mixed governments, nevertheless, remained absolute, uncontrollable and unlimited. If France was both *absolute* and *arbitrary*, England was only *absolute*, not *arbitrary*. The difference between the governance of New France and New England derived from that distinction.

Mansfield had expressed these controlling principles in 1766: "In Great Britain the legislative is in parliament, the executive in the crown." And he also spelled out the implication with admirable clarity: "That the British legislature, as to the power of making laws, represents the whole British empire and has authority to bind every part and every subject without the least distinction, whether such subjects have a right to vote or not, or whether the law binds places *within the realm or without*" (my emphasis).

Given this point of departure it should not be at all surprising that Hutchinson opened the substantive part of his Address by observing that it was "the Sense of the Kingdom" as well as the "Sense" of "our Predecessors" that they and their descendents were "to remain subject to the supreme Authority of Parliament." (He did qualify that historical generalization by adding, "except about the Time of Anarchy and Confusion in England which preceded the Restoration of King Charles the Second" in 1660.) Underneath that supreme Authority "subordinate Powers with legislative and executive Authority" had prospered and lived happily for generations, a fact that documented, according to Hutchinson's vision, how thoroughly "the Spirit of Liberty breathes thro' all the Parts of the English Constitution."

These "subordinate Powers" were of two different types. First, "a Variety of Corporations" had been "formed within the Kingdom with Powers to make and execute such Bylaws as are for their immediate Use and Benefit." These corporations had always remained "subject to the general Laws of the Kingdom." Second, the colonial governments exercised "more general and extensive Powers of Legislation" than these more limited corporations. But they remained "subject nevertheless, to all such Laws of the Kingdom as immediately respect them or are designed to extend to them."[35] He fully shared Mansfield's opinion that the various colonial governments were "all on the same footing as our great corporations in London."

The Answer of the House viewed the sense of the Kingdom in a profoundly different light. Regardless of how America had been acquired "by the Europeans," the English monarchs fully realized that the colonies were "not annexed to *the Realm of England*" (my emphasis).[36] The word *Realm* surfaced repeatedly in the argument, and it consistently meant *those regions that are represented in Parliament*. The fullest statement reads: "The Power and Authority of Parliament" is "constitutionally confined *within the Limits of the Realm* and the Nation collectively" (my emphasis).[37] And since the colonies were not represented in Parliament, it followed that "the

Colonies were *without the Realm and Jurisdiction of Parliament*" (emphasis in the original).[38]

Since the colonies were "at the absolute Disposal of the Crown," Parliament had nothing to do with Queen Elizabeth's grant of "the first American Charter" to Sir Walter Raleigh. Again, when King James I created the "two Virginia Companies," he had them vested "with all Liberties, Franchises and Immunities ... to all Intents and Purposes, as if they had been abiding, and born *within the Realm.*" These early colonial charters were granted precisely because the colonies were "not within the Realm, but only within the Fee and Seignory of the King." That meant that while the colonies were "within the Allegiance of the English Crown," they "were not intended or considered to be *within the Realm of England*" (my emphasis). Subject to and under the protection of "the King," yes; annexed to "the Realm of England," no.

In the opinion of the House, these early charters carried "all the Powers necessary to constitute them free and distinct States." While "certain Variations" in the wording did occur in these early charters, the general sense remained the same, namely, the colonial legislatures could pass laws "as nearly as conveniently might be conformable" to "the fundamental Laws of the English Constitution." Those fundamental laws "should be the certain and established Rule of Legislation" in the various colonies. That is why the phrases "consonant to Reason" and "not repugnant to the Laws of England" were included in these charters. Furthermore, the acts of the colonial legislatures were subject to review by the King-in-Council, not Parliament.

The House also thought Hutchinson's comparing colonies (without the Realm) to corporations (within the Realm) was "unjust" because Massachusetts was "a Corporation in no other Light, than as every State is a Corporation." From the beginning Massachusetts had been a free and distinct state "by a Grant and Charter from the Crown of England." Indeed, "to suppose a Parliamentary Authority over the Colonies ... would necessarily induce that Solecism in Politics *Imperium in Imperio.*" Because the colonies were *not within the Realm of England*, they could not be subject to "the Supreme Authority of the English Parliament," for "no Country, by the Common Law was subject to the Laws or to the Parliament, but the Realm of England."[39]

After arguing that "it *was not* and never had been the Sense of the Kingdom" that the people who migrated to New England "were to remain subject to the Supreme Authority of Parliament," the House turned to "what *was* the Sense of our Ancestors," and for this they quoted a few relevant passages from Hutchinson's own *History of the Colony of Massachusetts-Bay*. So the House concluded, "Thus we see, from your Excellency's History and Publications" that "the Sense our Ancestors had of the Jurisdiction of Parliament" under the Old Charter granted by Charles I in 1628 was "very different from that which your Excellency *in your Speech*" so erroneously claimed.

Turning to the New Charter granted by William and Mary after the Glorious Revolution, the House found that it did not alter the relationship between Massachusetts and Parliament whatsoever. Whereas the Governor maintained that Parliament retained "a Reserve of Power and Authority" in legislative matters, the Answer of the House argued that those who were "freely conversant with those who framed the Charter" of 1691 understood that "full Power and Authority" was vested in the General Court of Massachusetts. That meant that it not only had "a *sole* and exclusive Power" but "there was no 'Reserve in the Charter to the Authority of Parliament, to bind the Colony' by any Acts whatever."[40]

According to the House, the Governor followed Mansfield's reasoning in arguing what he called a "favourable Construction." To wit, after acknowledging that "it is an established rule of construction, that no parts *without the realm* are bound unless named in the act," Mansfield proceeded, "this rule establishes the right of parliament; for unless they had a right to bind parts *out of the realm*, this distinction would never have been made" (my emphases). The House was curious to know "by what Authority in Reason or Equity the Parliament can enforce a Construction so *unfavourable* to us."[41]

IN his Replication Hutchinson scoffed at the constitutional claims advanced by the House, especially its organizing principle that because the colonies had never been and "are not now annexed to the *Realm* they are not Part of the *Kingdom*, and consequently not subject to the Legislative Authority of the Kingdom." Given his world of discourse, the distinction between "within the Realm" and "without the Realm" was not relevant to the issue at hand. From his reading of "the Feudal System" it followed that "any new Countries" discovered by Englishmen became "Part of the State"; therefore, "the Lordship or Dominion" resided "in the Crown." When grants are made for "the Possession or Property of private Persons," they remain "Subjects of England," and, consequently, under "the Sovereign Legislative Authority of the English Empire."

Massachusetts was constituted as "a Corporation in England with Powers to create a subordinate Government" but this meant that the colonies "would always be Subjects of Taxes and Impositions *both in the Kingdom and in the Plantation*" (my emphasis). Hutchinson was convinced that "the Plantations, though not strictly *within the Realm*, have from the Beginning been constitutionally subject to the Supreme Authority *of the Realm* and so are annexed to it as to be, *with the Realm* and the other Dependencies upon it, *one entire Dominion*" (my emphases). And this was the context in which he evoked Lord Chief Justice Mansfield as "a very great Authority" to back up his constitutional claim that the colonies were "holden as feudatory of the Imperial Crown of England."[42]

Whereas the House argued that Massachusetts held charter rights that "granted or assured to the Inhabitants of the Province all the Liberties and Immunities of free and natural Subjects, to all Intents Constructions and Purposes whatsoever, as if they had been born within the Realm of England," the Governor from his opening Address put a different gloss upon that traditional claim. Although those Englishmen migrating to America retained "the Liberties and Immunities of free and natural Subjects," he interpreted that to mean that they "would not become Aliens." What it did not mean was that the colonists would be able to exercise all "the Rights of English

Subjects." That would simply be impossible because, for example, the colonists, by "their voluntary Removal" from the Kingdom, could no longer exercise their right to vote in an English election, but, of course, they could exercise that right again simply by returning to England.[43]

The limitations imposed upon colonial rights was Hutchinson's way of reading a key proposition articulated by Mansfield: "That the colonists, by the condition on which they migrated, settled, and now exist, are *more emphatically subjects of Great Britain than those within the realm*" (my emphasis). And recall that Mansfield's protégé, Sir William Blackstone, also shared the opinion that Parliament held "a Reserve of Power and Authority" over the colonies, while the full range of English liberties did not extend to the colonies.[44]

The House, on the contrary, was persuaded that Hutchinson's "Manner of Reasoning" would subvert any liberties "worth enjoying" by the people of Massachusetts. According to the House, "It was easily and plainly foreseen that the Right of Representation in the English Parliament could not be exercised by the People of this Colony." Since it was "an essential Right"—and here the House quotes the Governor himself—to be governed "by Laws made by Persons in whose Elections they from Time to Time have a Voice," it would necessarily follow that for Massachusetts to "have and enjoy all the Liberties and Immunities of free and natural Subjects within the Realm, as stipulated in the Charter, it was necessary" for "one Branch" of the legislature to consist of "Representatives chosen by the People, to make all Laws, Statutes, Ordinances, &c. for the well ordering and governing the same, not repugnant to the Laws of England, or, as nearly as conveniently might be, agreeable to the fundamental Laws of the English Constitution." The right to participate in the laws was the "most essential Right" of Englishmen—because *consent alone* "discriminates Freemen from Vassals."[45]

This theme was pursued in the Rejoinder of the House where it was directly stated that "the Construction" Hutchinson had put upon the limited liberties of the colonists "reduces us to a State of Vassalage, and exposes us to Oppression and despotic Power, whenever a Parliament shall see fit to make Laws for that Purpose, and put them in Execution." After reviewing the historical material the House concluded:

> The Question appears to us to be no other than Whether we are the Subjects of absolute unlimited Power, or of a free Government formed on the Principles of the English Constitution. If your Excellency's Doctrine be true, the People of this Province hold their Lands of the Crown and People of England, and their Lives, Liberties and Properties are at their Disposal.

The Governor's interpretation of colonial rights, in the judgment of the House, reduced the liberties of Massachusetts "into a mere Phantom."[46]

While the House maintained that as *free and distinct States* the colonies could never come under the jurisdiction of Parliament, the Governor maintained that the British Empire was *one entire Dominion* and, therefore, the colonies were "subject to one Supreme Legislative Power." As he emphasized in his opening Address, "It is impossible there should be two independent Legislatures in *one and the same State*, for although there may be but one Head, the King, yet the two Legislative Bodies will make two Governments as distinct as the Kingdoms of England and Scotland before the Union" (my emphasis).[47] Prior to the Union of 1707 Scotland and England had been two separate *realms*, each with its own Parliament. Because they were not *one and the same State*, the same person could serve as the King (or Queen in the case of Anne) of these two different kingdoms at the same time. That is precisely why King James I of England, for example, was simultaneously King James VI of Scotland.

The House responded to Hutchinson's claim that "two Legislative Bodies will make two Governments as distinct as the Kingdoms of England and Scotland before the Union" by saying, "Very true." Then it posed this question: "if they interfere not with each other, what hinders but that being united in one Head and common Sovereign, they may live happily in that Connection, and mutually support and protect each other?" Had not this been the lived experience of the British Empire—prior to 1764? The King was the "Head and common Sovereign" of each of the *free and distinct States*. Their own individual "Legislative Bodies" provided the polycentric British Empire with its prosperity and power.[48]

The House as well as Hutchinson distinguished between the King's own personal body ("natural Capacity") and his political body ("publick Capacity"). But the House insisted that by swearing allegiance to the King, one binds oneself to him "in his Natural Person." As "all but one" of the "Judges of England" ruled at the Union of 1707, "Allegiance followeth *the natural Person, not the politick*" body of the King (my emphasis). From this ruling—which reinforced the earlier ruling by Sir Edward Coke in the *Calvin* case—the House declared, "If then the Homage and Allegiance is not to the Body politick of the King, then it is not to him as the Head or any Part of that Legislative Authority" so dear to the heart of the Governor.[49]

Hutchinson responded directly that the House had fallen into "a fundamental Error" so egregious that it would "prove fatal to your System," for, while one can distinguish between the King's two bodies in theory, they cannot be separated in practice. In his Surrejoinder he pressed the point that "the natural Person of the King is ever accompanied with the Politick Capacity." Therefore, the distinction between the King's two bodies did not "amount to any Thing more than that Allegiance is not due to the Politick Capacity *only*."[50]

The Governor called the special session of the General Assembly because he believed the Boston Town Meeting as well as the Resolves passed by "several of the principal Towns in the Province" were "repugnant to the Principles of the Constitution" not only because "some of them deny the supreme Authority of Parliament," but also because "others speak of this supreme Authority, *of which the King is a constituent Part*" in ways that have "a direct Tendency to alienate the Affections of the People from *their Sovereign.*" The King "has ever been most tender of their Rights, and whose Person, Crown and Dignity we are under every possible Obligation to defend and support" (my emphases).[51]

It remains a curious fact that where one would expect to find the word *sovereignty,* Hutchinson systematically refers to *Supreme Authority.* Perhaps he realized that in ordinary discourse *sovereignty* was linked to the *sovereign,* and this connection would play into the hands of the General Assembly, for the House readily celebrated the "natural Person" of George III as "our rightful Sovereign." The Council even amplified the point: "we humbly look up to his present Majesty, our rightful and lawful Sovereign, as Children to a Father."[52] For George III to be *the sovereign* of Great Britain and, in turn, the British Empire was one thing everybody could agree upon. Hutchinson, however, located *sovereignty itself* in Parliament, precisely because the King's "Politick Capacity" made Parliament the Supreme Legislative Authority over the *entire dominion* as one consolidated state. And needless to say, that supremacy was unlimited, unbounded, and uncontrollable in all cases whatsoever.

ALTHOUGH the terms of this 1773 debate were set by the Address of the Governor, the confrontation turned upon much more than mutually exclusive *principles of government,* for Hutchinson also pressed an *inference* that cut to the heart of the matter. As Lord Chief Justice Mansfield in his 1766 oration had "repeatedly called upon the advocates for America to *draw the line,* to move their exceptions and to say *how far the sovereignty of the British Parliament should go and where stop,*" so in 1773 Hutchinson spelled out this *either/ or* choice for the General Assembly: "I know of *no Line that can be drawn* between the supreme Authority of Parliament and the *total* Independence of the Colonies" (my emphases).[53]

Hutchinson dismissed out of hand a pivotal distinction that the General Assembly thought was perfectly obvious, namely, that while the colony had formally consented to Parliament's supremacy over the colonial trade for the benefit of the whole empire, it had never consented to Parliament's jurisdiction over its internal affairs. He could never entertain so critical a distinction because *sovereignty* was indivisible. Likewise, it was impossible to claim that Massachusetts was subject to the King but not subject to Parliament, for one simply could never divide between the two. The essential nature of *sovereignty* demanded either complete submission or total independence. It was all or nothing—no conceivable *via media* was in the realm of possibility. Nevertheless, one should never lose sight of Hutchinson's opening statement that only rarely did Parliament interpose its vast authority in colonial affairs. All powerful, yes; frequently employed, no. And this power was only "occasionally" brought into play when "in its Wisdom" Parliament judged its intervention to be "necessary."[54]

Just how rare that intervention actually had been under the Old Charter was conceded in the Replication of the Governor: "From your Predecessors Removal to America until the Year 1640 there was no Session of Parliament and the first short Session of a few Days only in 1640, and the whole of the next Session ... being taken up in the Disputes between the King and Parliament, there could be no Room for Plantation Affairs." He then continued: "For 15 or 16 Years after the Restoration [in 1660], there was no Officer of the Customs in the Colony ... and the Acts of Trade were but little regarded."[55] A welcomed transformation in colonial attitudes occurred, however, "at the Time of the [Glorious] Revolution," for under the New Charter of 1691 "the People returned to a just Sense of the Supremacy of Parliament." Whereas under the Old Charter the Supreme Authority of Parliament had been almost completely inoperable—or perhaps one should say it was *latent but not manifest*—under the New Charter the interaction between Massachusetts and the mother country had proven to be pleasant as well as profitable—until the Stamp Act Crisis introduced so much turmoil.

According to the Governor's understanding of the lived experience throughout the Old Colonial System, "For more than seventy Years together"—that is, from 1691 to 1764—"the Supremacy of Parliament was acknowledged without Complaints of Grievance."

Yes, at times the "Unfitness of a Measure" had occurred, but that was in the nature of government. When America petitioned, Great Britain would reconsider, and often it repealed the offensive measure. But these disputes never approached "a Disavowal" of Parliament's "Right" and surely there was never so much as a hint of Parliament's "Relinquishment" of its "Right." Finally, Hutchinson pressed this challenge to the General Assembly: "I think I may very safely say that the oldest Person in the Province has never heard the Supremacy [of Parliament] called in Question until within a few Years past." He sincerely believed that Massachusetts had no reason to fear any "greater rigour of Government for seventy Years to come than what we and our Predecessors have felt in the seventy Years past."[56]

OVER against the submission to so benign a power, the Governor juxtaposed the terror of total independence. Surely it was transparent for all to see that without the "Protection" of Great Britain the colonies would "become the Prey of one or the other Powers of Europe." He even posed this probing question: "Is there any Thing which we have more Reason to dread than Independence?"[57] Given so clear-cut a choice between the benefits of submission and the costs of independence, he thought that the General Assembly would plainly see which option rational men, motivated by enlightened self-interest, would cheerfully choose. The structure of his rhetorical strategy could be diagrammed this simply: Either A or B; B is disastrous; therefore, reasonable men would surely embrace A.

Although very few Americans in early 1773 were eager to embrace the possibility of "Independence on the Crown," the House took up the issue in its Answer: "If there be no such Line, the Consequence is, either that the Colonies are the Vassals of the Parliament, or, that they are totally Independent." In the judgment of the House, "there is more Reason to dread the Consequences of absolute uncontrouled Supreme Power, whether of a Nation or a Monarch, than those of a total Independence." Should Hutchinson press his either/or and expect a formal answer on where to draw that "Line," the House directly informed the Governor that "could we conceive of such a

Line, we should be unwilling to propose it" without the consent of "all the other Colonies ... in Congress."[58]

The Council opened its analysis of where to draw the "Line" by saying, "it is necessary to guard against any improper Idea of the term *Supreme* Authority." And it promptly suggested that the Governor's "Idea" seemed "to include *unlimited* Authority," a claim that Hutchinson readily embraced in his Surrejoinder: "It is essential to the Being of Government that a Power should always exist which no other Power within such Government can have Right to withstand or controul: Therefore, when the word *Power* relates to the Supreme Authority of Government it must be understood *absolute* and *unlimited*." After laying down this fundamental principle he bluntly told the Council that if it could not accept something so obvious that "no sensible Writer upon Government has before denied," then "it can be to no Purpose to Reason or Argue upon the other Parts of your Message." So far as he was concerned, all the different types of government were "*absolute* and *unlimited*" by definition.

The Council rejected Hutchinson's "Idea" in theological terms taken straight from the traditional New England Mind:

> Supreme or unlimited Authority can with Fitness belong only to the Sovereign of the Universe: And that Fitness is derived from the Perfection of his Nature.—To such Authority, directed by infinite Wisdom & infinite Goodness, is due both active and passive Obedience: Which, as it constitutes the Happiness of rational Creatures, should with Chearfulness and from Choice be unlimitedly paid by them.—But with Truth this can be said of no other Authority whatever.

Because "the supreme Authority of every Government is limited," it necessarily followed that "the Supreme Authority of Parliament must be limited." The operative question then became, "what are the Limits of that Authority with Regard to the Colony?"

Although it would be "difficult" to fix the limits of Parliament's Authority "with Precision," the Council made it abundantly clear that the Charter was a potent constitutional limitation, one that secured for Massachusetts "all the Rights and Liberties of free and natural Subjects." And the most essential right to be protected at all costs was "a Freedom from all Taxes not consented to by themselves." Beyond that grounding in the rights of Englishmen, the Council pressed the more basic claim that "Life, Liberty, Property, and the Disposal of that Property with our own Consent, are *natural Rights*" (my emphasis). The Council moved effortlessly from a religious ground to the civil constitution, then concluded with "that great Law of Nature, Self-Preservation."[59] While the Council did not "presume to prescribe the exact Limits" to the authority of Parliament, it remained convinced that its authority "cannot constitutionally extend ... to the levying of Taxes in any Form, on his Majesty's Subjects in this Province." Furthermore, the current "Uneasiness and Unhappiness" that had descended upon "all the Colonies throughout the Continent" had derived from Parliament's novel "Regulations of Government."

By rejecting both "Independence" and the Governor's "Idea of ... *Supreme* Authority," the Council sought not only a restoration of that "Happiness and Tranquility" that had pervaded the Empire prior to 1763 but also "an Union established on such an equitable Basis" that neither Great Britain nor her colonies "shall ever wish to destroy." To that deeply desired end, the Council readily confessed: "We humbly supplicate the Sovereign Arbiter and Superintendent of human Affairs for these happy Events."[60]

HAPPY events were not gestating in the womb of time. Within a matter of weeks a packet of selected letters arrived in the hands of the Speaker of the House, Thomas Cushing. In late 1772 an unknown "gentleman of character and distinction" handed over these letters to Benjamin Franklin in London. After carefully reading them a shocked Franklin obtained permission from this mysterious gentleman to forward the packet to Massachusetts for the perusal of key members of the General Assembly, but only on condition that they not be copied and returned.[61]

These letters had been carefully selected from the correspondence between Thomas Whately and Thomas Hutchinson as well as his brother-in-law Andrew Oliver and a few others between 1768 and 1771. Whately, it should be recalled, was the principal promoter of the abandoned theory of "virtual representation," had played a critical part in the passage of the Stamp Act, and remained a close advisor to George Grenville. Along with a significant portion of Grenville's party, after the former Prime Minister's death in November 1770, he joined forces with the North Administration. Until he died in May 1772 he was the organizing center of an intimate circle of political activists dedicated to Lord Chief Justice Mansfield's imperial vision. In Franklin's judgment he was "the center to which flowed all the correspondence inimical to America."[62]

Although nothing in Hutchinson's letters was different from what he had been saying for years, the fact that he had been communicating these thoughts secretly to a British official so high in the imperial government seemed to explain many strange happenings over the recent past. Especially sinister was his 20 January 1769 statement that "there must be an abridgment of what is called English liberties."[63]

Needless to say, these letters caused a sensation that continued to swell as more people read them. When the General Assembly met on 26 May 1773, they were the talk of the town. After Samuel Adams had them read aloud in the House of Representatives, the House voted 105 to 5 that "the tendency and design of the letters ... was to overthrow the constitution of this government and to introduce arbitrary power." Directly contrary to the initial agreement, they were printed—several editions circulated throughout British North America before the year was out—and the House formally petitioned "our common Sovereign" to remove from office both Governor Thomas Hutchinson and Lieutenant Governor Andrew Oliver because they had "rendered themselves justly obnoxious to your loving subjects and entirely lost their confidence." Thomas Cushing summed up the obvious when he forwarded the Petition to

Benjamin Franklin: "it is universally apprehended that the G—v—r will never be able to recover the Confidence of this People and that his Usefullness is at an End."[64]

AS early as March, Lord Dartmouth had expressed his displeasure with the way the Governor had rushed into an unfortunate controversy over the proper understanding of the Constitution.

Before Hutchinson had time to respond, the American Secretary conferred with Benjamin Franklin on how the ministry should proceed now that it had been put into an impossible position by the open denial of the Supremacy of Parliament by the House of Representatives. Franklin advised him simply to ignore Hutchinson's "imprudence" as well as Massachusetts's "declaration of independence" from Parliament. "It is *Words* only," Franklin noted; any response—especially any use of "Violent Measures" or "Force"—would only worsen the unfolding situation. When Dartmouth pressed him to try to persuade the House to voluntarily withdraw its statement of principles, Franklin politely declined to pursue so lost a cause.[65]

GOVERNOR Hutchinson held an impressive command over how tea—both legal and illegal—was being marketed in New England. Not only was his crown salary of £1,500 covered by the tea tax, most of his liquid capital was also invested in the East India Company. Furthermore, *Thomas & Elisha Hutchinson* (a firm owned by two of his sons) as well as *Richard Clarke & Sons* (a firm closely related to his extended family) had sold English tea in defiance of the boycott of tea over the last few years—and these firms were selected as consignees to receive the tea in Boston. (*Faneuil & Winslow* was also selected because it followed closely the direction of the former two firms.)

The sheer fact that throughout the summer of 1773 Hutchinson remained blissfully unaware of any imminent danger speaks volumes about how slowly the colonial opposition would begin to gather against the coming explosion.[66] The few garbled reports from London that did dribble in over the summer were either inaccurate or incomplete, leading many to suppose that Parliament had actually repealed the Townshend Duty on tea. That illusion dissolved after the *New York Gazette* published the full text of the Tea Act for the first time on 6 September 1773. Opposition picked up momentum, however, only after a handbill called *Alarm No. I*—distributed under the name of that seventeenth-century worthy, HAMPDEN— appeared on the streets of New York City on 7 October.[67]

As a much fuller understanding of the East India Company's involvement surfaced in colonial consciousness, it became transparent that three distinct yet interlocking dimensions were moving through the novel arrangement. First, the constitutional contention was supercharged—because North's handling of the debate emphasized the importance of retaining the trifling three pence per pound tax imposed by the Townshend Duties Act. Second, the plan promised to generate vastly more revenue to pay the colonial salaries—because the removal of the 10% *ad valorem* duty for another five-year experiment, plus the commitment by the East India Company to sell below the market price, was consciously designed to increase rather dramatically the amount of English tea sold in America. And that brought into play the third dimension, for the direct sale by the East India Company to American consignees transparently threatened to set up a *monopoly*—because the price of English tea would be lowered to the point where it would drive out of business not only the smugglers but also those legitimate merchants not chosen as consignees.

John Dickinson—the chairman of the Stamp Act Congress and the author of the FARMER'S LETTERS—brought the American protest against the novel arrangement to a fitting climax when he published, under the name of RUSTICUS, "A Letter from the Country to a Gentleman in Philadelphia." As Pennsylvania's leading constitutional lawyer, he carefully noted that America's opposition did not rest upon "the paltry Sum of Three-pence"—it rested upon "the Principle" at the core of the constitutional conflict. And given the underhanded tactics of the East India Company, he pressed this telling rhetorical point: "It is something of Consolation to be overcome by a Lion, but to be devoured by Rats is intolerable." After counseling perseverance, RUSTICUS instructed the "Watchmen … as they go their Rounds, to call out every Night, *past Twelve O'Clock, beware of the East India Company.*"[68]

AFTER much soul searching and more hesitation, as early as 26 June Hutchinson had written Dartmouth requesting a leave of absence for six to nine months to go to England in search of a new, less demanding position in the imperial government of Massachusetts. The American Secretary granted him this leave in a letter written on 12 August, but the letter did not reach Boston until 14 November. During the two weeks prior to receiving this long-awaited news, the local situation had grown much more alarming, but because all the ocean-going vessels had already departed for "home"—and a winter crossing in a smaller boat was not to Hutchinson's liking—he decided to wait until spring to leave his post. One can only speculate on what might have happened over the next month had Dartmouth's letter not taken three full months to cross the Atlantic and Hutchinson had taken leave in, say, early October.[69]

Three days after receiving Dartmouth's letter, the news arrived on the *Hayley* that four tea-bearing ships were already on their way toward Boston. The *Hayley*, moreover, also brought with it from London the younger son of the firm *Richard Clarke & Sons* and the brother-in-law of Thomas Hutchinson, Jr. As the Clarkes gathered later that evening at their stately house on School Street to welcome the return of young Jonathan Clarke, the Boston mob gathered outside for a different kind of welcoming party. In the commotion someone—probably Jonathan—fired a pistol from an upper floor to disperse the crowd. In response "the people below went wild, smashing in the windows, frames and all. Stones, brickbats, and other debris flew in through the openings, badly damaging the furniture and injuring several of the occupants." This explosive confrontation brought immediately to mind how eight years earlier the Boston mob had destroyed Thomas Hutchinson's town house during the Stamp Act Crisis.[70]

At this critical junction the Governor still lacked any official information from the North Administration, and he could not look for guidance from the actions of the other colonial governors because Boston, as the closest port to England, would presumably be the first to receive the tea. He was on his own, and he knew it. He also knew that the stakes were incredibly high—for the Empire and for himself. Politically isolated, physically exhausted, and emotionally crippled though he surely was, the gathering storm focused the mind and marshaled the energies of the Royal Governor of Massachusetts.

FROM the moment the *Hayley* arrived both Governor Hutchinson and the neighborhood of Boston knew it was merely a matter of time before critical decisions would have to be made, for according to received practice the duty on East Indian Company tea would have to be paid within twenty days of its arrival or it would be seized by the custom officers. When the first of the four ships carrying tea—ironically named the *Dartmouth*—anchored in Boston harbor on Sunday 28 November, the clock began ticking toward Day Twenty—17 December 1773.[71]

The day after the arrival of the *Dartmouth* an extra-legal meeting of "the Body" from Boston and the neighboring towns convened in Faneuil Hall. Because the number of protesters grew to 5,000 or more protesters, this meeting had to be shifted to the much larger Old South Meeting House. (Given Boston's population of around 20,000 persons, there would have been approximately 2,500 eligible voters for a regular town meeting.) Although this meeting on Day Two demanded that the tea be shipped back to England without paying the Townshend Duty, Hutchinson and the consignees were determined not to surrender to this demand—and they apparently believed that time was on their side, for they had both the law and the British military to back them up. But the situation had grown more than threatening. According to Labaree,

> In mid-afternoon the two Clarke sons, Benjamin
> Faneuil, and Thomas Hutchinson, Jr., fled to Castle
> William for safety. Old Mr. Clarke was apparently

in Salem; Hutchinson's other son remained at the lieutenant-governor's home in Middleborough; and the last consignee, Joshua Winslow, was safe at his house in Marshfield. Even Governor Hutchinson found it necessary from 29 November on to stay at his Milton estate whenever possible.[72]

When the *Eleanor* arrived on Day Five, it was ordered to join the *Dartmouth* along side Griffin's Wharf, where John Hancock's militia stood guard. The *Beaver* joined the other two ships on 15 December. The last of the tea-ships, the *William,* crashed off Cape Cod. Although these later arrivals intensified the conflict, the *Dartmouth* set the temporal agenda.

On Day Sixteen news arrived that Philadelphia had joined New York in forcing the consignees to resign, but that option was not available to Boston because their consignees were under the protection of the British military. Forcing the *Dartmouth* to leave also was not an option, for Castle William with its 32-pounders guarded the primary passages in and out of Boston harbor, and it was common knowledge that Admiral Montagu—in response to a directive from Hutchinson—had positioned the navy so as to block the various minor routes in and out as well.

Regardless of Boston's demand that the ship that brought the tea to Boston carry it back to England, Francis Rotch, the young owner of the *Dartmouth*, was in an acute bind. What he had at stake was more than the rather serious loss of his ordinary business—his ship itself was in serious jeopardy. Even if he could somehow slip out of the harbor, he knew that he risked having it seized if he carried the tea back to England against the law. What Rotch desperately needed was a clearance from the custom officers, but by Day Eighteen it became utterly transparent that a clearance was not in the cards.

During the morning of Day Nineteen a huge congregation crowded into the Old South Meeting House. Francis Rotch explained yet again why he could not carry the tea back to England without a clearance from the custom officials. The gathered host then sent him to Milton in a final attempt to persuade the Governor to grant him a permit to leave the harbor. Knowing that the journey would take an appreciable amount of time—Milton was seven miles away—the meeting adjourned to 3 in the afternoon.

After discussing some technical points and trivial options, Rotch could not come to an agreement with Hutchinson. So, the die was cast for the final act in the drama. By the time he arrived back at the Old South Meeting House at 5:45 the assembly had become more than restive. According to Labaree's detailed account,

> The shipowner was then asked two final questions. Would he order his vessel back to England with the tea on board? Rotch replied that he could not do so, for it would result in his ruin. Did he intend to unload the tea? He replied that he would attempt to do so only if properly called upon by the authorities and then only to protect himself. Samuel Adams rose at that point to proclaim that he did not see what more the inhabitants could do to save their country.

That was the signal for a picked number of men in disguise to move into action aboard the *Dartmouth*, the *Eleanor*, and the *Beaver*. Before Day Nineteen was over 340 chests of tea—90,000 pounds of tea worth £9,000—were dumped into Boston harbor.[73]

John Adams recorded this comment in his *Diary* on Day Twenty: "The malicious Pleasure with which Hutchinson the Governor, the Consignees of the Tea, and the officers of the Customs, have stood and looked upon the distresses of the People, and their Struggles to get the Tea back to London, and at last the destruction of it, is amazing." But was this action necessary? Adams entertained no doubts: "They could not send it back, the Governor, Admiral and Collector and Comptroller would not suffer it." So, "there was no other Alternative but to destroy it or let it be landed."

As Adams peered into what could be coming in the near future his musings took on a somber tone:

> What Measures will the Ministry take, in Consequence of this?—Will they resent it? will they dare to resent it? will they punish Us? How? By quartering Troops upon Us?—by annulling our Charter?—by laying on more duties? By restraining our Trade? By Sacrifice of Individuals, or how?

While Adams entertained dire measures in the future, the stunned Governor immediately called a meeting of the Council, but when a quorum could not be rounded up, he fled to the safety of Castle William on Day Twenty.[74]

AS he anxiously waited for intelligence from London, Governor Hutchinson's personal agony was radically intensified by the onset of a serious illness that promised to kill his brother-in-law, Lieutenant Governor Andrew Oliver. The two were more than close friends—they had married sisters, Margaret and Mary Sanford. To compound their grief, the Assembly resolved that Chief Justice Peter Oliver, the younger brother of Andrew, should be removed from office. In this dreadful situation Hutchinson poured out his heart to Dartmouth in a lengthy eleven-paragraph letter on "the general state of the province." Ranging over the collapse of authority so far as "the county of Berkshire, adjoining to the province of New York," this letter veritably reeks with despair. He even enlarged upon the sentiment pulsing throughout the Atlantic seaboard: "The people, my Lord, in every Colony, more or less, have been made to believe that, by firmly adhering to their demands, they may obtain a compliance with every one of them."

So far as the Governor could see, the Council had been captured by the people and even surpassed the House in "indecent reflections upon His Majesty's Ministers of State." Even the Associate Justices of the Superior Court had renounced their crown salaries. And the friends of Chief Justice Oliver, who lived "forty miles from town," had "dissuaded him from coming to Court" out of a lively concern for his personal safety. Regular government had come to a complete standstill—anarchy reigned over the province. In abject despair he confessed that those who had been supportive of government were now thoroughly intimidated:

> They all give one and the same answer. Matters, they say, are now carried to such a length, that either order will be restored to the Government by the interposition of the authority in England, or we shall take it for granted they intend to yield to the demands of the leaders of the people here, and suffer the independency they lay claim to: and as soon as we see, as we shall do in the spring, which is the case, so we shall govern ourselves; if the latter, we must join with those from whom we have hitherto kept separate, and submit to them on the best terms they will grant us.

Needless to say, Hutchinson could see no way to restore law and order in Massachusetts "without the interposition of the authority of England."

Yet once again the Governor revealed his hand in regard to the root cause of the contemporary confusion in the governance of the Empire: "All the present disorder in the Colonies is undoubtedly owing to neglect in suffering that sense of the supreme authority of Parliament, which, seven years ago, in every colony, it was thought treason with force and violence to oppose, gradually to go off from the minds of the people, until it is entirely lost." Lost it was, but how to restore that authority was beyond Hutchinson's penetration, though he did "humbly submit" that it might be expedient to leave "to the subordinate legislature in the Colonies, the raising monies by Taxes or Duties, whenever it shall be thought fit that requisitions should be made from them." Then he added, "only I beg leave to suggest that it would greatly tend, if it is not absolutely necessary, to conciliate the affections of the Colonies to the parent state."

Hutchinson still wanted to leave for England as soon as possible, but the Lieutenant Governor's "bilious disorder" had placed that in serious jeopardy, for "if he should die, I shall be in doubt whether … His Majesty would approve of my leaving the province until a successor be appointed." While Andrew Oliver continued his decline until he died on 3 March, tensions were running so high that Chief Justice Peter Oliver did not consider it safe to attend his brother's funeral. Although Hutchinson managed to keep his wits about him in his retreat in Milton, he confessed in a letter to an earlier governor, Sir Francis Bernard, "Five years constant scene of anxiety would weary a firmer mind than mine." As his situation became increasingly unstable, he plunged ever deeper into the pit of despair: "If we have not passed the Rubicon this winter, we never shall."[75]

THE North Administration first heard about the Boston Tea Party when the *Hayley* arrived with the initial report on 19 January 1774, a report confirmed by Governor Hutchinson's official version of events when the *Dolphin* arrived on 27 January. At this moment the government was taken up with a Petition requesting the removal of both Governor Hutchinson and Lieutenant Governor Oliver from office because of the suspicious letters they wrote in the late 1760s.

William Whately—the brother of the late Thomas Whately, who had died in the summer of 1772—had challenged John Temple to a duel because he wrongly assumed that Temple was the one who had forwarded these letters to Massachusetts. A fortnight after Whately and Temple fought an inconsequential duel, Benjamin Franklin publicly acknowledged in the *London Chronicle* that Whately and Temple were "totally ignorant and innocent" in the Hutchison Letters Affair and that he alone was the person responsible for transmitting the letters in question to Boston. William Whately, in turn, sued Franklin in the Court of Chancery in a vain attempt to force him to reveal who gave him the letters. That was the immediate background for the hearing on the Massachusetts Petition by the Privy Council's Committee for Plantation Affairs, originally set for 8 January, but at Franklin's request was postponed to 29 January 1774.

Except for Chancellor Apsley, the entire Cabinet, as well as "an immense crowd of other auditors" witnessed the hearing in the Cockpit. Alexander Wedderburn opened the argument by heaping praise upon "the high character" of Governor Hutchinson. Rehearsing his splendid contributions to the Crown provided Wedderburn with a platform on which to venture widely "into what he called a history of the province for the last ten years," an excursion punctuated with plenty of abuse upon the disloyal Bostonians. Needless to say, Hutchinson was vindicated and the Petition was unanimously rejected. With Hutchinson cleared of the charges, Wedderburn then turned and savagely assaulted Benjamin Franklin's character as a violator of sacred trust:

> He has forfeited all the respect of societies and of men. Into what companies will he hereafter go with an unembarrassed face, or the honest intrepidity of virtue. Men will watch him with a jealous eye, they will hide their papers from him, and lock up their escrutoires. He will henceforth esteem it a libel to be called *a man of letters*.

As the assembled crown roared with laughter, Dr. Franklin stood ramrod straight in his finest Manchester velvet suit, with his eyes rigidly fixed straight ahead, and not a shadow of turning in his composure.[76]

THE INTOLERABLE
ACTS OF 1774

I MMEDIATELY AFTER THE CASTIGATION OF BENJAMIN FRANKLIN IN THE COCKPIT, THE North Administration held its initial meeting on how to respond to the Boston Tea Party. Its first decision was that leniency had to be replaced by firmness but this alteration in policy should be based on the authority of the Crown alone. With this end-in-view, Dartmouth presented to the Cabinet on 4 February 1774 a three-point plan prepared by John Pownall, an Under Secretary of State in the Colonial Office. First, the seat of government should be removed from Boston. Second, the Custom House should be moved to another location, thereby closing the Port of Boston to all significant commerce. Third, "Adams, Molineux, and other principle Incendiaries" should be arrested, brought to England, tried, and "if found guilty, put ... to death."[1]

While the Cabinet readily accepted the first two points, before proceeding with the third part it was deemed prudent—especially in light of how this procedure had proven so ineffective after the burning of the *Gaspée* on 10 June 1772—to obtain the legal opinion of Solicitor General Alexander Wedderburn and Attorney General Edward Thurlow. Was the destruction of the tea in Boston Harbor an act of treason? If yes, what would be "the proper and legal method of proceeding against such persons" primarily responsible for the crime?

A week later the law officers declared that the ministry could act on the authority of the Crown alone, but sufficient evidence did not yet exist to proceed against those guilty of this act of treason. Dartmouth, Wedderburn and Thurlow then proceeded on 16 February to interview many more witnesses of the events in Boston and obtained what they considered to be much more reliable and compelling evidence. Six of these witnesses were examined under oath before the Privy Council on 19 February.[2]

Given the more compelling evidence now compiled by Dartmouth, Wedderburn and Thurlow, the ministry had warrants prepared for the arrests of Thomas Cushing, John Hancock, Joseph Warren, and Samuel Adams, according to the recollection of William Knox, another Under Secretary of State. When the warrants were brought before the Privy Council for signing, "the Lords of the Privy Council actually had their pens in their hands, in order to sign the Warrant to apprehend [the] principle Incendiaries." A later report claims that John Pownall "repeated it … literally, they had their pens in their hands, prepared to sign the Warrant." At this dramatic moment, however, "Lord Mansfield diverted it by urging the *other measures*" (my emphasis).[3]

While these "other measures" were not specified, from the context it would appear that they concerned an alteration of the 1691 Charter of Massachusetts. Dartmouth had presented the alteration to the Cabinet in this way:

> That it be moved in the House of Commons to resolve that it is necessary to alter the constitution of the Province of the Massachusetts Bay, and that the Governor be directed to inform the General Court that a Bill will be brought in for that purpose *in the next session of Parliament*, in order that they may depute proper persons in the name of the said

Province to show cause why such alteration should
not be made [my emphasis].

The Cabinet, however, changed "in the next session of Parliament"
to read "in the present session or suspended to the next session of
Parliament." It is easy, however, to overlook the critical point that *this
was the moment when the ministry decided to proceed, not through
the Crown alone, but through an Act of Parliament, thereby radically
escalating the constitutional issue by involving Parliament directly in
the internal affairs of a colony.*[4]

Pownall as well as others "were for seizing six or eight persons,
and sending them over for trial; and for a time this seemed to be
the determination" of the North Administration. At some point,
however,

> Lord M[ansfield], *whose opinion in such cases carries
> all before it*, declared for the necessity of the first
> measure [i.e., the alteration of the Charter] and was
> much inclined that the last [i.e., the seizing of six or
> eight persons] should accompany it, and steered the
> business in such a channel, as that the last has not
> been given up, though it was not absolutely entered
> upon as had been proposed [my emphasis].[5]

So, according to Pownall, the third part of the original plan was to
set an example by arresting the ringleaders, carry them to England
to be tried, and this was to proceed through warrants signed by the
Privy Council. But this third part was set aside because Mansfield
diverted the action, even though he was "much inclined" to support
the signing of the warrants, presumably at a later date.

Mansfield's own version of what actually happened before the
Privy Council is slightly different. He did allow that "the Lords of
Council had their pens prepared to sign a warrant for apprehending
persons in Boston." So, both Mansfield's and Pownall's versions
agree that the Privy Council was ready to proceed on the authority of
the Crown alone. Furthermore, Mansfield "said things never would

be right" until some of the ringleaders were arrested and brought to England to be tried, but he "wished to see examples made here first for the like offences." In his opinion one of the problems with this part of the plan was, "if they were convicted, a way might be found to keep the affair pending seven years, by motions in arrest of judgment upon error in proceedings, &c." That too was consonant with Pownall's report. But according to Mansfield's version the Lords laid down their pens because "the Attorney and Solicitor General were in doubt whether the evidence was sufficient to convict them."[6]

Why then did Wedderburn and Thurlow change their minds? They certainly came in with what they believed was compelling evidence obtained under oath, and the Cabinet had most certainly wanted those warrants signed. Assuming that Pownall's version is at least close to the mark, it would seem that Mansfield threw up so many uncertainties that the law officers reversed their opinion on the spot. While that reversal is surely what caused the Lords of Council to put their pens down, it is more than plausible to believe Mansfield did bring up "another measure" in order to divert the action. Note—this third part had *not* involved Parliament, as Mansfield clearly wanted it to be. And he prevailed.

When the Attorney General walked out, William Knox and John Pownall were expecting to hear that the warrants had been signed. According to Knox's later recollection the following exchange occurred between Thurlow and Pownall:

> "Well," said Pownall, "is it done?" "No," answered Thurlow, "nothing is done. Don't you see," added he, "that they want to throw the whole responsibility of the business upon the Solicitor -General and me, and who would be such damned fools as to risk themselves for such—fellows as these. Now if it was George Grenville, who was so damned obstinate that he would go to hell with you before he would desert you, there would be some sense in it." He walked off, and the project was dropped.

Much to the consternation of Dartmouth and the King the law officers had changed their minds at the last moment, in all probability under the prodding of Mansfield.[7]

On 1 March the Cabinet revisited its 19 February decision "to alter the constitution" of Massachusets during "the present session or suspended to the next session of Parliament." Now it was decided to "seize this opportunity when all persons of all parties were of the same mind" to act during this session of Parliament, and *not proceed through the Crown alone.*[8]

According to Pownall's report to Hutchinson months later, "he did everything he could to prevent the Bill for altering the [Massachusetts] Council" from being considered during this session of Parliament. At a critical point he even produced Hutchinson's own letters to Hillsborough and to himself in order to prove that Hutchinson was "not for breaking in upon, or taking away the Charter" before hearing from Massachusetts, but that was to no avail, for "Lord Mansfield pushed the matter, and upbraided them with their late irresolution." Presumably their late irresolution referred to the Cabinet's initial decision to proceed through the Crown alone.[9]

Although the American colonies had consented to the regulation of the imperial trade by Parliament, they forthrightly rejected Parliament's right to become involved in their internal affairs. While they readily acknowledged that they were subject to the King-in-Council, they rejected from top to bottom Mansfield's notion that the internal affairs of a colony were subject to the jurisdiction of Parliament.

THE King's Message on 7 March 1774 signaled a major change in the legislative agenda for the remainder of this session of Parliament. Over the next three and half months Parliament would pass five Bills that have come down in history as the Intolerable or Coercive Acts—the Boston Port Act (31 March), the Massachusetts Government Act (20 May), the Massachusetts Justice Act (20 May), the American Quartering Act (2 June), and the Government of Quebec Act (22 June).

The proceedings in Commons were opened by George Rice with this sobering statement: "I very much fear the question now brought to issue will be nothing less than whether the colonies of America are, or are not, the colonies of Great Britain. That, Sir, is a question that goes to very being of this constitution, as a powerful though commercial people." The House did not need to be convinced by this expert on the colonial trade that Great Britain "cannot subsist without the advantages which are derived from our commerce in America."

The opening speeches accurately predicted that over the next few months the various parties would divide along a fault line created by the Repeal of the Stamp Act. Speaking for the Rockingham party, William Dowdeswell maintained that the Repeal put in place a system that did bring quiet, but the following year Parliament "would go in search of a peppercorn" so as to "establish taxes as tests of obedience" by vainly attempting to "collect from peppercorn to peppercorn." Such a misguided "system has brought in destruction, commotions, fruitless expedients, timidity at one time, violence at another time."

General Henry Seymour Conway was convinced that "if the Stamp Act had been insisted upon" America would have been lost forever. He informed the House that after examining American colonial "history with some attention," he had concluded that the Americans "have always held that universal language not to be taxed by Great Britain." After he "lamented that we have had no plan at all with regard to America," he emphasized how the government had limped along in a "confused jumble" that is "visible now to all mankind." Although Parliament had enacted one year and repealed the next, he still was bold to say at this late date, "I think [the Americans] have been ready, I think they are ready to pay all due obedience to the Parliament of Great Britain," *if Parliament would surrender its absurd attempt to tax them.*

George Germain, however, insisted that the confused situation was due to the fluctuating policies ever since 1766. He was quoted in the *Middlesex Journal* as saying, "A different system must be embraced, and when embraced must be executed vigorously, and in a more manly method than that in which we have hitherto trifled. Relaxation certainly will not do; we have experienced that from the Repeal of the Stamp Act to the present hour. Had that repeal never been made, I believe these disturbances would never have happened." That expressed the position of the Administration. The various participants, nevertheless, did share a common opinion. Regardless of whether one was for repealing the tax on tea or advocated a consistent firmness in order to show the Americans that Great Britain was now serious, both thought that *the imperial policy had been an incoherent mass of inconsistent stances ever since the New Colonial System was inaugurated in 1764.*[10]

BECAUSE the 109 American Papers that were laid before the House would take considerable time to digest, it was agreed that a full week would be granted before taking up legislation on 14 March 1774. Prime Minister North opened the debate by observing that Boston deserved to be singled out for punishment because she had "invariably been the ringleader and promoter of all the disorders, the discontents, the disturbances" in America. The intent of the forthcoming legislation was to make "an example" of Boston so as to prevent the other colonies from following in her steps. While North refused to spell out the details of the full plan of action, he did provide one insight into what was to come, for he proposed, "it shall not be in the power of the King to re-establish the custom-house at Boston till such time as a just and adequate satisfaction has been made to the East India Company for the damage they have sustained."

After rehearsing the troubled history since the Repeal of the Stamp Act, North wanted the House to understand that the quarrel with the colonies had reached far beyond the familiar points of contention in the recent past: "We are not entering into a dispute between internal and external taxes, not between taxes laid for the purpose of revenue and taxes laid for the regulation of trade, not between representation and taxation, or legislation and taxation."

While those were the principal lines of argumentation over the last decade, they now needed to be set aside so as to face squarely "the question whether we have or have not any authority in that country." So far as he could see, Massachusetts had already issued its "Declaration of Independence." What he wanted to be decisively rejected was the colonial claim that Parliament had "no legislative right" over the colonies.

Given the gravity of the situation, North stressed the urgent need for something approaching unanimity. He thought it would be "a wise plan" for "Members of Parliament, peers, merchants, all ranks and degrees of people, to proceed steadily and universally in one course." Instead of altering direction "by the accidental shifting of ministers" or "the change of Parliaments," all the different political factions should keep constantly in mind that the primary aim was "to maintain the authority of this country" over America.

John Yorke reported to Hardwicke that North's performance was "one of the coldest, and most unanimated speeches, I ever heard." Then he added that it was "received as coolly as it was delivered, but nobody much opposed it." When he sat down, according to the report in the *London Evening Post*, "there was a perfect silence for some minutes." After the House regained its composure, not much of a debate ensued. By and large the House simply lined up in support of punishing Boston for the *destruction of private property*. Even Isaac Barré supported coercive measures with a "hearty and determinate affirmative," although he did observe, "In 1764 [you] made one revenue act, in 1765, made another revenue. 1766 repealed. In 1767, made another." Then he dropped the humorous remark, "You have been taxing and scratching ever since."[11]

THE Boston Port Bill was formally presented to the House for its first reading on 18 March.[12] Rose Fuller of the Rockingham party asked a pointed question about its place within some overall "great plan." While North confessed that other Bills would be forthcoming this session, he stressed that the Boston Port Bill addressed a singular event with what he surmised would be "a temporary measure," but it definitely was not "part of any plan." At the second reading on 21 March it passed on a voice vote, over the loud but lonely "No" shouted by George Byng.[13]

The Committee of the House considered a few amendments on 23 March. Rose Fuller now thought the Boston Port Bill was "too severe for the first offence." After saying that the Americans "will look upon it as a foolish act of oppression," he proposed instead that Boston be fined £25,000, and if not paid by Christmas, then the harbor should be closed.

North answered, "Would to God it was the first offence!" On the contrary, "during the whole seven years past there has been a series of offences breathing throughout defiance to the authority of the House and a total independence to the laws of this country." In his opinion, "Those who lead the people of Massachusetts Bay have undoubtedly construed all our lenity, either as want of power or want of resolution." What was urgently needed was a Bill that would "Produce a conviction throughout America that all lenient measures are now at an end, that we are really in earnest."

George Dempster, responding for the Rockingham party, did not believe that "lenient measures" were what encouraged the Americans to resist, as North had asserted. The real cause of "all the disorder risen in America" was rooted in "our attempt to tax them contrary to the general policy of this country" prior to 1764.

Charles Jenkinson would have none of this Rockingham nonsense. He thought the Stamp Act was "a wise measure," because taxing the colonies promised to be a key part in the entire plan. "Jenkinson broke out in the true spirit of the Court," according to Walpole's *Journal*, "and, full of prerogative and vengeance, called on all the friends of the Stamp Act to join in humbling America."[14] But the prize for the most provocative comment of the day went to a little known backbencher, Charles Van. From his odd perspective the legislation did not go far enough! Instead of temporarily closing Boston's harbor, he proposed demolishing the port entirely: "Make it a mark that shall never be restored"—"*Delenda est Carthago*."[15]

Needless to say, North did not have any trouble sailing a middle course between these extremes. No amendments were even considered. While there were numerous speakers that day, North confessed to George III, "it is difficult to say which spoke for and which against" the Bill.[16]

When the motion to pass the Boston Port Bill came two days later, Dowdeswell denounced the Bill as "unjust, unwise and dangerous." It was *unjust* because "All commerce may safely be carried on at Boston, but that in tea." It was *unwise* because taxing America was folly. It was *dangerous* because it would "unite all the colonies against us."[17]

Former Governor Johnson expressed satisfaction for being in the right when he had "told the East India Company what would be the consequence of their sending tea" to America. Now he predicted that the Bill would "sow the seeds of resistance and rebellion." Then he pressed beyond the Bill itself: "We should have *the whole intended plan* laid open to us, or how can we judge of any part of it. We should not give our assent to this Bill till we know how *the plan* was to proceed" (my emphases). North, though, sidestepped the larger issue of *the whole intended plan* by insisting that this Bill was "a particular law to punish a particular violence." The House of Commons, furthermore, was in no mood to listen to the Opposition. Without a division the House passed the Boston Port Bill on Friday 25 March 1774.[18]

WHEN the House of Lords engaged in the debate, it was noticed that the ministry did not present a united front. According to Shelburne's report to Chatham, some of the ministers called "what passed in Boston *commotion*, others *open rebellion*" (my emphases). So far as he could penetrate the inner-workings of the North Administration, that difference disclosed that a majority of the Cabinet disregarded Dartmouth and even shared similar points of disagreement with North, even though he "declared very plainly, that other very determined measures should be offered, before the end of the session."

The Lord Chief Justice of King's Bench thoroughly agreed, for Shelburne reported, "Lord *Mansfield* took upon himself a considerable lead." After declaring the Boston Tea Party to be the result of "over-lenity and want of foresight," Mansfield enlightened the remarkably full House with the insight that the destruction of the tea was *"the luckiest event that could befall this country"* (my emphasis). Why so lucky? Because "all might be recovered" now that this "last overt act of high treason" had finally occurred. The ministry would be forced to assert *Parliament's jurisdiction over the internal affairs of the colonies.* In his opinion "compensation to the India Company" was not the object of the Bill, as the Prime Minister had insisted. The real object was to let the Americans know "that we should temporise no longer."[19]

In his *Journal* Walpole maintained, "Lord Mansfield was ... the soul of the intended exertion against the colonies." As "the true instigator of violence," he exploited "the obscure chicanery of law" before avowing that the Bill was "as decisive *as passing the Rubicon.*" If the Bill "passed with tolerable unanimity," he was even convinced that the Americans would finally submit. From this moment forward there could be no turning back—the point of no return had been reached. Without a division the House of Lords forwarded the Bill to George III, who signed it on 31 March 1774.[20]

THE April edition of the *London Magazine* featured a political cartoon, "The Able Doctor, or America Swallowing the Bitter Draught." Lord North, with the "Boston Port Bill" hanging out of his pocket, is pouring tea down the throat of a topless Indian Maiden—symbolizing America—defiantly spewing the Bitter Draught back into the Able Doctor's face. Moving clockwise from the left of this central focus, Lord Sandwich, First Lord of the Admiralty, is holding Miss America's ankles with his right hand as he lasciviously peeks up her skirt, gingerly held aloft by his left hand. Two dandies representing France and Spain are pointing at the spectacle as they confer on so delicious an opportunity for fishing in the troubled waters of the British Empire. And on the distant horizon "Boston cannonade" appears above the town's mast and spires. Further on the right Britannia averts her head so as to shield her delicate eyes from so shameful a scene. On the extreme right Lord Bute wearing a Scottish kilt holds a sword marked "Military Law." Returning to the central focus, one finds Miss America forced down with her hands pulled behind her back by none other than Lord Chief Justice Mansfield.

EVEN before the King had signed the Boston Port Act, North moved for leave to bring in the Massachusetts Government Bill. Regardless of what he had told the House of Commons three days before, on 28 March 1774 he revealed that a much larger plan was to be put into motion.

Since the Massachusetts magistrates had been "uniformly inactive for years past," it followed that something was "radically wrong in their constitution." George Germain fleshed out the needed corrections for "the internal government of the Province." He thought the Council should be appointed by the Crown, as was the case in the other Royal Colonies, not elected by the Assembly and the outgoing Council. Town meetings should be done away with, for "men of a mercantile cast" ought not to be "every day collecting themselves together, and debating about political matters." Indeed, he "would have them follow their occupations as merchants, and not consider themselves as ministers of that country," now bogged down in "anarchy and confusion." Finally he rhetorically asked, "Shall charters stand in our way?" The Prime Minister happily responded, "Charters ought not to stand in the way of Parliament." He went even further and expanded upon the theme: "the constitution of this [Massachusetts] charter ought not to prevent Parliament from *interfering to regulate those matters in America*, which the indigested measures of their charter have, perhaps, precipitately been, in some degree, a means of preventing the peace and quietness of that country from being restored," according to the *London Evening Post* (my emphasis).[21]

DURING the Easter Recess, North apparently became afflicted with serious doubts about the alteration of the Massachusetts Governor's Council. Perhaps Dartmouth's objections were still causing him some uncertainty over the Cabinet's decision to go forward. In any event, he reported to George III on 13 April that he had become so troubled that he had conferred with Lord Chief Justice Mansfield on the issue. The King responded the next day: "I am confirmed in the propriety of altering the Council and I find it so much the wish of the cabinet that … [I can] not too strongly express my preferring your introducing the Bill tomorrow that is drawn up for vesting the nomination of the councilors in the Crown."[22]

John Pownall, it should be recalled, "did everything he could to prevent the Bill for altering the [Massachusetts] Council" from being considered during this session of Parliament, but "Lord Mansfield pushed the matter, and upbraided them with their late irresolution." The fingerprints of the Lord Chief Justice of King's Bench were all over the policy formation of the Massachusetts Government Bill.

The Bill was introduced on 15 April 1774, along with a motion for leave to bring up the Massachusetts Justice Bill. After North cursorily laid out the proposed transformation of the 1691 Charter, William Dowdeswell let the House know that the Opposition wished "to see no new charter granted" to the Massachusetts Bay, especially in light of the fact that the Charter had proven to be such an outstanding success. After praising "the spirit of liberty" that breathes through the Charter, this spokesman for the Rockingham party expressed his disgust with "that absurd obstinacy, of *you shall*, and *I won't*, between parent and child." He concluded by accusing the North Administration of "struggling to obtain a most ridiculous superiority, to which I hardly know a name base enough to stamp it with."

The House, however, was in no mood to hear praises of the Bay Colony. The House promptly reconfigured itself into the American Committee so as to consider the Massachusetts Justice Bill. Given time, the Americans would call this "the Murdering Act," for if a soldier or official were accused of murder or any capital crime while carrying out orders, the Bill provided the Governor with the discretionary authority to shift the trial to either another colony or to Great Britain, where the case would be tried "before his Majesty's court of *King's Bench*."

North directly warned that "everything valuable [is] now at stake between us and America." With the stakes so high he deemed it necessary to proceed with this "temporary" measure, just as it would be necessary "to suspend the Habeas Corpus and many other defences of liberty ... for a little while ... in order to preserve the whole entire."

In response, Colonel Isaac Barré ironically expressed his gratitude for the way the Justice Bill came dressed with "the aid of those lawyers which are to bring about all perfection." With sarcasm dripping from his lips, he proclaimed, "I am at the same time apt to augur, however great the abilities of those long-robed gentlemen may be, that the present plan before us will not turn out so fruitful of justice, and square itself with the line of constitution, as those gentlemen may apprehend." But after "continually goading and teazing America for these ten years past," Barré thought "these act of violence" would finally drive the Americans to a "real rebellion." What was the prospect facing General Gage on his arrival as the Royal Governor of Massachusetts? "Your Governor will be at eternal war with your colonies, and your colonies never satisfied with his administration." Whereas North entertained the fanciful vision that these necessary measures would prove to be "advantageous and happy to this country," Barré entertained the diametrically opposite prospect, for he saw "it pregnant with every mischief to this country."[23]

General Henry Seymour Conway was not alone in hoping that an olive branch would also be extended to the Americans. More than a few members of the House of Commons wrongly assumed that the ministry would balance the passage of the Boston Port Bill with a conciliatory repeal of the tea tax, thereby opening the way for Boston to make amends by paying the East India Company for the loss of its private property and publicly promising to return to obedience to His Britannic Majesty. Dartmouth, in fact, had let it be known in March that he would use "the utmost of his power" to persuade the Cabinet to repeal the tea tax. With this possibility in mind, Conway inquired, "if his Majesty's ministers have the least thoughts of putting an end to the taxation, let them adopt it now at once, and it will put an end to every thing."[24]

After it became abundantly clear that Dartmouth had failed to persuade the North Administration to balance its coercive policy with an olive branch, Rose Fuller announced that he would move to take up the issue of American taxation in committee. The stage was set for an extensive debate in the House of Commons on the Constitution of the British Empire.

ON 19 April 1774 upwards to twenty speakers joined in the Commons Debate on the American Tea Duty. Although the full spectrum of opinion was represented in this Commons Debate, of particular concern is the extensive exposition of the Rockingham party's understanding of the Constitution given by Edmund Burke. The *London Evening Post* reported that Burke "made the most masterly speech that has perhaps been ever uttered in a public assembly. He spoke upwards of two hours, and the attention of the House continued as fixed at the last moment as at the first."

Edmund Burke opened his sweeping review of the entire historical development of colonial policy as well as the shifting policies of the recent ministries by saying, "For nine long years, session after session we have been lashed round and round this miserable circle of occasional arguments and temporary expedients." What was the result? "Invention is exhausted; reason is fatigued; experience has given judgment; but obstinacy is not yet conquered." So far as Burke could fathom, what had "shaken the solid structure of this empire to its deepest foundations" was "departing from the maxims" plainly visible in the Repeal of the Stamp Act and the passage of the Declaratory Act in 1766.

Burke's understanding of the doctrine of Parliamentary Supremacy turned upon a distinction he drew between "the constitution of Britain" and "the constitution of the British Empire." Parliament was "the local legislature of this island" with sovereign jurisdiction over "all things at home." But in its *"imperial character"* Parliament "superintends all the several inferior legislatures, and guides and controls them all, without annihilating any." In his opinion, ever since 1767 the various ministries had collapsed Parliament's two distinct roles by construing its imperial capacity through the prism of its local authority. So far as he was concerned, the very idea of "the unlimited and illimitable nature of supreme sovereignty" that had bedeviled so much of the recent formation of imperial policy should be left "to the schools" where monkish professors could safely pursue at their leisure the "subtle deductions" of metaphysical notions. Statesmen should not act under the influence of abstract reasons or precious refinements—they should be guided by *experience*.

The lived experience under Old Colonial System that thrived "from the year 1660 to the unfortunate period of 1764" centered upon the fact that it was "purely commercial" from the beginning. Indeed, this "commercial system was wholly restrictive," or to speak plainly, "a monopoly." There were "no less than twenty-nine Acts of Parliament" that documented how this commercial monopoly operated with its "detailed enumerations" and "innumerable checks." There were an "infinite variety of paper chains" to "bind together this complicated system" into the amazingly successful and overwhelmingly powerful British Empire. According to his careful reading of the historical record, "during that whole period, a parliamentary revenue from thence was never once in contemplation." And the Americans were "confirmed in obedience" to this commercial system "more by usage than by law."

What Burke saw while the government pursued trade, not revenue, moved him to rhapsodize over the extraordinary development of British North America: "Nothing in the history of the world is like their progress. For my part, I never cast an eye on their flourishing commerce, and the cultivated and commodious life, but they seem to me rather ancient nations grown to perfection through a long series of fortunate events, and a train of successful industry, accumulating wealth in many centuries, than the colonies of yesterday." Indeed, they were nothing more than "a set of miserable outcasts, a few years ago, not so much sent as thrown out, on the bleak and barren shore of a desolate wilderness, three thousand miles from all civilized intercourse." Given this lived experience, America "had, except the commercial restraint, every characteristic mark of a free people in all her internal concerns. She had the image of the British constitution. She had the substance. She was taxed by her own representatives." America had ever enjoyed the most precious foundational principle of English liberty, the right to consent in matters of taxation.

Soon after the Peace of Paris, however, Charles Townshend "in a brilliant harangue" charmed the House of Commons, especially the country gentlemen, with "the image of a revenue to be raised in America." From these "first glimmerings of this new colonial system," Prime Minister George Grenville then proceeded to implement "this fatal scheme into form" by the American Revenue Act of 1764, commonly known as the Sugar Act. At this critical juncture "the scheme of a regular plantation parliamentary revenue was adopted in theory, and settled in practice."

Admittedly, "our colonies were backward to enter into the present vexatious and ruinous controversy" simply because they were new at exploring the ramifications of the novel system expressed in the Preamble of the Sugar Act. Yes, at first the Americans touched "very tenderly" upon the constitutional principle involved, for they had grown accustomed to bear regulations of trade, and the Sugar Act treated these new taxes as if they were simply an extension of the Navigation Acts. With the passage of the Stamp Act of 1765, however, that ambiguity utterly dissolved and in short order a "mighty tempest" swept through the British Empire.

Contrary to the insinuations of the defenders of the imperial policy exhibited in the Stamp Act, Burke boldly declared that the Rockingham Administration did not come into office with the intention of repealing the Stamp Act. Only after the alarming situation became known in October did the ministry even consider that option. And they did not rush into their decision precipitously. "They weighed this matter as its difficulty and importance required. They considered maturely among themselves. They consulted with all who could give advice or information." The deliberations within the ministry were guided by two basic principles of the most substantial nature:

> One, that the legislative rights of this country, with regard to America, were not entire, but had certain restrictions and limitations. The other principle was, that taxes of this kind were contrary to the fundamental principles of commerce on which the colonies were founded; and contrary to every idea of political equity; by which equity we are bound, as much as possible, to extend the spirit and benefit of the British constitution to every part of the British dominions.

Granted these "principles of policy, of equity, and of commerce," the Rockingham Administration forthrightly committed itself to a total Repeal of the Stamp Act, and the ministry prevailed "by an independent, noble, spirited, and unexpected majority" in the House of Commons. Tranquility returned, commerce revived, and universal joy spread throughout the British Empire.

Had Great Britain retained the colonial policy expressed in the Repeal of the Stamp Act, Burke believed a lasting peace would have been secured for generations to come. That peace was not lasting arose from the fact that in 1766 the new Earl of Chatham created a ministry without any semblance of coherence. When he soon fell ill and "withdrew ... from public cares," leadership within the Chatham Administration devolved upon the delightful Charles Townshend, who had introduced the idea of deriving revenue from the colonies a few years earlier. Now he proposed a new set of taxes for America. According to the Preamble of the Townshend Duties Act these new taxes were designed to "support the civil government" in America.

How had that worked out? Well, beginning in 1767 the various ministries have "enacted, repealed, enforced, yielded, and now attempt to enforce again." Not many months passed before the Grafton Administration committed itself to repealing five of the "six branches of duties," reserving the tax on tea alone, and the North Administration had delivered on that commitment, thereby reducing the yield to a pittance: "Five-sixths repealed—abandoned—sunk—gone—lost for ever." Those five taxes were repealed "on commercial principles." But "this commercial motive never was believed by any man, either in America … or in England." Indeed, "If commercial principles had been the true motives to the repeal [of the Townshend Duties], or had they been at all attended to, tea would have been the last article we should have left taxed for a subject of controversy."

Burke accused the various ministries since 1767 "of not having large and liberal ideas in the management of great affairs." Without any system, they "only invented occasionally some miserable tale for the day, in order meanly to sneak out of difficulties, into which they had proudly strutted." The result? The Empire has endured "the loss not only of peace, of union, and of commerce, but even of revenue," where the Exchequer could have received "at least a million of free grants since the peace" in 1763. "So paltry a sum as three-pence in the eyes of a financier, so insignificant an article as tea in the eyes of a philosopher, have shaken the pillars of a commercial empire that circled the whole globe."

Just to preserve "the opprobrium of an empty, absurd, and false recital" in the Preamble to the Townshend Duties, Parliament had retained this trifling tax on tea. Even if the Americans were willing to accept the three pence per pound tax on tea, the revenue would be "utterly insufficient" to meet the objective of the Preamble. The policy was in pursuit of "a phantom; a quiddity; a thing that wants, not only substance, but even a name; for a thing, which is neither abstract right, nor profitable enjoyment." Call it then, "*a preambulary tax*," for it is "a tax of sophistry, a tax of pedantry, a tax of disputation, a tax of war and rebellion."

After citing Hillsborough's authoritative circular letter of 13 May 1769, Burke thundered, "the idea of taxing America for the purpose of revenue is an abominable project," for "it yields nothing but discontent, disorder, disobedience." The last thing it would ever yield was any revenue sufficient for the stated purpose. The only way to resolve the conflict was to "leave America, if she has taxable matter in her, to tax herself." In brief, "Leave the Americans as they anciently stood" before the enactment of the Sugar Act of 1764.

Not only did Burke pour down rational scorn upon the ministry's pursuit of a pitiful peppercorn to preserve the propriety of Parliament. He also sought to distance the Rockingham party's position from the Earl of Chatham's understanding of the doctrine of Parliamentary Supremacy. While both agreed that Parliament had the right to regulate the imperial trade, they did not share identical views on policing the British Empire.

Burke's exposition of Parliament's *imperial character* began with a commonsensical observation: "As all these several inferior legislatures are only co-ordinate to each other, they ought all to be subordinate to her; else they can neither preserve mutual peace, nor hope for mutual justice, nor effectually afford mutual assistance." From that foundation Burke proceeded to spell out some *necessary* implications that followed from the nature of the "several inferior legislatures":

> It is necessary [for Parliament] to coerce the negligent, to restrain the violent, and to aid the weak and deficient, *by the overruling plenitude of her power.* She is never to intrude into the place of the others, whilst they are equal to the common ends of their institution. But in order to enable Parliament to answer all these ends of provident and beneficent superintendence, *her powers must be boundless* (my emphases).

To preserve that *overruling plenitude of her power* was precisely the point of the Declaratory Act.

Although Parliament's power was boundless, it was a "reserved power," simply because "the legislative rights of this country, with regard to America, were not entire, but had certain restrictions and limitations." The *overruling plenitude of Parliament's reserved power* would come into play only when subordinate powers failed to act responsibly. For example, in time of war it was standard operating procedure for the colonies to contribute men and money through *requisitions*—issued by the King-in-Council. While most of the colonies "would cheerfully furnish whatever is demanded," suppose some would "hang back, and, easing themselves, let the stress of the draft lie on the others." In situations such as this, Parliament could rightfully employ its coercive power, saying, in effect, "Tax yourselves for the common supply, or Parliament will do it for you." Nevertheless, "this ought to be no ordinary power; nor ever used in the first instance." Indeed, in Burke's understanding of the Declaratory Act, Parliament's reserve power of coercing a delinquent colony was simply "an instrument of empire, and not ... a means of supply."

While discussing the Declaratory Act Burke confessed, "I never came with so much spirit into this House. It was a time for a *man* to act in. We had powerful enemies; but we had faithful and determined friends; and a glorious cause." That was eight long years ago, "not as now, when our arms are tied behind us." Assuming he derived this image from "The Able Doctor" cartoon, it would seem that he was suggesting that Lord Chief Justice Mansfield's theoretical axiom of "the unlimited and illimitable nature of supreme sovereignty" was the pivotal reason why our arms were now tied behind our backs.[25]

THREE days after Edmund Burke's oration the Second Reading of the Massachusetts Government Bill came before the House of Commons. In this 22 April Commons Debate General Conway implicitly evoked the Declaratory Act when he advanced this principled objection to the Bill, loaded with italics in the report in the *London Evening Post*:

> I do think, and it is my sincere opinion, that *we* are the *aggressors* and *innovators,* and *not* the *colonies*. We have *irritated* and *forced* laws upon them for these six or seven years last past. We have enacted such a *variety* of laws; with these new taxes, together with a refusal to repeal the *trifling* duty on tea; all these

> things have served no other purpose but to *distress*
> and *perplex*. I think the Americans have done *no*
> *more* than *every* subject *would* do in an *arbitrary*
> state, where laws are imposed against their will.

Conway was the Secretary of State when the Declaratory Act was passed. He knew what the issues had been. He also knew what the implications for the future promised to yield.

Richard Rigby, however, dismissed General Conway's argument out of hand: "it is a matter of astonishment to me, how an honourable gentleman (Mr. Conway) can be the author or bringer in of a *declaratory law* over all America, and yet say at one and the same time, that we have no right to tax America." Increasingly, the Declaratory Act had become a convenient bludgeon for exposing the supposed contradictions in the Rockingham party's understanding of the doctrine of Parliamentary Supremacy. Their notion that Parliament could rightfully employ its authority to tax as "an instrument of empire, and not … a means of supply" was wasted upon the North Administration, given its maximal understanding of the doctrine of Parliamentary Supremacy advocated by Lord Chief Justice Mansfield.

Not only did the North Administration believe that Parliament could rightfully raise revenue from the Americans, it also embraced the notion that Parliament could rightfully intervene in the domestic affairs of a colony, thereby radically increasing the pressure. Since both the Massachusetts Government Bill and the Massachusetts Justice Bill required an alteration in the 1691 Charter, the question arose over whether Parliament had the authority to modify what had been granted exclusively by the King alone.

Welbone Ellis argued affirmatively that "the supreme power which the constitution has vested in Lords and Commons in Parliament assembled" took precedence over the royal prerogative.[26] Later that day James Harris pressed the point that to hold charter rights to be "superior to the Act of the King, Lords and Commons" would be "saying there may be a partial sovereignty," which, of course, was absurd in the world of discourse championed by Sir William Blackstone and his mentor, Lord Chief Justice Mansfield.[27]

THE Opposition steadily hardened its formal position as the full scope of the coercive policy became more transparent. A major challenge was launched during the Third Reading of the Massachusetts Government Bill on 2 May 1774.

Two months earlier Isaac Barré had supported coercive measures against Boston with a "hearty and determinate affirmative," but by 15 April he thought the fuller plan was "pregnant with every mischief to this country." Now on 2 May he noted, "In the one House of Parliament we have passed the Rubicon, in the other *delenda est Carthago*." Instead of these coercive measures, Barré celebrated Chatham's "lenient and palliative" approach as he "always went cap in hand" seeking support from the colonies during the Seven Years War.

General Conway pointedly asked, "Where is this olive branch I have heard so much talk about?" After telling the House "as long as you continue the doctrine of taxing America, you will never be at rest," this respected military authority pressed the strategic situation: "I think it is better to have peace with America, and war with the world, than be at war with America, because, if they are in peace with us, they will continue to support us in time of war."

Some of the most telling observations by the Opposition came in the speeches of the former Solicitor General, John Dunning. He had been "a sharp thorn in the sides of Lord Mansfield" ever since he published *An Inquiry into the Late Doctrine on Libels* in late 1764. Like many others, he initially had not deemed the Boston Port Bill of "sufficient magnitude to oppose it," but now that the ministry had introduced these two other Bills, he thought the House had gained "possession of the whole of that fatal secret," namely, that the aim of the policy was "war, severe revenge, and hatred against our own subjects." In his opinion, "We are now come to that fatal dilemma, resist and we will cut your throats, submit and we will tax you."

This opened the way for Dunning to attempt to puzzle out the conceptual origin of the whole general plan. After saying he did not believe the Prime Minister was "the immediate actor of all this," he openly confessed, "I know not the age, the person, or the *sex*, but that I may not be wrong, I will use the language of acts of Parliament ... and will say, *he, she,* or *they,* to the person or persons alone do I mean to address myself."

To grasp what Dunning was driving at in this frankly bizarre pronouncement, one needs to know the meaning of the word *macaroni* in the polite society of contemporary London. The June 1770 edition of the *Oxford Magazine* expressed the meaning this way, according to the *OED*: "There is indeed a kind of animal, neither male nor female, a thing of the neuter gender, lately started up amongst us. It is called a *Macaroni*. It talks without meaning, it smiles without pleasantry, it eats without appetite, it rides without exercise, it wenches without passion." While discussing a technical issue in the Massachusetts Justice Bill, Dunning turned to how it provided a most dangerous precedent that threatened "as a remnant of Barbarism and Gothicism" a "great pillar of the constitution." This led one of the most prominent legal authorities to ask: "Is it then the present idea to destroy every part of that Gothic constitution, and adopt a *Macaroni* one in its stead? If so, it is a system of ministerial despotism that is adopted here."

Constantine John Phipps pursued the topic by attacking "whatever doctrines gentlemen may imbibe from Mr. Blackstone." Phipps could not conceive how Blackstone's doctrines could "be of that authority which ought to guide and direct us." Indeed, "There is not a more insidious way of gaining proselytes to his opinion than that dangerous pomp of quotations which he has practiced; it conveys some of the most lurking doctrines to lead astray the minds of young men." Nevertheless, the House of Commons had been led astray by the lurking doctrines emerging from the legal establishment. Commons passed the Massachusetts Government Bill on 2 May by a margin of 239 to 64. Four days later it passed the Massachusetts Justice Bill 127 to 24. The Opposition never came close to reaching even a third of the votes in the House of Commons.[28]

WHERE John Dunning had left the originator(s) of this macaroni constitution in the realm of mystery, Camden brought the accusation down to earth when the Massachusetts Government Bill came up for its Third Reading in the House of Lords on 11 May. After declaring the Bill to be "a wanton exercise of power … which will infallibly alienate the minds and affections of the colonists," the former Lord Chancellor "warmly attacked *Lord Mansfield, whom he treated as author of the bills and of all the present measures*," according to Walpole's *Journal*. Then Walpole added, "Lord *Mansfield*, in a speech of an hour and a half, very artful but very timid, returned no attack, but purged himself of the bill, *which he protested he had never seen till printed*—a falsehood too gross and incredible for any art to palliate."

Mansfield also responded to the Duke of Richmond in a sharp exchange. According to the *London Evening Post*, "a *noble Duke*, remarkably distinguished for his popularity, in the course of his speech said, *that if the Americans were thus to be treated, he could not help wishing them success in their resistance.* Upon which Lord *Mansfield* got up, and after apologizing for expressions spoken in the heat of argument, said, *he was very sure the noble Duke would correct himself.*" Instead of correcting himself the Duke shot off another volley by referencing Matthew 11:28 as he "formally appealed to the Bench of Bishops, whether it did not well become a Christian to wish relief to all those who were *heavy laden*." The magnitude of that burden was wasted upon the King. George III signed the second and third Intolerable Acts on 20 May 1774.[29]

ON 29 April Lord Barrington brought up the obvious need for British troops to be moved back to the town of Boston from Castle William far out in the harbor, where they had been isolated since Governor Hutchinson had them removed in the wake of the Boston Massacre. The fourth Intolerable Act—the American Quartering Act—empowered the new military Governor, General Gage, with the authority to requisition "so many uninhabited … or other buildings" to house the army.[30]

Although the Bill passed the House of Commons without a division, the long absent Earl of Chatham caused something of a stir when the Bill came up for its Third Reading in the House of Lords on 26 May.[31] Instead of addressing the Bill directly, Chatham took it upon himself in a speech lasting an hour and a quarter to expand on the unfolding situation. In what Walpole called "a long feeble harangue," he first "blamed the violence of the Bostonians," then turned around and blamed "every step that had provoked them or been taken to chastise them." After talking "high for the sovereignty of this country," he "condemned the taxes." So far as Walpole could tell, "he meant to insinuate ... that he alone could assert the authority of England, and compose the differences in America." And truth to tell Chatham ended up confusing almost everybody on where he stood or what he thought should be done. What captured Walpole's attention, however, was how he played "a comedian, even to his dress, to excuse his late absence." To exhibit his anguish, he entered the House of Lords with "his legs wrapped in black velvet boots, and as if in mourning for the King of France he leaned on a crutch covered with black."[32] (Two weeks earlier the long reign of King Louis XV had come to an end on 10 May 1774.)

HORACE Walpole had noted while visiting Paris years before that the Parlements of France "were filled with many great, able, and steady magistrates" whose eyes had been opened to "the rights of mankind" by "the philosophy and studies of the age." So taken by the term *Parliament*, "they chose to believe, at least to inculcate the belief, that they were possessed of the rights of a British senate." Their pretension to being more than "courts of judicature" even led them to attempt "with heroic firmness to shake off the chains that galled their country."

In response to these pretensions, however, Louis XV "suddenly and very early in the morning" entered the Parlement of Paris, "called for the registers" and "torn out their remonstrances." The magistrates were appalled, but they could only respectfully sigh in utter defeat. Not content with silencing the Parlement of Paris in 1766, the King then abolished all the Provincial Parlements in 1771. Finally, His Most Christian Majesty—with the support of His Most Catholic Majesty of Spain—pressured Pope Clement XIV into dissolving the Jesuit Order in 1773. The dominance of the State over the Church so closely intertwined Throne and Altar that on meeting "the sacrament" in the street after tearing out the remonstrances of the Parlement of Paris, Louis XV "alighted from his coach, knelt in the dirt, and received the blessings of all the old beggar women."[33]

WITH its French Catholic faith Quebec fully shared the interpenetration of piety and politics that shaped the *Ancien Régime*, a fact that was not disturbed by the Peace of Paris.[34] According to the Preamble to the Royal Proclamation, George III "thought fit, with the advice of our said Privy Council, to issue [this Proclamation] under our Great Seal of Great Britain." General Assemblies would be established "so soon as the state and circumstances … will admit thereof." Until then, the people "may confide in our royal protection for the enjoyment of the benefit of the laws of our realm of England."[35]

While it is widely known that the Royal Proclamation of 1763 was resented by the Americans because it was consciously designed to hem them in between the seacoast and the mountains—and exclude them from the vast territories beyond—it is seldom noticed how the British legal establishment under Lord Chief Justice Mansfield also thoroughly despised it. Why? Because it was issued by *the Royal Prerogative when it should have proceeded through an Act of Parliament.*

According to the imperial vision of Mansfield, all colonial legislation was *subordinate* to the King-in-Parliament. The constitutional issue surfaced initially when the Rockingham Administration sought to prepare a proper government for Quebec. In the Cabinet deliberations, Lord Chancellor Northington insisted upon the need for the legislation to proceed by Act of Parliament. When the ministry ignored Northington's advice, George III seized upon this opinion to replace the Rockingham Administration. As Lord President of the Council Northington then repeated this opinion during the Chatham Administration. But for all the initiatives and inquiries during the late 1760s, the Rockingham, the Chatham, as well as the Grafton Administrations never troubled to bring forward the slightest legislation on Quebec.[36]

A proper government for Quebec, quite obviously, could not be postponed indefinitely, and the North Administration took it up in 1771. The Privy Council directed the Attorney General, the Solicitor General, and the Advocate General to render their opinions on what to do about Quebec. Because no action followed from that directive, the Privy Council renewed its request on 31 July 1772, and this time it did get some written opinions that put serious planning into motion within the lethargic imperial bureaucracy.

After examining the three briefs prepared by the law officers, on 4 August 1773 Lord Chancellor Apsley—after consulting with Lord Chief Justice Mansfield—forwarded the briefs to Dartmouth to "enable his Lordship to form a plan of government for [Quebec] fit to be laid before Parliament." His Lordship, however, did not seem to be in a hurry to act—until early December, when North "begged that he may have ... a précis of the affairs of Quebec" from the American Department.[37]

While Dartmouth introduced the Government of Quebec Bill in the House of Lords on 2 May, the decisive argument was joined during the Second Reading in the House of Commons on 26 May. That a Bill of such importance originated in the House of Lords caused more than a little concern. North, however, tried to calm the situation by arguing that the Quebec Bill "was the result of the opinion of the noble lord who offered what he conceived to be the best plan for Canada, the best plan for Great Britain after considering, and weighing every information, and every light it could receive from every quarter."

After promptly pointing out that North had failed to name this noble lord, John Dunning aggressively announced, "I am glad it is imputable to any House but ourselves. I believe no individual in that House will own it. I believe I shall not do injustice to my learned friends, I shall not be found a false prophet, when I take leave to say, they will disown it." Dunning proved to be a true prophet, for nobody would "venture to own himself the parent" of the Quebec Bill.

Regardless of who was the author—it surely looks like a collective effort of the legal establishment as a whole under the guidance of Lord Chief Justice Mansfield—it was designed to stabilize the rather chaotic situation of French Canada still operating under the Royal Proclamation of 1763. Attorney General Thurlow tagged that situation as "the grossest, and absurdist, cruelest tyranny" that "a conquering nation ever practiced over a conquered country." In Mansfield's opinion, "The history of the world don't furnish an instance of so rash and unjust an act." Four contentious issues now stood in need of urgent resolution: the boundaries of the Province, the position of the Roman Catholic religion in Quebec, the proper mixture of English and French law, and the establishment of a (partial) provincial legislature.

The Quebec Bill basically restored the disputed boundaries that France had claimed prior to the opening of the French and Indian War in 1754, namely, the vast territory west of the ill-defined border of Pennsylvania to the Mississippi River and north of the Ohio River to the Hudson Bay Territory. The Province of Quebec, in other words, was expanded to encompass the present states of Ohio, Indiana, Illinois, Michigan, Wisconsin, plus portions of Minnesota!

During the Commons Debate on 26 May, one speaker observed, "You have given Canada almost all that country which was the subject of dispute" leading into the French and Indian War. He even noted, "We went to war calling it the province of Virginia." (At Fort Le Boeuf next to Lake Erie, Major George Washington had personally delivered the Governor of Virginia's ultimatum demanding French withdrawal from the contested area to Le Gardeur de Saint-Pierre on 12 December 1753.)

Colonel Barré pressed even harder, claiming that two decades ago the government had insisted upon no boundary other than "the River St. Lawrence, and the lakes," but now the North Administration was saying that old boundary line was "the center, not the frontier."

He wanted to know "why the noble lord has taken this sweep from North America, runs a frontier at the back of almost all our capital settlements," and brought Quebec "so close to all our frontiers." The suspicious Barré thought this new boundary "carries in its breast something that squints, and looks dangerous to the other inhabitants of that country, our own colonies."

Solicitor General Wedderburn, however, made it abundantly clear that the ministry, for a variety of reasons, wanted to preserve the standing policy of confining the Americans to areas easily accessible to the Atlantic seacoast. He even admitted that he would not say to them, "cross the Ohio, you will find an Utopia, some entire great and mighty empire." On the contrary, his message was this candid—"this is the border, beyond which for the advantage of the whole empire, you should not extend yourself."

Besides radically enlarging the territory of Quebec, the Bill altered the position of the Catholic Church within the Province. While the French Canadians had enjoyed the "free exercise" of their faith from the moment Quebec was admitted into the British Empire, the 1774 Bill introduced the provision ("subject to the King's Supremacy") that the Catholic clergy "may hold, receive, and enjoy their accustomed Dues and Rights."

John Dunning did not object to the "full toleration" granted to Catholics. What was objectionable was this fact: "The Roman Catholic religion is established by law." Or as Colonel Barré noted, "it is very singular how this poor Roman Catholic religion has been treated. In Maryland it has been tolerated, in Ireland persecuted, in Canada you choose to give it an establishment."

Hard on the heels of the religious issue came the retention of the French Civil Law. That led Barré to point out that "many thousands of English subjects are established some hundred miles beyond the Endless Mountains upon that very spot, which you are going to make a part of this country of Canada." After saying he did not find it "a grievance … to give them the English laws," he evoked the authority of his own certain knowledge to buttress his claim that "they wish to have the *habeas corpus*." Furthermore, the French

Civil Law was "founded upon … the Custom of Paris," which was composed of "30 folio volumes." How all that arcane material could ever be administered in North America struck the knowledgeable Barré as simply incomprehensible.

Finally, "for the Peace, Welfare, and good Government" of Quebec, the Royal Governor would rule with "a Council … to consist of such Persons resident there, not exceeding Twenty-three, nor less than Seventeen." The civil government of Quebec, in other words, would function *without a representative Assembly of the people*.[38] (Quebec did not obtain an Assembly until 1791.)[39]

In the opinion of Sergeant-at-Law John Glynn the government of Quebec would be "as absolute, as any King of France can make it." Charles Fox thought it was "contrary to the genius" of Great Britain, "to go at once, and establish a government perfectly despotic." And the Bill established "a tax," a point picked up by yet another speaker who said, "Laying a tax, or repealing a tax, should not be suffered to originate in the House of Lords."[40]

When the issue was revisited on 31 May, Captain Phipps saw "nothing in this Bill but the language of despotism." Edmund Burke could not remember a time when he "came with so little information to decide a question of this degree of magnitude." George Cavendish found the entire legislation "cruel and impolitic to the highest degree." In his report to Lord Hardwicke, Soame Jenyns claimed the plan was "to establish popery and arbitrary power in so large a part of America." Colonel Barré thought it was probably of good thing that the House was "left in the dark" about the origins of the Quebec Bill, for he knew "of no way of defending despotism." After a very thin House passed the Government of Quebec Bill 56 to 20, it was forwarded to the House of Lords for a final vote.[41]

In the Lord's Debate on 17 June, Chatham condemned the legislation as "*a breach of the [Protestant] Reformation, of the [Glorious] Revolution, and of the King's Coronation Oath.*" According to Walpole, he finished off by charging that "*the mask was now thrown off,* and arbitrary power openly aimed at." Mansfield, however, did not hear this fiery blast simply because he had "with his usual poltroonery *absented himself*" after Camden had accused him of being "*the real Prime Minister.*" As Walpole reported in his *Journal,* "nobody doubted" that our Scottish Law Lord was the author of the Government of Quebec Bill.[42]

This parliamentary session lasted much longer than usual. Most of the members had gone home when the Quebec Bill passed the House of Lords 26 to 7. On 22 June 1774 the King assented to the fifth Intolerable Act. Needless to say, Lord Chief Justice Mansfield was a prime instigator of more than a few of these Intolerable or Coercive Acts.

THOMAS JEFFERSON: A SUMMARY VIEW

THOMAS JEFFERSON (1743-1826) WAS A PRECOCIOUS YOUNG ATTORNEY AT LAW WHEN he received the news in the spring of 1774 that the Boston harbor was "to be stopped by an armed Force." With several other Virginians—after rummaging through "the revolutionary precedents & forms of the Puritans" in seventeenth-century England—they "cooked up" a Resolution that was adopted by the House of Burgesses and forwarded to the respective colonies throughout North America. After protesting the violation of "our just, antient, and constitutional rights" by Parliament's embracing "a determined system" to reduce "the inhabitants of British America to slavery," the statement claimed that an attack upon "one of our sister colonies ... is an attack made on all British America." The Committee of Correspondence then communicated with the entire Atlantic seaboard "on the expediency of appointing deputies from the several colonies of British America, to meet in general congress, at such place annually as shall be thought most convenient."

Governor Dunmore, the haughty Scottish Earl of the Murray clan, promptly dissolved the Assembly for passing this supportive

Resolution, but "89 MEMBERS OF THE LATE HOUSE OF BURGESSES" simply moved to the Raleigh Tavern and in short order recommended a boycott of "any kind of East India commodity whatsoever, except saltpetre and spices, until the grievances of America are redressed." This proposal was also endorsed by 21 "clergymen and other inhabitants of the colony and dominion of Virginia."

Soon letters on the "alarming Crisis" arrived from "*Boston, Philadelphia,* and *Maryland,*" but "so small a Proportion of the late Associates" remained in Williamsburg that the Moderator, Peyton Randolph, "resolved to invite all the Members of the late House of Burgesses to a general Meeting in this City on the first Day of *August* next" to address how to pursue "the Common Cause." To prepare the way for this event, the various communities in Virginia were asked to hold Fast Days.

By focusing the collective mind of Virginia on imploring "the diving interposition in behalf of an injured and oppressed people" in Massachusetts, these Fast Day services transformed the political landscape in the Old Dominion. In Jefferson's own words, "The people met generally, with anxiety & alarm in their countenances, and the effect of the day thro' the whole colony was like a shock of electricity, arousing every man & placing him erect & solidly on this centre."[1]

LONG before Parliament passed the Intolerable Acts of 1774, George Wythe had persuaded Jefferson that the constitutional crisis was rooted in the maximal doctrine of Parliamentary Supremacy at the heart of Mansfield's Project and Blackstone's *Commentaries.* Vast historical and legal research prepared our advanced thinker as he was composing what soon came to be known as *A Summary View of the Rights of British America.*

The importance of English history for a proper understanding of American institutions was an enduring principle in Jefferson's universe of discourse. As early as March 1764 he bought David Hume's *History of England from the Invasion of Julius Caesar to the*

Revolution of 1688.[2] Before the Stamp Act Crisis began to clarify the issue, the young law student was quite taken by Hume's *History.* Years later he disclosed to William Duane, "I remember well the enthusiasm with which I devoured it when young, and the length of time, the research and reflection which were necessary to eradicate the poison it had instilled into my mind." His reasoning is quite instructive:

> It was unfortunate that [Hume] first took up the history of the Stuarts, became their apologist, and advocated all their enormities. To support his work, when done, he went back to the Tudors, and so selected and arranged the materials of their history as to present their arbitrary acts only, as the genuine samples of the constitutional power of the crown, and still writing backwards, he then reverted to the early history, and wrote the Saxon and Norman periods with the same perverted view.[3]

From the long perspective of his extraordinary political career Jefferson firmly believed that this *History of England* by Scotland's empiricist philosopher turned revisionist historian—plus "the wily sophistries" of Blackstone's *Commentaries*—had "done more towards the suppression of the liberties of man, than all the millions of men in arms of Bonaparte and the millions of human lives with the sacrifice of which English books, English prejudices, English manners, and the apes, and dupes, and designs among our professional crafts."[4]

While Jefferson said nothing of consequence in his *Autobiography* about his legal studies under the guidance of George Wythe, it is only fair to assume that every law student in Williamsburg in the 1760s kept abreast of the transformation in British Colonial Policy. And pirated copies of Blackstone's "Analysis" had circulated widely for the better part of a decade before the first volume of his celebrated *Commentaries on the Laws of England* was published in 1765.[5]

Exactly when Jefferson set his heart against the toxic influence of Lord Chief Justice Mansfield's far reaching innovations will never be settled satisfactorily simply because almost all the documentary evidence on his early life went up in smoke in the Shadwell fire of February 1770. Of the sixteen letters that have been recovered, half were to his dear friend, John Page. And it was to Page that the twenty-six-year-old Jefferson wrote the distressing news, "Of papers too of every kind I am utterly destitute. All of these, whether public or private, of business or of amusement have perished in the flames." What so deeply troubled him was the loss of his books on the English Common Law Heritage, except for one he had lent out.[6]

Also surviving—probably because the budding architect had taken his notebooks up to Monticello, now in an early stage of construction—is what Douglas L. Wilson refers to as Jefferson's *Legal Commonplace Book*. Following the lead of Marie Kimball's careful analysis of his evolving handwriting, Wilson has determined that he began making entries somewhere around the time he passed the Virginia Bar Exam.[7]

Entries in Jefferson's *Legal Commonplace Book* made during the late 1760s and early 1770s reveal that he had studied William Salked's *Reports of the cases in the King's Bench, 1689-1712,* Robert Raymond's *Reports,* Lord Kame's *Historical Law Tracts,* Sir John Dalrymple's *Essay towards a General History of Feudal Property in Great Britain,* and Bernard Hale's *History of the Common Law.* And surely Jefferson had remained fully abreast of the indictment of Mansfield in the *Letters of Junius,* and nobody of consequence overlooked the Lord Chief Justice's role in the trials and tribulations of John Wilkes. In any case, Mansfield's initial appearance in Jefferson's extant papers began to appear in the 1770 case of Bolling v. Bolling.[8]

AFTER the freeholders of the county of Albemarle reappointed Thomas Jefferson and John Walker to represent them at the August Convention in Williamsburg, Jefferson prepared a twenty-two paragraph "Draft of Instructions" to guide this Convention in preparation for the forthcoming Continental Congress to be held in

Philadelphia in September. On the way to Williamsburg, however, he fell sick with dysentery and had no choice but to return to Monticello. Two copies of his "very hasty production, intended to have been put under a course of severe correction" were forwarded, and Peyton Randolph, who chaired the Convention, laid a copy "on the table for perusal." Although it was "thought too bold for the present state of things," the Draft by "A NATIVE, and MEMBER of the HOUSE of BURGESSES," was soon published in Williamsburg with this full title: *A Summary View of the Rights of British America, set forth in some Resolutions for the Inspection of the present Delegates of the People of Virginia now in Convention.*[9]

Before reaching the end of the opening sentence in *A Summary View* the reader is introduced to a key pillar in Jefferson's understanding of the Constitution of the British Empire, namely, that the King as "the chief magistrate" was duly bound to protect British North America from the "many unwarrantable encroachments and usurpation, attempted to be made by the legislature of one part of the empire, upon those rights which God and the laws have given equally and independently to all." Since the various entities within the British Empire shared "the same common sovereign, who was thereby made the central link connecting the several parts of the empire," he boldly concluded the opening section by "earnestly entreat[ing] his majesty, as yet the only mediatory power between the several states of the British empire, to recommend to his parliament of Great Britain the total revocation" of all those recent Acts that defined the New Colonial System at the root of the constitutional conflict. According to his vision, "Parliament has no right to exercise authority" over America at all. That was the "true ground" he was intent upon standing to defend the Rights of British North America.[10]

Jefferson opened the historical groundwork for his understanding of the Constitution of the British Empire by reminding George III "that our ancestors, before their emigration to America, were the free inhabitants of the British dominions in Europe." During the Dark Ages these "Saxon ancestors ... left the native wilds and woods in North of Europe" and "possessed themselves of the island of Britain."

Barbarians though those pagans were, they somehow hit upon "trial by peers," and they "held their lands, as they did their personal property in absolute dominion." Over time these Anglo-Saxons created "a system of laws which has so long been the glory and protection of that country."[11]

Because the Common Law was challenged when "William the Norman" brought the feudal system across the channel from France in 1066, Jefferson spelled out the implications in some detail: "The lands which had belonged to those who fell in the battle of Hastings, and in the subsequent insurrections of his reign, formed a considerable proportion of the lands of the whole kingdom. These he granted out, subject to feudal duties, as did he also those of a great number of his new subjects, who by persuasions or threats were induced to surrender them for that purpose." He candidly acknowledged that "by express laws, enacted to render uniform the system of military defence," King William came very close to imposing this new order upon merry England. Although many of the estates remained unencumbered by "feudal conditions," it remained the case that they, too, were "made liable to the military duties as if they had been feuds." Indeed, "the Norman lawyers soon found means to saddle them also with the other feudal burthens."

Nevertheless, the conquerors failed in their long-range project. In Jefferson's reading of the historical record, "Feudal holdings were therefore but exceptions out of the Saxon laws of possessions, under which all lands were held in absolute right." As "feudal holdings" were derived from the Norman Civil Law, so those native "allodial" lands were rooted in "the basis, or ground-work, of the common law."

Given this historical preparation, Jefferson emphatically maintained that since "America was not conquered by William the Norman, nor its lands surrendered to him, or any of his successors," it followed that the possession of land was "undoubtedly of the allodial nature." But he did acknowledge that the early settlers of Virginia were persuaded to accept "the fictitious principle that all lands belonged originally to the king … and accordingly took grants of their own lands from the crown." To explain how this *usage* became solidified, he resorted to saying, "Our ancestors … were farmers, not lawyers."[12]

When Edmund Pendleton pressed him on the current implications of his understanding of land and property rights, Jefferson responded by saying directly, "The opinion that our lands were allodial possessions is one which I have very long held, and had in my eye during a pretty considerable part of my law reading which I found always strengthened it." Furthermore, "the happy system of our ancestors … as it stood before the 8th century" still remains "the wisest & most perfect ever yet devised by the wit of man."[13]

Jefferson's reading of the past showed that the Early Stuarts were a blemish in the historical record of the English people:

> A family of princes was then on the British throne, whose treasonable crimes against their people brought on them afterwards the exertion of those sacred and sovereign rights of punishment reserved in the hands of the people for cases of extreme necessity, and judged by the constitution unsafe to be delegated to any other judicature. While every day brought forth some new and unjustifiable exertion of power over their subjects on that side of the water, it was not to be expected that those laws here, much less able at the time to oppose the designs of despotism, should be exempted from injury.

Not only did the Stuarts parcel out various territories in America "by an assumed right of the crown alone," it was not long before they made an "unjust encroachment" upon America's "free trade with all parts of the world." And he explicitly said that the Americans possessed a "natural right" to this "free trade."

After the execution of Charles I, Parliament continued this "high offence" and "assumed upon themselves the power of prohibiting" the American trade "with all other parts of the world, except the islands of Great Britain." But on 12 May 1651 Parliament retreated from this arbitrary action and reached an accommodation with the Virginian House of Burgesses. The eighth article of this treaty explicitly stated that Virginia should have "free trade as the people of England do enjoy to all places and with all nations." Alas, "upon the restoration of his majesty king Charles the second" in 1660, Virginia's "rights of free commerce fell once more a victim to arbitrary power."

While Jefferson argued that the Old Colonial System was less than constitutional, he did have the grace to acknowledge that from 1660 to 1764 "the violations of our rights were less alarming ... than that rapid and bold succession of injuries" under the New Colonial System. With rising anger he filed this report:

> Scarcely have our minds been able to emerge from the astonishment into which one stroke of parliamentary thunder has involved us, before another more heavy, and more alarming, is fallen on us. Single acts of tyranny may be ascribed to the accidental opinion of a day; but a series of oppressions, begun at a distinguished period, and pursued unalterably through every change of ministers, too plainly prove a deliberate and systematical plan of reducing us to slavery.

Even though the contending factions in London could find precious little consistency whatsoever in the countless ministerial reversals over the previous decade, Jefferson saw a "connected chain of parliamentary usurpation" under the control of an "unseen hand" guiding "the momentous affairs of this great empire."[14] Given time, he would track down the source of these novel powers to *"all Mansfield's innovations, or civilisations of the common law"* (my emphasis).[15]

Shining through Jefferson's list of grievances was his own vision of a splendid British Empire. He asked King George III to open his breast "to liberal and expanded thought," explicitly asking, "Let no act be passed by any one legislature which may infringe on the rights and liberties of another." In regard to the vexed issue of trade, he openly advanced this proposal: "Accept of every commercial preference it is in our power to give for such things as we can raise for their use, or they make for ours. But let them not think to exclude us from going to other markets to dispose of those commodities which they cannot use, or to supply those wants which they cannot supply." And he did make it abundantly clear that America was "willing, on our part, to sacrifice every thing which reason can ask to the restoration of that tranquility for which all must wish. On their part, let them be ready to establish union and a generous plan."[16]

Although Thomas Jefferson went much further than the Convention was prepared to go, some were more than impressed by how he worked up his Draft "with that freedom of language and sentiment which becomes a free people claiming their rights, as derived from the laws of nature, and not as the gift of their chief magistrate." Then he pointedly concluded his disquisition: "Let those flatter who fear; it is not an American art."[17]

FEW things could be more transparent than how utterly different Lord Chief Justice Mansfield's reading of medieval and early modern English history was from that of Thomas Jefferson. Whereas Mansfield could cite endless authorities from the Norman Conquest to the Glorious Revolution and beyond so as to exhibit the control of the government over the affairs of the state, Jefferson reached further back in time and concluded that the people never surrendered their own authority over policy, though the contest had been severely challenged at different times. In his outlook, the Glorious Revolution formed the climax where it was supposedly fixed forever that the people's rights would be respected. Lord Chief Justice Mansfield's reading of the deep past remains as a mirror image of Thomas Jefferson's. Strangely, they both shared a similar aesthetic sensibility, for both Kenwood and Monticello were shaped by one of the most influential architects of the age, Robert Adams.

THOMAS HUTCHINSON'S ENTRY INTO ENGLAND

T HOMAS HUTCHINSON CROSSED THE ATLANTIC IN GOOD TIME, ARRIVING IN THE IMPERIAL capital "between 8 & 9 o'clock" on the evening of 30 June 1774.[1] Within moments he was swept up in a whirlwind of activity, conferring with George III, consulting with officials, responding to dinner invitations. After the last few years when his every word as the Governor of Massachusetts had been challenged, he was now more than pleased with his welcome. His opinions were actively solicited. Civilities were extended. Kind words were spoken. As an acknowledged expert intimately versed on American affairs, he enjoyed a prominent place in polite society. At the close of his first week in London he informed his son, "a great number of persons of the first rank are continually calling upon me." Especially gratifying was the fact that "Lord Mansfield has desired to see me as soon as the sittings are over."[2]

One cannot read Thomas Hutchinson's *Diary and Letters*, edited so lovingly by his great-grandson Peter Orlando Hutchinson in 1884, without becoming acutely aware of how he moved almost exclusively within official circles that summer and fall. Indeed, in a letter he identified "Lord Chancellor [Apsley], Lord Suffolk, Lord

Dartmouth, Lord Mansfield, and Lord North" as "those Ministers who most concern themselves in American affairs." By simply adding Dartmouth's Under-Secretaries, John Pownall and William Knox, one would have the most important points of contact in his political world during his entry into London.[3]

Hutchinson's organizing intention was to figure out a way for Massachusetts to make amends for the Boston Tea Party and restore a working harmony with Great Britain. His prescription for reconciliation was based on two principles. First, "The supremacy of Parliament must never be given up." Second, "the legislatures of the Colonies" should have "the full enjoyment, and especially in matters of taxation, of every power consistent with this supremacy." And he was convinced that "there never was an administration more disposed to adopt both parts of this plan" than the current ministers, especially the American Secretary, Lord Dartmouth.[4]

On his first day in London Hutchinson responded to an invitation from Dartmouth "to see him at his Lordship's house … before noon." After bringing him up to date on some of the more recent Intolerable Acts—the Boston Port Act alone was known in Massachusetts when he left Boston—Dartmouth "proposed introducing me immediately to the King." Even though not dressed for the occasion, he was persuaded to attend when Dartmouth observed that "the King would not be at St. James's again until Wednesday." His Lordship, nevertheless, took so much time getting dressed that the King's Levée was over by the time they finally arrived. Against standard protocol though it was, the two were immediately ushered into the King's Closet, where for two long hours George III pressed for detailed answers to one question after another from the still rather seasick and humbly dressed Governor of Massachusetts.

While the political situation in Massachusetts commanded the central focus of the interchange, the King's curiosity spread over an incredible range of topics. When he asked about particular persons, Hutchinson would clarify or politely correct him. For example, Doctor Winthrop was "not a Doctor of Divinity," but "a Professor of Mathematicks and Natural Philosophy at the College." And John

Adams was not the brother of Samuel Adams, but "a relation" who was a lawyer. Hutchinson even noted that the proper phrase was "tarr & feather" when the King had said, "I see they threatened to pitch and feather you."

Much attention was given to uncovering how Benjamin Franklin had obtained Hutchinson's private letters to Thomas Whately. In regard to the rapid growth of the colonial population, Hutchinson said that at first he doubted the accuracy of Franklin's calculation that "the inhabitants of America, from their natural increase, doubled their number in 25 years," but he had soon come to the conclusion that the ambassador was basically right. Ecclesiastical matters were also canvassed, with Hutchinson stating, "The body of the people are Dissenters from the Church of England—what are called Congregationalists." He openly acknowledged, "My education, Sir, was with the Dissenters." The King even wanted to know what kind of bread the ordinary people ate in New England. Hutchinson's response: "In the country towns the people … live upon coarse bread made of rye and corn mixed"; and they "prefer this to flour or wheat bread," because "the Rye keeps it moist." And how were the Indians in Massachusetts faring? Hutchinson claimed there were around "50 or 60 families at most upon the Eastern Frontier," plus "near 100 families" living mostly in Mashpee under the care of a Congregational missionary, but he did not attempt to disguise his conviction that "in a few years the Indians would be extinct in all parts of the Continent."

And so it went, touching on points of interest, but the burden of the interview fell upon the developing political situation in Massachusetts. (In his *Diary* "K" indicates "King" and "H" himself, with "D" specifying Lord Dartmouth.)

> K.—How did you leave your Government, and how did the people receive the news of the late measures in Parliament?

> H.—When I left Boston we had no news of any Act of Parliament, except the one for shutting up the port, which was extremely alarming to the people.

(*Lord* D. said, Mr. H. came from Boston the day that [the Boston Port] Act was to take place, the first of June. I hear the people of Virginia have refused to comply with the request to shut up their ports ... and Mr. H. seems to be of opinion that no colony will comply with that request.)

K.—Do you believe, Mr. H., that the account from Virginia is true?

H.—I have no other reason to doubt it, except that the authority for it seems to be only a newspaper; and it is very common for articles to be inserted in newspapers without any foundation.

Hutchinson noticed that the King smiled at the suggestion that the other colonies would not comply with Massachusetts's request "to shut up their ports" so long as Boston's harbor remained closed.

Soon the conversation turned to the planned appointment of the Council by the King, as was the case in all the other Royal Colonies. In particular George III wanted his opinion on whether "the new appointed Councillors" would be "agreeable to the people." Hutchinson responded cautiously because he had just arrived "late last evening," had only now found out about the Massachusetts Government Act, and did not know who had been chosen. But he did say, "If the Council shall have been generally selected from the Episcopalians, it will make the change more disagreeable."

Hutchinson recorded the various entries from "what remained the clearest upon my mind," but he candidly admitted, "the King was particular in many other enquiries relative to my Administration, to the state of the Province, and the other Colonies."[5] And apparently he omitted much of what he said, or perhaps the King heard more than was actually said. In any event, the King reported to Prime Minister North that very evening that Hutchinson was of the opinion that "the Boston Port Bill was the only wise effectual method that could have been suggested for bringing them to a speedy submission, and that the change in the legislature will be a means of establishing some government in that province which till now has been a scene of anarchy." For whatever reason Hutchinson's testimony had apparently convinced George III that Massachusetts would soon submit to the Supreme Authority of Parliament.[6] That the King was "so intimately acquainted with the affairs of America" astonished Hutchinson. As he confided in a letter to his son a few days later, he came away from this encounter—he had stood the entire two hours—not only thoroughly enthralled but deeply convinced that the King was "more his own minister than is generally imagined."[7]

DURING those first few weeks the only discordant note to disturb Hutchinson's peace of mind came when he visited a former Governor of Massachusetts, Thomas Pownall. He had given a speech, recently published in the *London Evening Post*, in which he declared "that when he was Gov. of the Mass_____s, he never made any scruple of acting without the Council, in civil as well as military matters of government." Hutchinson viewed this as "implying blame upon me for declining to act in the affair of the Tea without the advice of Council." Since he was intimately aware of the inner working of the Massachusetts government during Pownall's tenure as Governor during the 1750s, he pressed for some substantiation for the claim: "I asked him if he could recollect any instance wherein he had acted, or could act, without the Council in any civil matter? He answered—In every instance. Mention one—In all. But recollect one—He repeated— All." Preposterous though Pownall's assertions were, Hutchinson politely changed the subject because he deemed Pownall's own house to be "an unfit place to carry the dispute any further."[8]

Although this serious disagreement over proper procedures did more than upset Hutchinson, he was gratified with what another former Governor related to him. When he dined with Sir Francis Bernard, the two intimate friends had a "long conversation upon old affairs in New England," a conversation in which Bernard amused him by telling how he had "apologized to Ld Mansfield for appointing me Chief Justice, not having been bred to the law," only to have Lord Chief Justice Wilmot exclaim, "By _____ he did not make a worse Chief Justice for that!"[9]

AMONG the numerous officials conferring with Hutchinson, the most helpful in filling him in on the critical details of the evolution of the planning for the Intolerable Acts was Under-Secretary of State John Pownall. He surely was the "authority" evoked in Hutchinson's report to General Gage that the alterations in the 1691 Charter were "not what was intended by the Ministry as the first plan."[10] And John Pownall was the one who informed him of the decisive role Mansfield had played in that alteration.

Hutchinson had already received an elegant invitation to dine with the Lord Chief Justice at Kenwood on Sunday 17 July. For this splendid dinner a host of dignitaries were present, including "[Robert] Adams, his Lordship's Architect and Planner," who had enlarged and extensively remodeled Kenwood in the 1760s. When *Works in Architecture* was published in 1773, the Adams brothers pronounced Kenwood, with its magnificent vistas, as the model for a new aesthetic that "brought about … a kind of revolution in the whole system of English architecture."[11] The most fascinating guest on this occasion, however, was "the famous Bruce" whose recent travels in Abyssinia "engrossed all the conversation."

In the midst of this festive occasion Mansfield expressed his deep appreciation for Hutchinson's steady loyalty under the most trying circumstances:

> After the highest encomiums upon every part of my conduct, and particularly the controversy upon Independency, he expressed his surprise at my perseverance, when I had *no assurance of support from the Ministry, their councils being fluctuating and undetermined*: but, says he, they are at last determined, and they are now gone too far to recede; and at all events the supremacy of P[arliament] will be maintained [my emphasis].[12]

Hutchinson was more than a little pleased to hear Mansfield declare that the reinvigorated resolution of the Administration expressed "the sense of the whole nation," for "there was not a man in any party but what agreed to the necessity of Parliament interposing to support its authority." The only disagreement within Parliament concerned "the mode" of interposing its authority. Mansfield claimed that even Chatham had reversed his opinion and was now maintaining that "he never did say what was attributed to him—*that Parlia___t had no right to tax America*: and never intended any more than *that a scheme of taxation of Amer[ica] was utterly inexpedient*." A few weeks later Mansfield told him that Chatham had asserted that the authority of Parliament to tax America "ought not to be suffered to be called in question." Hutchinson had heard similar words from Lord Chancellor Apsley. To imagine that "the King and his Ministers" would ever countenance a denial of the authority of Parliament was "contending for a phantom, or for a mere shadow."[13] The crux of the matter turned not upon the trifling amount of money in dispute. What needed to be preserved was the maximal doctrine of the Supremacy of Parliament. All this fit neatly into his two principles so essential to restoring harmony within the beloved Empire.

In the posthumously published third volume of his *History of the Colony and Province of Massachusetts-Bay*, Hutchinson noted that "a person of the first rank, as well as reputation, in the laws of England" congratulated him by saying the principles he had articulated in his controversy with the Massachusetts General Court were "a very succinct and judicious digest of the argument upon the relation of the colonies to the metropolis." While it is impossible to know the identity of this unnamed person, Mansfield's compliments on this occasion would seem to suggest that he could have been referring to none other than the Lord Chief Justice himself.[14]

WHETHER Chatham had actually reversed his opinion on American taxation, however, is quite problematical, for his rhetorical style had a way of confusing people, perhaps misleading them on purpose. For example, Lord Sandy's report to Lord Hardwicke on one of

Chatham's orations explicitly states that he supported "the legislative authority of Great Britain over the colonies, *even to the power of taxation*," precisely Mansfield's claim. But Walpole's report in his *Journal* on this same speech claims that Chatham "talked high for the sovereignty of this country, but *condemned the taxes*."

The fuller report in the *London Evening Post* also supports Walpole, not Sandy and Mansfield. It has Chatham calling attention to what he considered "an established fact, that the principal towns in America are learned and polite." Given their development "not only in arms, but in arts also," it should not come as a surprise that the Americans would maintain "a watchful eye over their liberties" and would oppose "the least encroachment on their *hereditary rights*." And he pressed the point that the Americans "*understand the constitution of the empire* as well as the noble Lords who are now in office." The policy that provoked the Boston Tea Party was "*contrary to all the principles of justice and civil policy*." After appealing to "his received and unalterable opinion," an opinion that he vowed to carry "to my grave," he asserted, "this country had *no right under heaven to tax America*" (my emphases).[15]

There remains some evidence, however, that Chatham had been dropping hints of a change in his opinion, for he was positioning himself to form a new ministry. Nevertheless, if Mansfield's testimony on his reversal is taken at face value, then (in the words of Peter D. G. Thomas) "Either Chatham's veracity or his memory must be in question," for all the known evidence over the last decade clearly documents Chatham's long-standing conviction that Parliament did not have the right to tax America.[16]

Throughout those debates the Chathamites also never wavered in their opposition to taxing the Americans as a matter of principle, and the Rockingham party never wavered in opposing the taxation of the Americans as a matter of expediency. It would appear that Mansfield wanted Hutchinson to believe that the crucial constitutional differences so conspicuously displayed in these debates had been leveled out. And Chatham did in fact distance himself from the Rockingham party and its interpretation of the 1766 Declaratory

Act, which of course divided the Opposition, much to the delight of the ministry.

WHILE Hutchinson was enjoying himself by making the rounds in England, General Thomas Gage was struggling to stay afloat as the new Governor of Massachusetts. He had thought he knew the Americans very well, for he had arrived with General Braddock in 1754, been rescued by Virginian forces after the crushing defeat at Fort Duquesne, and had succeeded Jeffrey Amherst as Commander-in-Chief of British forces in 1763. He was the one who confidently told George III shortly after the Boston Tea Party that the colonials "will be lions, whilst we are lambs, but if we take the resolute part they will undoubtedly prove very meek." All it would take to restore law and order would be a little roaring of the British Lion.

On his return to Massachusetts, however, Gage soon discovered that he needed more troops on the ground and more ships off shore to maintain his position. By 5 July he would be writing Dartmouth with the news that for all intents and purposes the civil government had been usurped by the mob and that the court system could no longer function. Not only had legal authority in Massachusetts utterly collapsed, the armed militias of the neighboring colonies were actively training for action.

Of course, it took time for urgent messages to cross the Atlantic. When several arrived on 2 August Dartmouth was so distressed he spoke "with great emotion" when he called upon Hutchinson. Although Hutchinson thought they contained "not very agreeable news," the King apparently misread the implications, for he is reported as saying to Richard Jackson, "Well: matters go on well in America: they are coming right." Jackson, who knew better, responded, "I hope, Sir, they will come right, but it may require some time."[17]

AFTER Hutchinson happened to meet the Lord Chief Justice at "the Chapel at Highgate" on 14 August, Mansfield graciously invited him and his daughter to join him for a fine dinner at Kenwood after the Sunday service. Their conversation ranged widely over a variety of topics—"the Feudal tenures" of the hereditary "Grants of Jurisdiction" given to the proprietors of Maryland and Pennsylvania, the "principles" involved in the 1772 *Somerset Case*, William Franklin's public letter condemning "his father's whole conduct in the affair of the letters," as well as what actually happened when the Lords of the Privy Council put their pens down without signing the warrants to arrest the Boston troublemakers. And Chatham's supposed reversal was also extensively reviewed.

Of particular notice was how Hutchinson opened his report with a rather chaotic rendering that captured the transparent agitation over the unfolding situation in America that so profoundly disturbed the Lord Chief Justice:

> [Mansfield] talked very largely and fully upon the state of America, particularly on the proposed Congress. Something, he said, must be done immediately, to-morrow—without delay—in the most formal way: he would not determine what: whether the King's Proclamation ordering Council—but something ought to be done.[18]

According to his imperial vision the Continental Congress was absolutely illegal by definition and should not be allowed to meet. Both Mansfield and Hutchinson fully realized that imperial matters had now reached a critical turning point.

THE FIRST CONTINENTAL
CONGRESS

A S THOMAS HUTCHINSON WAS PREPARING TO LEAVE
FOR LONDON, JOHN ADAMS RECORDED in the privacy of
his *Diary*, "There is a new, and a grand Scene open before me—a
Congress." Within a matter of days, however, he openly confessed,

> I wander alone, and ponder.—I muse, I mope, I
> ruminate.—I am often In Reveries and Brown
> Studies.—The Objects before me, are too grand, and
> multifarious for my Comprehension.—We have not
> Men, fit for the Times. We are deficient in Genius,
> in Education, in Travel, in Fortune—in every Thing.
> I feel unutterable Anxiety.—God grant us Wisdom,
> and Fortitude![1]

As he surveyed the extended landscape of America, he knew the
people were not united—and the questions were so monumental.
Many were confused; all were alarmed; some were committed. But
something had to be done.

Disturbed though he was, Adams went on the court circuit
in July in what today is the state of Maine. (Maine was part of

Massachusetts until 1820.) During a break in the court Adams and Attorney General Jonathan Sewall hiked up a hill overlooking Casco Bay for a personal exchange over the evolving crisis. They had much to discuss.

During the late 1750s Sewall had seen "some juvenile Letters" that Samuel Quincy had shown him that Adams had written, writings that caught Sewall's fancy because they "discovered a Mind awake to the love of Litterature and Law." A few years older than Adams and Quincy—as well as "somewhat advanced" in the legal profession—Sewall befriended Adams and by the early 1760s the two had become such close collaborators and dear companions that they were sometimes compared to Jonathan and David of biblical lore. In Adams's own words, Sewall "possessed a lively Wit, a pleasing Humour, a brilliant Imagination, great Subtlety of Reasoning and an insinuating Eloquence." Sewall had "Virtues to be esteemed, qualities to be loved and Talents to be admired." Adams even acknowledged, "I know not that I have ever delighted more in the friendship of any Man." Sewall spent numerous weekends in Braintree—before marrying Ester Quincy in 1764. This provided the intimate circle of rising lawyers "frequent Opportunities of Meeting, besides those at Court in Boston, Charlestown and Cambridge."[2]

Happy times, however, were not to last, for soon the Stamp Act Crisis seriously divided the friends into opposite camps. After Sir Francis Bernard and Thomas Hutchinson selected Sewall to be Attorney General of Massachusetts, he even offered Adams the "Office of Advocate General in the Court of Admiralty," a lucrative office not only in "the most profitable Business in the Province" but also "a first Step in the Ladder of Royal Favour and promotion." Adams, however, turned down the offer without hesitation, because it would have violated his "political Principles" to participate in "a System, wholly inconsistent with all my Ideas of Right, Justice and Policy."[3]

Early on their irreconcilable differences over political principles did not abate their "mutual Esteem" or cool "the Warmth" of their friendship, but the intensifying constitutional crisis placed them upon a collision course that reached a poignant climax in 1772. The rupture between these dear friends had become so acute that Adams was moved to confide in his *Diary*: "At this Moment I look upon him [as] the most bitter, malicious, determined and implacable Enemy I have." Adams, though, did have the grace to add, "God forgive him the Part he has acted, both in public and private Life! It is not impossible that he may make the same Prayer for me."

Now in the summer of 1774 Sewall was determined to make a last, final appeal to Adams not to represent Massachusetts in the forthcoming Continental Congress. As they were overlooking Casco Bay, Sewall argued that Great Britain would never retreat from its new Colonial Policy. If America persisted in its folly, the superiority of British arms would settle the contest in short order. While Adams agreed that Great Britain was "determined on her system," it simply remained the case that their "very determination, determined me on mine." So, "Swim or sink, live or die, survive or perish," he would take his stand "with my country."[4] Much later John Adams would confess that Thomas Hutchinson had "Seduced from my Bosom, three of the most intimate Friends I ever had in my life, Jonathan Sewall, Samuel Quincy, and Daniel Leonard."[5]

JOHN Adams resolutely set his face toward Philadelphia on 10 August 1774.[6] When the delegates met in Carpenters Hall from Monday 5 September to Wednesday 26 October 1774, only nine of the fifty-six delegates had known each other since participating in the Stamp Act Congress of 1765. The rest knew precious little about the various members of the other delegations. Because this heterogeneous assortment of "strangers" was "not acquainted with each other's language, ideas, views, designs," Adams deemed them to be "jealous of each other—fearful, timid, skittish."[7]

Although the delegates from South Carolina to New Hampshire were eager to listen, especially about their respective plans for the future, they had so much to learn from and about each other. How the diverse colonies could stand together was the hidden agenda for much of the proceedings, for broadly construed there were at least three different types of social organization among them.

The South was shaped by its vast plantation system. A master headed the plantation, with slaves concentrated on relatively isolated parcels of land. The towns were small. The parishes were enormous. The Anglican Church held sway as an establishment, but numerous groups of Dissenters, especially Baptists, agitated the population. But the leadership seemed decidedly aristocratic.

In New England a completely different social organization prevailed. The Puritans lived in towns and went out to their farms. This provided for intense interaction among the people, where a consensus was relatively easy to obtain, ordinarily. Connecticut, for example, was a most homogeneous colony.

The Middle Colonies were primarily founded later in the seventeenth century. The Quakers lived largely on their individual farms, but Philadelphia had grown so prodigiously that it now was the second or third most populous city in the Empire. Given time, the Middle Colonies had developed into a polyglot society of all the different groups of Christians and free spirits.

Less than ten years had passed since John Dickinson chaired the Stamp Act Congress. In the letter he wrote to William Pitt, he had stressed what would transpire after a war with Great Britain, a war he was sure the Americans would win. The situation was this grim: "A Multitude of Commonwealths, Crimes, and Calamities, of mutual Jealousies, Hatreds, Wars and Devastation; till at last the exhausted Provinces shall sink into Slavery under the yoke of some fortunate Conqueror." That is why Dickinson dreaded *independence*. Nevertheless, independence was better than submission. And most of the participants—many arriving in Philadelphia in late August— were quite foreign to each other but yet eager to learn from each other. This occasioned that they meet and measure each other over good food and much drink, which Philadelphia supplied with abundance.

IN his *Diary* John Adams recorded about forty different dinners he enjoyed while in Philadelphia, frequently calling these late afternoon occasions "elegant" and once even "a most sinfull Feast." At Chief Justice Chew's mansion on 22 September the assembled guests were served a formidable dinner: "Turtle, and every other Thing—Flummery, Jellies, Sweetmeats of 20 sorts, Trifles, Whip'd Syllabubbs, floating Islands, fools—&c., and then a Desert of Fruits, Raisins, Almonds, Pears, Peaches—Wines most excellent and admirable." On a more personal note Adams admitted, "I drank Madeira at a great Rate and found no Inconvenience in it." The Continental Congress dined very well, indeed.[8]

After feasting with a host of other delegates at the "grand, spacious, and elegant house" of Thomas Mifflin, Adams heard Benjamin Harrison of Virginia give this rousing toast: "A constitutional Death to the Lords Bute, Mansfield and North."[9] *North* was the person primarily responsible for carrying the Intolerable Acts through Parliament. Nobody needed to be reminded that *Mansfield* had been a major mover behind the new Colonial System since its inception in 1764. But why *Bute*? Although the despised Earl of Bute had retreated into obscurity, he still functioned within the popular imagination on both sides of the Atlantic as the iconic Scotsman who symbolized that "Military Law" now hovering over Boston—a stance graphically featured in the political cartoon, "The Able Doctor."[10] So, in proposing his toast the Virginian was defying the military *programs* (Bute) that flowed from the governmental *policies* (North) rooted in the constitutional *principles* exhibited in the maximal understanding of the doctrine of Parliamentary Supremacy (Mansfield).

THE Continental Congress received the news of the passage of the Suffolk Resolves by Massachustts when "Paul Revere arrived Express from Boston" with the document in hand. The next day they were approved unanimously, and against the rules of secrecy the Congress voted to have them published for the world to see. That evening John Adams wrote in his *Diary*, "This was one of the happiest Days of my Life. In Congress We had generous, noble Sentiments, and manly Eloquence. This Day convinced me that America will support the Massachusetts or perish with her."[11]

Before many days had passed the conversation became "swallowed up" in "the great Question of Parliamentary Jurisdiction."[12] As early as the Lords Debate on 3 February 1766 Mansfield had "repeatedly called upon the advocates for America to *draw the line*, to move their exceptions and to say how far the sovereignty of the British Parliament should go and where stop."[13] In the 1773 debate between the Governor and the General Assembly of Massachusetts, Thomas Hutchinson had emphatically declared, "I know of *no Line that can be drawn* between the supreme Authority of Parliament and the *total* Independence of the Colonies" (my emphases). The House responded to Hutchinson's extreme formulation by claiming it would be unwilling to draw that line without consulting "the other Colonies ... in Congress."[14]

While all the participants on this Committee rejected the maximal reading of the doctrine of Parliamentary Supremacy, they quickly split into two predictable groups on where to draw the critical constitutional line. While some utterly denied the authority of Parliament to interfere in the colonial affairs across the board, more than a few supported the need for Parliament "to regulate the Trade of the Empire." The two sides, however, fully realized that they would have to reach a compromise in order to preserve the Union. Although Adams believed that "not one of the Committee were fully satisfied" with the compromise, "they all soon acknowledged that there was no hope of hitting on any thing, in which We could all agree with more Satisfaction." In his opinion, the compromise "demanded as little as could be demanded, and conceded as much as could be conceded with Safety, and certainly as little as would be accepted by Great Britain."[15]

The compromise appeared in the decisive fourth article of the Resolves of the First Continental Congress, divided here into two parts. First:

> That the foundation of English liberty, and of all free government, is a right in the people to participate in their legislative council: and as the English colonists are not represented, and from their local and other circumstances, cannot properly be represented

> in the British parliament, they are entitled to
> a free and exclusive power of legislation in their
> several provincial legislatures, where their right of
> representation can alone be preserved, in all cases
> of taxation and internal polity, subject only to the
> negative of their sovereign, in such manner as has
> been heretofore used and accustomed.

Having registered that foundation, the Congress then acknowledged as a matter of *necessity* that Parliament should regulate the imperial trade. So, second:

> But, from the necessity of the case, and a regard to
> the mutual interest of both countries, we cheerfully
> consent to the operation of such acts of the British
> parliament, as are bona fide restrained to the
> regulation of our external commerce, for the purpose
> of securing the commercial advantages of the whole
> empire to the mother country, and the commercial
> benefits of its respective members excluding every
> idea of taxation, internal or external, for raising a
> revenue on the subjects of America without their
> consent.

The Preamble to their Declaration and Resolves rehearsed the historical record "since the close of the last war" before lining out the "Rights" of the colonies based upon "the immutable laws of nature"; "the principles of the English constitution"; as well as "the several charters or compacts" of the various colonies. They also declared it was against the law to keep "a Standing army in these colonies, in times of peace, without the consent of the legislature." As loyal subjects they had the right to peaceably assemble, file their grievances, and petition the King.

After lining out these articles, the Congress listed all the Acts of Parliament since 1764 that were "infringements and violations of the rights of the colonies." In brief, "in order to restore harmony between Great Britain and the American colonies," it was "essentially necessary" to repeal all Acts designed to raise revenue for the British Exchequer and return to the governing principles of the Old Colonial System. (Earlier infringements were deliberately passed over in "an ardent desire that harmony and mutual intercourse of affection and interest may be restored.")[16]

In order to "obtain redress of these grievances, which threaten destruction to the lives, liberty, and property of his majesty's subjects," the Congress then adopted a Non-Importation, Non-Consumption, and Non-Exportation Association. The Non-Importation agreement would forbid any "goods, wares, or merchandize whatsoever" to be imported "from Great Britain or Ireland" beginning on 1 December 1774. The Non-Consumption agreement would go in effect as soon as possible but no later than 1 March. But given the needs of "our fellow-subjects in Great-Britain, Ireland, or the West-Indies," it was decided that the Non-Exportation agreement would not commence until 10 September. Unless a redress of grievances had been met, the Continental Congress agreed to reconvene on 10 May 1775.[17]

Satisfied with their collective effort, the fifty-six delegates returned home feeling much more comfortable with each other. They would talk with their neighbors, stressing the need to compromise, to listen, and be prepared to act. They knew they were sitting on a powder keg. They would have to stand together, come what may.

XXI

THE FINAL DESCENT

BEFORE ANY SIGNIFICANT INFORMATION ON THE CONTINENTAL CONGRESS ARRIVED AT THE capital in London, George III laid out his reading of the evolving situation with Prime Minister North: "*The dye is now cast.* The colonies must either submit or triumph. I do not wish to come to severer measures but we must not retreat. By coolness and an unremitted pursuit of the measures that have been adopted I trust they will come to submit. I have no objection afterwards to their seeing that there is no inclination for the present to lay fresh taxes on them, but I am clear there must always be one tax to keep up the right, and as such I approve of the tea duty."[1] Trivial though the tea tax had proven to be, its removal was simply non-negotiable. What was at stake was the principle involved. What should not be overlooked, however, was how the King actually thought the issue turned on this tiny tax, while in fact the situation had moved radically beyond taxation itself.

As Prime Minister North informed the House of Commons when he introduced the Intolerable Acts in March, what needed to be faced squarely was how the situation had changed over time. To be precise, he said: "We are not entering into a dispute between internal and external taxes, not between taxes laid for the purpose of revenue and taxes laid for the regulation of trade, not between representation and taxation, or legislation and taxation." The situation now was "whether we have or have not any authority" over America. And before terminating that session Parliament had passed the five Intolerable Acts, which carried Great Britain directly into closing the Port of Boston, rewriting the Constitution of Massachusetts, and radically expanding the geography of Province of Quebec, much to the disadvantage of the Americans. And there were hints of much more to come.

Recall how Lord Mansfield had said in the House of Lord that passing the Boston Port Act would be "as decisive *as passing the Rubicon.*" He had opposed Townshend's entire plan, simply because it caved in on permitting a tax to be considered *external*, when in fact it was not at all designed to regulate trade but to raise revenue for the British Exchequer. He wanted to pursue the original plan, namely, to tax America as George Grenville had originally proposed. And the Intolerable Acts paved the way toward that goal. They were a clear first step promising to transform the British Empire into the liking of the Lord Chief Justice of King's Bench.

AS the Continental Congress was getting under way, Mansfield very privately slipped away to Paris to confer with his nephew, David Murray, the seventh Viscount Stormont and the British Ambassador to the Court of his Most Christian Majesty since 1772. During this excursion to France under the given name of William Murray, Louis XVI and Marie Antoinette received him at Versailles. In Lord Campbell's romantic narrative, he was presented to the King and the young Queen, still "glittering like the morning star, full of life and splendor and joy." He was even treated "with marked civility." Indeed, "his reputation as a great magistrate had spread over Europe, and his noble appearance and manners added to the interest which this had excited." Marie Antoinette even presented the British Ambassador with her writing table as a token of friendship and respect.[2]

While one can only guess about what the Ambassador and the Lord Chief Justice were so intent upon discussing in the British Embassy located in the Hotel de Brancas on rue de l'Université on the

Left Bank of the Seine, Horace Walpole was prepared to conjecture that the rapidly unfolding situation with the colonies were front and center in Mansfield's mind as he attempted "to fathom the new views of the French Court." After noting that before the Glorious Revolution Charles II and James II "were apt to court France when they meditated subversion of the Constitution at home," Walpole posed this rhetorical question: "who can doubt but Lord Mansfield went to endeavour to persuade the French Court not to interfere in our differences with America?"[3]

BECAUSE the Continental Congress had agreed to a code of silence, the North Administration was reduced to reading bits and pieces of information about what was transpiring in Philadelphia. When Dartmouth and Hutchinson had a conversation "upon the affairs of America" immediately prior to the opening of the Congress, the American Secretary seemed quite relaxed, even relatively optimistic. Indeed, he told Hutchinson, "until the result of the Congress was known" the ministry would do precious little.[4]

On 21 September Hutchinson learned that North "fancied" the Continental Congress would do nothing more serious than "agree upon a non-importation and non-consumption" strategy. And he clearly thought such a plan "could never last." Nevertheless, "If they refused to trade with Great Britain, G. B. would take care they should trade no where else." He was so confident that both New York and Pennsylvania would "break through" any collective agreement that he did not appear to be very concerned about the prospect facing the Empire.[5]

While visiting Norwich, Hutchinson heard "very alarming and distressing news from Boston," followed by even "more and more alarming" accounts a few days later. Given such disturbing news, he left Norwich sooner than expected and set out "direct for London." In his conversations with John Pownall and Dartmouth it became utterly transparent that they all had received the same information, namely, "Gage thought more force necessary" to control the situation in Massachusetts. But in response, "nothing more was determined than to send three ships of the line, which would carry 600 Marines: that there would be a Cabinet [meeting] this week, and the *Scarborough* immediately be sent back with orders to Gage."

In letters written on 10 October Hutchinson confided that his hopes for reconciliation had been "blasted by the late doings in America. At present the prospect is dark." Furthermore, he would "conjecture, from observations made from time to time," that the ministry had become concerned that the Empire was "in danger of a French or Spanish war, if the disturbance in the Colonies continues." Official circles had begun to take the unfolding situation much more seriously. Because the amiable Dartmouth "seems to despair," Hutchinson promised that he would not "go into the country again ... without first acquainting his Lordship."[6]

On 28 October London received news of the Suffolk Resolves, in which Massachusetts declared that "no obedience is due" to the Intolerable Acts; no public money should be collected "until the civil government of the province is placed upon a constitutional foundation"; trade with Great Britain should be terminated; and a provincial Congress should be called "to consult such measures as may be adopted, and vigorously executed by the whole people" of the Province. Diplomatically, the Resolves also promised to "pay all due respect and submission" to the recommendations of the Continental Congress "for the restoration and establishment of our just rights, civil and religious, and for renewing that harmony and union between Great Britain and the colonies, so earnestly wished for by all good men."[7]

The moment the Suffolk Resolves arrived in London, they radically transformed the mood in the imperial bureaucracy. Hutchinson thought both Dartmouth and John Pownall "seemed thunderstruck with the American news." At first the American Secretary could not believe what had really happened. He even questioned Hutchinson closely on their authenticity, adding: "Why, Mr H[utchinson] ... if these Resolves of your people are to be depended on, they have declared War against us: they will not suffer any sort of Treaty." In a letter to his younger brother, Hutchinson wrote: "If I knew what was to be done here, I would not tell you in a letter, but I do not know. I dare say Ld North does not know." In other letters he reported that he often heard people say, "Something decisive must be done." Important people kept asking him, "How shall an entire separation of the Colonies from the Kingdom be prevented?" So far as he could tell, "The general voice is, that so important an affair has not come before Parl[iamen]t since the [Glorious] Revolution. Indeed, I do not think that affair was of so great importance."[8]

Early on Dartmouth had told Hutchinson, "until the result of the Congress was known" the ministry would do nothing of consequence, a claim reinforced when the Prime Minister told him "no particular measure could be determined" before details were "known of what was doing at Philadelphia." But North thought the situation had grown so "desperate" that "it must come to violence."[9]

On 2 November Hutchinson wrote his son, "The storm thickens every time any vessel arrives from America," but official London had to wait for more than two weeks before letters from General Gage finally arrived with the news that his authority had utterly dissolved throughout Massachusetts; that there was an open discussion among the provincial leadership of "fixing a plan of government of their own"; and that both Rhode Island and Connecticut were also up in arms, literally. In General Gage's considered opinion, "there is no prospect of putting the late Acts in force but by first making a conquest of the New England provinces."[10]

After receiving these reports from General Gage, George III wrote North, "I am not sorry that *the line of conduct seems now chalked out*." Indeed, "*blows must decide* whether they are to be subject to this country or independent" (my emphases).[11] North informed Hutchinson, "it was to no purpose any longer to think of expedients," for Massachusetts was "in actual rebellion and must be subdued." The government would employ whatever force may be necessary for the Intolerable Acts to be "carried into execution."[12]

BECAUSE the Septennial Act dictated that a new Parliament had to be elected no later than March 1775, it was deemed prudent to move the General Election forward. As North told Hutchinson, "Parliament was dissolved ... that we might, at the beginning of a Parliament take such measures as we could depend upon a Parliament to prosecute to effect." The Election of 1774 did not strengthen the North Administration, but it did weaken the Rockingham party, reducing its supporters from 55 to 43.[13]

IN the rapidly changing context triggered by the news of the Suffolk Resolves, Hutchinson learned that "Lord Mansfield enquired after me, and that he will let me know one day this week when to wait upon him." The invitation, however, never came, in all probability because Mansfield was too busy preparing for the opening of the Michaelmas Term in Westminster Hall. From Dartmouth's office, Hutchinson witnessed the grand procession: "There were 3 state coaches, the Ld Chancellor's, Ld Chief Justice of the K. Bench, and a gentleman by me said the third was the Master of the Rolls. The coaches of the other Judges and Lawyers scarcely exceeded a dozen. Constables and other civil officers in plenty, marched by the sides."[14]

Two days before the opening of the new Parliament, Hutchinson paid a return visit to Westminster Hall where he "spent an hour most agreeably in the Court of King's Bench hearing Ld Mansfield give judgment in the Grenada Cause," that is, the pivotal case of *Campbell v. Hall*. Because this case exhibits the *fundamental principles* informing Mansfield's understanding of the Constitution of the British Empire, it deserves detailed attention.[15]

Campbell v. Hall was up for action before the Court of King's Bench because *by the royal prerogative alone* the imperial government had "imposed a tax of 4 per cent on all exports" from the newly acquired island of Grenada in the 1763 Peace of Paris. Years later Alexander Campbell directly challenged the Collector of Customs, William Hall, on the constitutionality of this export duty. Now in November 1774 Lord Chief Justice Mansfield ruled in favor of Campbell's challenge of this tax.

In his ruling in *Campbell v. Hall* Mansfield cited the 1722 opinion of Solicitor General Clement Wearge and Attorney General Philip

Yorke (the future Lord Chancellor Hardwicke) on the status of the Island of Jamaica: "If Jamaica is still to be considered as a conquered island, the King has a right to lay taxes upon the inhabitants; but if it is to be considered in the same light as the other plantations, no tax can be imposed on the inhabitants but *by an assembly of the island, or by an act of parliament*" (my emphasis).[16] Mansfield had thoroughly shared this opinion for a very long time, too. In 1744 when he was the Solicitor General he had straightforwardly argued, "a colony of English subjects cannot be taxed but *by some representative body of their own or by the Parliament of England*" (my emphasis).[17]

Mansfield laid out six propositions in support of his understanding of the Constitution of the British Empire:

1. A country conquered by the British arms becomes a dominion of the King in the right of his crown; *and therefore necessarily subject to the legislature—the Parliament of Great Britain.*

2. The conquered inhabitants, *once received under the King's protection, become subjects,* and are universally to be considered in that light; *not as enemies or aliens.*

3. The articles of capitulation upon which the country surrendered, and the articles of peace by which it is ceded, are *sacred and inviolable* according to their true intent and meaning.

4. The law of every dominion annexed to the crown equally affects all persons and all property within the limits thereof, and is the rule of decision for all questions which arise therein. Whoever purchases, lives, or sues there, puts himself under the law of the place. An Englishman *in Ireland, Minorca, the Isle of Man, or the plantations,* has no privilege distinct from the natives.

5. The laws of a conquered country continue in force until they are altered by the conqueror. The absurd exception as to Pagans mentioned in *Calvin's case* shows the universality and antiquity of the maxim; in all probability it arose from the mad enthusiasm of the Crusades.

6. The last proposition is, if the King (and *when I say the King, I always mean the King without the consent of parliament*) has a power to alter the old and to introduce new laws in a conquered country, this legislation being subordinate, that is, *subordinate to his own authority in parliament*, he cannot make any change contrary to *fundamental principles*; he cannot exempt an individual in that dominion from the power of parliament, or give him privileges exclusive of his other subjects [my emphases].[18]

Before a conquered country was annexed to the crown it was subject to *the King without the consent of Parliament*; the King ruled through the executive orders of his Privy Council completely independent of Parliament. After coming under the King's protection, however, the people were to be treated as fellow-subjects, *not as enemies or aliens*. From this moment forward all legislation for the entity became *necessarily subject to the Parliament of Great Britain*.

Mansfield's reasoning is this straightforward. Major Premise: the King promised Grenada an Assembly the moment the island was ceded to the British Empire. Minor Premise: neither Grenada's Assembly nor the Parliament of Great Britain had imposed this export duty. Ergo: the imposition of this tax by royal authority alone was unconstitutional.[19] According to Mansfield's understanding of the Constitution of the British Empire, the Parliament of Great Britain held the right to legislate and tax *outside the realm*.

On Monday 28 November 1774 Mansfield handed down this famous ruling in *Campbell v. Hall*. Parliament met two days later. The imperial capital received notice of the actions taken by the Continental Congress shortly before the Christmas break.

BY the time the declarations of the Continental Congress arrived in the imperial capital, it had become crystal clear that the policy of focusing on Massachusetts alone had proven to be a serious mistake. Instead of isolating Massachusetts, all New England had rallied to her defense. And now Great Britain had more than New England to cope with. The maladroit policy of the North Administration had brought into an organized resistance the entire Atlantic seaboard from South Carolina to New Hampshire.

When Parliament reopened on 19 January 1775, Chatham presented a proposal "to send immediate orders for removing the forces from Boston." Although the proposal was supported in a rare show of solidarity by Rockingham, the motion was roundly defeated. Chatham was behind the times, and frankly rather isolated. As Peter D.G. Thomas expressed it, "Chatham's plan was a mass of specific proposals, about which no coherent discussion was possible." On 1 February he laid out "A Provisional Act for settling the Troubles in America and for asserting the supreme legislative Authority and superintending Power of Great Britain over the Colonies." While Dartmouth had agreed to accept the proposal for discussion, he quickly changed his mind, leading Benjamin Franklin to comment that the American Secretary "has in reality no will or judgement of his own, being with dispositions for the best measures, easily prevailed with to join in the worst."

The next day North compared the relative burden of the taxes in Britain and America, i.e., "£100,000,000 were paid annually by 8,000,000 Britons, a mere £75,000 by 3,000,000 Americans. The average tax was fifty times that in America, 25s. a head compared with 6d." So far as he could penetrate, Massachusetts was in rebellion— her neighbors supported her—and the law would be enforced.[20]

THE contest in the House of Lords was much more exciting. Mansfield weighed in with the observation, "we were reduced to the alternative of adopting coercive measures, or of forever relinquishing our claim of sovereignty or dominion over the colonies." He even mentioned Thomas Hutchinson's stated belief that "the supremacy of the British legislature must be compleat, entire, and unconditional; or on the other hand, the colonies must be free and independent." For proof, he "examined very minutely the several acts of Parliament complained of in the Congress" to show "that every one of them, more or less, confirmed the principles he had laid down and the conclusions he had drawn." To be precise, "He more particularly adverted to the acts for the establishing the admiralty courts in that country; for regulating the rates of postage of letters; for ordering persons in any part of the dominions of the crown to be tried in any English county; for being charged with setting his Majesty's dock-yards on fire; for quartering the soldiers." Giving up on any one of these laws "would be a total renunciation of sovereignty." What the Americans were demanding violated "any principle of civil government, reason, experience, or common sense." Sovereignty dictated that "it was to the last degree monstrous and absurd to allow they had a right distinct from the British legislature in any one particular, and not in all." So the question boiled down to this—"whether we should relinquish our rights, or resolve at all events to resolutely persist in their assertion?"

In Mansfield's judicial worldview, "it was utterly impossible to say a syllable on the matter of expediency, till the right was first as fully asserted on one side, as acknowledged on the other." He then "loudly condemned the bad policy of laying the taxes on in 1767." That maladroit measure had "laid all our present troubles and political confusions at that door." Yes, the Townshend Duties had proven to be a serious mistake. Charles Townshend, so far as Mansfield could tell, was the chief villain who had pointed Great Britain down the garden path.

After claiming the Americans were not in rebellion, Camden challenged "the very extraordinary measure of blocking up the American ports." Furthermore,

> sending an army thither in a hostile manner, was insanity the first; but were the present proposed measures adopted, it would indeed be insanity the second. It would be no less than a political *felo de se*; and would be like a man, who, to be revenged of a person that he supposed had injured him, should sheath a poniard in his own bosom. Our commerce ... is at once the source of our wealth

and our power; it both gives us seamen to man our
fleets, and money to pay them; without commerce
this island … is but a small insignificant spot: it is
from our commerce alone that we are entitled to
that consequence we bear in the great political scale.

Camden then cited Shakespeare: England is "no more than a bird's
nest floating on a pool. What, then, would be the consequence of
adopting so wild and dangerous an expedient?"

After the Duke of Grafton claimed "that the administration he
was connected with was the only one who wanted the assistance of
the noble and learned Lord," Mansfield answered with precision. Yes,
he had been "a cabinet minister part of the late reign, and the whole
of the present," but that missed the critical distinction between "a
nominal and an efficient cabinet." In regard to the efficient cabinet,
he had indeed "deliberated with the King's minister," but that had
terminated "a short time previous to the administration in which the
noble Marquis [of Rockingham] presided at the head of the treasury."
Mansfield labored the point, saying, "from that day to the present he
had declined to act as an efficient cabinet minister."

But Mansfield pressed on to claim that he had "never refused
his advice when applied to." In fact, Rockingham "must recollect
his giving him every assistance his poor abilities were capable of
affording." After readily admitting that he voted against the Repeal
of the Stamp Act, he now even claimed to have highly approved the
Declaratory Act, especially the way the North Administration had
put it "into execution." But, alas, Grafton never asked his opinion,
"for had he been applied to, he would have cheerfully rendered him
every assistance in his power."

The Earl of Shelburne quickly responded that "his situation
gave him an opportunity of knowing the sentiments of a very high
Personage, and he could affirm, from his own knowledge, that they
were extremely favourable towards America." And everybody knew
that neither Chatham nor Camden was the author of "that despotic
system which has governed our councils for some years past." He

wanted to know "by what over-ruling, fatal influence this great empire was brought to the eve of being plunged into all the miseries and horrors of civil war."

Lord Lyttelton would have none of this nonsense. He praised Mansfield's "talents, integrity, and political conduct." On the defining issue, "he contended without reserve for the legislative supremacy of Parliament over every part of the British dominions in America, the East and West Indies, in Africa, in Asia, in every part and quarter of the globe, nay over Ireland itself, if it should become necessary; the right of taxation and legislation being indivisible and unconditional, over every place in which our sovereignty extended." That expresses rather thoroughly the mentality of the Lord Chief Justice of King's Bench.

The Duke of Richmond challenged Lord Lyttelton, castigating "the inflammatory and ill-grounded representations" thrown out in debate. "He said it was very unbecoming the gravity and dignity of his situation … to endeavour to inflame and mislead at so alarming a crisis." And he pointed out, "The measure which had been originally the cause of our present dangerous situation was now openly disavowed by three cabinet ministers." He claimed that these three had "solemnly declared it was no measure of theirs, jointly or separately." He was intent upon learning, "Whence then … are we to suppose it originated"? He then pointedly added: "when I came to office I saw several foreign dispatches, on the margin of which were written observations in that noble Lord's hand writing. I need not tell his Lordship, but I shall take the liberty to inform the House, that the correspondence with our foreign ministers … is sent round in little blue boxes to the efficient cabinet ministers; and that each of them give their opinions on them in writing."

Mansfield now "rose in great warmth." He began by asking, "What do their Lordships insinuate, that I have been *the author of the present measures*, and it is I that direct them?" He would have proudly owned them, because he thought they were "*wise, politic, and equitable*" (my emphases). But since the dismissal of the Grenville Administration, he had removed himself from the executive council.

Defiantly, he finally asserted, "I am threatened! I dare the authors of those threats to put any one of them in execution. I am ready to meet their charges."

After Lord Lyttelton defended Mansfield a second time, the Earl of Shelburne "returned to his general charges of a fatal and over-ruling influence":

> We cannot, cannot suppose it was the minister who framed them. We are almost certain that none of the members of the administration drew them up. We know they were fabricated by some person conversant in the law. It is impossible we can hesitate a minute, therefore, to pronounce them to be the work of some hand who is unwilling to own them. The law officers of the crown have disavowed them. Who then framed them? The public naturally look at a law lord, notoriously high in favour in the cabinet, with whose sentiments and doctrines they perfectly agree.

Shelburne pressed on, furiously:

> The noble and learned Lord has confessed, that though for some years he has ceased to act in the character of an efficient cabinet minister, there was a time when it was otherwise; there was a time when he united in his character two things in the English constitution, the most repugnant in their nature, that of an acting cabinet minister, and a lord chief justice of England. For my part, I always imagined ... that it was the great, pervading principle and excellence of it, to keep the judicial and executive powers as separate and distinct as possible.

He then put the knife in:

I hope the time will come when those matters will undergo a full and impartial discussion, without a personal allusion to any man, when we shall be able to point out, with certainty, the real author of the present measures; and be at the same time informed, where the judges in Westminster-hall have kept within their own province, and where they have invaded the constitution, by substituting their own prejudiced and partial opinions for the law of the land.

Then he turned the knife:

The noble and learned Lord has disclaimed having any direct concern in the present business, and endeavours to strengthen his bare assertion, by shewing what little or no temptation he could have to interfere. But the noble Lord knows, every noble Lord in this House knows, a court has many allurements. His Lordship denies any obligations or personal favours whatever. I am ready to give his Lordship full credit for this declaration; but he will permit me at the same time to observe, that smiles may do a great deal; that if he had nothing to ask for himself, he has had friends, relations and dependants amply provided for; I will not say beyond their deserts, but this I may say, much beyond their most sanguine expectations. Independent however of these considerations, I think the pride of directing the councils of a great nation, to certain favourite purposes, and according to certain preconceived principles, may possibly effect great things, and tempt to great hazards, considering the frame and temper of some men's minds.

Shelburne had plunged the dagger all the way into Mansfield's heart. Mansfield now proceeded to castigate the entire indictment "in great passion." Besides accusing Shelburne of "uttering the most gross falsehoods," he "totally denied that he had any hand in framing *all* the bills of the last session" (my emphasis). It simply was the case that "the law officers of the crown never asserted that they had no hand in them; but whether they had or had not, was of no consequence to him, for he was clear, the charge ... was as unjust as it was maliciously and indecently urged."

Walpole's account reads slightly differently. When Shelburne accused him of being "*the confidential Minister,*" he made no reply, even though Shelburne had actually shouted at one point, "That is a falsehood."

Camden now engaged Mansfield in a dispute over the doctrine of treason, explicitly citing his bold claim that "the ministers of the Church of England were persecuted by the Fanatics of Boston, and other parts of New England." To the contrary, Camden argued the object of the disputed measure was "to bring the unhappy Americans to England to be tried, under the act of Henry VIII, and have them butchered in the King's Bench."

Dartmouth finally brought the debate to a close. After saying that he was "directed by his own judgement, not by Lord Mansfield's," he pressed on to claim, "Lord Mansfield was totally unconnected with the present administration."[21]

In Camden's report to Chatham, the ministry was "proceeding with the most mischievous expedition, to plunge the nation irrecoverably into a civil war." He did not have to add that the Opposition overwhelmingly lost when votes were tallied, 27 to 87.[22]

HAVING won the round rather handsomely, the North Administration proceeded to prepare for the enforcement of the laws. Since the Americans refused to trade with Great Britain, Great Britain would not allow them to trade anywhere else. What began as the New England Trade and Fishery Bill was now extended to Pennsylvania, New Jersey, Maryland, Virginia, and South Carolina.

The Admiralty Board then proposed an increase in the navy by two thousand men, followed by an expansion of the army by four thousand. Before long North revealed that the government would treat with the colonies individually, not collectively, for he seriously thought that the colonies were separate and distinct entities, held together solely through Britain. When any colony proposed to pay for its own civil government as well as its own defense, Parliament would no longer tax it for revenue.[23]

THE policy of the North Administration came in for more severe criticism. Consider, for example, what the young Marquis of Granby had to say. After being educated by his grandmother, the Duchess of Somerset—the sister of Mansfield's wife—he boldly announced that he had "entered these walls with prejudices against the system administration was pursuing." He then proceeded to clarify his misgivings:

> As to the bill, immediately the object of our consideration, I think in every respect so arbitrary, so oppressive, and so totally founded on principles of resentment, that I am exceedingly happy at having this public opportunity of bearing my testimony against it, in the strongest manner I am able. In God's name, what language are you now holding out to America! Resign your property, divest yourselves of your privileges and freedom, renounce every thing that can make life comfortable, or we will destroy your commerce, we will involve your country in all the miseries of famine; and if you express the sensations of men at such harsh treatment we will then declare you in a state of rebellion, and put yourselves, and your families, to fire and sword.

Before finishing Granby said, "From the fullest conviction of my soul, I disclaim every idea both of policy and right internally to tax America. I disavow the whole system. It is commenced in iniquity;

it is pursued with resentment; and it can terminate in nothing but blood."

Or consider what Mr. Cruger said in the Commons Debate on 15 May. After North had pontificated, "no paper should be presented to that House, which tended to call in question the unlimited rights of parliament," his response was to the point:

> Every lover of this liberal constitution cannot but (at least) forgive the apprehension and disquietudes of freemen, under a claim which stamps them with the character of *slaves*. I mean the claim held up by this country of binding them, without the consent or security of their own representatives, in all cases whatever—than which there cannot be a more compleat description of the most ignominious servitude; and it is reserved to distinguish the administration of this day—to assign as a reason for rejecting a petition from a British subject and in an English House of Commons, that they claimed a right of giving and granting their own money by their own representatives. And, Sir, as a refutation of many unjust charges alledged against them, they particularly disclaim all intentions and desires of independence. They confess the necessity of a superintending power in parliament, and explicitly state their conviction of its utility and equity when exercised for the regulation of trade.

That summarized the situation rather nicely, but it all was in vain. Soon it was announced that "it was contrary to every idea of the supremacy of parliament to receive a paper in which the legislative rights of parliament were denied."[24]

SO it went until 17 May, when Camden brought up the question of Quebec again. He thought the Act passed the previous year was "so thoroughly impolitic, pernicious, and incompatible with the religion and constitution of our country" that nothing would suffice but "a total repeal" of the Act itself. He mentioned, first, "that there could be no good reason for so extending the limits of Quebec." Then, second, "that the Popish religion, though not in express terms, is in effect really and fully established in the province of Quebec." Finally, Camden asked how Quebec could be "subjected to the civil law of France, and to the despotism of a governor and a dependent council, instead of being allowed an assembly, and laws made by the representatives of the people."

Mansfield answered by arguing that to repeal the Act would leave the people with "nothing but a sense of anarchy and confusion" until a new law came into effect the following year. And everybody knew the "old maxim" that "a bad constitution was better than none." To which Camden responded, "if the noble lord objected to the repeal of this bill, only because no better could be produced, he would be bound to produce to that house in twenty-four hours, nay, in half the time, a bill founded on better policy, and much wiser regulations ... than the bill which had taken the Ministry ten years to frame." But the debate was much beside the point. It was defeated 88 to 28 when the proxies were added. In Commons the vote was 174 to 86.[25]

On 26 May 1775 Parliament voted to recess for the summer. Edward Gibbon captured the situation best when he confessed, "In this season and on America the Archangel Gabriel would not be heard."[26]

LORD Mansfield repeatedly denied that he was responsible for the present measures. Although he did not hold a responsible office in the administration, and, therefore, could not be blamed, it remains the case that the recent legislation documents just how far the government had adopted his positions on policy. When the Empire was preparing to go to war his influence permeated the highest levels of the administration as it came to embrace wholeheartedly the longstanding position he had promoted in season and out ever since the opening of the Stamp Act Crisis. Great Britain would now act firmly, decisively. As the dark horse of the American Revolution, no single person so thoroughly symbolized the ultimate British stance better than Lord Chief Justice Mansfield.

The magnitude of these events was graphically exhibited in the May edition of the Westminster Magazine. A cartoon features a chariot drawn by two horses, Pride and Obstinancy, racing straight toward an abyss. At the rear Bute is holding a placard, "Places, Pensions, Revisions." Chatham and Camden are furiously chasing after the chariot. In the foreground a crowd is offering bribes. On the left five Scots are drawing plans on a table. In the sky a devil is carrying away "National Credit." North and some bishops are cheering the chariot on. In the center George III is holding a placard, "I glory in the name of Englishmen." Furiously driving the chariot over Magna Charta and the Constitution is none other than the Lord Chief Justice of King's Bench.[27]

XXII

NOVANGLUS V.
MASSACHUSETTENSIS

A BOUT THE TIME THE DECISIONS BY THE CONTINENTAL
CONGRESS ARRIVED IN LONDON, a letter appeared in the
Massachusetts Gazette under the signature of *Massachusettensis*
that spelled out the dire consequences of the American rejection
of the maximal reading of the doctrine of Parliamentary
Supremacy promoted by Lord Chief Justice Mansfield. The *Letters
of Massachusettensis* "were well written, abounded with Wit,
discovered good Information, and were conducted with Subtlety
of Art and Address, wonderfully calculated to keep Up the Spirits
of their Party, to depress ours, to spread intimidation and to make
Proselytes among those, whose Principles and Judgment give Way
to their fears, and these compose at least one third of Mankind,"
according to the *Autobiography* by John Adams.[1] After the first
six letters by *Massachusettensis* had appeared, Adams took it upon
himself to respond under the signature of *Novanglus*, beginning 23
January 1775. For every Monday over the next three months the
two antagonists addressed each other in rival newspapers. What
brought this interchange to an abrupt halt was the opening of armed
hostilities on the Lexington Green on 19 April 1775. (The last letter

by *Novanglus* appeared on 17 April; *Novanglus* did pen parts of another letter but it was not published until later.)

Novanglus was convinced that *Massachusettensis* was none other than Jonathan Sewall, once a close friend, but now a supporter of the government. Only much later did he discover that the writer of these papers was Daniel Leonard. As a successful lawyer from Taunton, Leonard was elected to the Massachusetts House in 1769. Initially he sided with the Patriots, actually voting for the recall of Governor Bernard, and joining the popular revulsion against both Chief Justice Peter Oliver and Governor Hutchinson. The Boston Tea Party, however, altered his political orientation completely, and by the summer of 1774 he had become one of the new appointees to the Council, a decision that so upset the good people of Taunton that Leonard decided to move his family to Boston under the protection of General Gage's Red Coats.

According to a letter Leonard wrote a few years later, he was "solicited by several of the principal gentlemen" in Boston "to point out the criminality and ruinous tendency of the opposition to the authority of parliament." Or positively, "to convince the people of the justice of the measures of Administration."[2] It is more than reasonable to assume that Jonathan Sewall was among those "principal gentlemen" advising Leonard as he wrote. In any event, the ensuing disputation in the Boston press brought the foremost legal talent in New England into open conflict on the public stage.

THE *Novanglus-Massachusettensis Controversy* covered the issues in the conflict by penetrating the constitutional argument with conceptual breadth as well as historical depth. And before the end of the controversy *Novanglus* had tracked down the decisive precedent that now defined the constitutional impasse to a ruling Lord Chief Justice Mansfield handed down in the Court of King's Bench in 1759.

In Letter I *Massachusettensis* contended that events had gradually proceeded so far from the Stamp Act Crisis through the decisions of the First Continental Congress that "we have passed the Rubicon" and now faced a shooting war with "the most powerful nation upon the globe," an Empire that "triumphed over the united powers of France and Spain, and whose fleets give law to the ocean." The Americans would be incapable of uniting their forces, because "the colonies south of Pennsylvania" would be hard pressed "to govern their numerous slaves, and to defend themselves against the Indians." New England should anticipate that "our trade, fishery, navigation and maritime towns [would be] taken from us the very day that war is proclaimed" and "our back settlements a prey to our ancient enemy, the Canadians." He was "certain that when ever the sword of civil war was unsheathed, devastation will pass through our land like a whirlwind, our houses be burnt to ashes, our fair possessions laid waste, and he that falls by the sword will be happy in escaping a more ignominious death." The only way to avoid so monumental a catastrophe was for the Americans to come to their senses and resolve the impasse by acknowledging the authority of Parliament.

The American Patriots cling to the proposition that "Parliament has no right to tax or legislate" for the colonies, while the British maintain that because the American colonies are "a part of the British Empire" their legislatures are subordinate to the King-in-Parliament. From the premise that "every state from the nature of government must have a supreme uncontrollable power," it followed necessarily that the denial of Parliament's right led inextricably to independence. But independence would never be granted because Great Britain would never surrender its sovereignty over the British Empire, period.[3]

Letters II, III, and IV rehearse the historical development from the Stamp Act through the Intolerable Acts. According to the narrative advanced by *Massachusettensis*, "At first we did not dream of denying the *authority* of Parliament to tax us, much less to legislate for us." As far as he was concerned, "We had always considered ourselves, as a part of the British Empire, and the Parliament, as the supreme legislature of the whole." But that traditional loyalty soon gave way to resistance because the Whigs, the printers and the clergy "flattered the people with the idea of independence." Over time "the political balance of the province was destroyed" because the council

LORD CHIEF JUSTICE MANSFIELD: CHIEF AUTHOR OF THE AMERICAN REVOLUTION

was emasculated. Both Governor Bernard and Governor Hutchinson were made "obnoxious" in the eyes of the people by a systematic misreading of the true import of their private letters to influential persons in the imperial government. So, by this means, "disaffection to Great-Britain being infused into the body of the people, the subtle poison stole through all the veins and arteries, contaminated the blood, and destroyed the very stamina of the constitution." Then the reduction of the price of tea "by near one half" brought about "the foulest, subtlest and most venomous serpent that ever issued from the eggs of sedition," Committees of Correspondence. Once in motion these committees "assume a dictatorial style," wreak "private revenge" on those who disagree with their opinions, and "frequently erect themselves into a tribunal, where the same persons are at once legislator, accusers, witnesses, judges and jurors, and the mob the executioners."[4]

All this preparation led into an exposition of standard political theory. Governments have "simple" or "complex" forms. The simple forms are "monarchy, aristocracy and democracy," each with its own strengths but more especially with its own weaknesses. To be explicit, "monarchy is apt to rush headlong into tyranny, aristocracy to beget faction and multiplied usurpation, and democracy, to degenerate into tumult, violence and anarchy." To avoid these dreadful possibilities, "the British constitution, consisting of King, Lords and Commons ... includes the principal excellencies, and excludes the principal defects" of these simple forms of government. The complex mixing of the three simple forms results in a splendid balance: "The distributions of power are so just, and the proportions so exact, as at once to support and controul each other." And that is precisely why the British constitution is readily acknowledged "to be the most perfect system that the wisdom of ages has produced." Indeed, "An Englishman glories in being subject to and protected by such a government." And that had traditionally been the sentiment of the Americans as proud participants in the successful British Empire.

Regardless of the various forms of government, every government must, in principle, command unlimited sovereignty.

Massachusettensis spelled out the doctrine in these terms: "Two supreme or independent authorities cannot exist in the same state. It would be what is called *imperium in imperio*, the height of political absurdity." His explanation: "The analogy between the political and human body is great. Two independent authorities in a state would be like two distinct principles of volition and action in the human body, dissenting, opposing and destroying each other." Given that foundational principle, he then drew the obvious:

> If then we are a part of the British Empire, we must
> be subject to the supreme power of the state, which is
> vested in the estates of Parliament, notwithstanding
> each of the colonies have legislative and executive
> powers of their own, delegated or granted to them for
> the purposes of regulating their own internal policy,
> which are subordinate to, and must necessarily be
> subject to the checks, controul and regulation of the
> supreme authority.

With the Whig denial of colonial subordination to Parliament—or the favorite theory that the colonies owe allegiance to the "person" of the King alone—the predictable result was this clear: the British Empire was dissolved into "distinct states, as compleatly so as England and Scotland were before the Union [of 1707], or as Great-Britain and Hanover are now." Furthermore, Whig political thought would also dissolve all connection among the American colonies as well, regardless of what the Continental Congress might pretend.[5]

Massachusettensis advanced his argument with the "self-evident proposition" that before 1764 nobody but fools or madmen would have denied that "the colonies were a part of the British empire and dominion, and as such subject to the authority of the British Parliament." And this held "whether they send members to Parliament or not, and whether they have legislative powers of their own or not." And he even cited the "predicaments" of Ireland as well as the islands of Guernsey and Jersey as cases in point.[6] The organizing intent of these opening six letters is succinctly captured in one sentence: "It is our highest interest to continue a part of the British Empire, and equally our duty to remain subject to the authority of Parliament."[7]

THIS was the moment when *Novanglus* decided to respond—forcibly. In his opening letter on 23 January 1775, he argued that the Tories were "the aggressors in the conflict," while the Whigs "acted on the defensive from first to last." It was an old game, too, one that pitted "some of the most intrigueing and powerful citizens" against the people who were "accustomed to confide in certain persons, and could never be persuaded to believe, until prophecy, became history." Even though the people had been warned ten or twelve years ago, only now was the plan transparent for all to see. And the plan was old, very old, indeed. After siding with the worthies, Plato, Aristotle, Livy, Cicero, Sydney, Harrington, and Locke, *Novanglus* lined up *Massachusettensis* with Philip, Alexander, Caesar, Charles V, Louis XI, and "ten thousand others" such as Hobbes, Filmer, Andross, Randolph, and Dudley. In brief, *Novanglus* spoke for "Liberty" while *Massachusettensis* spoke for "Power."[8]

By Letter II *Novanglus* zeroed in on Dr. Franklin's altercation with Governor Shirley in 1754 over "the great design of taxing the colonies by act of parliament." After that plan was laid aside, liberty loving Thomas Pownall became Governor, but Thomas Hutchinson and Andrew Oliver made life so uncomfortable that Pownall asked to be reassigned. The upshot? Soon Francis Bernard was appointed Governor in 1760. Early on Bernard aimed at a transformation in colonial politics, which became visible when he "transmitted home to different noblemen and gentlemen four copies of his principles of law and polity, which proves incontestably, that the project of new regulating the American colonies were not first suggested to him by the ministry, but by him to them." Nobody in America, however, knew the first thing about Bernard's proposal—except, of course, the junto. And so it went until *Novanglus* finally asserted, "There are but two sorts of men in the world, freemen and slaves." Alas, "when luxury, effeminacy and venality are arrived at such a shocking pitch in England," what could one expect? That was the canvas on which he launched his critique of the source of the conflict.[9]

BERNARD of course came in for criticism as starting the quarrel, but Hutchinson received the brunt of the analysis. As the argument grew wider and deeper, however, it finally reached Lord Chief Justice Mansfield. To be precise, on 10 April 1775 *Novanglus* rather casually commented, "We must now turn to Burrow's reports, vol. 2. 834. Rex vs. Cowle. Lord Mansfield has many observations upon the case of Wales, which ought not to be overlooked." While the argument centered on a medieval text, its present relevance turned upon a decision Mansfield handed down in the Court of King's Bench in 1759.

In ruling on this case, Mansfield argued that "the principality of Wales"—just like "the counties palatine of Chester and Durham"—was "holden of the imperial crown of England." The King "treated the prince of Wales as a rebellious vassal; subdued him; and took possession of the principality." From this foundation, it followed that "Wales ever hath been incorporated, annexed, united and subject to, and under the imperial crown of this realm, as a very member, and joint of the same." Then he added, "Edward I. having succeeded as to Wales, maintained likewise that Scotland was holden of the crown of England." The key passage reads:

> In conformity to the *system* contained in these words, my lord Mansfield, and my lord North, together with their little friends Bernard and Hutchinson, have "conceived the great design of annexing" all North-America "to the realm of England" and "the better to effectuate this idea, they all maintain, that North-America is holden of the crown."

So, "they all maintain that America is dependent on the imperial crown and parliament of Great Britain." Given this historical foundation it followed that "they are all very eagerly desirous of treating the Americans as rebellious vassals, to subdue them and take possession of their country."

Novanglus drew out the implication: "no doubt America will come back as parcel of the realm of England, from which (by fiction of law at least) or by virtual representation, or by some other dream of a shadow of a shade, they had been originally severed." But he had had enough: "But these noblemen and ignoblemen ought to have considered that Americans understand the laws and politicks as well as themselves." With "600 men" in arms, it will be quite difficult to float "fictions of law" to convince the Americans to surrender "their liberties."

At this point *Novanglus* indulged in a fantasy that was located in 1759 and placed in Lord Chief Justice Mansfield's mouth:

> We are now in the midst of a war, which has been conducted with unexampled success and glory. We have conquered a great part, and shall soon compleat the conquest of the French power in America. His majesty is near 70 years of age, and must soon yield to nature. The amiable, virtuous and promising successor, educated under the care of my nearest friends, will be influenced by our advice. We must bring the war to a conclusion, for we have not the martial spirit and abilities of the great commoner: but we shall be obliged to leave upon the nation an immense debt. How shall we manage that? Why, I have seen letters from America, proposing that parliament should bring America to a closer dependence upon it, and representing that if it does not, she will fall a prey to some foreign power, or set up for herself. These hints may be improved, and a vast revenue drawn from that country and the East-Indies, or at least the people here may be flattered and quieted with the hopes of it. It is the duty of a judge to declare law, but under this pretence, many we know have given law or made law, and none in all the records of Westminster hall more than of

late. Enough has been already made, if it is wisely improved by others to overturn this constitution. Upon this occasion I will accommodate my expressions, to such a design upon America and Asia, and will so accommodate both law and fact, that they may hereafter be improved to admirable effect in promoting our design.

Novanglus then whimsically added, "This is all romance, no doubt, but it has as good a moral as most romances."[10]

IN a slightly earlier context *Novanglus* had discussed three distinct ways in which "a person or a country might be subjected to a king, a feudal sovereign." First, "It might be subject to his *person*." What this would imply was that "it would continue so subject, let him be where he would, in his dominions or without." Second, "To his *crown*, and in this case subjection was due, to whatsoever person or family, wore than crown, and would follow it, whatever revolutions it underwent." Third, "To his *crown and realm or state*, and in this case it was incorporated, as one body with the principal kingdom, and if that was bound by a parliament, diet, or cortes so was the other" (my emphases). After lining out these options, *Novanglus* "humbly conceived" that the subjection of America to the British King fell under "the second sort."[11]

To be explicit, *Novanglus* clearly believed that the Americans had their own governments *under the King's sovereignty.* They were subject to his *Crown*, not to the British *State.* While the colonies had agreed to give Parliament control over the imperial trade *out of necessity*, this most emphatically did not give Parliament the right to levy taxes upon America or in any measure to interfere with the internal order of a colony. Taxes could be levied only on those *within the realm or state*, and America had always been *out of the realm or state*. To tax those outside of the realm would reduce them to *a vassal state*. That was precisely the constitutional error that initially surfaced in the Sugar Act of 1764 and the Stamp Act of 1765. Prior to then Parliament had "no authority over them, *excepting to regulate their trade*, and this not by any principle of common law, but merely by the consent of the colonies, founded on the obvious necessity of the case" (my emphasis).[12]

The British Empire began descending into confusion from the moment when the government attempted to collapse the distinction between those *out of the realm* and those *within the realm*. The Lord Chief Justice of King's Bench clearly championed precisely this confusion. Although the idea had been moving in the circles around him for decades, it never once made it into law prior to 1764. And the Americans had argued the issue ever since Prime Minister Grenville introduced the idea in the legislation during the Stamp Act Crisis. Now time was fast running out.

THE EMPIRE GOES TO WAR

STRANGE THOUGH IT MAY SEEM, DURING THE EARLY MONTHS OF 1775, THE AMERICANS knew precious little about what was happening in London. Some even imagined that the British government would climb back down once again. Events began to pick up rather rapidly, however, after General Gage finally received word from Lord Dartmouth urging action. Although Dartmouth had written on 27 January, the letter had been delayed by bad weather as well as some rather serious afterthoughts by British officials. This letter, actually a copy, did not arrive until 14 April 1775.[1]

During the early dawn on 19 April seven hundred British soldiers encountered seventy armed Americans at Lexington, Massachusetts. Both sides were under orders not to fire, but someone did, and before it was over eight Americans had been killed. The British marched on to Concord without incident, but on their return heavy fighting broke out, leaving considerable causalities—73 British soldiers killed and 174 wounded, 49 Americans killed and 39 wounded. Two days after Parliament had gone home for the summer, London received an unofficial report on what had happened at Concord and Lexington, but the official report did not arrive until 10 June.[2]

Once the truth was known, the mood changed in the imperial capital rather dramatically. Some called for "changing the ministry," but Chatham had relapsed yet once again, and Rockingham was not in the mood for action. All the talk about change was really nothing more than talk. On the day the official news arrived George III wrote Dartmouth, "America must be a colony of England or treated as an enemy. Distant possessions standing upon an equality with the superior state is more ruinous than being deprived of such connections."[3] As the King expressed it, "I am certain any other conduct but compelling obedience would be ruinous and culpable; therefore no consideration would bring me to swerve from the present path which I think myself in duty bound to follow."[4] The war had begun, though few dreamed how long it would last.

On 17 June a fighting force of 2,200 British soldiers engaged 4,000 to 5,000 Americans in the Battle of Bunker Hill. After suffering almost 50 per cent casualties, the British finally prevailed. When the news arrived in London, the British public celebrated their triumph, but the government quickly realized that several more such triumphs would surely spell defeat. As William Eden put it, "if we have eight more such victories there will be nobody left to bring news of them."[5]

When North told the King, "the war is now grown to such a height, that it must be treated as a foreign war," George III responded: "I am clear as to one point, that we must persist and not be dismayed by any difficulties that may arise on either side of the Atlantic. I know I am doing my duty and therefore can never wish to retract."[6] Soon the ministry was championing the war as vigorously as they would have against France or Spain. Indeed, the War Office was already planning to send five regiments from Ireland. By the opening of August George III had ordered 2,355 men in Hanover, Germany, to prepare for action.[7]

ON 6 July 1775 the Continental Congress issued *A Declaration of the Causes and Necessity for Taking Up Arms*. After a rather tedious opening, the declaration plunges into the crux of the matter:

> The Legislature of Great-Britain ..., stimulated by an
> inordinate Passion for a Power not only unjustifiable,
> but which they know to be peculiarly reprobated

by the very Constitution of that Kingdom, and desperate of Success in any Mode of Contest, where regard should be had to Truth, Law, or Right, have at Length, deserting those, attempted to effect their cruel and impolitic Purpose of enslaving these Colonies by Violence, and have thereby *rendered it necessary for us to close with their last Appeal from Reason to Arms.*

The declaration then cryptically covered the long history since the founding of the colonies, how the colonists, without the slightest help from England, "effected Settlements in the distant and inhospitable Wilds of America" so as to secure their "civil and religious Freedom." Next it moved directly to the Seven Years War and how William Pitt (now Lord Chatham) "publicly declared, that these Colonies enabled her to triumph over her Enemies." Nevertheless,

Towards the Conclusion of that War, *it pleased our Sovereign to make a Change in his Counsels.* From that Moment, the Affairs of the British Empire began to fall into Confusion, and gradually sliding from the Summit of glorious Prosperity to which they had been advanced by the Virtues and Abilities of one Man [i.e., William Pitt], are at length distracted by the Convulsions, that now shake it to its deepest Foundations.

After noting that nothing spared them from "the meditated Innovations" that had been planned for several years, they issued this proclamation: "Parliament was influenced to adopt *the pernicious Project,* and assuming *a new Power* over them, have in the Course of eleven Years given such decisive Specimens of the Spirit and Consequences attending this Power, as to leave no Doubt concerning the Effects of Acquiescence under it."

399

The imperial legislation was grounded directly upon the Declaratory Act that stated how Parliament could "*of right make Laws to bind us in all Cases whatsoever.*" Against "so enormous, so unlimited a Power," America was more than alarmed: "We saw the Misery to which such Despotism would reduce us." For years the Americans had "incessantly and ineffectually besieged the Throne as Supplicants; we reasoned, we remonstrated with Parliament in the most mild and decent Language." Then on 5 September 1774 the Continental Congress issued "an humble and dutiful Petition to the King, and also addressed our Fellow Subjects of Great-Britain," but it was placed in "a Bundle of American Papers, and there neglected."

In February 1775 Parliament openly declared, "a Rebellion at that time actually existed within the Province of Massachusetts-Bay." In response, "the commercial Intercourse of the whole Colonies … was cut off"; General Gage received "large Reinforcements of Ships and Troops." Then Parliament "adopted *an insidious Manoeuvre* calculated to divide us, to establish a perpetual Auction of Taxation." On 19 April British forces attacked Lexington, "murdered eight of the Inhabitants, and wounded many others." Then in Concord, "they set upon another Party …, killing several and wounding more." Again, in Boston the Americans had been deceived into surrendering their arms as the price for leaving the town, only to discover that their families were divided. "By this perfidy Wives are separated from their Husbands, Children from their Parents, the aged and the sick from their Relations and Friends." Finally, on 12 June General Gage declared "the good People of these Colonies … to be Rebels and Traitors."

After this recital of the key events, *A Declaration of the Causes and Necessity for Taking Up Arms* openly declared, "We are reduced to the alternative of chusing an unconditional Submission to the tyranny of irritated Ministers, or resistance by Force. The latter is our choice. We have counted the cost of this contest, and find nothing so dreadful as voluntary Slavery." Then came this fitting climax: "*Our cause is just. Our union is perfect. Our internal resources are great, and, if necessary, foreign Assistance is undoubtedly attainable.*"

Nevertheless, the Continental Congress wanted the world to know that "Necessity has not yet driven us" to declare independence, "or induced us to excite any other Nation to War" against Great Britain. But defiantly the Americans threw into the face of the irritable ministers in London this ultimate challenge: "*They boast of their Privileges and Civilization, and yet proffer no milder Conditions than Servitude or Death*" (emphases altered throughout this document).[8]

A FEW days after addressing Parliament in *A Declaration of the Causes and Necessity for Taking Up Arms*, the Continental Congress addressed its *Olive Branch Petition* to the King. The tone was remarkably different, indeed, deferential. After the opening comments this declaration moved directly to a brief statement covering the deep past:

> The union between our Mother Country and these colonies, and the energy of mild and just government, produced benefits so remarkably important, and afforded such as assurance of their permanency and increase, that the wonder and envy of other Nations were excited, while they beheld Great Britain riseing to a power the most extraordinary the world had ever known.

"At the conclusion ... of the late war," however, "a new system of Statutes and regulations [were] adopted for the administration of the colonies." To the "inexpressible astonishment" of the Americans, "the dangers of a foreign quarrel [were] quickly succeeded by domestic dangers." So, "the unhappy differences between Great Britain and these colonies ... have *flowed from this fatal source*" (my emphasis).

Since the Stamp Act Crisis the situation had deteriorated "to the impossibility of reconciling the usual appearances of respect with a just attention to our own preservation against those artful and cruel enemies, who abuse your royal confidence and authority for the purpose of effecting our destruction." Parliament was the enemy against whom the Americans have been compelled "to arm in our own defence." Nevertheless, the Americans still remain "Attached to your Majestys person, family and government with all the devotion that principle and affection can inspire, connected with Great Britain by the strongest ties that can unite societies, and deploring every event that tends in any degree to weaken them." Furthermore, "we not only most ardently desire the former harmony between her and these colonies may be restored but that a concord may be established between them." Indeed, "our breasts retain too tender a regard for the kingdom from which we derive our origin to request such a reconciliation as might in any manner be inconsistent with her dignity or her welfare."

Sincerely the Americans pressed on to say, may it please your Majesty "to direct some mode by which the united applications of your faithful colonists to the throne ... may be improved into a happy and permanent reconciliation." Furthermore, may "such statutes as more immediately distress any of your Majestys colonies be repealed." In a word, graciously return the British Empire to the situation the Americans were in prior to 1763 and they would become "the most dutiful subjects and the most affectionate colonists."[9]

THE radical difference in tone between the *Olive Branch Petition* and *A Declaration of the Causes and Necessity for Taking Up Arms* lies right on the surface, for the Americans still acknowledged the King as the lynch pin of the entire system. The King stood above the conflict with Parliament. He surely would impose his authority the moment he understood what was actually going on. What was needed was clarity on the usurpation advanced by Parliament.

The *Olive Branch Petition* arrived in England on 13 August. An advanced copy was sent to Dartmouth on 21 August, with the proviso that the original would be officially presented to him two days later. The messengers informed the President of the Continental Congress, "We thought it our duty to press his Lordship to obtain an answer; but we were told, as his Majesty did not receive it on the throne, no answer would be given."[10] The very day that the *Olive Branch Petition* was supposed to be delivered—23 August 1775—the King signed the *Proclamation of Rebellion*. The mask then fell abruptly from the King's face.

DURING September and October around eighty Addresses from across England and Scotland were sent to the government in support of action against the colonies. As Prime Minister North said to George III, "One or two Addresses may perhaps not be of much importance, but a general run of Addresses just before the opening of Parliament will be of great service."[11] The King's Speech at the opening of Parliament on 26 October was this blunt: "The rebellious war now levied has become more general, and is manifestly carried on for the purpose of establishing an independent empire." In the discussion the situation was clarified: "Those who have long too successfully laboured to inflame My People in *America* by gross Misrepresentations, and to infuse into their Minds a system of Opinions repugnant to the true Constitution of the Colonies, and to their subordinate Relation to *Great Britain*, now openly avow their Revolt, Hostility, and Rebellion." They needed to learn that "to be a Subject of *Great Britain* ... is to be the freest Member of any Civil Society in the known World."[12]

The Duke of Grafton, however, entertained a different opinion entirely. According to him what was needed was "to bring in a bill for repealing every act ... which has been passed in this country since the year 1763, relative to America." Indeed, "nothing less will effect any effectual purpose, without scenes of ruin and destruction, which I cannot think on without the utmost grief and horror." To that end he pledged, "if necessity should require it, and my health not otherwise permit it, I mean to come down to this House in a *litter*, in order to express my *full* and *hearty disapprobation* of the measures now pursuing."

The Earl of Shelburne soon took up the challenge, calling attention to how the ministry had already pronounced "the funeral oration of their addresses." The public had been "deceived by these very ministers." He then pressed this burning question: "How comes it, that the colonies are charged with planning independency in the face of their explicit declaration to the contrary?" The ministry's conception of independence grew from a misguided source, namely, *independence from Parliament*, not independence from the King. So far as Shelburne could see, "it is a plain and incontestable fact, that the commerce of America is the vital stream of this great empire." Why not leave things alone? Indeed, "I have ever found them and their correspondents constant and earnest in the wish for conciliation, upon the terms of antient connection." And he pinpointed the source of the confusion: "There wants only a similar acknowledgement from *a certain law lord*, who was forward to pledge himself last year for the success of their plans" (my emphasis). He even confessed that he had heard "two of his Majesty's ministers acknowledge, they were deceived in their information."

Shelburne then labored an obvious point. Why must the ministry "support the measure of another administration"? They "lament" this task, which suggests "the measure was wrong." Then the knife goes in:

> What secret influence has compelled them to heap errors on errors, grievance upon grievance, till they have shaken the constitution to its foundation, and brought the whole empire into danger and confusion. The Americans judge from facts. They have seen an uniform lurking spirit of despotism pervade every administration. It has prevailed over the wisest and most constitutional counsels; it has precipitated us into the most pernicious of all wars; a war with our brothers, our friends, and our fellow subjects. It was this lurking spirit of despotism, that produced the Stamp Act of 1765; that fettered the repeal of that act in 1766; that revived the principles of it in 1767; that has accumulated oppression upon oppression since, till at length it has openly established, by the Quebec Bill, popery and arbitrary power over half America.[13]

THE EMPIRE GOES TO WAR

Shelburne, it should be recalled, had served as the Secretary of State for the Southern Department, prior to the establishment of the American Department.

IN the House of Commons, Governor Johnson supported America by raising some critical questions, such as, why are the Americans taxed without representatives? Then he asserted in their behalf, "that one of the unalienable consequences of that situation, is the giving and granting of aids for the support of government, according to the exigency that shall appear to their own understanding." Has not "the essential right of a British subject to trial by jury ... been abrogated in many cases by the late acts of Parliament, and totally destroyed in all civil causes in the extensive province of Quebec?" Had not Habeas Corpus been done away with in Quebec? Then he pressed on: "The people in America wisely foresee the suppression of all their rights, in the train of those iniquitous innovations."

The government's plan, in fact, "demonstrates a perfect ignorance of the history of civil society." Why? Because it assumes "two independent legislatures cannot exist in the same community." Are we "to destroy the whole fabrick of those governments which have subsisted for so many years"? Is it plausible to believe that "any man assuming the character of a statesman, should proceed in this mad career, to destroy in a few years that beautiful system of empire our ancestors have been raising with so much pains and glory?"

People speak of the "*dignity of Parliament!*" That would be "best supported by humanity and justice, and maintaining the freedom of the subject." Using "unintelligible jargon" more than a few insist upon the "*supremacy* of the legislative authority of Great Britain!" On the contrary,

> gentlemen should consider that the very first principles of good government in this wide-extended dominion, consist in sub-divining the empire into many parts and giving to each individual an immediate interest, that the community to which he belongs should be well regulated. This is the

> principle upon which our ancestors established those different colonies or communities; this is the principle on which they have flourished so long and so prosperously; this is the principle of which alone they can be well governed at such a distance from the seat of empire.

Even though the ministry had asserted that the Americans "aim at independence," Johnson levied the counter-assertion that they "wish for nothing more than a constitutional dependence on Great Britain." That is how "Ireland depends on the British legislature at this moment." To a man, "America is unanimous in resisting the power of taxing them ... where they have no representatives." He finally punctuated his claim by saying "they will never yield this point."

For years Johnson had canvassed the American scene with wonder, unable "to see the end of our glory from the same causes which have destroyed other states, little dreaming that one infatuated minister could tempt, seduce, and persuade a whole nation to cut the strings of such harmony." But instead of preserving the "institutions favourable to the freedom of mankind," the nation had been seduced into destroying them, thereby committing "the greatest evil." He wanted to know "to what motive then can these innovations be imputed?" So far as Johnson could see, the government had drawn its information from a single source—the Governor of Massachusetts, Thomas Hutchinson. "The civil war now raging in America seems, step by step, to have been carried on by his advice."

John Wilkes pronounced the entire procedure "fatal and ruinous." Conway called it "a butchery of his fellow-subjects." Barré argued that ten thousand troops could never conquer America. Burke recalled that North had wished to see America at his feet. Fox advocated the repeal of all American legislation since 1763 after accusing North of being a "blundering pilot," who had lost "a whole continent."

Serjeant Adair called attention to the fact that the war was "staking the fate of a great empire against a shadow." The contest

THE EMPIRE GOES TO WAR

had begun over "the assertion of a right," a dubious right where "this country can never derive a single shilling of advantage." And what was the result? "This doubtful and unprofitable right, has been attempted to be asserted and enforced by a series of laws, the most oppressive, the most violent, the most arbitrary, unjust and tyrannical, that ever disgraced the annals of any civilized nation upon earth." Do the Americans actually desire "absolute independence"? Are they not demanding only a return to "the ancient constitution of the empire"? And the Americans were explicit: "place us in the situation we were in the year sixty-three, and we will submit to your regulations of commerce, and return to our obedience, and constitutional subjection." "Were they independent of this country in the year sixty-three, or at any preceding period?" No. "Is this a claim of absolute independence?" No. "Repeal the acts that have passed since sixty-three, and put them on the footing of their old system of colonial administration."

Prime Minister North was of a completely different opinion. So far as he was concerned, "many of the acts were framed for the necessary support of the superiority of the mother country." And that superiority had "never been questioned till America was refactory." The ministry had only advocated this superiority as "acts of justice," not "cruelty." Defiantly he pronounced: "if the scheme of repealing every American act passed since 1763 were adopted, there was *certainly an end to the dispute*, for from that moment America would be *independent of England*" (my emphases).[14]

Regardless of what had been said, Parliament refused to listen. War with America was planned and the King committed. When the votes were counted, the government prevailed almost three to one in the House of Commons.

IN the Lord's Debate on 15 November 1775 Camden and Mansfield engaged in an extended altercation. Camden bluntly stated, "I will prove Great Britain has been the aggressor; that America has only acted on the defensive." "America has been driven, by cruel necessity, to defend her rights from the united attacks of violence, oppression, and injustice." Indeed, "if I were an American, I should resist to the last," because "there has not been a single step nor consequence throughout this whole business, that did not originate from the principle of laying taxes on America, for the purpose of raising a revenue."

Mansfield now rose, and this is what he said. "My Lords, I did not intend to speak to the question, for you will perceive by my voice that I am not well." Sick though he happened to be, he covered the history of New England with an eye toward, say, revisionist history:

> The bad consequences of planting northern colonies were early predicted. Sir Josiah Child foretold, before the [Glorious] Revolution, that they would, in the end, prove our rivals in power, commerce, and manufactures. Davenant adopted the same ideas, foresaw what has since happened; he foresaw that whenever America found herself of sufficient strength to contend with the mother country, she would endeavour to form herself into a separate and independent state. This has been the constant object of New England, almost from her earliest infancy.

From there he proceeded to the reign of William and Mary, emphasizing how the King was compelled "to recall their former charter, and give them a new one; and towards the conclusion of his reign, to get an act passed, that no law enacted in the colonies should be valid, if contrary to any law at the time existing in England." Then in 1733 "Mr. Talbot (afterwards Chancellor) proposed a set of resolutions in the House of Commons, in which the nature of the disputes then subsisting were directly pointed at, and similar doctrines to those maintained at present by the British Parliament fully asserted."

Before the Seven Years War began, Mansfield claimed "the ministry were extremely unwilling to engage in a war on account of America." The new Administration, however, was "brought about by a coalition … I had the honour of being an instrument." After the war came, "Whatever form the war might have afterwards assumed, the preservation of America was what originally brought us into it."

When Peace was restored in 1763, "the inconveniences which have since arisen were then partly foreseen; but they were, however, balanced with a suitable degree of wisdom against those which might have been produced by embracing the other part of the alternative." For example, "If Canada was restored to France, it would have been the source of future disputes, and future wars; it would have been the source of endless contention between both nations. This was the precise state of the case, previous to the laying on the Stamp Act." The Stamp Act, however, proved to be a decisive threshold in the ongoing saga: "An idea then prevailed, that America, from her increased power and ability to pay, should contribute to alleviate the burdens she had been instrumental in loading this country with." Nevertheless, "as things have since turned out, I am sorry the Stamp Act ever passed," but he hastened to add, "no person at the time so much as offered to say a word against it." Again, "The next year the Declaratory Act was passed, without any opposition." And yet once again, "the noble and learned Lord [Camden], who spoke last, being then at the head of the Majesty's counsels, and presiding on the woolsack, was present when the Port-Duties were laid on, and never said a word against them."

Mansfield was not through with his recital of the relevant history: "Much about the same time, the act for extending the act of Henry the Eighth, relative to the trial of persons for offences committed out of the realm, was passed." But neither Camden nor Grafton said a word against the measure. Again Mansfield added: "I am sorry that bill was passed." And to finish this tale of woe, he added yet another episode "relative to stopping up the port of Boston," which passed "without any manner of opposition." In concluding this tale of inconsistency, he added this clincher: "Of the succeeding acts I shall say nothing, but that if the others were justifiable, I think the latter were equally so."

Turning now to the heart of the controversy, he proceeded to reveal his understanding of the critical issues involved:

> I do not think that America complains of particular injuries, so much as she does the violation of his rights. If I do not mistake, in one place, the Congress sum up the whole of their grievances in the passage of the Declaratory Act, which asserts *the supremacy of Great Britain, or the power of making laws for America in all cases whatsoever.* That is *the true bone of contention.* They positively deny the right, not the mode of exercising it. *They would allow the King of Great Britain a nominal sovereignty over them, but nothing else.* They would throw off the dependency on the Crown of Great Britain, but not on the Person of the King, whom they would render a cypher. In fine, they would stand in relation to Great Britain as Hanover now stands; or, more properly speaking, as Scotland stood towards England, previous to the Treaty of Union [my emphases and capitalizations].

Mansfield then proceeded to show through "a variety of detailed reasonings" how limited the options really were. To be precise, he wanted it to be fully understood "that the views of America were directed to independence; that Great Britain could not concede without relinquishing the whole, which he supposed was not intended; and that consequently, any measure of conciliation, in the present situation of affairs, and the declared intentions of America, would answer no end, but furnishing her with grounds to erect new claims on, or to hold out terms of pretended obedience and submission." So far as he could see, there was no option other than war.

The Earl of Shelburne now rose to challenge the entire range of reasons the Lord Chief Justice had advanced. He began modestly enough: "I do not pretend, particularly at this late hour, to follow the noble and learned Lord over the very wide circuit he has taken."

Before long he cut to the quick: "The principal, and fundamental right, is that of granting their own money. The Irish have always exercised that right uninterrupted, so has America till very lately." Then he pressed: *"this invaluable privilege is going to be wrested from them, I take to be the true grievance*; remove that away, and every thing, I dare say, will soon return into its former channel" (my emphasis).[15]

A FEW days later North unveiled his Peace Commission, stating directly that his proposals were appropriate for a state of war but framed so as to "open the door of peace." Indeed, he would be willing, for example, to "suspend every exercise of the right of taxation, if the colonies themselves would point out any mode by which they would bear their share of the burden and give their aid to the common defence." Attorney General Thurlow then clarified how North's plan "retained the habitual exercise of taxation, and left an opening to America, of a permission to raise her share of supply to the common defence, by granting it in her own assemblies, and giving it in her own way."[16] In a word, Parliament would fix the amount and America could choose how to pay.

On the Second Reading of the Bill to prohibit American Trade, Mansfield forthrightly asserted that "it would be impossible to make distinctions in favour of the innocent," for in cases such as these "every individual is concerned in and abetting every act of public hostility."[17] Shelburne then challenged Mansfield yet once again. In this interchange he declared: "Instead of being directed against individuals, who are the supposed authors of this rebellion, it is carried on as if against foreign enemies; war is made on the community at large." In his opinion, "the principle of the bill is to punish the innocent, as well as the guilty." And he concluded, "On the whole, I think the principle of the bill wrong, the provisions absurd, oppressive, cruel, and contradictory, and the measure taken together, to the last degree, hasty, rash, unjust, and ruinous." So far as Shelburne could see, this was "a constitutional war," not as Mansfield maintained, a "war against a foreign enemy."

Mansfield was quick to respond that he "always was of opinion that the people of America were as much bound to obey the Acts of the British Parliament, as the inhabitants of London and Middlesex." There was no distinction between England and America; they both were cut from the same cloth. Nevertheless, "ever since the Peace of Paris, the Northern Colonies were meditating *a state of independency on this country*" (my emphasis). He entertained not the slightest doubt on that score—because prior to 1763 France alone held them in check. With France removed from the scene, the Americans had an open field on which to play. After once again reviewing the past twelve years, Mansfield then asked, "what are we to do?" "Are we to rest inactive, with our arms across, till they shall think proper to begin the attack, and gain strength to do it with effect? We are now in such a situation, that we must either fight or be pursued." He then brought up a saying from Sweden during the reign of Gustavus Adolphus: "My lads, you see those men, yonder, if you do not kill them, they will kill you."

Mansfield pressed the larger issue as well: "what will be the fate of the Sugar Islands; what will be the fate of our trade to that country." The Sugar Islands were "the best feather in our wing." The Americans "are preparing to raise a navy; they have begun in part; trade will beget opulence, and by that means they will be enable to hire ships from foreign powers." Whereas some people maintained "the present war is only defensive on the part of America," he asked: "Is the attack on Canada, or the attempt on Halifax a defensive war? Is the prohibiting all trade and commerce with every other part of the dominions of the British Empire, with Ireland, for whom they express such friendly sentiments; is starving the Sugar Islands, acting on the defensive?" No. The Americans were the aggressive party, but suppose they were justified:

> Are we, in the midst of all the outrages of hostility, of seizing our ships, entering our provinces at the head of numerous armies, seizing our forts, to stand idle, because we are told this is an unjust

war, and wait till they have brought their arms to our very doors. The last Dutch war was generally understood to be unjust; yet that did not prevent us from repelling the invaders, when they came up to burn our navy at Chatham. The causes of the late war were much condemned, but that did not prevent us from pursuing it with vigour.

The acknowledged Head of Jurisprudence finally reached this extraordinary climax: "I do not therefore consider who was originally in the wrong; we are now only to consider where we are." Indeed, "The justice of the cause must give way to our present situation; and the consequences which must ensue, should we recede, would, nay must, be infinitely worse than any we have to dread by pursuing the present plan, or agreeing to a final separation."[18] The issue had gone beyond ordinary morality, come what may.

FOR some time Dartmouth had been plainly discouraged, taking so much time off that others noticed. "Our Office makes a most pitiful figure," complained John Pownall to William Knox in October. Always hoping to be a conciliator, Dartmouth now would be a war minister and that did not suit his temperament. When Grafton lost his position by rebelling, Dartmouth asked for his office as Lord Privy Seal, but Weymouth had already been promised that position. So, North now talked Rochford into resigning, thereby opening the office of the Southern Secretary to Weymouth, who readily accepted. Hard charging George Germain now became the American Secretary—and Dartmouth ended up becoming Lord Privy Seal after all![19]

GENERAL Washington had hemmed in British forces at Boston, but there was precious little either side could do, other than wait for warmer weather. Washington, though, had designs on how to cope with the stalemate. In November he ordered the big guns from Fort Ticonderoga to be brought from New York, a formidable task. Then on 31 January 1776 he said, "the troops in Boston should be destroyed if possible before they can be reinforced or removed." Determined to drive the British out, on 4 March the heavy artillery from Fort Ticonderoga was positioned on Dorchester Heights with a commanding view of Boston and its harbor.

Within hours General Howe began planning for the evacuation of Boston. Though Howe had prepared for the destruction of Boston, he held his fire, with the tacit understanding that the Americans would not attempt to interfere. So, on 17 March the British left Boston on around 125 ships, carrying 8,900 soldiers, plus several thousand Loyalists. After hovering off Boston for ten days just to vex the Americans, the British navy set sail for Halifax in order to rest and recoup.[20]

THE Duke of Grafton had been nursing his wounds for quite some time before proposing on 14 March 1776 that the King should issue a Royal Proclamation declaring a suspension of hostilities until the Americans had time to submit a petition of rights and grievances. For a former Prime Minister to act so precipitously at this late date was more than unusual. The move was frankly desperate. He began by explaining what had happened in 1769 "when it was proposed in the cabinet to procure a repeal of [the Tea Act], along with the other duties laid on in 1767." He openly confessed that he had been "over-ruled and out-voted by a majority on the proposition of repealing that tax," adding pointedly that he viewed that decision as "productive of the worst consequences," for it would provide "the occasion of the present unhappy disputes, that threaten to overwhelm this country in ruin and destruction." Things, however, had grown worse "since the new doctrine of an *unconditional* submission had been broached," a position that had never been "openly avowed or maintained in either House of Parliament."

Grafton then went even further into the mystery of how things had developed over time. This is what he said: "if the new-adopted system has not a most unfavourable appearance, an appearance full of mischief, and big with that *over-ruling secret influence*, those dark and dangerous designs, which every now and then betray themselves to public view, and which create the justest jealousies and suspicions in the breast of every man who is not deaf and callous to the feelings and interests of this devoted country." America lacked any confidence "in ministerial promises, in *loose* and *undefined* claims, which every successive administration have explained their *own way*." Indeed, "scarcely any two of the members of the present seem to be agreed in." After this pointed preparation, he proceeded with this substantive claim. The doctrine advanced by George Germain—mark the words—had been "repeated in this House by persons who, though *not in responsible offices, are nearly connected with those in power*." To be precise, "it is plain that the person who advised or framed this clause, and who, I presume, has had *the chief hand in directing and advising the present measures from their commencement,* by his personal influence, *though not called by his office to a participation of this species of power,* had a view to that unconditional submission which is now contended for" (my emphases). So the nation was left with "an eternal war and resistance on the one hand, till both or either party are destroyed; or that America shall instantly disarm, surrender, and submit." Grafton did everything but mention by name the Lord Chief Justice of King's Bench.

A variety of Lords spoke before the Earl of Hillsborough rose to clarify the situation in 1769. What he had said was that "his majesty's then ministers engaged for themselves, and desired the respective governors to assure the several assemblies, that it was not the intention of this country to lay any tax on America, for the purpose of raising a revenue." Having made that good confession, he proceeded to say that he presumed that nobody would ever think that this bound successive administrations. Nevertheless, will anybody "produce a single instance in which this promise has been violated or departed from?" After saying that no new taxes had been levied, he laid out his own understanding: "If sovereignty includes every thing essential to its inherent power and exercise, it is to the last degree absurd and ridiculous, to distinguish between the general legislative right to govern, direct and controul, and the partial limited object of taxation, which is clearly included in that right, and necessarily forms a part of it." After rehearsing the history of the period, Hillsborough forthrightly revealed his hand:

> A full, clear, and specific acknowledgement of the right, I thought necessary; when that was perfectly and completely secured, I was willing to concede on the ground of expediency alone. I am still of the same opinion, and shall ever continue to resist, to the utmost of my power, in whatever form it may be brought forward, every proposition for concession or accommodation, short of submission and acknowledgment, such as I have described; because, I am perfectly convinced, that if the right of taxation be surrendered, every other beneficial right of sovereignty will soon follow, and America in the end be totally separated from this country.

As Hillsborough contended, "all corporations are under the controul of Parliament; that it is competent for Parliament to alter, amend, or abridge the privileges thus granted, whenever they see that the interests of the empire demand it."

Mansfield soon rose and addressed the larger situation facing the extensive Empire: "This country … is now arrived at a very tremendous crisis, just commencing a war of a nature entirely new." He acknowledged that this war "must necessarily be very expensive, and the issue of which no man can foretell. It is true, that the kingdom will in a great measure be left defenceless; that we can have *no* certainty that France and Spain will *long preserve* their present *pacific dispositions.*" But there was no way to avoid these facts: "America has rebelled; America is in arms; not defensively, but offensively; even if we were willing to cease hostilities, they are not." So, given this situation Great Britain must "act with vigour, and we must at least show ourselves determined to surmount their opposition."

After spending so much money, without saving a cent, the proposal "agrees that the troops should proceed," but then what?

The forces are "to remain with their arms folded across," while "commissioners are to treat with the Congress"? The Americans are "to prepare a petition of grievances" and bring them to England? *The Congress will laugh in their sleeves at our folly*" (my emphasis). A whole season would be lost and "the next spring we shall *have* the whole to begin again." So far as he could see, Mansfield pronounced the motion "nugatory, ill-timed, and ineffectual." And he prevailed.[21]

Rockingham was discouraged. Chatham was sick. Grafton was in a rage. Regardless of their differences over details, the three Prime Ministers from 1765 to 1770 were radically opposed to the decision to proceed against the Americans. With the Empire held in balance, the Opposition was thoroughly eclipsed by Lord Chief Justice Mansfield.

BEFORE sending Admiral Howe off to war the only thing left to do was instructing him on the terms involved in his Peace Commission. The issue had been floating in the background for months, largely out of public view, and it had become vexed in the ministry's plans because of George Germain. The American Secretary had become quite uneasy about allowing Admiral Howe to serve as the sole minister. He wanted William Eden or William Knox added to the Peace Commission, but Howe would have none of it. He did, however, agree to have his brother, General Howe, on the Commission.[22]

But the controversy escalated into what terms Admiral Howe should pursue. George Germain wanted America to agree to the Declaratory Act of 1766 *as a precondition for talks.* According to Under-Secretary Knox, "The truth was, Lord George having now collected a vast force, and having a fair prospect of subduing the colonies, he wished to reduce them before he treated at all." Howe, nevertheless, insisted that the Declaratory Act should be a condition for *final approval,* and not a precondition for talks. Finally, Dartmouth got involved, arguing against any conditions at all. Dartmouth, Howe, and Germain became so divided over this issue that each of them threatened to resign![23]

When Germain refused to back down, Wedderburn suggested that he and North go talk to Lord Chief Justice Mansfield. The upshot? This compromise was reached: "Instead of instructing the Commissioners to demand of the colonies, they were now to wait for the colonies making offers, and in case the colonies did not make the declaration the Commissioners were not to restore them to peace until they received further instructions, but if they did so offer, they were then to receive them." When Howe saw the draft of these instructions, he rebelled. They went too far, radically reducing his role. Officially, the record reads: "But observing that a method directly the reverse [of what he had believed], it is with infinite concern he finds himself obliged to confess that he is disqualified from engaging as a Commissioner in the execution of instructions framed on that plan."[24]

Although Germain proposed dropping Howe from the Commission, the Cabinet had other plans in mind. The compromise that had been worked out with the Lord Chief Justice was withdrawn, and Germain was forced to agree with Howe's overall plans. To wit, the Commissioners held the complete power of discretion in granting pardons, the rebellion had to be suppressed, and finally each colony had to "pledge itself for the sum apportioned to be raised by such mode of taxation as each colony shall in its own discretion find most convenient and least burthensome." Connecticut and Rhode Island, furthermore, were now to become Royal Colonies.[25] Nevertheless, before Parliament went home for the summer recess, Germain openly stated in the House of Commons, "A revenue some way or other must be had from America."[26]

The final version of the instructions arrived at Spithead on 10 May. Before Admiral Howe arrived in Halifax, British forces had already left Nova Scotia. Not until 12 July 1776 did he finally reach New York.

THE WAR OF
INDEPENDENCE

ON FRIDAY 7 JUNE 1776 RICHARD HENRY LEE OF VIRGINIA MOVED THIS RESOLUTION IN THE Continental Congress: "That these United Colonies are, and of right ought to be, free and independent States, that they are absolved from all allegiance to the British Crown, and that all political connection between them and the State of Great Britain is, and ought to be, totally dissolved." On Saturday and the following Monday this resolution was debated by Congress acting as a committee of the whole.[1] James Wilson, Robert R. Livingston, Edward Rutledge, and John Dickinson were for postponing action, because "the people of the middle colonies ... were not yet ripe for bidding adieu to British connection but that they were fast ripening & in a short time would join in the general voice of America." Nevertheless, they made sure it was understood that "they were friends to the measures themselves, and saw the impossibility that we should ever again be united with Gr[eat] Britain." (Thomas Jefferson listed 19 reasons in support of this position.)[2] John Adams, George Wythe and others argued for acting *now*. Indeed, they thought the Congress should have engaged France at least "six months sooner." (Thomas Jefferson listed 26 reasons presented for this position.)[3]

While it was prudent to postpone action on the resolution "in order to give the Assemblies of the Middle Colonies an opportunity to take off their restrictions and let their Delegates unite in the measure," so as not to lose time, John Adams, Benjamin Franklin, Roger Sherman, Robert R. Livingston, and Thomas Jefferson were appointed to prepare an initial draft. After Jefferson was chosen to make a rough copy, he "reported it to the house on Friday the 28th of June when it was read and ordered to lie on the table."[4]

During the arguments on the first and second of July, a few minor changes were made, plus two massive ones, namely, Jefferson's denunciation of slavery and any mention of the word "Parliament" were excised from the text. The *Declaration of Independence*, nevertheless, remains a neatly argued document. The underlying principles are laid out conceptually:

> We hold these truths to be self-evident, that all men are created equal, that they are endowed by their Creator with certain unalienable Rights, that among these are Life, Liberty, and the pursuit of Happiness. That to secure these rights, Governments are instituted among Men, deriving their just powers from the consent of the governed, That whenever any Form of Government becomes destructive of these ends, it is the Right of the People to alter or to abolish it, and to institute new Government, laying its foundation on such principles and organizing its powers in such form, as to them shall seem most likely to effect their Safety and Happiness.

It then directly focuses upon "the present King of Great Britain" who is responsible for "repeated injuries and usurpations." Eighteen are spelled out in detail—one explicitly mentions how he has "combined with others to subject us to a jurisdiction foreign to our constitution," which is amplified with ten additional charges, the last of which reads, "For suspending our own Legislatures, and declaring themselves invested with power to legislate for us in all cases whatsoever." With majestic power it shifts the argument to a full recital of his failures: "A Prince whose character is thus marked by every act which may define a Tyrant, is unfit to be the ruler of a free people."[5] The document was approved on 2 July 1776. The *Declaration of Independence* was formally endorsed on the Fourth of July. After a parchment was prepared, it was officially signed on 2 August.

OXFORD University conferred upon Thomas Hutchinson "the Degree of Doctor, *in Jure Civili, honoris causa*" on 4 July 1776. Little did he know that the *Declaration of Independence* would also be released on the same day across the Atlantic. But when it first became available in London in August, he told Lord Hardwicke, it was "a most infamous paper" and to prove it he recited "a great number of pretended tyrannical deeds of the King." Its facts were all wrong and "to the last degree frivolous."[6]

WHEN Great Britain learned that British forces had decisively forced General George Washington and the American army to evacuate Long Island, George III elevated Baron Mansfield to the position of the *Earl of Mansfield*. As the new Earl looked over the Atlantic during the coming months, the scene pleased him. Not only had the British captured New York City, the Americans were clearly on the defensive. Things were moving along quite nicely. Soon the war would be over, or so he thought. Thomas Paine managed to express the situation quiet accurately when he opened the *American Crisis* with the provocative line, "These are the times that try men's souls."[7]

Needless to say, nothing could have prepared Mansfield for the reversals in 1777. They truly staggered Great Britain. Even though General Howe successfully moved the British Army from New York to Philadelphia during the summer, even defeating General Washington at Brandywine on 11 September, the army under

General John Burgoyne—cut off from Howe in Philadelphia and St. Leger out West—capitulated on 17 October at Saratoga, New York.

On 2 December 1777 word finally arrived that Burgoyne had been utterly defeated and his entire army taken prisoners. New England was not isolated. The army was not triumphant. Nothing had worked out the way those in command had thought it would. The King fell into agony, only to pretend to be merry the next day. In something of a panic, North informed the House, "I trust we have still force enough to bring forward an accommodation." He even offered his resignation, only to have it reject by the King. While North clearly wanted to sue for peace, others in the administration pressed on—after a Christmas break of six weeks.[8]

By early February 1778 Mansfield "went and sat by Lord Camden, and told him he thought we were undone, and he could not sleep for uneasiness." Surely it was "a time for all men to join for the common cause." Camden's response? He "did not think he ought to *join* with the author of all the mischief." And according to Chatham's report, "he had heard of five places where Lord Mansfield had been crying." Cry as often as he liked, it proved to be of no avail.[9]

The reason Mansfield had been weeping turned on much more than Burgoyne's defeat. He was upset because he already knew the British government was going to propose a reversal in its American policy—as it promptly did on 17 February when North revealed his "conciliatory plan." What the Americans had wanted from the beginning would now be granted. If the Americans would only renounce their separation, the Empire was prepared to return to the situation it had occupied before 1763. North was now fully prepared to accept what he had so casually dismissed for four long years.

Time, however, does matter, plus the new American treaty with France, though North pretended not to be so sure it had been signed. Soon Mansfield openly asserted, "the Ministers did not speak truth if they denied the treaty, for it was certainly signed!"[10] Not until 13 March did the news officially arrive that France had indeed "concluded a Treaty of Commerce and Amity with the Independent States of America." In response Lord Stormont was ordered to come home, immediately.[11]

Chatham still believed that he could talk the Americans into returning to obedience. Referring to the blundering ministry, he pronounced: "I do not call for vengeance on the heads of those who have been guilty; I only recommend retreat; let them walk off, and let them make haste, or speedy and condign punishment will overtake them." Wild though his plan happened to be, Chatham quite seriously announced his decision, though seriously ill, to make his case against the North Administration in the House of Lords. When the day arrived in April, he slowly rose, cast his eyes toward heaven, and began with these words: "I thank God that I have been enabled to come here this day to perform my duty, and to speak on a subject which has so deeply impressed my mind. I am old and infirm—have one foot, more than one foot, in the grave. I am risen from my bed to stand up in the cause of my country—perhaps never again to speak in this House."

For some time Chatham spoke with commanding authority, but he soon collapsed, never to finish. Camden, who was sitting beside him, filed this report:

> He fell back upon his seat, and was to all appearances in the agonies of death. This threw the whole House into confusion; every person was upon his legs in a moment, hurrying from one place to another, some sending for assistance, others producing salts, and others reviving spirits. Many crowding about the Earl to observe his countenance, all affected, most part really concerned; and even those who might have felt a secret pleasure at the accident, yet put on the appearance of distress, *except only the Earl of M[ansfield]*, who sat still, almost as much unmoved as the senseless body itself [my emphasis].

In John Singleton Copley's historical painting, *The Death of Chatham*, Mansfield is the only person not standing in the entire spectacle. He is the tiny figure on the far left, opposite the enormous figure of the fallen Chatham on the right. The radical difference in scale actually focuses attention so as to emphasize the centrality of Mansfield in the drama. Chatham did not die, however, until 11 May 1778.

The funeral for the great orator caused yet another scandal, for in the debate on whether to attend as a collective body, Mansfield absented himself, only to have the House of Lords turn down the proposal by a single vote. He even declined to participate privately, as did many of the other Lords. When a bill was introduced to add £4,000 a year to Chatham's title, his opponents in the House of Lords openly attacked his career, his character, as well as his policies, while the Lord Chief Justice remained rigidly silent. Their furious antagonisms had no end, so deep had their hatred for each other grown since it all began during their school days at Oxford so many long years ago.[12]

DAVID Murray, the seventh Lord Stormont, returned from Paris in March. Soon be became the Secretary of the Northern Department, where he could report directly to the Lord Chief Justice. And the news was not good. After Sir Henry Clinton replaced General Howe, the British army moved back to New York, only to be attacked by Washington at Monmouth in June 1778. While the British prevailed in Savannah, the international situation turned increasingly against Great Britain. France induced Spain to enter the war in 1779. Soon Great Britain and the Netherlands were in open conflict. Then the Russians formed the League of Armed Neutrality to protect their vessels. Great Britain found herself isolated in Europe.

At the opening of Parliament in November 1779, Rockingham contrasted the current situation with the splendid condition the King had inherited in 1760. He then openly declared, "if anything could prevent the consummation of public ruin, it could only be new councils and new counsellors." Mansfield responded with a sweeping review of the troubled history ever since the Stamp Act by arguing that every Administration had been responsible for the current state of affairs. After this rather feeble defense, he launched his proposal: "I say that nothing but a full and comprehensive union of all parties can effect [the country's] salvation." He even brought up his own participation in the formation of William Pitt's First Administration and how it resulted in "the immense accession of territory made in the course of the late glorious war." All this was in preparation for the finale:

> How far the temper of the nation or the state of parties may admit of a coalition at present, I will not pretend to determine; but, my Lords, it is an event most earnestly to be desired, for the country requires the assistance of every heart and hand; and with such cooperation, although I am far from desponding, I shall still anxiously await the event. My resolution is firm, but my confidence staggers.

Mansfield's proposal, however, did not stand a chance in the House of Lords. It was voted down 82 to 41.[13]

Come April 1780, John Dunning shocked the House of Commons by announcing, "*That the influence of the Crown has increased, is increasing, and ought to be diminished.*" In the argument it was decided to alter the phraseology by adding, "*It is necessary to declare,*" before the pronouncement. Whereas the ministry expected this addition to change the import of the declaration, needless to say, it changed nothing. After a lively debate, the motion finally carried 233 to 215.[14]

THOMAS Hutchinson's mood had deepened considerably over the last winter. When he visited Kenwood the previous fall he seemed quite relaxed. He even troubled to notice that Dido "came in after dinner and sat with the ladies, and after coffee, walked with the company in the gardens, one of the young ladies having her arm with the other." Her position in the family seems to have surprised him, for he was talking about the mulatto daughter of one of Mansfield's nephews, the one who had locked arms with Lady Elizabeth Murray in the portrait by Johann Zoffany. So far as Hutchinson could tell, she seemed to be "a sort of Superintendent over the dairy, poultry yard, &c." But she seemed more than a little attentive to Lord Mansfield's requests. This led into a lengthy discussion on slavery, with Mansfield drawing a nice distinction between setting a slave free and forbidding a master to "compel the slave to go into a foreign country."

A few days later, however, Hutchinson's mood changed, radically. With the French navy bearing down on Great Britain's coast, he openly confessed, "We are in a more critical state than anybody living has ever known." Five days later he again observed, "Never was the state of the British dominions more changed in so short a time, and all contrary to human appearances."[15] Soon things turned rather desperate. Gone was the feeling he had nursed earlier that things could have been significantly different—if only the government had listened to him. Vanished was his wish that he were young once again and could "rise in the world under [Mansfield's] protection." Now his youngest son was seriously ill, and the crisis was deepening, fast, very fast. As Billy lay dying, Hutchinson finally confessed, "My own catarrh and cough have been very troublesome today." But his health continued to decline. The last entry in his *Diary* came on 22 May. He collapsed on 2 June 1780 only to pass away the following day just as the Gordon Riots were sweeping through London with hurricane force.[16]

ALTHOUGH much remains unknown about what ultimately caused the ferocity of the Gordon Riots, one thing is certain—Lord Chief Justice Mansfield was a central focus in the uproar. For some time he had been extending the religious rights of Quakers and Dissenters. To be explicit, he had said, in regard to Dissenters, "There is no usage or custom independent of positive law which makes *Nonconformity* a crime." His reasoning is more than instructive: "any person reviling, subverting, or ridiculing them, may be prosecuted at common law"; nevertheless, "it cannot be shown from the principles of natural or revealed religion that, independent of positive law, temporal punishments ought to be inflicted for mere opinions with respect to particular modes of worship." Indeed, "The eternal principles of natural religion are part of the common law; the essential principles of revealed religion are part of the common law." From this foundation it followed, "Persecution for a sincere, though erroneous, conscience is not to be deduced from reason or the fitness of things."

Persecution surely was an abomination. Witness how the City of London had elected a Dissenter to serve as sheriff, simply because he could not take the sacrament as prescribed by the Church. And the City did this purposefully so as to collect a little money. The consequence? "If they accept, punish them; if they refuse, punish them: if they say yes, punish them; if they say no, punish them. My Lords, this is a most exquisite dilemma, from which there is no escaping; it is a trap a man cannot get out of." He compared it to Procrustes: "if they are too short, stretch them; if they are too long, lop them." He prevailed, but only at the cost of being set down among some as "little better than an infidel."

Mansfield had also provided the Roman Catholics with some severely limited rights, but this went too far, much too far for the aroused public. In Scotland the reaction became explosive, and the decision was severely challenged in Edinburgh. Riots erupted in the streets. Catholic churches were burnt. Sir George Gordon emerged as the fanatical leader after declaring "the religious constitution of Scotland was sacred against any law the parliament of Great Britain might enact." Convinced that the constitution was older than the Union, he predicted that the people "would prefer death to slavery, and perish with arms in their hands or prevail in the contest."

When the contagion spread to England in 1780, the people became excited to "a high pitch of frenzy." Some even imagined "the King himself was a Papist." A "monster petition" was prepared for Parliament to consider. Finally, it was announced, "on Friday, the 2d of June, the whole body of the Protestant Association would assemble in St. George's Fields, with blue cockades in their hats." With Sir George Gordon at their head, some 50,000 to 60,000 men crossed London Bridge, marched through London, and thoroughly dominated the area around the Parliament.[17]

427

With cries of "No Popery!" the assembled host stormed the House of Commons, which promptly adjourned, but the House of Lords resisted. In Walpole's moving narrative, "A prodigious riot began, and fell especially on the Peers, many of whom were insulted and torn out of their chariots." To be precise, "Lord President Bathurst ... behaved with great firmness." Then "Lord Stormont, Lord Hillsborough, Lord Townshend, Lord Willoughby de Broke ... came into the House disheveled." When the Bishop of Lincoln had his carriage broken completely apart, he "escaped over the leads of the House."[18]

As Mansfield was recognized on his way to the House of Lords, the windows of his carriage were smashed, his wig was upset and his robe torn. After suffering verbal abuse, he made his way to the House—with the aid of the Archbishop of York—where he presided as the Speaker, because Lord Chancellor Thurlow was ill. Stoically, the House decided to proceed, but Lord Montfort broke into the meeting and shouted that Lord Boston had been assaulted and must be rescued. Order broke down utterly. This was proposed, and that. Finally, Lord Boston himself appeared in remarkably good shape— because he had engaged the mob in an argument over "whether the Pope really be Antichrist?" But he gave "a very formidable account of the increasing numbers and fury of the assailants."

After lengthy arguments that lasted for hours, the House finally adjourned, leaving the mob in control, only mysteriously to depart for other targets of opportunity. The Lord Chief Justice, however, remained seated in his chair. After the crowd dissipated, he drank a cup of tea, and went peacefully home.

With Parliament closed down on this Friday, what followed were several days of the worst riots in eighteenth-century British public life. Nothing like the extended frenzy had happened in conscious memory. In the chaos, events spun completely out of control.

On Tuesday 6 June 1780 Mansfield conferred with Sir John Hawkins on what to do about the angry crowd forming outside his house on the northeast corner of the fashionable Bloomsbury Square. Should armored guards be posted outside? No, thought Mansfield, that would only entice the crowd to advance. He believed it would be better to rely upon the traditional reverence for judges in England. For about half an hour the plan did seem to work, but then distant shouts were heard as a huge crowd of angry rioters poured into Bloomsbury Square and set his house ablaze. As he and his Lady fled out the back, leaders of the mob could be seen "at the upper windows, tearing down and throwing over furniture, curtains, hangings, pictures, books, papers, and everything they could lay their hands on." Nothing was left but "the bare and blackened skeleton of the walls."

On Wednesday 7 June, the Bank of England barely escaped. Then prisoners in Newgate and the King's Bench prison were set free and the buildings seriously damaged. Roman Catholic distilleries were torched. The Inns of the Court were attacked. A mob set out to burn Kenwood, but they were lured into a local drinking club and stopped.

On Thursday 8 June, "near thirty persons were killed rioting in Fleet-street," and "a popish chapel was burnt at Bath and another at Hull," according to Walpole. Finally, "Lord George Gordon was seized by messengers in his own house, and carried to the Horse-Guards."

With the army now arriving in force, 800 or more of the rioters were killed or injured. Twenty-two were executed. The Gordon Riots were soon over, but Mansfield suffered the utter destruction of his princely house and everything within it—all his papers, notes, and books. Nothing whatsoever survived, except the dinner bell the mob took so as to guide them ever onward in their plundering rage. Whereas many filed for recompense, he refused to ask for anything.[19] Benjamin Franklin commented from Paris on the upheaval across the Channel: "A Mob of fanatics join'd by a mob of Rogues have burnt and destroy'd Property to the amount it is said of a Million Sterling." Fifty houses had been torched, but he zeroed in on Lord Mansfield's house, saying it had been "burnt with all his furniture, Pictures, Books and papers." And the moral was not missed: "Thus he who approved the Burning American Houses, has had fire brought home to him. Had the mob burnt none other, we might have more easely excused them." After saying Mansfield had been "horribly scar'd"

429

he proceeded to add that Thomas Hutchinson had "died outright of the Freight."[20]

ACROSS the Atlantic, Spain entered the war in 1779. Baton Rouge and Natchez were the first to fall into the hands of the Spanish, followed by Mobile and then Pensacola. Galveston in Texas was named for the young leader of Spanish forces, Bernardo de Gálvez. The British, however, captured General Benjamin Lincoln with his army of 5,500 or so American soldiers at Charleston, South Carolina—the greatest American loss in the entire war. Moving up the Santee River, British forces decisively defeated General Horatio Gates and his hastily formed American army at Camden on 16 August 1780. The Americans, though, reverted to guerrilla warfare to harass the British, thereby keeping them from consolidating their victory.

A new American army formed under Nathanael Greene refused a direct engagement, thereby forcing General Cornwallis to divide his forces. As the main British army pressed forward, their left flank was defeated at King's Mountain. Falling back to regroup, when Cornwallis pressed forward again, he left Tarleton and his American Tories exposed on his far left, with the result that a contingent of American forces wiped out Tarleton at Cowpens, South Carolina on 17 January 1781. Cornwallis then pursued the elusive American army into North Carolina where the two armies collided in an indecisive battle at the Guilford Court House. After the battle the British retreated to Wilmington, North Carolina on the coast to rest, while the Americans regained control of most of the South.

With his army still intact, Cornwallis set his sights upon Virginia, advancing all the way to Charlottesville, where Thomas Jefferson barely escaped capture. From the interior of Virginia the British army made its way down to Yorktown on the coast, expecting to be picked up by the British fleet, but Admiral de Grasse arrived with the French navy first, turned back the British fleet, and had Cornwallis blocked in the Chesapeake Bay. The trap was set.

General Washington and Comte de Rochambeau were positioned with the main American and French armies outside New York City.

As they began to stir, it was assumed that they were preparing to attack the British in the City, but the armies marched past New York City and rushed down to the Chesapeake Bay. After sailing straight to Yorktown, they had the British vastly outnumbered. When the contest began in earnest the British commanded around 7,000 or so troops over against the combined French and American force of around 16,000 troops. After a fierce fight, Cornwallis capitulated on 19 October 1781. When the British marched out in defeat, their band played "The World Turned Upside Down." Although the war was not over, everybody realized that the Americans—with massive help from the French—had won a most decisive battle. When the news arrived in London, Prime Minister North repeatedly cried out, "Oh God! Its all over!"[21] It was noticed, however, that Lord Chief Justice Mansfield chose to remain rigidly silent. For some time he had refused to attend the Cabinet meetings, so intense were his opposition to North's attempts to resolve the conflict.

WHEN the Prime Minister finally resigned in March 1782, Lord Rockingham for the second time became the new Prime Minister, but only three months later he "expired calmly, and perfectly in his senses." To pick up the pieces, the Earl of Shelburne—the enduring opponent of the Lord Chief Justice in so many parliamentary debates—was then selected to lead the government over the next eight months.[22]

Great Britain initially wanted to block the Americans behind, say, the Proclamation Line of 1763. Although both France and Spain desired this outcome, especially the latter, this early plan soon shifted dramatically. Did not Great Britain receive the territory all the way to the Mississippi River in the 1763 Peace of Paris? In a reversal that utterly ignored the earlier decision to grant to Quebec the territory from the Ohio River to the Great Lakes, Great Britain now wanted to turn over to the Americans the entire area East of the Mississippi, South of the Great Lakes, and North of Florida and points West to New Orleans. To have so vast a region added in the final negotiations was an extraordinary development, but this radical extension prevailed when the Treaty of Paris was signed on 3 September 1783.

THREE JUDGMENTS
AGAINST LORD
MANSFIELD

JOHN ADAMS ARRIVED IN LONDON ON SUNDAY 26 OCTOBER 1783 AS THE NEWLY appointed Ambassador to the Court of Saint James. Within a matter of days he attended the opening of Parliament to hear the King's speech. While waiting in the lobby, "Sir Francis Molineux, the gentlemen usher of the black rod, appeared suddenly in the room with his long staff, and roared out with a very loud voice—'*Where is Mr. Adams, Lord Mansfield's friend!*'" After being conducted to his place, Adams "found more politeness and good humor in him than in Richmond, Cambden, Burke or Fox." The Lord Chief Justice was more than gracious in accepting the reality of defeat, but as Adams troubled to note, "*His politics in American affairs I had always detested*" (my emphasis). Such are "the vicissitudes of life, and the whimsical antithesis of politics."[1]

THOMAS Jefferson was much more detailed on Lord Mansfield's influence over political affairs. The Scottish Law Lord handed down "many good" decisions in the Court of King's Bench, his work on contract law was excellent, and much of his life work would endure the test of time, or so Jefferson thought. Nevertheless, the fact remained "that a man first & thoroughly initiated into the principles of one system of law can never become pure & sound in any other." The reason? Because he "can never so far eradicate early impressions as to imbibe thoroughly the principles of the other system." Furthermore, Mansfield's insistence upon deliberating in secret before disclosing the judgment of the court was completely foreign to Jefferson's mentality. Late in life the Sage of Monticello emphatically rejected the very idea "first introduced into England by Lord Mansfield." Jefferson pressed on immediately: "An opinion is huddled up in conclave, perhaps by a majority of one, delivered as if unanimous, and with the silent acquiescence of lazy or timid associates, by a crafty chief Judge, who sophisticates the law to his mind, by the turn of his own reasoning." So far as Jefferson could determine, Mansfield ventured opinions "on his own authority."[2]

Shortly after being appointed the American Ambassador in Paris, Jefferson received a letter from his Italian friend, Philip Mazzei, asking for clarification on "the Origin and Object of our court of Chancery" in Virginia. In November 1785 he responded to Mazzei's request, even though he was without books which would have enabled him "to enter into details" more fully. Although he settled for a "general description only," he realized that such a procedure "would furnish matter for abundant exceptions" by learned students of the material.

Even without the benefit of his outstanding library at Monticello, Jefferson still commanded an impressive control over the distinctive rules operative in the Court of Chancery, principles that he sharply differentiated from those governing the Common Law Courts. In the latter "the letter of the law" was "sufficiently known to guide the decisions of the courts," precisely because the substance of the Common Law "has been retained in the memory of the people and committed to writing from time to time in the decisions of the judges and treatises of the jurists." The Chancery Court, on the other hand, had to pursue "the spirit and reason" of the law by necessity in those unusual cases which were not adequately addressed by the Common and Statute Law.

Jefferson was convinced that it was necessary to resort to "the equity of the law" in the Court of Chancery—in certain clearly defined situations, especially "where it would do injustice by comprehending within its letter cases not within its reason, nor intended to have been comprehended." Of course, in medieval times things were not so complex, but as things developed there arose "a general desire that a power should be found somewhere which would redress" the wrongs flowing from a strict reading of the letter of an obsolete law. What actually happened in England was that fixed law with its "certainty" was reserved for the Courts of Common Law, while discretionary law with its "equity" was differentiated out into the Chancery Court.

> History renders it probable that appeals were made to the king himself in these cases, and that he exercised his power sometimes in person, but more generally by his Chancellor ... This was most commonly an Ecclesiastic, learning being rare in any other class at that time. Roman learning, and a prejudice in favour of Roman institutions, are known to have been a leading feature in the ecclesiastical character. Hence it happened that the forms of proceeding in the court of Chancery and the rules of its decisions were *assimilated to those of the Roman law* (my emphasis).

In his historical judgment, "the Chancellors of England, finding the ordinary courts in possession of the administrations of general law, assumed to themselves by degrees that of the *jus praetorium*, and made theirs be considered as a court of conscience, or of equity."

Jefferson, nevertheless, insisted that "the two distinct departments" in the judicial system should be rigorously and permanently divided. Few things could be worse, he wrote to Mazzei, than to "relieve the judges" within the Common Law Courts "from the rigour of text law, and permit them, with pretorian discretion, to wander into its equity," for then "the whole legal system becomes incertain." (Following the Latin roots, Jefferson systematically writes "incertain" for "uncertain.") "This has been its fate in every country where the fixed, and the discretionary law have been committed into the same hands."

Alas, that blunder is precisely what Great Britain stumbled into when Lord Chief Justice Mansfield was placed at the head of the Court of King's Bench in 1756.

> Ld. Mansfield, a man of the clearest head and most seducing eloquence, coming from a country [i.e., Scotland] where the powers of the common law and the chancery are united in the same court, has been able since his admission to the bench of judges in England, to persuade the courts of Common Law to revive the practice of construing their text equitably.

As a result "a very unexpected *revolution* is working in their laws of late years" (my emphasis).

Lord Mansfield's talent for removing landmarks "on his own authority" was clearly on Jefferson's mind when he immediately explains: "The object of the former judges has been to render the law more and more certain, that of this personage to render it more incertain under the pretence of rendering it more reasonable: no period of the English law, of whatever length it be taken, can be produced wherein so many of its settled rules have been reversed as during the time of this judge." By extending the rules appropriate for the Court of Chancery to the Court of Common Law, this Scottish Law Lord had compounded the distinct functions of each.

Jefferson clearly thought that both types of courts were essential in a sound judicial system. Indeed, those American states that had "chosen to be without" a Chancery Court were caught on the horns of a dilemma so acute that they could not long maintain so absurd a position. He minced no words, however, when he claimed that trying to "avoid Charybdis" by "running on Scylla" spelled shipwreck for liberty. Lord Chief Justice Mansfield's entire orientation collapsed the distinction, thereby driving the First British Empire directly on the rocks.[3]

Writing to John Brown Cutting from Paris in 1788, Jefferson remained more than convinced that "there is so much sly poison instilled into a great part of [Mansfield's decisions], that it is better to proscribe the whole." And he was more than emphatic, too, for he proceeded to add: "I hold it essential to forbid that any English decision should ever be cited in a court, which has happened since the accession of Lord Mansfield to the bench."[4]

On 17 June 1812—the eve of America's Second Declaration of War against Great Britain—Jefferson wrote a powerful letter to his old friend from school days, Judge John Tyler. In this letter he covers the long history of the conflict with the mother country, beginning with this observation: "On our arrival here [in Virginia], the question would at once rise, by what law will we govern ourselves? The resolution seems to have been, by that system with which we are familiar, to be altered by ourselves occasionally, and adapted to our new situation." Yes, at the opening of the controversy he shared the opinion that "we brought with us from England the *Common Law rights,*" simply because "this narrow notion was a favorite in the first moments of rallying to our rights against Great Britain." But as the conflict deepen the Americans pressed on to "the truth," namely, "that we brought with us the *rights of men,* of expatriated men."

> We may doubt, therefore, the propriety of quoting in our courts English authorities subsequent to ... the Declaration of Independence, or rather to the accession of that King, whose reign, *ab initio,* was the very tissue of wrongs which rendered the Declaration at length necessary. The reason for it had inception at least as far back as the commencement of his reign. The relation to the beginning of his

reign, would add the advantage of *getting us rid of all Mansfield's innovations, or civilisations of the common law* [my emphasis].

Thomas Jefferson's anachronistic usage of *civilisations* directly documents the original jurisprudential meaning of this eighteen-century neologism.[5]

HORACE Walpole had been tracking Lord Mansfield from the moment he first entered the government, and now he was beside himself as he acidly commented on the outcome of the American Revolution. In his own self-understanding, the youngest son of Sir Robert Walpole was "without the least tincture of ambition, had a propensity to faction, and looked on the mischief of civil disturbances as a lively amusement." His "warm conception, vehement attachments, strong aversions" issued forth in a "satiric" style that sheltered "a most compassionate heart." This gossiping gadfly also candidly admitted that he was "no historian"—"I write casual memoirs, I draw character; I preserve anecdotes." And he fully understood that "no man is acquainted with the whole plot; as no man knows all the secret springs of the actions of others. His passions and prejudices warp his judgment, and cast a mist before the most penetrating sagacity." Nevertheless, as he made a steady attempt "to trace the stream of events to their secret sources," he remained persuaded that the most prominent of those secret sources undermining traditional English liberty was none other than the Lord Chief Justice.[6]

At one point Walpole claimed that Mansfield "had more weight with the King than Lord North himself," even though he had not served in the executive branch of the government since 1765. When our Scottish Law Lord was appointed the Earl of Mansfield, he added that the new Earl "chose to be thought now *the Chief Author of the American War.*" Then he concluded, "*as I believe he was*" (my emphases and capitalizations).[7] Walpole's final bitter statement reads:

Lord Mansfield was by birth, education, principle, cowardice, and revenge for the public odium, a bigot to tyranny. He would have sacrificed the universe, and everything but his personal safety, to overturn the constitution and freedom of England. But in the blindness of that rage, and from not daring to open the attempt where the danger to himself would have been imminent, he was *the Author of the Liberty of America*, and the instrument of Providence to bless a whole continent, whose destruction he sought to involve with that of his country [my emphasis and capitalizations].[8]

Walpole's fury over Mansfield's decisive interventions knew no end. He even entertained the thought of moving to the United States, but decided against it, given his age.

XXVI

LORD MANSFIELD'S
FINAL YEARS

FROM THE RESIGNATION OF LORD NORTH IN 1782, IF NOT SLIGHTLY BEFORE, LORD CHIEF Justice Mansfield's political career within the nation at large came to an abrupt halt. He had gambled and lost America. There was little that he could do about it, other than accept the inevitable, which he did with grace.

When William Pitt the Younger made a bid for power after the American Revolution, Lord Mansfield at first disapproved, for he was clearly too young, only a mere twenty-four years of age. And he was the son of his ancient foe. Surely he could not last. Pitt's administration would soon collapse, or so Mansfield thought. But this very fact soon led him into thinking perhaps it was not so good an idea to oppose him, at least not yet. Let events play out their hand by destroying Pitt's lively pursuit.

With these notions held consciously in mind, Mansfield rose to speak in the last address he ever made in the House of Lords: "Every man who is called upon to consider a great measure ought to begin at the end; in other words, before he adopts it he ought to examine the consequences that will probably flow from it." Sound advice he could have wished he had always followed, but the situation now was overflowing with turmoil and something had to be done. "I have never risen to speak to a question with such anxiety in my life," he said. What was needed was *union*. He reached to heaven, exclaiming, "I hope God Almighty in His goodness will instill concord into the hearts of the inhabitants of this ill-fated country, and thus effect our salvation from almost certain perdition." Public affairs were indeed urgent. Time was short. "The ship sinks while we are deliberating on what course we should steer."

After this preamble the Lord Chief Justice revealed his hand. The extreme peril Great Britain found herself in was not due to this or that administration. While he wished the current regime had "more strength," were there not "able and respectable men" to be found in it? "At this moment the strongest administration is the best, and any administration competent to deliver us from the appalling dangers with which we are environed shall have my support." Then turning his attention to the resolution before the House of Lords, he calmly asked why so many were for chasing after wind. It was perfectly transparent for all to see "that neither House of Parliament has power to suspend or alter the law of the land." All that could be done was dissolve Parliament, and he laid out the evils that lay in store were that to happen. So, to "pass a resolution which can neither prevent nor punish crime, which can only be meant as an insult to the representatives of the people," would be to invite "universal confusion in the country."[1]

Although it was a powerful speech, he went down to defeat. The resolution was adopted by a majority of 47. He never again spoke in the House of Lords. Parliament was dissolved. A new election held. And William Pitt the Younger returned to power. He even remained Prime Minister for longer than anyone else during the long reign of George III. Few events could have revealed more clearly just how far the Lord Chief Justice's influence over political affairs had simply dissolved.

LADY Mansfield died abruptly on 10 April 1784, throwing Lord Mansfield into a deep depression that lasted for months. The therapy advised for his recovery was to try the waters at Tunbridge Wells, a suggestion he warmly embraced. That is where the very sick, sixty-nine year old Lord George Germain paid his last respects, for he wanted Mansfield to know how he deeply appreciated his support during the late war.

By early 1785 Mansfield retreated full time to Kenwood House where his larger family took care of him. That summer he went on a short circuit near London, but he was fading fast. Come June 1786 he was escorted to the Court of King's Bench. Given the fact that his rheumatism had become so bad that he could hardly remove his hat, he brought it off with aplomb, but all was vain display.

For his successor Mansfield chose Sir Francis Buller. He would preserve his orientation in the law, combining Civil with Common Law precedents so as to render the latter more nimble in the chaotic developments of the time. He had promoted Buller since 1778, and he had grown more than fond of him, the youngest judge to ever serve on the court. Although Buller now served as the head of the court, the government would not consider him as Chief Justice. Its choice fell on the Master of the Rolls, Sir Lloyd Kenyon. As a known opponent of Mansfield's judicial philosophy, Kenyon promptly insisted upon preserving the ancient distinction between Civil and Common Law, a popular position among the legal profession.[2]

IN his final appearance in the House of Lords, Lord Mansfield refused to support either side in the raging controversy over who should serve as regent now that George III had been declared insane. When the issue simply dissolved on the King's recovery, he orchestrated a magnificent show with splendid fireworks to charm the neighborhood around Kenwood.[3]

After John Wilkes forwarded a copy of his rather splendid Latin edition of *Catullus*, Mansfield congratulated him for pursuing "those enjoyments which an early taste for the Classics has put in his power." Wilkes also sent him his Greek edition of *The Characters of Theophrastus* as well. Yes, Wilkes was an advanced classical scholar, publishing a good 188 books and pamphlets on classical literature.

Surprisingly, Mansfield made peace with his ancient foe who had caused him so much grief, saying, "Mr Wilkes was the pleasantest companion, the politest gentleman, and the best scholar he knew."[4]

As the Head of Jurisprudence the Lord Chief Justice carried extraordinary weight. His contributions to the improvement of British industry and international commerce had been more than impressive. His understanding of contract law has stood the test of time. Over all, he remains by far the one eighteenth-century jurist most frequently quoted by later generations. Needless to say, a few of his decisions have been reversed. The long controversy over the right of juries to decide the law as well as the fact in cases of libel was finally resolved against his judgment. Lord Camden himself expressed the issue quite nicely, though somewhat beyond the evidence, when he said: "Though so often opposed to [Mansfield], I ever honored his learning and his genius; and, if he could be present, he would bear witness that personal rancor or animosity never mixed with our controversies."[5] An issue ever so close to the surface of public affairs was finally resolved, never to return. In the unfolding situation he found himself repeating the adage, "YOUNG FRIENDS AND OLD BOOKS."[6]

WHEN the federal Convention hammered out a constitutional framework for the United States of America in 1787, one of the most signal principles was to secure a permanent separation of powers among the three branches of government. One could not serve, for example, in both the judicial and executive branches at the same time, precisely the troublesome position of Lord Chief Justice Mansfield.

AFTER the French Revolution had begun and its first constitution was ratified, Mansfield's apothecary was moved to say to him, "Well, my Lord, the troubles in France are now over." He would have none of it, however, for he responded immediately, "Over, sir, do you say? My dear sir, they are not yet begun!"

On another occasion, Lord Mansfield had a rather lengthy conversation on the meaning of the French Revolution with a doctor attending him. He began the conversation innocently enough, asking, "what do you think of this wonderful French Revolution?" The physician had the insight to turn the question around by asking for his own opinion. This is what he heard:

> My dear Turton, how can any two reasonable men think differently on the subject? *A nation* which, for more than twelve centuries, has made a conspicuous figure in the annals of Europe: *a nation* where the polite arts first flourished in the Northern Hemisphere, and found an asylum against the barbarous incursions of the Goths and Vandals: *a nation* whose philosophers and men of science cherished and improved civilization, and grafted on the feudal system, *the best of all systems*, their laws respecting the descents and various modifications of territorial property:—to think that *a nation* like this should not, in the course of so many centuries, have learned *something* worth preserving, should not have hit upon some little *code* of *laws*, or a few principles sufficient to form one! Idiots! Who, instead of retaining what was valuable, sound, and energetic in their constitution, have at once sunk into barbarity, lost sight of first principles, and brought forward a farrago of laws fit for Botany Bay! It is enough to fill the mind with astonishment and abhorrence! A constitution like this may survive that of an *old man*, but nothing less than a miracle can protect and transmit it down to posterity![7]

Lord Mansfield proved to be a prophet, for when Louis XVI was executed in January 1793 the Old Regime was over and he knew it.

IN his own handwriting, the Lord Chief Justice had already prepared his will. It began rather plainly: "Whenever it shall please Almighty God to call me to that state to which, of all I now enjoy, I can carry only the satisfaction of my own conscience and a full reliance upon

443

his mercy through Jesus Christ." After making provision for those depending upon his estate, he gave the remainder to his nephew, David Murray, Lord Stormont. Then he concluded: "Those who are dearest and nearest to me best know how to manage and improve, and ultimately in their turn to divide and subdivide, the good things of this world which I commit to their care, according to events and contingencies which it is impossible for me to foresee, or trace through all the mazy labyrinths of time and chance."[8]

On Saturday 9 March 1793 Lord Chief Justice Mansfield talked clearly on a legal case Lord Stormont was facing in the House of Lords. The next morning, however, he had difficulty speaking. After complaining about feeling heavy, he was taken to bed, where his pulse remained quite low. On Monday he seemed to be much better, but on Tuesday he said, "Let me sleep! Let me sleep!" He never spoke again. For a full week he remained in bed, apparently not conscious, though "he breathed freely and softly like a child, and as calm and serene a countenance as in his best health." On Wednesday 20 March he died without so much as a groan. He was buried shortly thereafter in a private ceremony in the North Transept of Westminster Abbey.[9]

NOTES

I. Introduction

1   Thomas Jefferson: *Writings*, ed. Merrill D. Peterson (Library of America, 1984), 28.

2   Robertson's recollection is recorded by Horace Walpole in his *Journal of the Reign of King George the Third, from the year 1771 to 1783*, ed. Dr. Doran (London, 1859), II, 251 (4 April 1780). Inferring from so casual a comment Robertson convinced himself—but precious few historians—that Franklin had already set his mind upon securing the Independence of the United States of America.

II. Background

1   For the historical background of Chambers's exposition, see J. G. A. Pocock, *The Ancient Constitution and the Feudal Law: A Study of English Historical Thought in the Seventeenth Century* (Cambridge, 1957; reissued, 1987).

2   Lord John Campbell, *The Lives of the Chief Justices of England, from the Norman Conquest till the Death of Lord Tenterden*, revised edition by James Cockcroft (New York, 1894, 1899), III, 392ff..

3   David Hume, *History of England* (Liberty Press, 1983), V, 59-60.

4   James Lees-Milne, *The Last Stuarts: British Royalty in Exile* (Charles Scribner's Sons, 1984), 2.

5   The range of opinion is mapped in historical detail by J. P. Kenyon, the Ford Lectures for 1975-6, *Revolution Principles: The Politics of Party, 1689-1720* (Cambridge, 1977). See also J. C. D. Clark, *English Society: 1688-1832* (Cambridge, 1985), especially chapter 3 for a statement of the unfolding "patriarchal" argument.

6   J. P. Kenyon, *Revolution Principles: The Politics of Party, 1689-1720* (Cambridge, 1977), 36-7.

[7] Sir Charles Petrie, *The Jacobite Movement: the First Phase, 1688-1716* (Eyre & Spottiswoode, 1948), 124-7.

[8] For a detailed narrative of the unfolding argument over the succession, see the trenchantly argued analysis by J. P. Kenyon in *Revolution Principles: The Politics of Party, 1689-1720* (Cambridge, 1977), chapters 7-9.

[9] Sir Charles Petrie claims "there is no foundation" for this crowning at the Scone Palace, *The Jacobite Movement: the First Phase, 1688-1716* (Eyre & Spottiswoode, 1948), 194. Nevertheless, as recently as 1989 Paul Kléber Monod cautiously suggests in *Jacobitism and the English People: 1688-1788* that "James Francis Stuart may in fact have been crowned at Perth on 23 January 1715-16, in a makeshift ceremony … ." In the footnote Monod then cites: "Martin Hale, *James France Edward, the Old Chevalier* (London, 1907), p. 210, suggest that a coronation took place; Shield and Lang, *The King over the Water*, p. 251, cast doubt on it. See also Farquhar, 'Royal Charities, Part IV', p. 166."

[10] James Lees-Milne, *The Last Stuarts: British Royalty in Exile* (Charles Scribner's Sons, 1984), 33, 36, 46; Alistair Tayler and Henrietta Tayler, *1715: The Story of the Rising* (Thomas Nelson, 1936), 50-3, 111, 126, 192; Sir Charles Petrie, *The Jacobite Movement: the Last Phase, 1716-1807* (Eyre & Spottiswoode, 1950), 26-7.

III. Early Years

[1] Basil Williams, *The Whig Supremacy: 1714-1760* (Oxford, 1939; revised, 1942, 1945), 170.

[2] John Trenchard and Thomas Gordon, *Cato's Letters: or, Essays on Liberty, Civil and Religious, and Other Important Subjects*, ed. Ronald Hamowy (Liberty, 1995), xx. According to Bernard Bailyn's study of the "Sources and Traditions" informing the *Ideological Origins of the American Revolution* (Harvard, 1967), 36, "the writings of Trenchard and Gordon ranked with the treatises of Locke as the most authoritative statement of the nature of political liberty and above Locke as the exposition of the social sources of the threats" facing the American people during the 1760s and 1770s. On the importance of *Cato's Letters*, see also the extensive comments by Caroline Robbins in *The Eighteenth-Century Commonwealthman* (Harvard, 1959), especially 115ff.

3   Ibid., 405-6. The spelling of this "unalienable Right" is carried forward in the Declaration of Independence, even though "inalienable" is the proper spelling according to Samuel Johnson's 1755 *Dictionary of the English Language*.

4   Ibid., 408. The phrase occurs only seven times: 87, 236, 370, 408, 411, and two times on 414.

5   Ibid., 427, 236.

6   Ibid., 180-6; see also 540-1, 586, 706, 804, and 914.

7   Ibid., 742, 772, 858.

8   Ibid., 239.

9   Ibid., 181-6, 260.

10   Ibid., 189, 920.

11   Ibid., 124-6, 172, 195.

12   Ibid., 158, 258-9. According to Paul Kléber Monod, *Jacobitism and the English People, 1688-1788* (Cambridge, 1989), 274, "Of the great national schools, Winchester and Westminster were the Jacobite favourites."

13   *Cato's Letters*, 599-601, 867.

14   On the Atterbury Plot of 1722, see Ibid., 681, 802, 864ff, 872, 880, 889, 920-1, 932.

15   John Richard Alden, *General Gage in America: A History of His Role in the American Revolution* (Louisiana, 1948), 11-2.

16   Romney Sedgwick, *The History of Parliament: The House of Commons, 1715-1754* (Oxford, 1970), I, 34-5; II, 283-5.

17   James Lees-Milne, *The Last Stuarts: British Royalty in Exile* (Charles Scribner's Sons, 1984), 33-42.

18   Campbell, *Chief Justices*, III, 414-27.

19   Campbell, *Chief Justices*, IV, 1-15.

20   *Boswell's Life of Johnson*, ed. George Birkbeck Hill, revised by L. F. Powell (Oxford, 1934), II, 155 (27 March 1772). Johnson's statement is derived from Prior's *Chameleon*: "But if, at first, he minds his hits,/And drinks champagne among the wits."

21   Campbell, *Chief Justices*, III, 429ff; IV, 29. In David Martin's portrait of Lord Mansfield, this bust of Homer is prominently displayed in the background. Both the sculpture and the painting are now on display in the library of the Scone Palace. During Lord Mansfield's life-time they were at Kenwood House.

22   Campbell, *Chief Justices*, III, 392-405.

23   Romney Sedgwick, *Letters from George III to Lord Bute: 1756-1766* (Macmillan, 1939; reprinted, 1981), xxvii. See also Sedgwick, *Commons*, II, 449-51.

24   Campbell, *Chief Justices*, IV, 16-9.

25   Ibid., IV, 204-5.

26   Paul Langford, *The Eighteenth Century: 1688-1815* (St. Martin's, 1976), 115; Sedgwick, *Bute*, xxvii; Sedgwick, *Commons*, I, 46-50.

27   *The Yale Edition of Horace Walpole's Correspondence*, ed. W. S. Lewis (Yale, beginning in 1937), XVIII (9 Dec. 1742).

IV. Solicitor General in the Whit, Establishment

1   Romney Sedgwick displaces Murray to Aldborough in *Letters from George III to Lord Bute: 1756-1766* (Macmillan 1939; reprinted, 1981), xxviii; xxvii, note 4.

2   John B. Owen, *The Rise of the Pelhams* (Methuen, 1957; reissued, 1971), 142-3; Campbell, *Chief Justices*, IV, 20-2.

3   Walpole, *Correspondence, XVIII* (9 Dec. 1742).

4   Sedgwick, *Commons*, II, 286.

5   Campbell, *Chief Justices*, IV, 32-7; Basil Williams, *The Life of William Pitt: Earl of Chatham* (Longmans, Green, 1915), I, 105.

6   Lord John Campbell, *Lives of the Lord Chancellors and Keepers of the Great Seal* (Estes & Lauriat, 1874), VI, 110-15.

7   Campbell, *Chancellors*, IV, 135.

8   See chapter XLIII in *Waverley; or, 'Tis Sixty Years Since*, an historical novel Sir Walter Scott began writing in 1805 and published anonymously on 7 July 1814.

9   James Lees-Milne, *The Last Stuarts: British Royalty in Exile* (Charles Scribner's Sons, 1984), 58ff.

10   Michael A. Bellesiles, *Arming America: the Origins of a National Gun Culture* (Knopf, 2000), 145.

11   R. L. Mackie, *Scotland* (Frederick A. Stokes, no date), 494.

12   John Prebble, *Culloden* (Secker & Warburg, 1961), 236.

13   Campbell, *Chief Justices*, IV, 37-49; Walpole, *Correspondence*, XIX, 379-80; John Prebble, *Culloden* (Secker & Warburg, 1961), 270, 283-4, 288-90.

14   R. L. Mackie, *Scotland* (Frederick A. Stokes, no date), 474, 496, 469; John Prebble, *Culloden* (Secker & Warburg), 330-1.

[15]   *The Parliamentary History of England*, XIV, 3.

[16]   Ibid., XIV, 34ff.

[17]   Ibid., XIV, 50.

[18]   Baron de Montesquieu, *The Spirit of the Laws*, trans. Thomas Nugent (Hafner, 1949), I, 161-3.

[19]   Paul Langford, *The Eighteenth Century: 1688-1815* (St. Martin's, 1976), 128-9.

[20]   Campbell, *Chief Justices*, IV, 49-53.

[21]   Sedgwick, *Bute*, xx; Campbell, *Chief Justices*, IV, 53-7.

[22]   Walpole, *Correspondence*, XX, 323 (27 July 1752).

[23]   Walpole, *George II*, I, 203-7; Walpole, *Correspondence*, XX, 342-5, 360-1; IX, 144-5; Sedgwick, *Bute*, xxx.

[24]   See *Dodington's Diary* quoted by Campbell, *Chief Jiustices*, IV, 377n. Campbell's claim (IV, 58) that Fawcett was one of the "intimate associates" of Johnson, Stone and Murray at Westminster Public School is probably inaccurate, for Fawcett was considerably younger than the others.

[25]   For Fawcett's letter to Johnson see Campbell, *Chief Justices*, IV, 61n.

[26]   Sedgwick, *Bute*, xxxii; Campbell, *Chief Justices*, IV, 61f.

[27]   Sedgwick, *Bute,* xxxvi-xxxcii; Campbell, *Chief Justices*, IV, 62-3; Walpole, *Correspondence*, XX, 360-4.

[28]   Basil Williams, *The Life of William Pitt: Earl of Chatham* (Longmans, Green, 1915), I, 188, 225-6.

[29]   James Alan Renne, *The Scottish People* (Hutchinson, 1960), 103; John Prebble, *Culloden* (Secker & Warburg, 1961), 244-5, 309. See also Sedgwick, *Commons*, 62-78; Namier, *Commons*, I, 184ff.

[30]   Paul Kléber Monod, *Jacobitism and the English People: 1688-1788* (Cambridge, 1989), 238; J. C. D. Clark, *Dynamics of Change: The Crisis of the 1750s and the English Party System* (Cambridge, 1982), 39; Paul Langford, *A Polite and Commercial People: England, 1727-1783* (Oxford, 1989), 221-2; Campbell, *Chief Justices*, IV, 57, 65; *The Letters of Junius*, ed. John Cannon (Oxford, 1978), 207n.

[31]   Jack P. Greene, *Peripheries and Center: Constitutional Development in the Extended Polities of the British Empire and the United States, 1607-1788*, (Georgia, 1986), 34, 61, 73.

[32]   William Edward Hartpole Lecky, *The American Revolution*, ed. James Albert Woodburn (New York, 1917), 64.

[33] Sir Lewis Namier and John Brooke, *Charles Townshend* (St. Martin's, 1964), 7, 13-5, 37, 179. Namier did not live to finish this portrait of the person he thought was most responsible for the disastrous policy of taxing the American colonies. Townshend's acknowledgement that he advised these instructions came in a Commons Debate on 20 February 1756. See also Richard B. Morris, *The American Revolution Reconsidered* (Greenwood, 1967), 19-21.

[34] Leonard Woods Labaree, *Royal Government in America: A Study of the British Colonial System before 1783* (Yale, 1930; reissued Ungar, 1958), 269, 404.

V. Attorney General in the Newcastle Administration

[1] Walpole, *Correspondence*, XX, 411-2 (7 March 1754); Walpole, *George II*, II, 1-4.

[2] In 1713 there were 358 Tories in the House of Commons over against 200 Whigs; after the contested seats were resolved in the 1715 Election, that decisive Tory majority fell radically to a minority of 186. Expressed in terms of percentages, the Tories controlled only 30.3% of the seats in Commons after the Election of 1722; 22.9% after the Election of 1727; 26% after the Election of 1734; 24.8% after the Election of 1741; and only 20.6% after the Election of 1747. See Sedgwick, *Commons*, I, 19, 34, 37, 42-3, 46, 57.

[3] J. C. D. Clark, *The Dynamics of Change: the Crisis of the 1750s and English Party System* (Cambridge, 1982), 43, 457.

[4] Basil Williams, *The Life of William Pitt: Earl of Chatham* (Longmans, Green, 1915), I, 188, 255-6; Clark, *Dynamics*, 7.

[5] Williams, *Pitt*, I, 234; Clark, *Dynamics*, 88-90.

[6] Clark, *Dynamics*, 90; Namier, *Commons*, III, 189.

[7] Benjamin Franklin, *Writings*, ed. J. A. Leo Lemay (Library of America, 1987), 375-7. It should not go unnoticed that Georgia was not included.

[8] Ibid., 367-74.

[9] Ibid., 383-4.

[10] Ibid., 1466.

[11] Ibid., 386-9.

[12] Bernhard Knollenberg, *Origin of the American Revolution: 1759-1766* (Macmillan, 1960; revised, Liberty, 2002), 96-7, see especially

notes 33-7. For Townshend's and Murray's responses to Newcastle, see Herbert L. Osgood, *The American Colonies in the Eighteenth Century* (Columbia, 1924), IV, 325-8.

13   Franklin, *Writings*, 405-6.

14   *Proceedings and Debates of the British Parliaments Respecting North America: 1754-1783*, ed. R. C. Simmons and R. D. G. Thomas (Kraus, beginning in 1982), I, 36 (16 December 1754).

15   Walpole, *George II*, II, 14-5; Clark, *Dynamics*, 99; Lawrence Henry Gipson, *The British Empire before the American Revolution: The Great War for the Empire* (Alfred A. Knopf, 1946), VI, chapters 2 and 3.

16   Clark, *Dynamics*, 89, 99, 103, 115, 118; Julian S. Corbett, *England in the Seven Years War: A Study in Combined Strategy* (Longmans, Green, 1907), I, 10, 32.

17   Clark, *Dynamics*, 117; Williams, *Pitt*, I, 174.

18   Campbell, *Chief Justices*, IV, 66, 79; Williams, *Pitt*, I, 254-8, 273; Walpole, *George II*, I, 98; II, 27-8, 37, 100.

19   Clark, *Dynamics*, 186, 217, 242; Walpole, *George II*, II, 53, 68-70, 118-9, 162; Walpole, *Correspondence*, XXXV, 253; Jeremy Black, *Pitt the Elder* (Cambridge, 1992), 110-2; Simmons and Thomas, *Proceedings and Debates*, I, 91-109.

20   Namier, *Commons,* III, 189.

21   Paul Langford, *The Eighteenth Century: 1688-1815* (St. Martin', 1976), 135-42; Gipson, *Great War*, VI, chapters 11 and 12.

22   Julius Bryant, *The Iveagh Bequest: Kenwood* (English Heritage, 1990), 58-9.

23   Walpole, *George II*, II, 60n, 150-2.

24   Walpole, *Correspondence,* XXXV, 253.

25   Walpole, *George II*, I, 380, II, 162-4; Sedgwick, *Commons*, II, 286; Clark, *Dynamics*, 241; Campbell, *Chief Justices*, IV, 83ff; Namier, *Commons*, IV, 83.

26   Namier, *Commons*, III, 189; Campbell, *Chief Justices*, IV, 83-8; Walpole, *George II*, II, 164.

27   Campbell, *Chief Justices*, IV, 204 -5. For the context of Bute's remark in 1763 see Sedgwick, *Bute*, 195-213.

28   Sedgwick, *Bute*, xxviii; Walpole, *George II*, II, 164.

VI. The Rise of Pitt to Power

1.   Campbell, *Chief Justices*, IV, 179-80; Clark, *Dynamics*, 341, 358, 295.
2.   Walpole, *George II*, III, 43; II, 187, 1-2.
3.   Clark, *Dynamics*, 283-9, 295, 317; Jeremy Black, *Pitt the Elder* (Cambridge, 1992), 125; Walpole, *George II*, II, 185-8, 193, 254.
4.   Basil Williams, *The Life of William Pitt: Earl of Chatham* (Longmans, Green, 1915), I, 308; Walpole, *George II*, II, 176, 204, 233; Walpole, *Correspondence*, XXI, 64-5 (3 March 1757); Gipson, *Great War*, VI, 414; Clark, *Dynamics*, 363; Campbell, *Chief Justices*, IV, 183-4. A picture of this execution can be found opposite 131 in Julian S. Corbett, *The Seven Years War: A Study in British Combined Strategy* (reissued, Folio, 2001).
5.   Clark, *Dynamics*, 335, 340, 351.
6.   Ibid., 361-9.
7.   Ibid., 363-4, 367, 370, 372-3, 389, 405, 410.
8.   Ibid., 410-3.
9.   Ibid., 416, 421; Walpole, *George II*, II, 261.
10.   Sir Lewis Namier would have one believe that Mansfield was "out of office" in April 1757; see *England in the Age of the American Revolution* (Macmillan, 1930), 55.
11.   Campbell, *Chief Justices*, IV, 187-8; Clark, *Dynamics*, 423.
12.   Campbell, *Chief Justices*, IV, 280-2
13.   Richard Middleton, *The Bells of Victory: the Pitt-Newcastle Ministry and the Conduct of the Seven Years' War, 1757-1763* (Cambridge, 1985), 48.
14.   Lawrence Henry Gipson, *The Great War for the Empire*, VII, 118.
15.   Campbell, *Chief Justices*, IV, 184-5. When Campbell states, "it was chiefly owing [to Mansfield's interventions] that the reins of government were finally entrusted to Pitt, his former rival," this should not be taken to suggest that he thought that the "mortal enmity" between these two rivals had somehow been overcome. See "Inauguration of Pitt's 'System'" in Julian S. Corbett, *The Seven Years War: A Study in British Combined Strategy* (Longman, Green, 1907), chapter 8.

VII. The Transformation of the English Common Law Heritage

1.   Lord John Campbell, *The Lives of the Chief Justices of England, from the Norman Conquest till the Death of Lord Tenterden*, revised

edition by James Cockcroft (New York, 1894, 1899), III, 392-433, IV, 1-407. Mansfield's portrait opposite III, 256.

2 Campbell, *Chief Justices*, III, 393, 414-27; IV, 95, 108-14, 180.

3 Campbell, *Chief Justices*, IV, 146, 97-101. Brian Simpson, "The Common Law and Legal Theory," *Legal Theory and Common Law*, ed. William Twining (Basil Blackwell, 1986), 24. According to Simpson, "during the 30 years during which Lord Mansfield presided over the Court King's Bench it is said that there were only 20 dissenting opinions."

4 See Marcel Berlins and Clare Byer, *The Law Machine* (Penguin, 1990), 130.

5 Campbell, *Chief Justices*, III, 427; IV, 73, 95-7, 102, 114-6, 279.

6 See Stanley N. Katz's Introduction to the facsimile reproduction of the first edition of Blackstone's *Commentaries on the Laws of England* (Chicago, 1989).

7 Campbell, *Chief Justices*, IV, 70-1.

8 Blackstone, *Commentaries on the Laws of England* (Chicago, 1989), I, 91, 149, 155-6, 161. For the medieval origins of these distinctions, see George Duby, *The Three Orders: Feudal Society Imagined*, trans. Arthur Goldhammer (Chicago, 1980; original, 1978). For the contemporary setting of these distinctions, see J. C. D. Clark, "The Royal Prerogative: Constitutional Controversy from Blackstone to Holland House," *English Society, 1688-1832: Ideology, Social Structure and Political Practice during the Ancient Regime* (Cambridge, 1985), 201-16.

9 Ian R. Christie and Benjamin W. Labaree, *Empire or Independence: 1760-1776* (Phaidon, 1976), 58.

10 Pauline Maier, *From Resistance to Revolution: Colonial Radicals and the Development of American Opposition to Britain, 1765-1776* (Random House, 1972; reprinted Vintage, 1979), 41, 46-7. See H. Trevor Colbourn, *The Lamp of Experience: Whig History and the Intellectual Origins of the American Revolution* (Chapel Hill, 1965), 27.

11 Milton E. Flower, *John Dickinson: Conservative Revolutionary* (Virginia, 1983), 1-19.

12 Willard Sterne Randall, *A Little Revenge: Benjamin Franklin and His Son* (Little, Brown, 1984), 128-9.

[13]   Lord Campbell, *Lives of the Lord Chancellors and Keeper of the Great Seal*, ed. John Allan Mallory (New Edition, 1874), I, 12, note 2; Campbell, *Chief Justices*, III, 427; IV, 114-5. Horace Walpole, *Memoirs of King George II*, ed. John Brooke (Yale, 1985), III, 9-21.

VIII. Some Early Decisions

[1]   Campbell, *Chancellors*, IV, 92-3; VI, 295; Campbell, *Chief Justices*, IV, 337-9. Arthur M. Schlesinger, *Prelude to Independence: the Newspaper War on Britain, 1764-1776* (Knopf, 1957; reissued, Northeastern, 1980) systematically adopts Hardwicke's and Mansfield's reading of the received law, apparently not realizing that it was so bitterly contested in Great Britain that it became unenforceable and was quickly reversed soon after Mansfield retired; see especially xiv, 10, 44, 62f, 115f, 128, 137, 140f, 155, 216, 262, 267, 297, 300.

[2]   Walpole, *George II*, III, 9.

[3]   John Cleland, *Fanny Hill, or Memoirs of a Woman of Pleasure*, ed. Peter Wagner (Penguin, 1985), Introduction, especially section II, 11-6. It should be noted that this recent edition of the 1749 version reverses the original title and subtitle.

[4]   Walpole, *George II*, III, 39-40. Dr. Shebbeare had previously published *Letters on the English Nation, by Batista Angeloni, a Jesuit, who resided many years in London, translated from the original Italian, by the Author of the Marriage Act, a Novel* (London, 1755). His *Letters* were an explicit response to Voltaire's earlier *Letters concerning the English Nation* (London, 1733), written in praise of things English, which had upset John Shebbeare because he was a pugnacious opponent of the Whigs.

[5]   Basil Williams, *The Life of William Pitt: Earl of Chatham* (Longmans, Green, 1915), II, 37-40.

[6]   Walpole, *George II*, III, 9-21.

[7]   Campbell, *Chief Justices*, IV, 37-9.

[8]   Carl Bridenbaugh, *Mitre and Sceptre: Transatlantic Faiths, Ideas, Personalities, and Politics* (Oxford, 1962), 1, 30-1, 86, 93, 109-11, 119, 178, 194, 220, 315-23.

[9]   Charles M. Andrews, *England's Commercial and Colonial Policy* (Yale, 1938), 8, 168-9, 222-4, 261, 268-70, 333.

10   William Edward Hartpole Lecky, *The American Revolution*, ed. James Albert Woodburn (New York, 1917), 64.

11   Benjamin Franklin, *Papers*, VII, 38-9, note 1.

12   Ibid., VIII, 291-7; see also VII, 248-50.

13   For a cultural history of the emerging intellectual milieu that Franklin encountered in Scotland, see Richard B. Sher, *Church and University in the Scottish Enlightenment: the Moderate Literati of Edinburgh* (Princeton, 1985).

14   Benjamin Franklin: *Writings*, ed. J. A. Leo Lemay (Library of America, 1987), 1465-9.

15   Paul Langford, "Old Whigs, Old Tories, and the American Revolution," *The British Atlantic Empire before the American Revolution*, ed. Peter Marshall and Glyn Williams (Frank Cass, 1980), 116-7.

16   Walpole, *George II*, I, 1, 4; II, 118-9, 190-1; III, 1-2, 9-12, 43-5.

IX. Young King George III in the Hands of the Scots

1   Campbell, *Chief Justices*, IV, 376-9.

2   Horace Walpole, *Memoirs of the Reign of King George III*, ed. Derek Jarrett (Yale, 2000), I, 6.

3   *Boswell's Life of Johnson*, ed. George Birkbeck Hill, revised by L. F. Powell (Oxford, 1934), I, 363 (10 June 1761).

4   Richard B. Sher, *Church and University in the Scottish Enlightenment: the Moderate Literati of Edinburgh* (Princeton, 1985), see especially 75-6, 95, 110.

5   Campbell, *Chief Justices*, IV, 198-9.

6   Walpole, *George III*, I, 7, 11, 14-5.

7   Ibid., I, 10-1.

8   Willard Sterne Randall, *A Little Revenge: Benjamin Franklin and His Son* (Little, Brown, 1984), 177-82.

9   See the 1971 reprint of the 1894 edition of Walpole, *George III*, I, 64 note 1. Williams, *Pitt*, I, 333; II, 106-11.

10   Walpole, *George III*, I, 53-4, 56-7, 64.

11   Ibid., I, 87, 110.

12   For full scale biographies, see Peter D. G. Thomas, *John Wilkes: A Friend to Liberty* (Oxford, 1996), and Arthur H. Cash, *John Wilkes: The Scandalous Father of Civil Liberty* (Yale, 2006).

[13] Thomas, *The Stamp Act Crisis*, 21.

[14] Thomas, *Wilkes*, 4.

[15] Thomas, *Wilkes*, 19-21. Walpole, *George III*, I, 116-7; see also II, 57.

[16] Walpole, *George III*, I, 144-8.

[17] Thomas, *Stamp Act Crisis*, 23.

[18] *Letters from George III to Lord Bute, 1756-66*, ed. Romney Sedgwick (Macmillan, 1939; reprinted, 1981), #20, 4 November 1762.

[19] Walpole, *George III*, I, 86, 144, 152, 159.

[20] Ibid., I, 145.

[21] *Letters from George III to Lord Bute: 1756-1766*, ed. Romney Sedgwick (Macmillan, 1939; reissued, Greenwood, 1981), 196; Campbell, *Chief Justices*, IV, 204-5.

[22] Walpole, *George III*, I, 122, 128.

[23] See the article on Mansfield in the *Dictionary of National Biography*.

[24] Campbell, *Chief Justices*, IV, 198-204.

X. Thomas Hutchinson: Revisionist Historian

[1] For a full-scale biography, see Bernard Bailyn, *The Ordeal of Thomas Hutchinson* (Harvard, 1974).

[2] Edmund S. Morgan and Helen M. Morgan, *The Stamp Act Crisis: Prologue to Revolution* (North Carolina, 1953), 11.

[3] Jack P. Breene, ed. *From Colonies to Nation: 1763-1789* (MaCraw-Hill, 1967), 9-11/

[4] Thomas Hutchinson, *History of the Colony and Province of Massachusetts-Bay*, ed. Lawrence Shaw Mayo (Harvard, 1936), III, 60-4. Citations are to Mayo's edition. Hutchinson published volume one in Boston in 1764 and in London the same year; volume two in Boston in 1767 and in London in 1768; volume three was published posthumously.

[5] Hutchinson, *History*, I, Preface.

[6] Ibid., I, xxviii.

[7] Edmund S. Morgan, *The Gentle Puritan: A Life of Ezra Stiles* (North Carolina, 1962; reissued, Norton, 1983), 145, see also 137, 223, 238.

[8] Hutchinson, *History*, I, 71.

[9] Ibid., I, 13-4.

[10] Ibid., I, 39.

[11] Ibid., I, 381.

12   Ibid., I, 179-182.

13   Ibid., I, 449, 197.

14   Ibid., I, 230, 271-3.

15   Ibid., I, 272-3, 216-7; see also 79.

16   Ibid., I, 301-8.

17   Ibid., I, 311-4.

18   Ibid., I, 316-28.

19   Ibid., I, 351,

20   Hutchinson, *History*, III, 64.

XI. The Opening of the Constitutional Crisis

1   Campbell, *Chief Justices*, IV, 197-200; III, 393.

2   Walpole, *George III*, I, 222-6, 180; II, 106.

3   John Brooke, *The Chatham Administration: 1766-1768* (Macmillan, 1956), 28.

4   Peter D. G. Thomas, *John Wilkes: A Friend to Liberty* (Oxford, 1996), 26.

5   Ibid., 28-30. Walpole, *George III*, I, 182.

6   Ibid., 30-1.

7   Ibid., 35.

8   Walpole, *George III*, I, 74.

9   Peter D. G. Thomas, *British Politics and the Stamp Act Crisis: the First Phase of the American Revolution, 1763-1767* (Oxford, 1975), 10-3.

10   *The Yale Edition of Horace Walpole's Correspondence*, ed. W. S. Lewis (Yale), XXXVIII, 257-8; Walpole, *George III*, I, 192.

11   At least since 1899 when George Otto Trevelyan published *The American Revolution*, it has been known that Bute's influence was soon reduced to almost nothing. "It may be doubted," according to Trevelyan, "whether public opinion has ever been more profoundly affected by a more general and persistent illusion than in the case of the belief that Lord Bute was a motive power of George the Third's policy all the while that the American troubles were brewing, and as long as the war lasted." See condensed edition edited by Richard B. Morris (1964), III, 183-4. According to Campbell, *Chief Justices*, IV, 277-9, note 3, Macaulay thought that Bute "ceased to have any communication with the King on political matters some time before the dismissal of George Grenville" in 1765. According to

John Brooke, *The Chatham Administration: 1766-1768* (Macmillan, 1956), "Between 1763 and 1765 it [i.e., Bute's influence] waned slowly. When Rockingham came to power the King gave a promise that he would not permit Bute to interfere, a promise which he kept. By the autumn of 1766 Bute's influence was at an end and all correspondence between him and the King had ceased" (48).

[12] Thomas, *Wilkes*, 36.

[13] Ibid., 4, 24, 34, 38-42. Walpole, *George III*, I, 245ff.

[14] Walpole, *George III*, I, 206-7; Walpole, *Correspondence* XXXVIII, 230.

[15] Thomas, *Wilkes*, 43-5.

[16] Walpole, *George III*, I, 217-20; *Correspondence*, XXXVIII, 256-9. Thomas, 45-7. Arthur H. Cash, *John Wilkes: The Scandalous Father of Civil Liberty* (Yale, 2006), 159-61.

[17] Walpole, *George III*, II, 93. Fred Junkin Hinkhouse, *The Preliminaries of the American Revolution as seen in the English Press: 1763-1775* (Columbia, 1926), 67.

[18] Carl Ubbelohde, *The Vice-Admiralty Courts and the American Revolution* (Chapel Hill, North Carolina, 1960), 46.

[19] *Proceedings and Debates of the British Parliaments Respecting North America, 1754-1783*, ed. R. C. Simmons and P. D. G. Thomas, Commons Debates (7 and 9 March 1764), I, 485-92.

[20] Edmund S. Morgan and Helen M. Morgan, *Stamp Act Crisis: Prologue to Revolution* (Chapel Hill, North Carolina, 1953), 58-60.

[21] Edmund S. Morgan, *Prologue to Revolution: Sources and Documents of the Stamp Act Crisis, 1764-1766* (North Carolina, 1959), 4-17, 27-9.

[22] Thomas, *British Politics*, 87.

[23] Walpole, *George III*, I, 112-3.

[24] James Otis, *The Rights of the British Colonies Asserted and Proved*, 32, 54, 72n, 36. Reproduced in *Pamphlets of the American Revolution: 1750-1776)*, ed. Bernard Bailyn (Harvard, 1965), I, *309-82*.

[25] Morgan, *Prologue to Revolution*, 19-21.

[26] *Proceedings and Debates*, Commons Debate (6 February 1765) II, 9-17.

[27] Morgan, *Stamp Act Crisis*, 69.

[28] *Documents of American History*, ed. Henry Steele Commager (Appleton-Century-Crofts, New York and London, 1934; reprinted, 1948), 53-5; Morgan, *Stamp Act Crisis*, 57.

29 John Brooke, *The Chatham Administration: 1766-1768* (Macmillan, 1956), 27. Walpole, *George III*, III, 153.

30 John Brooke, *King George III* (Constable, 1972), 110-14. Walpole, *George III*, II, 116, 122-4, 135, 153, 156.

31 Paul Langford, *The First Rockingham Administration: 1765-1766* (Oxford, 1975), 40-5, 61.

32 Ibid., 39, 43-4, 67-71, 98.

33 Ibid., 65-6.

34 Daniel Dulany, *Considerations on the Propriety of Imposing Taxes in the British Colonies, for the Purpose of Raising a Revenue, by Act of Parliament*, 12-3. Reproduced in *Pamphlets of the American Revolution: 1750-1776)*, ed. Bernard Bailyn (Harvard, 1965), I, 608-58.

35 Dulany, *Considerations*, 31-8.

36 Ibid., 3, 9, 30-2, 41-6

37 Ibid., 25.

38 Martin Howard, *A Letter from a Gentleman in Halifax*, 19-22. Reproduced in *Pamphlets of the American Revolution: 1750-1776)*, ed. Bernard Bailyn (Harvard, 1965), I, 532-544.

39 James Otis, *A Vindication of the British Colonies*, 32. Reproduced in *Pamphlets of the American Revolution: 1750-1776)*, ed. Bernard Bailyn (Harvard, 1965), I, 554-579.

40 Carl Ubbelohde, *The Vice-Admiralty Courts and the American Revolution* (Chapel Hill, North Carolina, 1960), 56. See also 92, 125, 129, 133, 146, 154.

41 *Diary and Autobiography of John Adams*, ed. L. H. Butterfield (Harvard, 1961; reprinted Atheneum, 1964), I, 44-5.

42 Ibid., III, 271; I, 55.

43 Ibid., I, 124.

44 Morgan, *Prologue to Revolution*, 73.

45 *Diary and Autobiography of John Adams*, ed. L. H. Butterfield (Harvard, 1961; reprinted Atheneum, 1964), I, 124, 251.

46 Morgan, *Stamp Act Crisis*, 123-9. See also Bernard Bailyn, *The Ordeal of Thomas Hutchinson*, 69.

47 *Diary and Autobiography of John Adams*, I, 263, 300.

48 Morgan, *Prologue to Revolution*, 62-3; *Stamp Act Crisis*, 105-7.

49 John Dickinson, *The Late Regulations*, 31-5. Reproduced in *Pamphlets of the American Revolution: 1750-1776)*, ed. Bernard Bailyn (Harvard, 1965), I, 660-91.

50   Morgan, *Prologue to Revolution*, 118-22.
51   Langford, *Rockingham*, 76, 83, 127.
52   Ibid., 109-10, 126, 142-3.
53   Ibid., 118-9.
54   Ibid., 132-5.
55   *Proceedings and Debates*, Lords Debate (17 December 1765), II, 54-7.

XII. The Repeal of the Stamp Act

1   *Proceedings and Debates*, Commons Debate (14 January 1766) II, 80-92.
2   See, for example, the Parliamentary Debates on 9 May 1770, 26 April 1773, 7 March 1774, 19 April 1774, 18 May 1774.
3   On Pitt's denial in regard to Bute's influence, see Ross J. S. Hoffman, *The Marquis: A Study of Lord Rockingham, 1730-1782* (Fordham, 1973), 109. See King George III's comment: "Mr. Pitt said my declarations of last year [i.e., 1765] that Ld. Bute should not interfere in political matters made him quite easy on that head," John Brooke, *The Chatham Administration: 1766-1768* (Macmillan, 1956), 7.
4   Bernard Knollenberg, *Origin of the American Revolution: 1759-1766* (Macmillan, 1960), 97; (reissued, Liberty, 2002), 86.
5   *Proceedings and Debates*, Commons Debate (14 January 1766) II, 80-92.
6   For example, Daniel Dulany in America had asked this probing question, "Why did not some able friend intimate to him [i.e., Grenville] his Hazard on the Slippery ground, he chose, when the all powerful Sovereignty of Parliament might have afforded so safe a footing?"
7   *Proceedings and Debates*, Commons Debate (14 January 1766) II, 80-92.
8   *Proceedings and Debates*, Commons Proceedings (27 January 1766) II, 109-13.
9   *Proceedings and Debates*, Lords Debate (3 February 1766) II, 124-33; Appendix, 570.
10   *Proceedings and Debates,* Commons Debate (3 February 1766) II, 135-51.
11   *Proceedings and Debates*, American Committee (11-3 February 1766) II, 185-251.

[12] Ibid., XIII, 47.

[13] Ibid., XII, 413.

[14] *Proceedings and Debates*, Commons Debate (27 January 1766), II, 109-113.

[15] Franklin, *Papers* (Yale, 1969), XIII, 66-72.

[16] *Proceedings and Debates*, Commons Debate (21 February 1766) II, 280-9.

[17] *Proceedings and Debates*, Commons Debate (24 February 1766) II, 296-302.

[18] Walpole, *George III*, III, 28-9.

[19] *Proceedings and Debates*, Commons Debate (4 March 1766) II, 311-3.

[20] Walpole, *George III*, III, 31-2.

[21] *Proceedings and Debates*, Lords Debate (7 March 1766) II, 318-

[22] *Proceedings and Debates*, Lords Debate (11 March 1766) II, 335-46.

[23] Franklin, *Papers*, XIII, 207-225. In regard to emphases, the editorial procedure is followed here.

[24] Walpole assigns the names to this cartoon in *The Yale Edition of Horace Walpole's Correspondence*, ed. W. S. Lewis (Yale, 1960), XXII, opposite 400. The original print is reproduced in M. Dorothy George, *English Political Caricature to 1792: A Study of Opinion and Propaganda* (Oxford, 1959), plate 39. On page 135 George claims that Alexander Wedderburn is the person carrying the first black flag. Edmund S. Morgan is of the same opinion; see the frontispiece of *Prologue to Revolution: Sources and Documents of the Stamp Act Crisis, 1764-1766* (North Carolina, 1959). Walpole's designation, however, makes much more sense in the context of the Parliamentary Debates on the Repeal of the Stamp Act.

[25] *Proceedings and Debates*, Lords Debate (17 March 1766) II, 354.

[26] Franklin, *Papers*, XIII, 298-9.

[27] Thomas, *British Politics and the Stamp Act Crisis*, 279-81. See also Thomas, *Tea Party to Independence*, 90.

[28] Franklin, *Papers*, XIII, 384.

XIII. The Chatham Administration

[1] Walpole, *George III*, II, 60.

[2] Ibid., III, 61.

3   Ibid., III, 55-8, 75, 114.
4   Ibid., III, 65, 70-1. Walpole, *Correspondence*, XXII, 464.
5   Ibid., III, 90.
6   *Proceedings and Debates*, Lords Debate (10 April 1767) II, 448-54.
7   *Proceedings and Debates*, Lords Debate (6 May 1767) II, 459-61.
8   *Proceedings and Debates*, Lords Debate (22 May 1767) II, 493-6.
9   *Proceedings and Debates*, Lords Debate (26 May 1767) II, 498-501.
10   *Proceedings and Debates*, Lords Debate (22 May 1767) II, 493-6.
11   Walpole, *George III*, III, 77, 91, 94.
12   See Sir Lewis Namier and John Brooke, *Charles Townshend* (St. Martin's, 1964) for a full-scale biography. For an informative sketch see Peter D. G. Thomas, "Charles Townshend," in *The Oxford Dictionary of National Biography* (Oxford, 2004).
13   Walpole, *George III*, III, 130-1.
14   *Proceedings and Debates*, Commons Debate (17 January 1766) II, 97-9.
15   Peter D. G. Thomas, *The Townshend Duties Crisis: the Second Phase of the American Revolution: 1767-1773* (Oxford, 1987), 21-2.
16   *Proceedings and Debates*, Commons Debate (26 January 1767) II, 410-1.
17   *Proceedings and Debates*, Commons Debate (18 February 1767) II, 428-9.
18   Thomas, *The Townshend Duties Crisis*, 7n, 30. Walpole, *George III*, III, 98.
19   Benjamin Franklin, *Papers*, XIV, 119, 184. Thomas, *The Townshend Duties Crisis*, 22.
20   *Proceedings and Debates*, Commons Debate (13 May 1767) II, 463-72.
21   Walpole, *George III*, III, 114.
22   *Proceedings and Debates*, Commons Debate (15 May 1767) II, 473-485.
23   Benjamin Franklin, *Papers*, XIV, 109, 184. Thomas, *The Townshend Duties Crisis*, 22.
24   For a different reading of the situation, see Thomas, *The Townshend Duties Crisis*, 16, where he states, "on the key issue of Parliamentary sovereignty over America, British opinion was inflexible and virtually monolithic."

25   *Proceedings and Debates*, Lords Debate (7 March 1766) II, 318-23. See also Walpole, *George III*, II, 96.

26   *Proceedings and Debates*, Lords Debate (30 March 1767) II, 444-5.

27   Cited by Thomas, *The Townshend Duties Crisis*, 22.

28   Thomas, *The Townshend Duties Crisis*, 31.

29   *Proceedings and Debates*, Lords Debate (2 June 1767) II, 504-508.

30   Benjamin Franklin, *Papers*, XIV, 228-30.

31   Walpole, *George III*, III, 174; IV, 83.

32   *Empire and Nation: Letters from a Farmer in Pennsylvania: John Dickinson*, ed. Forrest McDonald (Prentice-Hall, 1962; reissued, Liberty, 1999), see especially the footnote on p. 24. Hereafter cited as Dickinson, *Letters*.

33   Dickinson, *Letters*, 13, 45, 67.

34   Ibid., 7-11.

35   Ibid., 23.

36   Ibid., 18-9.

37   Ibid., 11.

38   Ibid., 43-4, 81.

39   Walpole, *George III*, III, 176-8, 185-92; IV, 32.

XIV. The Grafton Administration

1   Peter D. G. Thomas, *The Townshend Duties Crisis*, 76.

2   Walpole, *George III*, IV, 8.

3   Peter D. G. Thomas, *John Wilkes: A Friend to Liberty* (Oxford, 1996), 70-9.

4   Walpole, *George III*, IV, 5-9.

5   Thomas, *Wilkes*, 79-82.

6   Walpole, *George III*, IV, 14n.

7   Walpole, *George III*, IV, 23-5; *Correspondence*, XXIII, 29 (9 June 1768).

8   Walpole, *Correspondence*, X, 263 (15 June 1768).

9   Thomas, *The Townshend Duties Crisis*, 78. Thomas strangely asserts that Dickinson and the Massachusetts Circular Letter represent a "new constitutional stance" by the Americans.

10   Ibid., 81-3.

11   Ibid., 98.

12   Ibid., 97.

13   Ibid., 103.

14   *Proceedings and Debates*, Commons Debate (8 November 1768), III, 1-13.

15   Thomas, *Townshend*, 108-11.

16   *Proceedings and Debates*, Commons Debate (7 December 1768), III, 32-43.

17   *Proceedings and Debates*, Lords Debate (15 December 1768), III, 47-50.

18   Thomas, *Townshend*, 136. From the beginning to 5 January 1769 the Townshend Duties netted a mere £11,136. That would not even cover the Lord Chancellor's income, estimated to be around £13,000 per annum. The military establishment in America was projected to cost well over £500,000 per annum.

19   Thomas, *Townshend*, 114-6.

20   *Proceedings and Debates*, Commons Debate (26 January 1769), III, 64-83.

21   Thomas, *Townshend*, 119.

22   Thomas, *Wilkes*, 87.

23   Arthur H. Cash, *John Wilkes: The Scandalous Father of Civil Liberty* (Yale, 2006), 171.

24   Thomas, *Wilkes*, 73-5.

25   Cash, *Wilkes*, 235-6; Thomas, *Wilkes*, 87-8.

26   Thomas, *Wilkes*, 116; Walpole, *George III*, IV, 55, 60, 62, but see also 80.

27   Thomas, *Wilkes*, 89-93.

28   Thomas, *Wilkes*, 93-4.

29   Thomas, *Wilkes*, 93-8; Walpole, *George III*, IV, 65.

30   Lord John Campbell, *Lives of the Lord Chancellors and Keepers of the Great Seal* (Estes & Lauriat, 1874), VI, 295, 310-3, 343.

31   Walpole, *George III*, IV, 56-8.

32   *Proceedings and Debates*, Commons Debate (8 February 1769), III, 87-112.

33   Thomas, *Townshend*, 119-22.

34   Thomas, *Wilkes*, 110-11; Walpole, *George III*, IV, 71.

35   Thomas, *Wilkes*, 98-101; Walpole, *George III*, IV, 77-9.

36   *Proceedings and Debates*, Commons Debate (14 March 1769), III, 134. Thomas, *Townshend*, 133.

37   *Proceedings and Debates*, Commons Debate (19 April 1769), III, 148-160.

38 Thomas, *Townshend*, 134-6.

39 Ibid., 137-8.

40 Ibid., 139.

41 Thomas, *Wilkes*, 97.

42 Thomas, *Wilkes,* 85-7; Walpole, *George III*, IV, 98.

43 Walpole, *George III*, IV, 87-8, 96.

44 Thomas, *Townshend*, 161; *Wilkes*, 104.

45 Walpole, *George III*, IV, 121.

46 Thomas, *Wilkes*, 103-4; Walpole, *George III*, IV, 81, 87, 91-2.

47 Campbell, *Chief Justices*, IV, 220; Walpole, *George III*, IV, 122-3.

48 See above, "Attorney General in the Newcastle Administration," at note 14.

49 Campbell, *Chief Justices*, IV, 221-2; *Proceedings and Debates*, Lords Debate (9 January 1770), III, 165-7.

50 Walpole, *George III*, IV, 122-3, 126-7; Campbell, *Chief Justices*, IV, 218.

51 Walpole, *George III*, IV, 127-31; *Correspondence*, XXIII, 174 (18 January 1770).

52 Walpole, *George III*, IV, 130-1; Campbell, *Chief Justices*, IV, 218-9.

53 *Proceedings and Debates*, Lords Debate (21 January 1770), III, 188-9.

54 Edmund Burke, *Thoughts on the Cause of the Present Discontents* (published 23 April 1770) is reprinted in *Pre-Revolutionary Writings*, ed. Ian Harris (Cambridge, 1993), 116-192.

55 Ibid., 118, 149, 181.

56 Ibid., 159-62.

57 Ibid., 161-2, 175.

58 Ibid., 127, 141.

59 Ibid., 142-3.

60 Ibid., 165-6, 171.

61 Ibid., 123.

62 Walpole, *George III*, IV, 134-5.

63 Ibid., IV, 137.

XV. The Opening Years of the North Administration

1 Campbell, *Chief Justices*, IV, 227-9.

2 Bernard Knollenberg, *The Growth of the American Revolutio: 1766-1775* (Free Press, 1975; reissued, Liberty, 2003), 76. For a full-scale biography see Peter D. G. Thomas, *Lord North* (St. Martin's, 1976).

[3]   Walpole, *George III*, IV, 141-2.

[4]   *Proceedings and Debates,* Commons Debate (5 March 1770), III, 209-42. On 21 February North had requested a postponement of the debate because of "the newness with which he entered on his post had made it impossible to be so complete a master of the points in dispute as he could wish." Ibid., III, 202.

[5]   Thomas, *Townshend,* 176, 198.

[6]   Knollenberg, *The Growth of the American Revolution,* 82-5.

[7]   Bernard Bailyn, *The Ordeal of Thomas Hutchinson* (Harvard, 1974), 156-63.

[8]   *Proceedings and Debates,* Commons Debate (26 April 1770), III, 256-262; Thomas, *Townshend,* 180-3.

[9]   *Proceedings and Debates,* Commons Debate (8 May 1770), III, 270-296.

[10]   *Proceedings and Debates,* Commons Debate (9 May 1770), III, 299-327.

[11]   *Proceedings and Debates,* Commons Debate (18 May 1770), III, 331-42.

[12]   Thomas, *Townshend,* 161, 191-5.

[13]   Campbell, *Chief Justices,* IV, 227-236. The *Letters of Junius* appeared in the *Public Advertiser* published by Henry Sampson Woodfall from 21 November 1768 to 21 January 1772.

[14]   Walpole, *George III,* IV, 178; *Junius,* 213n.

[15]   Adams, *Diary,* II, 7-8. The Mansfield reference on 5 June 1762 (I, 225) is rather casual.

[16]   *Junius,* Letter XXXIX (28 May 1770), 200-2. See also Letter XXXVII (19 March 1770), 184, and Letter XLII (30 January 1771), 217ff.

[17]   *Junius,* 365 (12 November 1770), 309 (22 October 1771), 341 (21 January 1772), 207 (14 November 1770).

[18]   *Junius,* Letter XLI (14 November 1770), 206-17; *The Yale Edition of Horace Walpole's Correspondence,* ed. W. S. Lewis (Yale), XXIII, 247; Walpole, *George III,* IV, 205n.

[19]   *Junius,* Letter XLI (14 November 1770), 206-17.

[20]   *Proceedings and Debates,* Commons Debate (13 November 1770), III, 342-4.

[21]   Campbell, *Chief Justices,* IV, 231, 239-40; Walpole, *George III,* IV, 203.

22 Campbell, *Chief Justices*, IV, 240-6; Walpole, *George III*, IV, 207-8.

23 Walpole, *George III*, IV, 145-6; Campbell, *Chief Justices*, IV, 246- 7.

24 Thomas, *Townshend*, 214.

25 Thomas, *Wilkes*, 126-7.

26 Ibid., 132.

27 Ibid., 135-40.

28 Reproductions of Grenville Sharp and his musical family are in Simon Schama, *Rough Crossings: Britain, the Slaves and the American Revolution* (BBC Worldview, 2005; reprinted HarperCollins, 2006), following 178.

29 Ibid., 28-32.

30 Ibid., 31-2.

31 Sharp's *Representation* occasioned "A Conversation on Slavery" that Franklin published in the *Public Advertiser* on 26 January 1770; Franklin, *Writings*, 646-653.

32 Schama, 39-44.

33 Ibid., 44-5.

34 Ibid., 46-7.

35 Ibid., 49-50.

36 Ibid., 50-2.

37 Ibid., 52-5.

38 Julius Bryant, *The Iveagh Bequest: Kenwood* (English Heritage), 63. A reproduction of a double portrait of Dido and Lady Elizabeth Murray by Johann Zoffany is included after page 178 in Schama, *Rough Crossings*.

39 Lord Campbell expended considerable energy refuting the thesis that Lord Chief Justice Mansfield "systematically disregarded the rules of the Common Law, and gave a preference to the Roman Law." But Campbell himself readily acknowledged that Lord Mansfield "did not sufficiently appreciate the merits of the old common law; overlooking the love of public liberty displayed by many of its maxims." And he proceeded to add that his hero "made ample use of the compilation of Justinian, and of the commentators upon it, but only for a supply of principles to guide him upon questions unsettled by prior decisions in England. He derived similar assistance from the law of nations, and from the modern continental codes." After conceding this much, Campbell remained

convinced that "while he grafted new shoots of great value on the barren branches of the Saxon juridical tree, he never injured its roots, and he allowed this vigorous stock to bear the native and racy fruits for which it had been justly renowned." (*Chief Justices*, III, 426; IV, 162-6.) That *Junius* did overstate the case in his racy journalistic fashion is transparently the case. But Lord Campbell's rejoinder obscures the larger point in his full exposition of Lord Mansfield's Jurisprudential Reform Project, namely, that his life-long ambition centered upon a gradual assimilation of the English Common Law Heritage to the Roman Civil Law Tradition through judicial decisions as concrete cases came before the Court of King's Bench.

[40] *Junius*, Letter LIX (5 October 1771), 296; Letter LXI (17 October 1771), 305; Letter LXIII (22 October 1771), 309-10; see also 334n.

[41] Walpole, *George III*, IV, 270.

[42] *Junius*, Letter LXV (2 November 1771), 314, see 313n; Letter LXVIII (21 January 1772).

[43] *Junius*, Letter XLI (14 November 1770), 216.

[44] *Junius*, Letter LIX (5 October 1771), 297.

[45] *Junius*, Letter LXIV (2 November 1771), 310-11.

[46] *Junius*, Letter XLI (14 November 1770), 216. Well into the nineteenth century the easiest way to destroy a dinner party was to ask, "Who was Junius?" Sixty-one different people have been suggested as the "Epistolary Sphinx" who wrote these scandalous but extraordinarily influential letters, and his identity surely ranks as one of the best-kept secrets of the age. The most plausible candidate for this high honor remains Sir Philip Francis. Thomas Babington Macaulay, the nineteenth-century Whig historian, marshaled five different reasons for his "firm belief" that Philip Francis could have been *Junius*. In the revised edition of *The Lives of the Chief Justices of England*, the editor weighed in on the controversial subject: "The weight of inferential evidence seems to point towards Sir Philip Francis, and it is certain that he was not unwilling to be considered as Junius, though he never admitted the claim in words. The test of handwriting seems to tend in the same direction." And since David McCracken's 1979 investigation, *Junius and Philip Francis*, the issue seems to have been settled but not conclusively proven that Philip Francis was *Junius*.

XVI. Thomas Hutchinson: Lord Mansfield's Foremost American Disciple

1   Benjamin Franklin, *Papers*, XVIII, 3-4.

2   Thomas, *Townshend*, 226; Bailyn, *Hutchinson*, 194.

3   Thomas, *Townshend, 226-9.*

4   Bernhard Knollenberg, *Growth of the American Revolution:1766-1775* (Free Press, 1975; reissued, Liberty, 2003), 72, 95.

5   Bailyn, *Hutchinson,* 169.

6   Ibid., 183.

7   Ibid., 202-5.

8   The legislature of Massachusetts was technically called "the General Court," but it was ordinarily referred to as "the General Assembly" in contemporary documents.

9   See *Sources and Documents illustrating the American Revolution,* ed. S. E. Morison (Oxford, 1923; second edition, 1929), 87-96.

10 See *Puritan Political Ideas,* ed. Edmund S. Morgan (Bobb-Merrill, 1965), 178-9.

11 Morison, *Sources and Documents*, 93.

12 *Proceedings and Debates,* Commons Debate (26 April 1773), III, 487-92.

13 Benjamin Woods Labaree, *The Boston Tea Party* (Oxford, 1964), 13.

14 Ibid., Table 1, 331. Since the price of tea continually fluctuated on the market it is impossible to say exactly how much a pound of tea actually cost in any given year, but it should be transparent that the price actually fell during the five-year period (1767-1772).

15 Thomas, *Townshend*, 246-7.

16 Labaree, *Boston Tea Party*, 60.

17 Ibid., 63-70.

18 Thomas, *Townshend*, 254, 234-5.

19 Labaree, *Boston Tea Party,* 70-3.

20 *The Briefs of the American Revolution: Constitutional Arguments Between Thomas Hutchinson, Governor of Massachusetts Bay, and James Bowdoin for the Council and John Adams for the House of Representatives*, ed. John Phillip Reid (New York University, 1981), 18. In the interests of clarity, I have taken the liberty to alter the spelling of a few words; for example, "dependance" has been rendered "dependence."

[21] Ibid., 154.
[22] Ibid., 147-8.
[23] Ibid., 85.
[24] For an overview of the controversy, see Bernard Bailyn, *Pamphlets of the American Revolution: 1750-1776* (Harvard, 1965), 131-3; reproduced in *The Ideological Origins of the American Revolution*, 219-22.
[25] Reid, *Briefs*, "The Address of the Governor," 17.
[26] Reid, *Briefs*, "The Answer of the Council," 33.
[27] Reid, *Briefs*, "The Answer of the House," 53.
[28] Reid, *Briefs*, "The Replication of the Governor," 86.
[29] Reid, *Briefs*, "The Replication of the Governor," 86-95.
[30] Reid, *Briefs*, "The Rejoinder of the House," 131.
[31] Reid, *Briefs*, "The Replication of the Governor," 152. John Adams tracked down the 1759 case of *Rex vr. Cowle*; he comments upon it extensively in his *Novanglus Paper* XI, 10 April 1775.
[32] Bailyn, *Hutchinson*, 317.
[33] Reid, *Briefs*, 16, 154.
[34] Reid, *Briefs*, "The Surrejoinder of the Governor," 149-50.
[35] Reid, *Briefs*, "The Address of the Governor," 15-18.
[36] Reid, *Briefs*, "The Answer of the House," 55.
[37] Ibid. 63.
[38] Ibid. 58.
[39] Ibid. 53-9.
[40] Ibid. 64-71. See also above, "Thomas Hutchinson: Revisionist Historian." The Governor and the House revisited Hutchinson's *History* with conflicting claims about the proper meaning of different passages. Hutchinson, though, did finally concede that "the Principles of Anarchy ... were avowed by many of the Inhabitants here for near twenty Years after they were exploded in England," that is, for two decades after the Restoration of 1660. Prominent though Hutchinson's *History* surely was in the dispute, the argument itself turned on incompatible constitutional doctrines, not historical facts. And that is why he still insisted, "at the Time of the [Glorious] Revolution the People returned to a just Sense of the Supremacy of Parliament." Reid, *Briefs*, "The Replication of the Governor," 97-101; "The Rejoinder of the House," 138-40; "The Surrejoinder of the Governor," 153.

41 Reid, *Briefs*, "The Answer of the House," 61.

42 Reid, *Briefs*, "The Replication of the Governor," 86-95.

43 Reid, *Briefs*, "The Address of the Governor," 18-9.

44 *Proceedings and Debates*, Lords Debate (3 February 1766) II, 124-33; Appendix, 570. On the same day that Mansfield was speaking in the House of Lords, Blackstone addressed whether "the right of imposing taxes arises from representation" in the House of Commons. After denying any connection between taxes and representation even in England, he pointedly added: "However this doctrine of representation held in this country, it certainly does not hold with respect to the colonies who are dependent upon us."

45 Reid, *Briefs*, "The Answer of the House," 61-3; see also 57.

46 Reid, *Briefs*, "The Rejoinder of the House," 137, 142-3.

47 Reid, *Briefs*, "The Address of the Governor," 20.

48 Reid, *Briefs*, "The Answer of the House," 71-2.

49 Reid, *Briefs*, "The Rejoinder of the House," 131-3.

50 Reid, *Briefs*, "The Replication of the Governor," 89; "The Surrejoinder of the Governor," 152-3.

51 Reid, *Briefs*, "The Address of the Governor," 17.

52 Reid, *Briefs*, "The Answer of the House," 73; "The Answer of the Council," 41.

53 Reid, *Briefs*, "The Address of the Governor," 20-2.

54 Ibid. 16-7.

55 Reid, *Briefs*, "The Replication of the Governor," 98.

56 Reid, *Briefs*, "The Replication of the Governor," 101; "The Surrejoinder of the Governor," 153.

57 Reid, *Briefs*, "The Address of the Governor," 15-21.

58 Reid, *Briefs*, "The Answer of the House," 71-2.

59 Reid, *Briefs*, "The Answer of the Council," 34-5, 40, 43; "The Surrejoinder of the Governor," 147, 154.

60 Reid, *Briefs*, "The Answer of the Council," 44.

61 Bailyn, *Hutchinson*, 224-5.

62 Ibid. 230.

63 Ibid. 243.

64 Ibid. 238-41. Benjamin Franklin from Thomas Cushing (14 June 1773), *Papers*, XX, 238.

[65] Ibid. 212-20. Benjamin Franklin to Thomas Cushing (6 May 1773), *Papers*, XX, 201.

[66] Labaree, *Boston Tea Party*, 76, 104-5.

[67] Ibid., 87-91.

[68] John Dickinson, *Writings*, ed. Paul Leicester Ford (Philadelphia, 1895), I, 460ff.

[69] Bailyn, *Hutchinson*, 219, 253-4, 258-9.

[70] Labaree, *Boston Tea Party*, 113-4.

[71] Ibid., 118-9, 127.

[72] Ibid., 120-4.

[73] Ibid., 133-41.

[74] *Diary and Autobiography of John Adams*, ed. L. H. Butterfield (Harvard, 1961; reissued, Atheneum, 1964), II, 86 (17 December 1773).

[75] Ibid., II, 112-7.

[76] Benjamin Franklin, *Papers*, XXI, 37-70.

XVII. The Intolerable Acts of 1774

[1] Walpole, *Journal*, I, 183.

[2] See Thomas, *Tea Party to Independence*, 30-7.

[3] Walpole, *Journal*, I, 183.

[4] Ibid., I, 185-6.

[5] Ibid., I, 189-91.

[6] Ibid., I, 218-9.

[7] For a different reading of the chain of events in late February, see Thomas, *Tea Party to Independence*, 36-8, especially footnote 62. See also 38, 50, 63-4.

[8] Bernhard Knollenberg, *Growth of the American Revolution: 1766-1775* (Macmillan, 1975; reissued Liberty, 2003), 136.

[9] Walpole, *Journal*, I,183, 189-91.

[10] *Proceedings and Debates,* Commons Debate (7 March 1774), IV, 36-51.

[11] *Proceedings and Debates,* Commons Debate (14 March 1774), IV, 55-85.

[12] Thomas, *Tea Party to Independence*, 53-4.

[13] Benjamin Franklin, *Papers* (22 March 1774), XXI, 152.

[14] Walpole, *Journal*, I, 336.

15   *Proceedings and Debates,* Commons Debate (23 March 1774), IV, 89-112.

16   Thomas, *Tea Party to Independence,* 54-6.

17   *Proceedings and Debates,* Commons Debate (25 March 1774), IV, 118-144.

18   Thomas, *Tea Party to Independence,* 57-8.

19   *Proceedings and Debates,* Lords Debate (28 March 1774), IV, 145-53.

20   Thomas, *Tea Party to Independence,* 59.

21   *Proceedings and Debates,* Commons Debate (28 March 1774), IV, 147-52.

22   Thomas, *Tea Party to Independence,* 70.

23   *Proceedings and Debates,* Commons Debate (15 April 1774), IV, 159-78.

24   Thomas, *Tea Party to Independence,* 61.

25   *Proceedings and Debates,* Commons Debate (19 April 1774), IV, 180-240.

26   *Proceedings and Debates,* Commons Debate (22 April 1774), IV, 262-81.

27   Thomas, *Tea Party to Independence,* 77.

28   *Proceedings and Debates,* Commons Debate (2 May 1774), IV, 329-83.

29   *Proceedings and Debates,* Lords Debate (11 May 1774), IV, 420-2.

30   Thomas, *Tea Party to Independence,* 79-80; Bernhard Knollenberg, *Growth of the American Revolution,* 139.

31   *Proceedings and Debates,* Lords Debate (26 May 1774), IV, 438-41.

32   Walpole, *Journal,* I, 369-71.

33   Walpole, *George III,* II, 193-4.

34   For a detailed treatment of the background of the Parliamentary Debates, see Thomas, *Tea Party to Independence,* "The Problem of Quebec," 99-104.

35   See *Documents of American History,* edited by Henry Steele Commager (Appleton-Century-Crofts, 1934; reprinted, 1948), 47-50.

36   Thomas, *Tea Party to Independence,* 90-1. See also Thomas, *British Politics and the Stamp Act Crisis,* 279-81.

37   Thomas, *Tea Party to Independence,* 94-7; Bernhard Knollenberg, *Growth of the American Revolution: 1766-1775* (Free Press, 1975; reissued, Liberty, 2003), 142-4.

[38] *Proceedings and Debates*, Commons Debate (26 May 1774), IV, 442-75.

[39] Knollenberg, *Growth of the American Revolution*, 143.

[40] *Proceedings and Debates*, Commons Debate (31 May 1774), IV, 485-98.

[41] *Proceedings and Debates*, Lords Debate (17 June 1774), V, 229-33; Thomas, *Tea Party to Independence*, 106.

[42] Walpole, *Journal*, I, 365.

XVIII. Thomas Jefferson: *A Summary View*

[1] Jefferson, *Writings* (Library of America, 1984), *Autobiography*, 8-9; *Papers*, I, 105-17.

[2] H. Trevor Colbourn, "Thomas Jefferson and the Rights of Expatriated Men," *The Lamp of Experience: Whig History and the Intellectual Origins of the American Revolution* (North Carolina, 1965), 158-9.

[3] Jefferson, *Writings*, 1228, to William Duane (12 August 1810).

[4] Jefferson, *Writings*, 967 (11June 1790), 1226 (26 May 1810); *Memoir, Correspondence, and Miscellanies, from the Papers of Thomas Jefferson*, ed. Thomas Jefferson Randolph (Boston, 1830), IV, 178-80 (17 June 1812); letter to Horatio G. Spafford, *Writings*, 1332-3 (11 March 1814).

[5] For a radically different interpretation of the scanty evidence, see Merrill B. Paterson, *Thomas Jefferson and the New Nation* (1970): "The completion in 1769 of William Blackstone's grand outline, *Commentaries on the Laws of England*, marked a tremendous advance. Within a few years Blackstone was as popular in America as in England. But *the work came too late for Jefferson*, and retrospect he was grateful for having missed the 'honeyed' smoothness and treacherous systematizing of Blackstone's packaged course in four volumes at the commencement of his studies" (my emphasis). That "honeyed smoothness" is derived from "the honied Mansfieldism of Blackstone," TJ to James Madison, *Writings*, 1513 (17 February 1826). Oddly, Peterson characterizes the very "legist" Jefferson most admired—Sir Edward Coke—as that "dreary and crabbed seventeenth-century legalist." "Legalist" and "legalism" are polemical terms in theological discourse, not jurisprudence.

6   Jefferson, *Papers*, I, 34-5.

7   Douglas L. Wilson, "Thomas Jefferson's Early Notebooks," *William and Mary Quarterly*, XLII (1985), 445; editor of *Jefferson's Literary Commonplace Book* (Princeton, 1989), 228. Although in his *Autobiography* Jefferson dates the opening of his "practice of the law at the bar of the General Court" in 1767, Wilson dates his calling to the bar in 1765, which seems a much more plausible date for when he finished his formal legal studies under the guidance of George Wythe.

8   *Thomas Jefferson and Bolling v. Bolling,* ed. Bernard Schwartz with Barbara Wilcie Kern and R. B. Bernstein (Huntington Library, 1997). Mansfield (or frequently, Solicitor General Murray) appears on 184, 208-9, 360, 367, 449, 451.

9   Jefferson, *Autobiography*, 9-10; Jefferson, *Writings*, 751, to Edmund Pendleton (13 August 1776); Jefferson, *Papers*, I, opposite 134.

10   Jefferson, *A Summary View*, paragraphs one, five, and thirteen; my capitalizations.

11   Compare Montesquieu's extraordinarily influential *Esprit des Lois*, which advances the thesis that among the various peoples of Western Europe the English alone had somehow managed to preserve the "beautiful system" of liberty that they brought with them from "the woods" of barbaric Germany. See Baron de Montesquieu, *The Spirit of the Laws*, trans. Thomas Nugent (Hafner, 1949), I, 161-3. *Esprit des Lois* is quoted in entries 775 to 802 in Jefferson's *Legal Commonplace Book.*

12   Jefferson, *A Summary View*, paragraphs two and nineteen. See Jefferson, *Papers*, I, 133 and note 35 on 137.

13   Jefferson, *Writings*, 751 -2, to Edmund Pendleton (13 August 1776). See items 557 through 584 in Jefferson's *Legal Commonplace Book.*

14   Jefferson, *A Summary View*, paragraphs seven through twelve.

15   Jefferson, *Papers, Retirement Series,* V, 134-7, to Judge John Tyler (17 May 1812).

16   Jefferson, *Papers*, I, 116; *A Summary View*, paragraphs one and twenty-two.

17   Jefferson, *A Summary View*, paragraph twenty-two.

XIX. Thomas Hutchinson's Entry into England

1. Hutchinson, *Diary and Letters*, I, 155.
2. Ibid., I, 180.
3. Ibid., I, 230.
4. Ibid., I, 189.
5. Ibid., I, 157-94. For another report, see the 4 July 1774 letter to General Gage, I, 175-8.
6. Cited in Bailyn, *Hutchinson*, 278.
7. Hutchinson, *Diary and Letters*, I, 179-80.
8. Ibid., I, 194-5. The punctuation has been slightly altered.
9. Ibid., I, 195.
10. Ibid., I, 177.
11. On the transformation of Kenwood by the Adams brothers, see Julius Bryant, *The Iveagh Bequest: Kenwood* (English Heritage, 1990), 44-5.
12. Hutchinson, *Diary and Letters*, I, 202. When Hutchinson related Mansfield's comment about how surprised he had been about Hutchinson's endurance to Lord Chief Justice De Grey several months later, De Grey interrupted Hutchinson to say, "I was not surprised." See 9 November *Diary* entry, I, 290.
13. Hutchinson, *Diary and Letters*, I, 191, 203-4, 213-9.
14. Hutchinson, *History of the Colony and Province of Massachusetts-Bay*, III, 275. John Phillip Reid suggests (*Briefs*, 158) that this unnamed person "may have been Edward Thurlow, attorney general and later lord chancellor." Support for Reid's suggestion can be found in Hutchinson, *Diary and Letters*, I, 266-7, entry on 19 October 1774: "In the evening received an extremely civil letter from the Attorney General, with the highest encomiums upon the part I took in the controversy with the House and Council upon the subject of their independency." But compare *Diary* entry on 15 November, I, 294.
15. *Proceedings and Debates*, Lords Debate (26 May 1774), IV, 438-41; Walpole, *Last Journal*, I, 369-71.
16. Thomas, *Tea Party to Independence*, 84-5, 140. Hutchinson clearly accepted Mansfield's version, for he writes, "even Ld Chatham, Burke, and Barré ... condemn ... the principles of the people there, and the actions consequent upon them" (I, 230; see also 213).

17 Ibid., 34, 119-22, 137. Hutchinson, *Diary and Letters*, I, 199, 201, 204.

18 Hutchinson, *Diary and Letter*, I, 218-9.

XX. The First Continental Congress

1 John Adams, *Diary & Autobiography*, II, 96-7.

2 Ibid., III, 278.

3 Ibid., III, 287-8.

4 See David McCullough, *John Adams* (Simon & Schuster, 2001), 71.

5 Adams to William Tudor (16 November 1816).

6 For a narrative account, see Edmund Cody Burnett, *The Continental Congress* (Macmillan, 1941), "The First Congress: Declaration of Rights, The Association."

7 Adams, *Diary & Autobiography*, II, 126-7.

8 Ibid., II, 136.

9 Ibid., II, 121.

10 See above, "The Intolerable Acts of 1774."

11 Adams, *Diary & Autobiography*, II, 134-5.

12 Ibid., II, 127.

13 See above, "The Repeal of the Stamp Act."

14 See above, "Thomas Hutchinson: Lord Mansfield's Foremost American Disciple." Hutchinson's all or nothing stance is powerfully repeated in his 8 August 1774 letter to an unknown patriot in Massachusetts, *Diary and Letters*, I, 213-7.

15 Adams, *Diary & Autobiography*, III, 309.

16 *Documents of American History*, ed. Henry Steele Commager (Fourth Edition, Appleton-Century-Crofts, 1948), 82-4.

17 Ibid., 84-7.

XXI. The Final Descent

1 Thomas, *Tea Party to Independence*, 138.

2 Campbell, *Chief Justices*, IV, 254-6. Bryant, *Kenwood*, 63f. For a picture of Marie Antionette's writing table, see *Scone Palace: Scotland*, 5.

3 Walpole, *Journal*, I, 394-5.

4 Hutchinson, *Diary and Letters*, I, 232.

5 Ibid., I, 245.

6 Ibid., I, 254, 256, 258-62.

[7]   Burnett, *The Continental Congress*, 42-3; Thomas, *Tea Party to Independence*, 158-9.

[8]   Hutchinson, *Diary and Letters*, I, 282-6.

[9]   Ibid., I, 232, 293.

[10]   Ibid., I, 285; Thomas, *Tea Party to Independence*, 159.

[11]   Thomas, *Tea Party to Independence*, 160.

[12]   Hutchinson, *Diary and Letters*, I, 292-3, 297; Thomas, *Tea Party to Independence*, 158-60.

[13]   Hutchinson, *Diary and Letters*, I, 298; Thomas, *Tea Party to Independence*, 143-9.

[14]   Hutchinson, *Diary and Letters*, I, 273, 281.

[15]   Lord Beloff, in his article, "American Independence and its Constitutional Aspects," in *The New Cambridge Modern History: The American and French Revolutions* (Cambridge, 1965), correctly maintained that in *Campbell v. Hall* "Lord Mansfield laid down the principle that once an assembly had been granted, the crown's prerogative right of taxation had lapsed." But Beloff failed to mention Mansfield's critical principle that taxes can be rightfully imposed upon an entity within the British Empire *by Parliament*. Selwyn H. H. Carrington addressed the case of *Campbell v. Hall* in his article, "The American Revolution and the Sugar Colonies, 1775-1783," published not only in *The Blackwell Encyclopedia of the American Revolution* (1991) but reprinted as well in *A Companion to the American Revolution* (2000). According to Carrington, *Campbell v. Hall* "came at the height of the dispute between Britain and her colonies in America" (which is true), but then he added, "the colonists welcomed it as supporting their struggle against subjugation by the British Parliament" (which is ludicrous).

[16]   Campbell, *Chief Justices*, IV, 126.

[17]   See above, "Solicitor General in the Whig Establishment."

[18]   Campbell, *Chief Justices*, IV, 124-7.

[19]   Hutchinson, *Diary and Letters*, I, 307-8.

[20]   Thomas, *Tea Party to Independence*, 195-6.

[21]   *Proceedings and Debates*, Lords Debate (7 February 1775), V, 379-404.

[22]   Thomas, *Tea Party to Independence*, 196.

[23]   Ibid., 196-201.

24 *Proceedings and Debates,* Commons Debate (5 April 1775), VI, 4-11;
    Commons Debate (15 May 1775), VI, 35-39.
25 *Proceedings and Debates,* Lords Debate (17 May 1775), VI, 39-58.
26 Thomas, *Tea Party to Independence,* 231-5.
27 See *The Blackwell Encyclopedia of the American Revolution,* ed. Jack
    P. Greene and J. R. Pole (Blackwell, 1991), 638.

XXII. *Novanglus V. Massachusettensis*

1   John Adams, *Diary and Autobiography,* III, 313.
2   Adams, *Papers,* II, 217, Editorial Note.
3   For a condensed but convenient version that edits out much of the
    technical material, see *The American Colonial Crisis: The Daniel
    Leornard-John Adams Letters to the Press, 1774-1775,* ed. Bernard
    Mason (Harper Torchbooks, 1972), Letter I, 3-7.
4   Ibid., 8-31.
5   Ibid., 32-7.
6   Ibid., 38-44.
7   Ibid., 37.
8   Adams, *Papers,* II, 226-32.
9   Ibid., 233-38.
10 Ibid., 369-72.
11 Ibid., 345.
12 Ibid., 246.

XXIII. The Empire Goes to War

1   Peter D. G. Thomas, *Tea Party to Independence,* 226.
2   Ibid., 227-8; 234.
3   Ibid., 238.
4   *The Correspondence of King George the Third,* III, 235; Peter D. G.
    Thomas, *Tea Party to Independence,* 235-40.
5   Ibid.
6   *The Correspondence of King George the Third,* III, 235.
7   Peter D. G. Thomas, *Tea Party to Independence,* 254-6.
8   *The Papers of Thomas Jefferson,* ed. Julian P. Boyd, I, 187-219.
    Emphases have been modified throughout this document.
9   Ibid., I, 219-223.
10 P. Force, *American Archives,* III, 627.

[11] *The Correspondence of King George the Third,* III, 255.
[12] *Proceedings and Debates,* King's Speech (26 October 1775), VI, 69-70.
[13] *Proceedings and Debates,* Lords Debate (26 October 1775), VI, 76-88.
[14] *Proceedings and Debates* Commons Debate (26 October 1775), VI, 88-94.
[15] *Proceedings and Debates,* Lords Debate (15 November 1775, VI, 245-258.
[16] Peter D. G. Thomas, *Tea Party to Independence,* 299-300.
[17] *Proceedings and Debates,* Lords Debate (15 December 1775), VI, 355-371.
[18] *Proceedings and Debates,* Lords Debate (20 December 1775), VI, 375-381.
[19] Peter D. G. Thomas, *Tea Party to Independence,* 282-84.
[20] Peter D. G. Thomas, *Tea Party to Independence,* 307-8.
[21] *Proceedings and Debates,* Lords Debate (14 March 1776), VI, 466-90.
[22] Peter D. G. Thomas, *Tea Party to Independence,* 313-4.
[23] Ibid., 314.
[24] Ibid., 315-6.
[25] Ibid., 317.
[26] Ibid., 325.

XXIV. The War of Independence

[1] Jefferson, *Papers,* I, 298.
[2] Ibid., 309-11.
[3] Ibid., 311-3.
[4] Ibid., 413ff.
[5] Ibid., 429-32.
[6] Hutchinson, *Diary and Letters,* II, 75; Bailyn, *The Ordeal of Thomas Hutchinson,* 356.
[7] Thomas Paine, *The American Crisis,* opening line.
[8] Walpole, *Journal,* II, 168-73.
[9] Ibid., II, 195-6.
[10] Ibid., 200-9.
[11] Ibid., 223-4.
[12] Campbell, *Chief Justices,* IV, 272-9.
[13] Ibid., IV, 280-2.
[14] Walpole, *Journal,* II, 392-3.

15   Hutchinson, *Diary and Letters*, II, 274-7.

16   Ibid., 312-3, 330, 342-7; Bailyn, *The Ordeal of Thomas Hutchinson*, 317.

17   Campbell, *Chief Justices*, IV, 282-93.

18   Walpole, *Journal*, II, 403.

19   Campbell, *Chief Justices*, IV, 293-308; Walpole, *Journal*, II, 407-10.

20   Franklin, *Papers*, XXXII, 541.

21   Walpole, *Journal*, II, 477.

22   Ibid., II, 544, 612.

XXV. Three Judgments Against Lord Mansfield

1   Adams, *Diary and Autobiography*, III, 150-1n. Adams provided this insight for the *Boston Patriot* in his last note on 17 February 1812.

2   Jefferson, *Papers: Retirement Series*, III, 125, 165. Jefferson, *Writings*, 1446, to Thomas Ritchie (25 December 1820); 1495, to Major John Cartwright (5 June 1825).

3   Jefferson, *Papers*, IX, 67-72., to Philip Mazzei (November 1785).

4   Ibid., XIII, 649, to John Brown Cutting (2 October 1788).

5   Jefferson, *Papers: Retirement Series*, V, 134-7, to John Tyler (17 June 1812). For some inexplicable reason this frequently quoted letter is omitted from *Thomas Jefferson: Writings*.

6   Walpole, *Memoirs of King George II*, III, 43-5; II, 1-2.

7   Walpole, *Journal*, II, 73.

8   Walpole, *George III*, IV, 145-6.

XXVI. Lord Mansfield's Final Years

1   Campbell, *Chief Justices*, IV, 329-31.

2   Ibid., IV, 357-8.

3   Ibid., IV, 360-1.

4   Peter D. G. Thomas, *John Wilkes: A Friend of Liberty* (Oxford, 1996), 209-21.

5   Campbell, *Chief Justices*, IV, 332-41.

6   Ibid., IV, 359.

7   Campbell, *Chief Justices*, IV, 361-2.

8   Ibid., IV, 367.

9   Ibid., IV, 364-5.

BIBLIOGRAPHY

PRIMARY SOURCES: BRITISH PARLIAMENTARY SPEAKERS

Proceedings and Debates of the British Parliaments Respecting North America: 1754-1783, ed. R. C. Simmons and P. D. G. Thomas (Kraus, beginning 1982). These indispensable volumes contain most of the Parliamentary citations included in the body of this study from the following:

Adair, Serjeant,
Barré, Isaac,
Barrington, Lord, William Wildman,
Bedford, Duke of, John Russell,
Blackstone, Sir William,
Burke, Edmund,
Camden, Lord, Charles Pratt,
Chatham, Earl of, William Pitt,
Colebrooke, Sir George,
Conway, Henry Seymour,
Dartmouth, Lord, William Legge,
Dempster, George,
Dowdeswell, William,
Dunning
Ellis, Welbore,
Fox, Charles,
Franklin, Benjamin,
Fuller, Rose,
Germain, George,
Glynn, John,

Grenville, George,

Grafton, Duke of, Augustus Henry Fitzroy,

Hardwicke, Lord, Philip Yorke,

Harris, James,

Hillsborough, Lord, Wills Hill,

Hussey, Richard,

Jenkinson, Charles,

Lyttelton, Lord,

Mackay, Colonel,

Mansfield, Earl of, William Murray,

Meredith, Sir William,

Newcastle, Duke of, Thomas Pelham-Holles,

North, Frederick,

Northington, Lord, Robert Henley,

Norton, Sir Fletcher,

Phipps, Constantine John,

Pownall, John,

Pownall, Thomas,

Rice, George,

Richmond, Duke of, Charles Lennox,

Rigby, Richard,

Rockingham, Lord, Charles Watson-Wentworth,

Shelburne, Earl of, William Fitzmaurice,

Stanley, Hans,

Temple, Lord, Richard Grenwille Temple,

Townshend, Charles,

Trecothick, Barlow,

Van, Charles,

Wedderburn, Alexander,

Whately, Thomas,

Wilkes, John,

Yorke, John,

PRIMARY SOURCES:

Adams, John, *Diary and Autobiography of John Adams,* ed. L. H. Butterfield (Harvated, 1961; reprinted Atheneum, 1964).

Adams, John, *The Papers of John Adams,* ed. Robert J. Taylor (Harvard, 1977).

Blackstone, Sir William, *Commentaries on the Laws of England*, ed. Stanley N. Katz (Chicago, 1989).

Boswell, James, *Life of Johnson*, ed. George Birkbeck Hill, revised by L. F. Powell (Oxford, 1934).

The Briefs of the American Revolution: Constitutional Arguments Between Thomas Hutchinson, Governor of Massachusetts, and James Bowdoin for the Council and John Adams for the House of Representatives, ed. John Phillip Reid (New York University, 1981).

Brown, John, *An Estimate of the Manners and Principles of the Times* (London, 1757).

Burke, Edmund, *Thoughts on the Cause of the Present Discontents*, reprinted in *Pre-Revolutionary Writings,* ed. Ian Harris (Cambridge, 1993).

Chambers, Ephraim, *Cyclopaedia* (1728).

Cleland, John, *Fanny Hill; or Memoirs of a Woman of Pleasure*, ed. Peter Wagner (Penguin, 1985).

Dickinson, John, *Empire and Nation: Letters from a Farmer in Pennsylvania*, ed. Forrest McDonald (Prentice-Hall, 1962; reissued, Liberty, 1999).

Dickinson, John, *The Late Regulations*, reproduced in *Pamphlets of the American Revolution*, ed. Bernard Bailyn (Harvard, 1965).

Dickinson, John, *Writings*, ed. Paul Leicester Ford (Philadelphia, 1895).

Dulany, Dulany, *Considerations on the Propriety of Imposing Taxes in the British Colonies, for the Purpose of Raising a Revenue, by Act of Parliament*, reproduced in *Pamphlets of the American Revolution: 1750-1776*, ed. Bernard Bailyn (Harvard, 1965).

Fortescue, Sir John, *On the Laws and Governance of England*, ed. Shelley Lockwood (Cambridge, 1997).

Franklin, Benjamin, *The Papers of Benjamin Franklin* (Yale)

Franklin, Benjamin, *Writings*, ed. J. A. Leo Lemay (Library of America, 1987).

George III, *Letters from George III to Lord Bute: 1756-1766*, ed. Romney Sedgwick (Macmillan, 1939; reissued, Greenwood, 1981).

Gibbon, Edward, *The Decline and Fall of the Roman Empire* (first volume, 1776).

Howard, Martin, *A Letter from a Gentleman in Halifax*, reproduced in *Pamphlets of the American Revolution: 1750-1776*, ed. Bernard Bailyn (Harvard, 1965).

Hume, David, *The History of England from the Invasion of Julius Caesar to The Revolution of 1688* (1778; reprinted, Liberty Classics, 1983).

Hutchinson, Thomas, *The Diary and Letters of His Excellency, Thomas Hutchinson, Esq.*, ed. Peter Orlando Hutchinson (Boston, 1884).

Hutchinson, Thomas, *History of the Colony and Province of Massachusetts-Bay*, ed. Lawrence Shaw Mayo (Harvard, 1936).

Jefferson, Thomas, *Memoir, Correspondence, and Miscellanies, from the Papers of Thomas Jefferson*, ed. Thomas Jefferson Randolph (Boston, 1830).

Jefferson, Thomas, *Jefferson's Literary Commonplace Book*, ed. Douglas L. Wilson (Princeton, 1989).

Jefferson, Thomas, *The Papers of Thomas Jefferson,* ed. Julian P. Boyd (Princeton, beginning 1950).

Jefferson, Thomas, *The Papers of Thomas Jefferson, Retirement Series,* ed. J. Jefferson Looney (Princeton, 2008).

Jefferson, Thomas, *Thomas Jefferson and Bolling v. Bolling,* ed. Bernard Schwartz (Huntington Library, 1997).

Jefferson, Thomas, *Writings* (Library of America, 1984).

Johnson, Samuel, *Dictionary of the English Language* (London, 1755).

Letters of Junius, ed. John Cannon (Oxford, 1978).

Montesquieu, Baron de, *The Spirit of the Laws,* trans. Thomas Nugent (Hafner, 1946).

Otis, James, *The Rights of the British Colonies Asserted and Proved,* reproduced in *Pamphlets of the American Revolution: 1750-1776,* ed. Bernard Bailyn (Harvard,1965).

Otis, James, *A Vindication of the British Colonies, against the Aspersions of the Halifax Gentleman, in His Letter to a Rhode Island Friend,* reproduced in *Pamphlets of the American Revolution,* ed. Bernard Bailyn (Harvard, 1965).

Paine, Thomas, *The American Crisis,* ed. Philip S. Foner, *The Life and Major Writings of Thomas Paine* (Citadel, 1948).

Puritan Political Ideas, ed. Edmund S. Morgan (Bobb-Merrill, 1965).

Reid, John Phillip, *The Briefs of the American Revolution* (1981).

Robertson, William, *History of the Reign of the Emperor Charles V* (1769).

Robertson, William, *History of Scotland, during the Reigns of Queen Mary and of King James VI* (1759).

Shebbeared, John, *Letters on the English Nation, by Batista Angeloni, a Jesuit, who resided many ears in London, translated from the original Italian, by the Author of the Marriage Act, a Novel* (London, 1755).

Sidney, Algernon, *Discourses Concerning Government* (1698).

Sources and Documents Illustrating the American Revolution, ed. S. E. Morison (Oxford, 1923; second edition, 1929).

Steele, Richard, *The Tatler* (1710).

Trenchard, John, and Gordon, Thomas, *Cato's Letters; Essays on Liberty, Civil and Religious, and Other Important Subjects,"* ed. Ronald Hamowy (Liberty Press, 1995).\

Walpole, Horace, *Memoirs of King George II*, ed. John Brooke (Yale, 1985).

Walpole, Horace, *Memoirs of King George III*, ed. Derek Jarrett (Yale, 2000).

Walpole, Horace, *Journal of the Reign of King George the Third, from the Year 1771 to 1783,* ed. Dr. Doran (London, 1859).

Walpole, Horace, *The Yale Edition of Horace Walpole's Correspondence,* ed. W. S. Lewis (Yale, beginning 1937).

SECONDARY SOURCES:

Alden, John Richard, *General Cage in America: A History of His Role in the American Revolution* (Louisiana, 1948).

Andrews, Charles M., *England's Commercial and Colonial Policy* (Yale, 1938).

Ashley, Maurice, *James II* (Minnesota, 1977).

Bailyn, Bernard, *The Ideological Origins of the American Revolution* (Harvard, 1967).

Bailyn, Bernard, *The Ordeal of Thomas Hutchinson* (Harvard, 1974).

Bellesiles, Michael A., *Arming America: the Origins of a National Gun Culture* (Knopf, 2000).

Beloff, Lord, "American Independence and its Constitutional Aspects," *The New Cambridge Modern History: The American and French Revolutions* (Cambridge, 1965).

Berlins, Marcel, and Byer, Clare, *The Law Machine* (Penguin, 1990).

Black, Jeremy, *Pitt the Elder* (Cambridge, 1992)

Bridenbaugh, Carl, *Mitre and Sceptre: Transatlantic Faiths, Ideas, Personalities, and Politics* (Oxford, 1962).

Brooke, John, *The Chatham Administration: 1766-1768* (Macmillan, 1956).

Brooke, John, *King George III* (Constable, 1972).

Burnett, Edmund Cody, *The Continental Congress* (Macmillan, 1941).

Campbell, Lord John, *The Lives of the Chief Justices of England, from the Norman Conquest till the Death of Lord Tenterden*, revised edition by James Cockcroft (New York, 1894, 1899).

Campbell, Lord John, *Lives of the Lord Chancellors and Keepers of the Great Seal* (Estes & Lauriat, 1874).

Carrington, Selwyn H. H., "The American Revolution and the Sugar Colonies, 1775-1783," *The Blackwell Encyclopedia of the American Revolution* (1991).

Cash, Arthur H., *John Wilkes: The Scandalous Father of Civil Liberty* (Yale, 2006).

Clark, J. C. D., *Dynamics of Change: The Crisis of the 1750s and the English Party System* (Cambridge, 1982).

Clark, J. C. D., *English Society: 1688-1720* (Cambridge, 1985).

Colbourn, H. Trevor, *The Lamp of Experience: Whig History ad the Intellectual Origins of the American Revolution* (North Carolina, 1965).

Corbett, Julian S., *England in the Seven Years War: A Study in Combined Strategy* (Longmans, Green, 1907).

Christie, Ian R., and Labaree, Benjamin W., *Empire or Independence: 1760-1776* (Phaidon, 1976).

Duby, George, *The Three Orders: Feudal Society Imagined,* trans. Arthur Goldhammer (Chicago, 1980).

Fifoot, Cecil Herbert Stuart, *Lord Mansfield* (Oxford, 1936).

Flower, Milton E., *John Dickinson: Conservative Revolutionary* (Virginia, 1983).

George, M. Dorothy, *English Political Caricature to 1792: A Study of Opinion and Propaganda* (Oxford, 1959).

Gipson, Lawrence Henry, *The British Empire Before the American Revolution: The Great War for the Empire* (Alfred A. Knopf, 1946)

Greene, Jack P., *From Colonies to Nation: 1763-1789* (McGraw-Hill, 1967).

Greene, Jack P., *Peripheries and Center: Constitutional Development in the Extended Polities of the British Empire and the United States, 1607-1788* (Georgia, 1986).

Hinkhouse, Fred Junkin, *The Preliminaries of the American Revolution as seen in the English Press: 1763-1775* (Columbia, 1926).

Hodgkin, Thomas, *The Barbarian Invasions of the Roman Empire* (1880-1899; revised, 1892; reprinted Folio Society, 2002, 2003).

Hoffman, Ross J. S., *The Marquis: A Study of Lord Rockingham, 1730-1782* (Fordham, 1973).

The Iveagh Bequest: Kenwood, ed. Bryant, Julius (English Heritage, 1990).

Kenyon, J. P., *Revolution Principles: The Politics of Party, 1689-1720* (Cambridge, 1977).

Knollenberg, Bernard, *The Growth of the American Revolution: 1766-1775* (Free Press, 1975; reissued, Liberty, 2003).

Knollenberg, Bernard, *Origins of the American Revolution: 1759-1766* (Macmillan, 1960; reissued, Liberty, 2002).

Labaree, Benjamin Woods, *The Boston Tea Party* (Oxford, 1964).

Labaree, Leonard Woods, *Royal Government in America: A Study of the British Colonial System before 1783* (Yale, 1930; reissued Ungar, 1958).\

Langford, Paul, *The Eighteenth Century: 1688-1815* (St. Martin's, 1976).

Langford, Paul, *The First Rockingham Administration: 1765-1766* (Oxford, 1975).

Langford, Paul, *A Polite and Commercial People: England 1727-1783* (Oxford, 1989).

Langford, Paul, "Old Whigs, Old Tories, and the American Revolution," *The British Atlantic Empire before the American Revolution*, ed. Peter Marshall and Glyn Williams (Frank Cass, 1980).

Lecky, William Edward Hartpole, *The American Revolution*, ed. James Albert Woodburn (New York, 1917).

Lees-Milme, James, *The Last Stuarts: British Royalty in Exile* (Charles Scribner's Sons, 1984).

Mackie, R. L., *Scotland* (Frederick A. Stokes, no date).

Maier, Pauline, *From Resistance to Revolution: Colonial Radicals and the Development of American Opposition to Britain, 1765-1776* (Random House, 1972; reprinted Vintage, 1979).

McCullough, David, *John Adams* (Simon & Simon, 2001).

Merryman, John Henry, *The Civil Law Tradition: An Introduction to the Legal Systems of Western Europe and Latin America* (Stanford, 1969; revised, 1985).

Middleton, Richard, *The Bells of Victory: the Pitt-Newcastle Ministry and the Conduct of the Seven Years' War, 1757-1763* (Cambridge, 1985).

Monod, Paul Kléber, *Jacobitism and the English People, 1688-1788* (Cambridge, 1989).

Morgan, Edmund S., *The Gentle Puritan: A Life of Ezra Stiles* (North Carolina, 1962; reissued, Norton, 1983).

Morgan, Edmund S., and Morgan, Helen M., *The Stamp Act Crisis: Prologue to Revolution* (North Carolina, 1953).

Morgan, Edmund S., *Prologue to Revolution: Sources and Documents of the Stamp Act Crisis, 1764-1766* (North Carolina, 1959).

Morris, Richard B., *The American Revolution Reconsidered* (Greenwood, 1967).

Namier, Sir Lewis, and Brooke, John, *Charles Townshend* (St. Martin's 1964); *Commons*

Namier, Sir Lewis, *England In the Age of the American Revolution* (Macmillan, 1930).

Namier, Sir Lewis, and Brooke, John, *The History of Parliament: The House of Commons, 1754-1790* (Oxford, 1964).

Osgood, Herbert L., *The American Colonies in the Eighteenth Century* (Columbia, 1924).

Owen, John B., *The Rise of the Pelhams* (Methuen, 1957; reissued, 1971).

Petrie, Sir Charles, *The Jacobite Movement: the First Phase, 1688-1716* (Eyre & Spottiswoods, 1948).

Petrie, Sir Charles, *The Jacobite Movement: the Last Phase, 1716-1807* (Eyre & Spottiswoods, 1950).

Poser, Norman S. *Lord Mansfield: Justice in the Age of Reason* ((McGill-Queen's University Press, 2013).

Pocock, J. G. A., *The Ancient Constitution and the Feudal Law: A Study of English Historical Thought in the Seventeenth Century* (Cambridge, 1957; reissued, 1987).

Prebble, John, *Culloden* (Secker & Warburg, 1961).

Randall, William Sterne, *A Little Revenge: Benjamin Franklin and his Son* (Little, Brown, 1984).\

Renne, James Alan, *The Scottish People* (Hutchinson, 1960).

Robbins, Caroline, *The Eighteenth-Century Commonwealthman* (Harvard, 1959).

Schama, Simon, *Rough Crossings: Britain, the Slaves and the American Revolution* (BBC Worldview, 2005; reprinted HarperCollins, 2006).

Schlesinger, Arthur M., *Prelude to Independence: the Newspapaer War on Britain, 1764-1776* (Knopf, 1957; reissued, Northeastern, 1980).

Scott, Sir Walter, *Waverley; or, 'Tis Sixty Years Since* (published anonymously, 1814).

Sedgwick, Romney, *The History of Parliament: The House of Commons, 1715-1754* (Oxford, 1970).

Sher, Richard B., *Church and University in the Scottish Enlightenment: the Moderate Literati of Edinburgh* (Princeton, 1985).

Simpson, Brian, "The Common Law and Legal Theory," *Legal Theory and Common Law,* ed. William Twining (Basil Blackwell, 1984).

Tayler, Alistair, and Tayler, Henrietta, *The Story of the Rising* (Thomas Nelson, 1936).

Thomas, Peter D. G., *British Politics and the Stamp Act Crisis: The First Phase of the American Revolution* (Oxford, 1975).

Thomas, Peter D. G., "Charles Townshend," *The Oxford Dictionary of National Biography* (Oxford, 2004).

Thomas, Peter D. G., *John Wilkes: A Friend to Liberty* (Oxford, 1996).

Thomas, Peter D. G., *Lord North* (St. Martin's, 1976).

Thomas, Peter D. G., *The Townshend Duties Crisis: the Second Phase of the American Revolution* (Oxford, 1987).

Thomas, Peter D. G., *Tea Party to Independence: The Third Phase of the American Revolution, 1773-1776* (Oxford, 1991).

Trevelyan, Sir George Otto, *The American Revolution* (1899; revised, Longmans, 1913).

Ubbelohde, Carl, *The Vice-Admiralty Courts and the American Revolution* (Chapel Hill, North Carolina, 1960).

Williams, Basil, *The Life of William Pitt: Earl of Chatham* (Longmans, Green, 1915).

Williams, Basil, *The Whig Supremacy: 1714-1760* (Oxford, 1939; revised, 1942, 1945).

Wilson, Douglas L., "Thomas Jefferson's Early Notebooks," *William and Mary Quarterly* (1985).

CPSIA information can be obtained
at www.ICGtesting.com
Printed in the USA
BVHW040257290323
661285BV00002B/351